FIFTY F...

A BELATED RECOGNITI[ON]
OF THE UNITED STATES A[IR FORCE]
WHILE FLYING EARLY WARNING SURVEILLANCE MISSIONS
IN THE NORTH ATLANTIC

A. J. Northrup
Senior Master Sergeant
United States Air Force - Retired

© Copyright 1998 - A. J. NORTHRUP
1976 Hickory Tree Lane
Tallahassee, FL 32303

Library of Congress Catalog Card Number: 98-92023

Edited by: Bonnie Williams
113 Ridgeland Road
Tallahassee, FL 32312

Jan Stetler
3168 Huntington Woods Blvd
Tallahassee, FL 32303

Printed in the United States of America

Cover designed by A. J. Northrup to honor the 50 officers and airmen, each represented by a star, who lost their lives during the "Cold War" while flying active Air Defense radar surveillance missions guarding the approaches to the East Coast of the United States.

ISBN: 0-9667486-0-3

THIS BOOK IS DEDICATED

To the fifty crew members who, while flying active air defense radar surveillance missions in the defense of our Country, lost their lives in three separate crashes of the Lockheed EC-121H "Warning Star" Super Constellation in the North Atlantic.

To the four crew members who survived.

To the families, friends, and co-workers of the fifty brave men whose lives were taken and of the four whose lives were spared.

To all the officers and airmen who were crew members on the radar surveillance planes in the 551st Airborne Early Warning and Control Wing at Otis Air Force Base, Massachusetts.

To all the maintenance and support personnel who in so many ways were involved with all the radar planes and the men who flew on them.

TO ALL THE BRAVE MEN

When the time came for the crew to say their goodbyes and go to the base to prepare to fly - none ever expected that they would die - they were brave men with their Nation to defend. To the very man they remained strong - having no hint that things soon would go wrong. In the late evening light they took off on their fatal flight - they soared overhead until out of sight - then flew away into the night. This blend of young men who flew with the wind never knew that many would never soar again - never see their kin - or friend and that many of them were soon to become missing men - never to be seen again. Their hope, future, and tomorrow all seemed to blend as they flew that night on the fatal flight in their Warning Star. There had to be tears - there had to be some fear - when side by side the crew did ride as the engines cried. Each lent their hand to their fellow man as they heard the engines roar and soon there would be a plane no more - as it began to lumber and pitch they prepared to ditch. They prayed to be saved from a watery grave and they were without smile as they flew their last mile - headed to a deep cold endless sleep - leaving their family and friends to weep. They felt the plane pitch and the shudder as the pilots fought the yoke and rudder. The flight soon ended into the waves where some feared they would forever remain in their watery graves. There was the crumble of metal as the structures tore - it did not resemble an aircraft anymore. Soon some were left to tend to a friend at their side and some watched as others died - and many drifted away with the wind and tide. Each and every man had made a valiant stand but don't look for their foot steps of those who were lost in the sand. Look instead to the Heavens - look afar - look beyond the evening star - there they all stand - hand in hand - to the very last man - they did fly again.

A. J. NORTHRUP

CONTENTS

TITLE PAGE	i
DEDICATION	ii
POEM BY A. J. NORTHRUP "TO ALL THE BRAVE MEN"	iii
CONTENTS	iv
FOREWORD	xvi
PREFACE	xvii
ABOUT THE AUTHOR	xviii
ACKNOWLEDGMENTS	xxi
SPECIAL THANKS	xxv
INTRODUCTION TO THE 551ST AIRBORNE EARLY WARNING AND CONTROL WING "ITS MISSION AND ITS MISHAPS"	28
SOME OF THE UNIT PATCHES OF THE 551ST AEW&C WING	32
RECOLLECTIONS OF THE FIRST 551ST AEW&C WING COMMANDER, COLONEL OLIVER G. CELLINI	33
PHOTOGRAPHS PROVIDED BY COLONEL CELLINI	36
SENTINELS ON GUARD	39
PHOTOGRAPH OF CONNIE	42
LOCKHEED EC-121 WARNING STAR SPECIFICATIONS	43
FLYING WITH THE 551ST AEW&C WING - A. J. NORTHRUP	44
THE AUTHOR FONDLY REMEMBERS MAJOR ROBERT A. BOSTICK OF THE 961ST AND NOTES FROM LT. COLONEL ROBERT A. BOSTICK - RETIRED - ABOUT THE 961ST	48
DUTIES OF THE TECHNICIANS ON THE EC-121H - DEAN BOYS	54
RADAR CREW DUTIES - JOHN N. PUOPOLO	55
A FLIGHT ENGINEER RECALLS - JOE BROSNAN	58

PHOTOGRAPH OF CONNIE OVER CAPE COD CANAL 62

RECOLLECTIONS OF THE 961ST AEW&C SQUADRON
OCT 62 - OCT 65 - ARTHUR D. KERR 63

RECOLLECTIONS OF THE 551ST AEW&C WING AND
CAPE COD JAN 1962 - AUG 1969 - DEAN BOYS 76

DEAN BOYS AND HIS WEB SITES 84

1ST MISHAP - THE LOSS OF 55-0136 ON JULY 11, 1965

CONSOLIDATED NEWS ARTICLES 55-0136

THREE PICKET PLANE SURVIVORS SPEND NIGHT
IN SEA - July 12, 1965 88

HUGE SEA SEARCH UNDERWAY - PLANE DOWN
OFF CAPE 19 ARE ABOARD - WASP IN HUNT - HOPE
IN SIGNALS - Record American July 12, 1965 90
CARRIER ON WAY
HAVE LIFE RAFTS
RADIO SOS GIVE HOPE

8 CREWMEN DIE, 11 SAVED BY ARMADA AS OTIS PLANE
DITCHES IN ATLANTIC -Cape Cod Standard-Times
July 12, 1965 92
BELIEVED TRANSFERRED
TO ARRIVE
PICKED UP SOS
HAMPER SEARCH

AIR FORCE LISTS CREW OF DOWNED AIRPLANE -
Cape Cod Standard -Times July 12, 1965 95

BAD COMMUNICATIONS, WEATHER ARE BLAMED -
Cape Cod Standard -Times July 13, 1965 97

HOPE WANES FOR 7 CREWMEN - BOARD OF INQUIRY
WILL SIT - Cape Cod Standard -Times July 13, 1965 97
WERE PICKED UP
UNUSUALLY RAPID
PILOT TOLD
NOT FOR SOME TIME

IT WAS HORRIBLE 20 HOURS, SAYS WIFE - Cape Cod
Standard -Times July 13, 1965 100

WAS AT HOSPITAL
NOT WAIT ALONE
RESPECT FOR OCEAN

LIKE HITTING A BRICK WALL - Cape Cod Standard -Times
July 13, 1965 101
WERE PICKED UP
SANK IN MINUTES

THIRD OF WISH REALIZED - Cape Cod Standard -Times
July 13, 1965 103

TIME LIKE THIS I WISH WE WERE CIVILIANS -
Cape Cod Standard -Times July 13, 1965 103
WAS DIRECTED
LAY SPRAWLED
ONE OF THREE SURVIVORS

SURVIVORS TELL STORY OF PLANE CRASH - Cape
Cod Standard -Times July 14, 1965 105
SEARCH CONTINUED
POSITION GIVEN
DRIFTED AWAY
8 IDENTIFIED

SPECIAL FLY-OVER RITE PLANNED AT OTIS BASE -
Cape Cod Standard -Times July 15, 1965 107
WERE SAVED
HEAD BACK
LIST THE DEAD
WARNING STAR

BIG AF PLANE IN OCEAN OFF CAPE - Record American
July 12, 1965 108

WARNING STAR IS FLYING RADAR SHIELD FOR U.S. -
Record American July 13, 1965 109

MY SWEETIE IS ALIVE - Record American July 13, 1965 110
HOSPITAL VISIT
SAD FOR VICTIMS

MOTHER AWAITING VISIT FROM SON - Record
American July 13, 1965 110

SISTER PLANE IS ALOFT AS FLYING RELAY POST -
Record American July 13, 1965 110

SEA SURVIVAL PROBLEMATIC - Record American
July 13, 1965 111

BIRTHDAY FETE BEFORE CRASH - BAY STATE KIN
WAIT WORD - Record American July 13, 1965 112
MISSING AIRMEN SEARCH IS ENDED
TO RECOVER WRECKAGE
TOLD OF RESCUE
SPOTTED JACKETS

HISTORY OF FLIGHT 115

BOARD OF INQUIRY 118

CREW MEMBERS 120

PHOTOGRAPHS 122

LOST MAN FLYOVER 138

MEMORIAL SERVICE 139

REMEMBERING CAPTAIN ANAKA 142

REMEMBRANCES OF CAPTAIN RICHARD BARBOLLA 146

POEM - TO A LOST AVIATOR - BY DIANE BARBOLLA 152

OUR WORLD AND CAPTAIN BARBOLLA 153

REFLECTION ON CAPTAIN MURRAY J. BRODY
BY DEBORAH A. BRODY 155

A SURVIVOR'S STORY - JOHN N. PUOPOLO - ONE OF
THREE WHO SURVIVED THE DITCHING OF 55-0136 159

A SURVIVORS STORY - DAVID A. SURLES - ONE OF THE
THREE WHO SURVIVED THE DITCHING OF 55-0136 177

MA-1 SURVIVAL KIT (INDIVIDUAL LIFE RAFT) 185

BLANK PAGES FOR NOTES, ETC. 191

2nd MISHAP - THE LOSS OF 55-5262 ON NOVEMBER 11, 1966

CONSOLIDATED NEWS ARTICLES 55-5262

IT WAS TO BE AN ORDINARY NIGHT FLIGHT - Boston Globe
Nov 12, 1966 197

THEY WERE ALWAYS AFRAID IT MIGHT HAPPEN -
Boston Globe Nov 12, 1966 198

PLANE HUNT PUSHED BUT HOPE SEEN DIM - Boston
Globe Nov 12, 1966 199

LIST OF 19 OTIS CRASH VICTIMS - Boston Globe Nov 12, 1966 200

SEARCH ENDS FOR FLIERS - Boston Globe Nov 13, 1966 201

OTIS BASE RADAR PICKET PLANE CRASHES,
EXPLODES; 19 CREWMEN BELIEVED DEAD - Cape Cod
Standard -Times Nov 12, 1966 202
3RD TRAGEDY
HAD DITCHED
FREIGHTERS AIDED
NOT TO CONTACT
SIGHTED DEBRIS

BRIEFING BEFORE FATAL FLIGHT CALLED ROUTINE -
Cape Cod Standard -Times Nov 12, 1966 206

OTIS SURE DEBRIS FROM LOST PLANE - Cape Cod
Standard -Times Nov 12, 1966 207

OTIS PLAQUE HONORS DEAD OF 1ST CRASH - UPI
[Cape Cod Standard -Times] - Nov 12, 1966 208

MEN LOST IN PLANE CRASH FROM OTIS AIR FORCE BASE
[Air Force Sergeants Magazine] - December 1966 209

HISTORY OF FLIGHT 210

BOARD OF INQUIRY 214

CREW MEMBERS 216

PHOTOGRAPH OF 55-5262 218

PHOTOGRAPHS 219

MEMORIAL SERVICE 223

WHAT HAPPENED TO 55-5262? 226

ELECTRICAL SYSTEM EC-121H 233

COLONEL JACK JANUARY, JR., RECALLS 235

3rd MISHAP - THE LOSS OF 53-0549 ON APRIL 25, 1967

CONSOLIDATED NEWS ARTICLES 53-0549

HERO PILOT HAD LONG RECORD OF BRAVERY -
Boston Traveler April 26, 1967 240

ENGINE DISINTEGRATING - HOLE IN WING -
WITNESSES WATCH IN HORROR - Boston Traveler 241
SEES FIREBALL SKIM WATER FOR 4,000 FEET

3RD PICKET PLANE CRASH PROBED - GRIM SEARCH
INTENSIFIES OFF NANTUCKET - Boston Traveler April 26, 1967 .. 242
SURVIVOR WEARING EMERSION SUIT
NAMES OF CREW MEMBERS ABOARD PLANE

BLAST SAVED PLANE SURVIVOR - FOUGHT THROUGH
FLAMES AS 15 AIRMEN DIED - Boston Traveler 245

AIR SURVEY SHOWS NO SIGN OF PLANE - Boston Traveler
April 26, 1967 247

PLANE BIG BALL OF FIRE BEFORE IT DISAPPEARED -
Boston Traveler April 26, 1967 248

RUBBER SUITS COULD SAVE MEN IN WATER -
Boston Traveler April 26, 1967 249

EVERY WIFE KNEW AND HAD TO WAIT -
Boston Traveler April 26, 1967 249

CRASH SPURS DRIVE FOR MEMORIAL PARK -
Boston Traveler April 26, 1967 250

WEATHER IS IDEAL AS SEARCH CONTINUES -
Cape Cod Standard -Times April 26, 1967 251

PILOT AVOIDS BEACHFRONT HOMES; HITS SEA IN
BALL OF FLAME - Cape Cod Standard -Times April 26, 1967 251
SAW BRIGHT LIGHT
AT THE SAME LEVEL
AIRCRAFT DISAPPEARED
PLUCKED FROM SEA
RUSHED TO DOOR
BURNED FOR 10 MINUTES

OTIS PLANE CRASHES AT SEA; 15 FEARED DEAD,
ONE SURVIVES - Cape Cod Standard -Times April 26, 1967 254

An Editorial - THOROUGH INQUIRY URGENT IN WAKE OF
3 CRASHES 254

LYLE LAUDED 19 CREWMEN - CONDUCTED SERVICE
AFTER 1966 DISASTER - Cape Cod Standard -Times
April 26, 1967 255

FISHING CREW AGAIN ON HAND FOR CRASH -
Cape Cod Standard -Times April 26, 1967 256

BATES, PHILBIN SEEN ON COMMITTEE - HOUSE UNIT
TO PROBE NANTUCKET AF PLANE CRASH -
Boston Traveler April 27, 1967 256

KEITH, KENNEDY DEMAND PLANE PROBE; AIR FORCE
INVESTIGATION UNDER WAY - HOUSE UNIT TO VISIT
OTIS - Cape Cod Standard -Times April 27, 1967 257

BOARD QUERIES LONE SURVIVOR - Cape Cod Standard -
Times April 27, 1967 258
TWO IDENTIFIED
50 LOST
RECORDS IMPOUNDED
BACKGROUND TOLD

HOPEFULLY IT PUTS OUT THE FIRE - Cape Cod Standard -
Times April 27, 1967 260

LOST WING COMMANDER OFTEN DEFENDED CONNIES -
Cape Cod Standard -Times April 27, 1967 260
CAREER OFFICER
HAD COMMAND IN ITALY
DECORATIONS LISTED

PROBE FOR CAUSE - Editorial - Boston Traveler
April 28, 1967 262

CONGRESSMEN TO OPEN CRASH PROBE MONDAY -
Cape Cod Standard -Times April 28, 1967 263
TALK TO SURVIVOR
SALVAGE TRY EYED
INTERVIEW SOUGHT
IS SATISFACTORY

MEMORIAL RITES HELD AT OTIS FOR 15 FLYERS -
Boston Traveler April 29, 1967 264

PLANE CRASH SURVIVOR TELLS OF ESCAPE -
NAVIGATOR WANTS TO FLY "CONNIE" AGAIN - Cape Cod
Standard -Times May 1, 1967 265
ONLY SURVIVOR
ROUTINE MISSION
VERY ORDERLY
NO TIME
A COINCIDENCE
NO CRIES FOR HELP
WILL BE ALL RIGHT

WARNING STARS INSPECTED - OTIS TAKES
PRECAUTIONARY ACTION - Cape Cod Standard -Times
May 1, 1967 267

STILL EARLY FOR DECISION ON CAUSES -
Cape Cod Standard -Times May 2, 1967 268
AWARE OF BOARD
COUNSEL LIAISON

CRASH OF GIANT AIR FORCE PLANE OFF MADAKET
BRINGS DEATH TO 15 AIRMEN - The Inquirer And Mirror -
Nantucket, Mass - April 27, 1967 269

LAST TRIBUTES PAID FLIERS AT OTIS BASE CEREMONY -
The Inquirer And Mirror - Nantucket, Mass - May 4, 1967 274
ISLAND CHURCHES OFFER PRAYERS FOR LOST FLIERS
RADAR PLANE WRECKAGE NOW BEING RECOVERED
INVESTIGATIONS OF PLANE CRASH TO BE HELD HERE

A LIFE-SAVING BOATHOUSE AT MADAKET - The Inquirer
And Mirror - Nantucket, Mass - May 11, 1967 278

ISLANDERS REMEMBER THE FIERY CRASH OF 1967 -
Cape Cod Times June 23, 1966 278

SUMMARY OF CIRCUMSTANCES 281

BOARD OF INQUIRY 283

CREW MEMBERS	284
PHOTOGRAPHS	286
MEMORIAL SERVICE	295
DEATH OF THE GREAT BIRD - A POEM BY CHRISTOPHER COBB	299
REMEMBERING DENNIS COLE - BY WALTER G. TROY II	301
REMEMBERING MY FATHER COLONEL JAMES P. LYLE - BY JAMES LYLE JR	305
I WILL ALWAYS REMEMBER MY FATHER - I WAS MY DADDY'S LITTLE GIRL - BY JANA [LYLE] TREVINO	307
CAPTAIN FRANK FERGUSON'S FAMILY REMEMBERS HIM AS A MAN YOU COULD LOOK UP TO...A GENTLE HERO	310
REMEMBERING MY FATHER - BY JAMES P. WALSH	316
MY MEMORIES OF MY DAD [A1C TED LaPOINTE JR.] BY TECHNICAL SERGEANT THEODORE LaPOINTE	319
MRS. MARIE LaPOINTE REMEMBERS HER HUSBAND - [A/1C TED LAPOINTE JR.]	321
IN MEMORY OF FRANK W. GARNER - AFSA MAGAZINE	333
A SENTINEL SLEEPS - A POEM BY JOE BROSMAN	334
WE WON'T FORGET YOU - AFSA MAGAZINE ABOUT MSGT FRANK GARNER	335
A SURVIVOR'S STORY - JOSEPH L. H. GUENET - THE ONLY SURVIVOR OF THE DITCHING OF 53-0549 ON APRIL 25, 1967	336
BLANK PAGE FOR NOTES	354

SUMMARY OF EVENTS AND EYE WITNESS ACCOUNTS
ABOUT THE CRASH OF 53-0549 PILOTED BY COLONEL
JAMES P. LYLE WHICH DEPICT HIS BRAVERY 355

CAN YOU RELY ON OFFICIAL RECORDS 358

CHANGES OF KEY PERSONNEL AT THE 551ST WING 364

THEY KNEW THEY WOULD RETURN 367

CONDOLENCES 369

CONDOLENCE LETTERS 370

THE SILENT BATTLEFIELD 387

LISTING OF CREW MEMBERS OF
53-0549 -- 55-0136 -- 55-5262 388

GRAVE MARKER FOR COLONEL JAMES P. LYLE 390

GRAVE MARKER FOR TSGT GORDON O. HAMMAN, JR 391

OTIS MEMORIAL PARK 392

PLAQUES HONORING THE DECEASED CREW MEMBERS
OF THE THREE EC-121H AIRCRAFT ACCIDENTS 393

AWARDS AND DECORATIONS 394

TOWN OF NANTUCKET, MA 408

MAP OF NANTUCKET ISLAND DEPICTING THE DITCHING
SITE OF 53-0549 411

MAP OF THE AREA OFF CAPE COD DEPICTING THE
DITCHING SITES OF 55-0136, 55-5262 AND 53-0549 412

HOUSE ARMED SERVICES COMMITTEE REPORT AND A
SPECIAL REPORT ORDERED BY THE SECRETARY OF THE
AIR FORCE ON THE THREE AIRCRAFT CRASHES 413

RELATIVES OF SOME OF THE DECEASED FLYERS WHO
WOULD LIKE TO MEET ANYONE WHO KNEW OR FLEW
WITH THEIR LOVED ONES 415

COLD WAR RECOGNITION CERTIFICATES 417

ABBREVIATIONS USED 418

USAF RANK USED 420

MILITARY AIRCRAFT REFERENCED 421

PHOTOGRAPHS AND ILLUSTRATIONS 422

GLOSSARY OF UNCOMMON WORDS & PHRASES 429

LISTING OF LOSSES OF MILITARY CONSTELLATIONS
1953-1978 430

LIST OF INDIVIDUALS WHO HAVE ATTENDED OR HAVE
AN INTEREST IN THE 551ST AEW&C WING REUNION 432

NOTES 443

ORDER FORM 448

FOREWORD

For many years during the "Cold War" period AEW&C crews of the Air Force and Navy, flying the Lockheed "Warning Star" EC-121, aircraft tirelessly complemented the North American Air Defense Command (NORAD) radar shield around North America by providing airborne radar surveillance off the East Coast of the United States and from Hawaii to the Aleutian Islands. This shield was maintained 24 hours a day in all weather conditions. The system required the training and employment of highly skilled units and personnel.

A. J. Northrup, in this book, unfolds some of the untold stories of this operation. This critical segment of the NORAD system touched the lives of many of the assigned personnel and their families.

Clearly, the NORAD radar shield story needs to be told. National Security consideration prevented the telling of this story to date. The American public should now understand how many dedicated military personnel and units worked tirelessly under hazardous conditions to help preserve our way of life. Their unsung courage, fortitude and devotion to duty should not go unrecognized. A loud "hurrah" for these brave Air Force and Naval EC-121 air crews and support personnel.

Colonel John H. Pease
United States Air Force - Retired

Colonel Pease, the Vice Commander of the 37th Air Division at Goose Bay, Labrador, headed the Board of Inquiry into the loss of 52-5262 on November 11, 1966. Colonel Pease, a fighter pilot, retired in 1971 after an Air Force career covering 30 years. He resides in Colorado.

PREFACE

This composite publication some additional details of the loss of three EC-121H Air Force aircraft and fifty of their crew members [four survived]. It has been compiled utilizing information from official Air Force documents and news articles. Additional information has been incorporated from recollections of those who maintained or flew those or similar aircraft on similar missions over the North Atlantic. Some information was provided by parents, by children of several of the men who died in those three crashes, and by some of the wives of the deceased flyers.

It is hoped that knowing some of the details of the three aircraft accidents it will give the reader a better understanding of what happened in those final minutes. Perhaps the reader will also have an understanding of the grief the families experienced when they learned of the death of their loved ones, and may sense the outpouring of sympathy and understanding along with those who lived on or near Otis Air Force Base, Massachusetts and whose lives were intertwined with the officers and airmen. Perhaps, just perhaps, an understanding of the significance of some of the many roles our military men play in preserving our freedom by their willingness to give their lives defending it, will be instilled.

ABOUT - A. J. NORTHRUP

Born December 15, 1936. Member of the USAF from 13 December 1954 - 1 July 1975 [Retired grade - Senior Master Sergeant]

After completion of Basic Training at Lackland AFB, Texas, was classified as a Airborne Radio Operator. Completed the Airborne Radio Operator Course at Keesler AFB, Mississippi, in August 1955 and was assigned to the 961st Airborne Early Warning and Control Squadron, 551st Airborne Early Warning and Control Wing, 8th Air Division (ADC) at Otis AFB, Massachusetts. Was assigned as a member of a flight crew on RC-121 (Super Connie) which was an airborne radar platform (similar to the present day AWACS).

Completed the Airborne Electronics Countermeasures Course at Keesler AFB, Mississippi, in May 1956, and performed those dual duties (Airborne Radio Operator/Electronic Countermeasures Operator) with the 961st AEW&C Squadron until November 1959.

In November 1959 was assigned to the 7405th Support Group, Headquarters United States Air Force Europe (USAFE), Wiesbaden AB, Germany, as an Airborne Radio Operator.

In April 1961 was assigned to the 7260th Support Group, United States Air Force Europe (USAFE), at Wiesbaden AB, Germany. This unit was the "sister" unit of the unit at Andrews AFB, Maryland, which had the mission of transporting VIPs' throughout the world. While serving as a Airborne Radio Operator on those missions visiting 23 foreign countries flew several missions into Moscow transporting VIP to or from that location and flying missions to support the US Embassy located there.

Accumulated 2877 flying hours in 14 various type aircraft.

Served one year as a Buyer in the Base Procurement office after returning to Otis AFB, Massachusetts, from Germany.

Was assigned to the Air Force Office of Special Investigations, OSI District 1, at Detachment 107 at Otis AFB, Massachusetts, in January 1964, and completed the Special Investigators Course (Class 64-B in May 1964. Completed the Procurement Investigators Course in December 1967.

Assigned to OSI District 50, Detachment 5002, Tan Son Nhut AB, Saigon, Vietnam from February 1968 until March 1969. Assigned to OSI District 1, Detachment 102 at Hanscom Field, Bedford, Massachusetts, from April 1969 until June 1973. Assigned to OSI District 1, Detachment 109, Griffiss AFB, New York, from June 1, 1973 until retiring in July 1975.

BRONZE STAR MEDAL
MERITORIOUS SERVICE MEDAL
VIETNAM AIR FORCE HONOR MEDAL SECOND CLASS
AIR FORCE LONGEVITY SERVICE AWARD RIBBON
AIR FORCE OUTSTANDING UNIT AWARD
GOOD CONDUCT MEDAL - ARMY
GOOD CONDUCT MEDAL - AIR FORCE - WITH TWO BRONZE LOOPS
USAF NCO ACADEMY GRADUATE RIBBON
AIRCREW MEMBER BADGE
NATIONAL DEFENSE SERVICE MEDAL
VIETNAM SERVICE MEDAL
REPUBLIC OF VIETNAM CAMPAIGN MEDAL
SMALL ARMS EXPERT MARKSMANSHIP RIBBON

Senior Ethics Investigator for the State of Florida Commission on Ethics 1976 - 1990. Private Investigator 1990 - 1996.

To get in touch with me write: A. J. NORTHRUP
                                    1976 Hickory Tree Lane
                                    Tallahassee, FL 32303
Telephone: (850)514-7441

E-Mail: north.north@att.net

A1C A. J. NORTHRUP [19 YEARS OLD] IN 1956 AT OTIS AIR FORCE BASE

A. J. NORTHRUP AT THE JOINT REUNION OF THE 551ST, 552ND AND 553RD WINGS AT OKLAHOMA CITY, OK - JUNE 30, 2001

WITH LOVE TO MY WIFE GRANDCHILDREN

**MARY THERESA [AVERSA] NORTHRUP
MICHELLE NICHOLE NORTHRUP - MAR 14, 1986
JENNIE ELENA NORTHRUP - FEB 17, 1988
LUKE ALAN NORTHRUP - JUL 17, 1992
JARED ROBERT NORTHRUP - JUL 16, 1995
HOPE JILLIAN NORTHRUP - OCT 20, 1997**

ACKNOWLEDGMENTS

Air Force Sergeants Association (AFSA)

Alan J. Northrup - Major - USAF - [My Son]

Amy Riley - Photographer - 102nd Fighter Wing Visual Information Office, Otis ANG, MA

Arthur D. Kerr - Former Pilot with the 961st AEW&C Squadron - Redmond, WA

Barbara P. Andrews - Librarian Emerita - Nantucket Atheneum - Nantucket, MA

Bill Richards - Airborne Early Warning Association

Boston Traveler

Boston Public Library

Boston Globe

Boston Herald

Bourne Massachusetts Public Schools [Lyle Middle School]

Cape Cod Standard-Times

Charolette Maison - Librarian - Atheneum Library - Nantucket, MA

Cottage Hospital - Nantucket, MA [President and CEO] Ms. Lucille C. Giddings

David A. Surles - Survivor of 55-0136 ditching on July 11, 1965

Dean Boys, Master Sergeant USAF - Retired

Deborah A. Brody - Washington, DC - whose father Captain Murray J. Brody, lost his life on July 11, 1965 on EC-121H number 55-0136

Diane Cheshire - Former wife of Captain Frank R. Ferguson who lost his life in the crash of 53-0549 at Nantucket Island on April 25, 1967

Diane Barbolla - Wife of Captain Michael R. Barbolla who lost his life in the crash of 55-0136 on July 11, 1965

Eric W. Benken, Chief Master Sergeant of the Air Force, HQ USAF

George Runkle - http://members.tripod.com/-CldWarHist/ArbnEW.html

Gloria J. Mick, CMSGT USAF, Chief of Air Force Casualty Branch

Jack January, Jr., Colonel USAF-Retired - Commander of the 961st at the time 55-5262 was lost with its 19 member crew on November 11, 1966

James L. Lyle Jr. - Hermosa Beach, CA - Son of Colonel James P. Lyle who lost his life on 25 April 1967 on EC-121H number 53-0549

James P. Walsh - Houston, TX - Son of A/1C William M. Walsh who lost his life on 25 April 1967 on EC-121H number 53-0549

Jana Trevino - Denton, TX - Daughter of Colonel James P. Lyle who lost his life on 25 April 1967 on EC-121H number 53-0549

Joanna DaSilva - 551st AEW&C Wing reunion coordinator

Joe Brosnan - Master Sergeant USAF - Retired - Flight Engineer

John H. Pease, Colonel USAF-Retired - Chairman of the Board of Inquiry regarding the loss of 55-5262

John M. Konosky - Colonel USAF - Retired - Former Commander of the 551st AEW&C Wing

John N. Puopolo - Survivor of 55-1036 ditching on July 11, 1965.

Joseph L. H. Guenet, Lt. Colonel USAF Retired - the only survivor of 53-0549

Juanita Lyle - [Deceased December 26, 1998] - Wife of Colonel James P. Lyle the Aircraft Commander who lost his life on 25 April 1967 on EC-121H number 53-0549

Judith C. Wallingford - Former wife of Captain Edward N. Anaka who lost his life on 55-0136 on July 11, 1965

Catherine Flanagan Stover - Town Clerk - Nantucket, MA

Linda Burnette - Staff Member - House National Security Committee

Marcia Haley - Chief Air Force Records - National Personnel Records Center

Marie LaPointe - Wife of A/lC Theodore LaPointe Jr., who lost his life on 25 April 1967 in the ditching of 53-0549

Mirror and Inquirer - Nantucket, MA

Oliver G. Cellini, Colonel - USAF - Retired - First 551st Wing Commander

Otis Notice - A newspaper published for and about Otis Air Force Base, MA

Record American

Robert A. Bostick - Lt. Colonel USAF - Retired

Theodore LaPointe - USAF TSGT - whose father A/1C Theodore LaPointe Jr., lost his life on 25 April 1967 on EC-121H number 53-0549

Town and County of Nantucket Board of Selectmen - County Commissioners Arthur L. Desrocher, Charles Gardner, Pamela L. Killen, Timothy M. Soverino, Vincent M. Vacca - Town & County Administrator C. Elizabeth Gibson - GIS Coordinator Hilliard Wood

United States Air Force Historical Research Agency - Maxwell AFB, AL

United States Air Force Safety Headquarters - Kirtland AFB, NM

United States Air Force Chief of Staff General Michael E. Ryan

Walter G. Troy - Newport News, VA - Friend of Airman Dennis Cole who lost his life in the crash of 53-0549 on April 25, 1967 at Nantucket

Wayne Minnick - Professor Emeritus [Florida State University] Tallahassee, FL

William R. Willner - Major USAF - Retired - Pilot Member of the Board of Inquiry of 55-5262 and 53-0549

NOTE: IF I HAVE FAILED TO ACKNOWLEDGE YOU BY NAME PLEASE FORGIVE ME - IT WAS AN OVERSIGHT

As the Author, I readily admit that what I have presented in this book is far from complete. There are so many stories that remain to be told. There also are photographs of individuals and events that were not available to me when I concluded my research that still need to be presented. I wish to apologize to the families of the 50 fallen flyers that I could not locate or whose locations came to my attention after the research had been concluded and whose stories and family photographs could not be included in the book.

When the book reached 448 pages I knew there had to be a stopping point in order to get it finished and printed.

Perhaps there will be enough interest shown by those of you, the readers of this book, who will be willing to contribute your personal stories, documents, and photographs to warrant another publication which would continue where this book left off. I would be interested in receiving your opinions, suggestions, ideas in that respect and any comments you wish to make about this book.

A. J. NORTHRUP
1976 Hickory Tree Lane
Tallahassee, FL 32303
E-Mail: north.north@worldnet.att.net

SPECIAL THANKS
TO
DEAN BOYS

Without your assistance this book never would have been possible. You were willing to share your extensive library dealing with the many aspects of the Air Force, its missions, personnel, and aircraft with me when I undertook this research project. If you did not have the information I wanted, you found it for me or directed me to the right place so I could make requests for it. I can never repay you for the time you graciously devoted to my project doing research, scanning documents and photographs, and exchanging information with me on a almost daily basis.

Although I have never met you, except through digital technology, I feel that I know you, and I look forward to one day meeting you. It is a pleasure to consider you as my best friend. Thank you, Dean, from the bottom of my heart for the friendship that automatically came along with your help.

A. J. NORTHRUP

SPECIAL THANKS
TO
THE PRESS

To the members of the press who reported the breaking news of the aircraft crashes and wrote follow-up articles as the events were occurring more than thirty years ago. Their reporting has provided a detailed history of the events as they unfolded.

Although some of the articles reporting the crashes, the searches, the rescue attempts, and the recovery operations are conflicting they nevertheless provide documentation for future generations what would not have been available from any other sources.

The confusion in the reporting of who survived, who died, those bodies that were found and not found was caused perhaps in part by the many and varied mixture of participants in the search and recovery operations (NATO member forces, the Air Force, the Coast Guard, the Navy, as well as the commercial and civilian vessels).

Secondly, the military does not routinely give out information when events such as the crashes occur. Perhaps had there been more openness on the part of the Air Force at that time the media could have reported events more accurately.

Surely the confusion involved in the reporting caused anguish, false hope and subsequent grief to some of the families who were awaiting news of their loved ones when data reported did not check out or was mistaken. I realize that reporting of events is necessary and in this case without the work of the reporters there would not exist today a detailed public record about the crashes as the Air Force does not release the testimony from survivors and/or eye witnesses. This material was reported by the media.

THANKS TO ALL THOSE WHOSE CONTRIBUTIONS MADE THIS TRIBUTE TO THE FLYERS POSSIBLE

I wish to thank the survivors who took the time and effort to document the accounts of their survival and to share their personal stories and photographs. Because of them we have a better understanding of what happened in the final minutes of their flight prior to ditching and the ordeal they experienced in the frigid waters of the North Atlantic while awaiting rescue.

I also wish to thank the many relatives who lost their loved ones but were willing to share their recollections of the flyers they obviously hold dear in their hearts. Even after all the years have passed since the loss of their loved ones the families have not forgotten them.

I thank each person (former commanders, acquaintances, fellow crew members, the many friends of the crew members, and every other person) who contributed in any manner in this memorial to the brave officers and airmen.

****

I ALSO WANT TO ESPECIALLY ACKNOWLEDGE MY LOVELY WIFE - MARY THERESA [AVERSA] NORTHRUP OF LEOMINSTER, MASSACHUSETTS, WHOM I MET ON HER VACATION AT CAPE COD IN JUNE 1956. WE WERE MARRIED JUNE 21, 1957, AT THE BASE CHAPEL AT OTIS AIR FORCE BASE, MASSACHUSETTS.

MARY, A MEMBER OF THE CHAPEL CHOIR AT OTIS, PARTICIPATED IN THE MEMORIAL SERVICES FOR THE FALLEN FLYERS.

HER ENCOURAGEMENT TO ME TO HONOR THESE MEN AND THEIR FAMILIES MADE THIS BOOK BECOME A REALITY.

INTRODUCTION

THE 551st AEW & C WING
ITS MISSION AND ITS MISHAPS

In January 1955, a strange-looking airplane, an RC-121D, a radar version of the famed C-121 Lockheed Constellation piloted by Colonel Oliver G. Cellini, landed at Otis Air Force Base, Massachusetts, after a cross country flight from McClellan Air Force Base, California. This was the first of many such aircraft assigned to Otis Air Force Base to be used in patrolling the eastern seaboard.

Otis Air Force Base, located on Cape Cod, was the only Air Defense Command base with units performing three of the Air Defense Command's prime missions: radar picket plane surveillance, fighter-interception, and ground-to-air missile operations.

With the completion of the Distant Early Warning (DEW) Line in 1958, the northern areas of the United States and Canada were still vulnerable. Consequently, the radar warning networks were extended seaward at Otis Air Force Base on the East Coast and McClellan Air Force Base on the West Coast by using the 551st and 552nd Airborne Early Warning and Control Wings, respectively. Those wings supplemented the radar protection along the entire coastal lengths of the United States.

The 551st Wing at Otis was the only Air Force organization flying the EC-121H **"Warning Star"** Super Constellation known as Airborne Long Range Input (ALRI) aircraft. Those aircraft carried more than six tons of complex radar and computer communications equipment on each flight.

The new integrated radar station on wings provided instantaneous automated relay of air defense surveillance and early warning information by data-link direct to ground based communications facilities. Then it was passed to high speed SAGE (Semi-Automatic Ground Environment) Air Defense Command and Control computers in the East Coast SAGE Direction Centers and to the NORAD (North American Air Defense Command) Combat Operations Center in Colorado Springs, Colorado, for air defense evaluation and action. ALRI permitted more versatile airborne control of interceptor missile and aircraft weapons systems.

The 551st Wing was composed of the 960th, the 961st, and the 962nd Airborne Early Warning and Control Squadrons, who flew their continuous missions over the Atlantic Ocean 24 hours a day. The three flying squadrons were supported by the 551st Combat Support Group and three maintenance squadrons - all of the 551st (Electronics Maintenance Squadron - EMS, Field Maintenance Squadron - FMS and Organizational Maintenance Squadron - OMS).

On March 2, 1965, the 551st AEW&C Wing celebrated its 10th anniversary. It was noted that the 551st Wing had progressed through many changes--some involving electronic equipment and other gear. There had been many assignments, reassignments and, in some cases, re-reassignments of Air Force members there to perform the radar surveillance mission. Still the mission continued to be an effective-- although more sophisticated--form of radar surveillance against the enemy. During that past decade the aircraft of the 551st Wing had accumulated more than 350,000 hours without an accident involving personal injury or a fatality. However, the fatality-free decade celebration didn't last long.

Some four months later, on July 11, 1965, an EC-121H Super Constellation (number 55-0136) with 19 crew members aboard ditched in the North Atlantic, resulting in 16 men losing their lives and three survivors being rescued. Of the 16 dead, nine bodies were recovered and seven never were located.

Then on November 11, 1966, [Veterans Day] another EC-121H Super Constellation (number 55-5262) ditched in the North Atlantic, resulting in all 19 crew members being killed and none of their bodies being recovered.

Again, on April 25, 1967, another EC-121H Super Constellation (number 53-0549) ditched in the North Atlantic near Nantucket, Massachusetts, resulting in 15 crew members being killed and one survivor being rescued. Of the 15 killed, 10 bodies were recovered and 5 apparently were not found.

Ironically, the Aircraft Commander on 53-0549 was the 551st Wing Commander, Colonel James Perkins Lyle, and he was one of the 15 crew members who lost their lives in that crash.

Colonel Lyle had assumed command of the 551st AEW&C Wing nine months earlier on July 22, 1966. It was Colonel Lyle who during memorial services for the victims of the November 11, 1966 crash of 55-5262, presented each of the next of kin with the United States Flag. Colonel Lyle's own death in an aircraft accident occurred five months later.

It was Colonel Lyle also who worked for the establishment of a memorial park at Otis Air Force Base in tribute to the 19 men who lost their lives in 1966 and the 16 other airmen who died in another crash on July 11, 1965. The Otis Memorial Park later became a reality, and plaques there honor the fifty officers and airmen who lost their lives in the three crashes.

The 50 flyers who lost their lives became "***FIFTY FALLEN STARS***" who individually and collectively deserve the highest recognition and honor for their sacrifice.

After a series of three crashes of the EC-121H "Warning Stars" in a period of twenty-one months took the lives of fifty crew members, an inquiry was reportedly directed by the then Secretary of the Air Force Harold Brown. Additionally, in April 1967 a special subcommittee of the House Armed Services Committee was appointed to investigate the causes of all three accidents.

An Air Force board of inquiry investigated the April 25, 1967 crash as similar boards had done when the two other EC-121H planes crashed. However, the Air Force's investigative board's "analysis, findings, and recommendations" regarding aircraft "mishaps" are "exempt from disclosure."

I asked Lockheed Martin Corporation, formerly known as Lockheed Aerospace Corporation (the manufacturer of the Super Constellation aircraft) to identify the cause of the three aircraft accidents. Lockheed responded that they could find no records identifiable with the aircraft in question.

The EC-121H "Warning Star" Super Constellation aircraft were phased out, and the 551st Airborne Early Warning and Control Wing at Otis Air Force Base, Massachusetts, was deactivated on December

31, 1969. Otis Air Force Base later was renamed Otis Air National Guard (ANG) Base.

[SOURCES] Some of the introductory information about the 551st AEW&C Wing was obtained partially from my recollection, from the web pages maintained by Dean Boys and from the handbook "This Is the 961st" provided by Art Kerr.

AIR DEFENSE COMMAND (ADC) EMBLEM

551ST AIRBORNE EARLY WARNING AND CONTROL WING EMBLEM - THE MOTTO *VIDERE EST PARARI* MEANS *VIGILANCE IS PREPAREDNESS.*

[NOTICE] - *For information about the 551st Airborne Early Warning & Control Wing reunions please contact Joanna DaSilva, P.O. Box 226, East Wareham, MA 02538 or telephone (508)295-2030*

For information about the 552nd Airborne Early Warning & Control Wing reunions please contact Tony Praxel, 3005 Prado, Sacramento, CA 95825 or telephone (916)487-1975 or e-mail TPraxel@aol.com.

THE AIR DEFENSE COMMAND AND THE 551ST AEW&W WING PATCHES FURNISHED COURTESY OF DEAN BOYS

TO LEARN MORE ABOUT THE 551st VISIT THE WEB SITE AT:

http://www.dean-boys.com/551aew/551 staew.htm

551st ORGANIZATIONAL MAINTENANCE SQUADRON

551ST FIELD MAINTENANCE SQUADRON

551ST SECURITY POLICE SQUADRON

551ST TRANSPORTATION SQUADRON

551ST SUPPLY SQUADRON

962ND AEW&C SQUADRON

960TH AEW&C SQUADRON

RECOLLECTIONS OF
THE FIRST 551ST WING COMMANDER
COLONEL OLIVER G. CELLINI

Dear Mr. Northrup.

I have read every word you have written. I don't know what I can add to your manuscript, because everything you covered occurred after my time [at Otis AFB]. Hopefully, I can fill you in on the period before you arrived in the wing [August 1955].

To set the record straight, I was originally the commander of the 4707th Air Defense Wing at Otis, long before the 551st. In the spring of 1954, I was fired as the commander and became the deputy commander. I was made a project officer for the A. E. W. & C. to be activated. March 10th, 1954, I was given a 1st Lt. and five very good enlisted men. We had our task cut out for us, and we worked our tails off.

At this point a bit on organization: I do not know what changes may have been made after I left. Eastern Air Defense Force (E.A.D.F.) was the parent command responsible for everything. It was located at Stewart A.F.B., New York. The 26th Air Division located at Syracuse, NY was responsible for operations.

The 4707th Air Defense Wing was responsible for operations and training of our area complex. The wing had two bases, Otis and Niagara Falls, NY. It also had a fighter squadron at Westover AFB, at that time a huge transport complex. The fighter squadron was a tenant on Westover. In addition to the above, the wing had five radar squadrons. Unless my memory fails, these squadrons were located at Truro (the end of Cape Cod), New Brunswick Naval Air Station, Maine; Albany, NY, Syracuse, and Niagara Falls.

As commander of the 4707th Air Defense Wing, my effectiveness report was made out by the commander of the 26th Air Division. My support came from EADF and from the Commander at Otis. The 4707th was actually a tenant on Otis. However, I made out the effectiveness report for the base commander at Otis, as well as the base commander at Niagara Falls, the Squadron C.O. at Westover, and the C.O.'s of five radar squadrons. Probably a bit confusing, but it worked.

When I became project officer of the 551st, I was really at the mercy of the 4707th, even though I was still the deputy. My full time job was getting things ready for the 551st. The commander of the 4707th, Col. Dick Legg, and I had been friends for many years. I can honestly say that the support from the 4707th was absolutely outstanding.

On October 1st, 1954, I was assigned as a provisional wing commander of the 551st, and on December 18th, 1954, I became the wing commander. I was relieved as of February 20th, 1956, and assigned overseas. Something else that was not recorded was the twelve hour days we put in.

When we finally activated as the 551st, we literally had nothing but the complete support of my ex-wing. Example: we were given office space, vehicles, typewriters, toilet paper, you name it. I had an airplane or airplanes available at all times. I personally made many trips to depots and the 8th Air Division.

In 1942, I activated a pursuit squadron. In 1947, I activated an all weather fighter group, and then the 551st in 1954. I can honestly say that I have had all sorts of assignments in my thirty-two years of service. The 551st required the most hours of work, the fewest (if any) days off, and with the least gratitude.

I was with the wing during most of the formative stage. You came in when things were beginning to roll; you missed the growing pains.

Many people sent into new organizations are often drudges not wanted by someone else. We received our share of both officers and airmen. We also received some absolutely outstanding people, and they became the backbone, or prime movers, of getting tasks done. As an example: Pan American tried very hard to get my panel engineer, Sgt. Crump, to go with them. Crump was super. Without the cooperation of those outstanding few, I could not have gotten the 551st out of first gear.

Our big task, of course, was to get the few aircraft we had operational and train combat crews. At the same time, we had to renovate barracks for incoming people, set up mess halls, office space for different activities, clamor for our organizational equipment list (OEL), tools, spare parts, test gear, support equipment, like vehicles, tugs, etc. The number of detailed time-consuming tasks could fill a few pages. We had to set up schools for *pilots, mechanics, electronics people, radio and radar operators, etc. In this respect, we did get some help from the 8th Air Division, primarily in the form of instructors, for which we were grateful.*

Sometimes the demands of the 8th Air Division were the same for the 551st as they were for the 552nd. The 552nd had been in business for a few years, and furthermore, was based at a major depot, McClellan AFB, CA.

By the time I left, I don't recall that we had a single designated combat crew. We did have a number of officers and airmen who individually were ready in their specific field. Example: we had some qualified pilots, navigators, radio operators, flight engineers, scope operators, etc. We sent many made-up crews on patrol, and we practiced quite a bit, controlling fighters from Otis and Westover. I would have loved to stay with the wing, about another year, in order to see the fruits of all our work. But unfortunately, the service moved us around frequently.

I don't know if I have helped you or not, but I hope I have. If nothing else, I've given you some history. My memory is not what it used to be, so please consider that everything I have written is at least forty-three years old. In closing, I want to commend and congratulate you for the tremendous amount of work you have done in researching and reviewing history and records, and in putting everything together.

Col. Oliver (Ollie) G. Cellini, USAF, Ret.
3020 E. Fuller Road
Colorado Springs, CO 80920-3630
(719)598-5463
E-Mail through my daughter:
BevFay@aol.com

**USAF PHOTOGRAPH FURNISHED BY
COLONEL OLIVER G. CELLINI**

[Left to Right] BRIGADIER GENERAL KEN GIBSON, COMMANDER 8TH AIR DIVISION - COLONEL OLIVER G. CELLINI, COMMANDER OF THE 551ST AEW&C WING; COLONEL FRED HOOK, COMMANDING OFFICER OF OTIS AFB; COLONEL ARTHUR A. McCARTAN, DEPUTY COMMANDER 551ST AEW&C WING; COLONEL HAVEY, OPERATIONS CHIEF OF THE 551st. COLONEL CELLINI BECAME THE COMMANDER OF THE 551ST WING ON DECEMBER 18, 1954.

USAF PHOTOGRAPH FURNISHED COURTESY OF COLONEL OLIVER G. CELLINI

THE LOCKHEED SUPER CONSTELLATION [RC-121D] SIMILAR TO THE FIRST ONE DELIVERED TO OTIS AFB BY COLONEL CELLINI IN JANUARY 1955.

THE CONSTELLATION IS FLANKED BY A COUPLE OF LOCKHEED F-94 "STARFIRE" INTERCEPTORS WHICH WORKED IN CONJUNCTION WITH THE RADAR PATROL AIRCRAFT OF THE 551ST AEW&C WING IN DETECTING AND INTERCEPTING UNKNOWN AIRCRAFT APPROACHING THE EAST COAST OF THE UNITED STATES.

Note: In September 1956, the Author was named the 961st AEW&C Squadron and the 551st AEW&C Wing Airman of the Month. The presentation of awards was made by Colonel Arthur A. McCartan, Commander of the 551st Wing. As a special favor the Author received a ride in an F-94C on October 3, 1956 (courtesy of the 60th Fighter Interceptor Squadron) for one hour and ten minutes.

USAF PHOTOGRAPH FURNISHED COURTESY OF COLONEL OLIVER G. CELLINI

[CENTER] SECRETARY OF THE AIR FORCE

[LEFT] GOVERNOR CHRISTIAN HERTER OF THE COMMONWEALTH OF MASSACHUSETTS

[RIGHT] COLONEL OLIVER G. CELLINI, COMMANDER OF THE 551ST AEW&C WING

CEREMONY ON THE FLIGHT LINE AT OTIS AFB

SENTINELS ON GUARD

THIS IS THE 551ST AEW&C WING

With the advent of thermonuclear weapons, the national security of the United States has depended greatly upon the Strategic Air Command's lead over the Soviet's ability to deliver these weapons to vital targets.

Recently, this lead was seriously diminished as the Russians began replacing their outmoded B-29 type bombers with new high speed, long range weapons carriers comparable to those used by the U.S. Air Force.

Realizing the increasing threat of Russian strategic air power, the United States has been striving to improve its air defenses, especially the radar detection system upon which it relies for vital advance warning of an enemy attack.

The detection system has been extended by building chains of far-flung radar sites, ranging from the Pinetree radar line just north of the U.S.-Canadian border to the Distant Early Warning Line near the Arctic Circle. At sea, picket ships patrol specific areas in the North Atlantic and Pacific and 'Texas Towers,' or radar islands, have been built on the coastal shelf off the eastern seaboard.

Complementing this warning system is the 551st Airborne Early Warning and Control Wing.

RC-121 Super Constellations, 'flying radar stations' built by Lockheed Aircraft Corporation, are utilized by the wing for its operations. The plane flies at a speed exceeding 285 miles per hour. Its maximum range exceeds 5,000 statute miles and it can remain aloft over 20 hours.

The RC-121's are four engine Super Constellations, equipped with five and one-half tons of radio and radar equipment. Operated by specially trained crews of Air Force technicians several hundred miles at sea, these airplanes extend the Air Force Coastal Detection Zones to provide early warning of any possible attack on the United States.

The RC-121 airborne radar search station and fighter-interceptor control center carries a maximum crew of 31 men, operates at altitudes up to 25,000 feet and flies at speeds up to 300 miles per hour. Since they remain on patrol over the ocean for extreme lengths of time, RC-121's are equipped with tip tanks which enable them to cover thousands of miles without refueling.

Initially, control of the fighter is the responsibility of the coastal radar station. When it moves into the range of the RC-121's radar, the airborne Intercept Director aboard the RC-121 assumes control of the fighter. On the radar screen, the Director charts the fighter's course and position. He speaks to the fighter pilot constantly by voice radio, giving him new ranges and courses at ten-second intervals, and instructs him as to altitude and speed of approach of the target.

Rapidly the target and fighter close, until the fighter pilot reports a 'Tallyho,' the word he uses to say he has sighted the target visually.

If the 'Bogey' is an enemy, the fighter engages it in battle; if the aircraft is friendly, identification information is relayed to the appropriate channels on ground and disciplinary action is taken against the pilot of the 'Bogey.'

From takeoff to landing, the fighter-pilot is constantly under vigilance and control of radar personnel, either through the airborne or ground stations. Repeated checks are made of the fighter's fuel supply and Air-Sea rescue units are alerted when the jet fighter reaches the shoreline, to be available immediately in case of an emergency occurring over water.

Thus, constant teamwork between both the fighter pilot and the airborne director is essential for the success of their respective missions. The Director is responsible for guiding the fighter to its prey and returning him to his home base before his fuel supply is depleted.

Before the airborne Director-Fighter team can go into action, every member of the numerous airborne crews must be thoroughly 'checked out' with the new RC-121 aircraft and equipment it carries. The Radar Controllers, Operators and Technicians can make use of their skills only when the Pilots, Navigators, Engineers, and Radio Operators all know completely their jobs and responsibilities. This applies especially to the pilots designated as Aircraft Commanders who shoulder the responsibility for the safety of the aircraft and crew from the preflight briefing to the postflight physical conditioning exercises.

The 551st AEW&Con Wing was organized on October 1, 1954 as a provisional unit. On December 18, 1954 it was designated as the 551st Airborne Early Warning and Control Wing and assigned to the 8th Air Division under the Western Air Defense Force.

Much of its early activity was devoted to training. By the fall of 1956 the wing was ready to assume its mission responsibilities and it became fully operational in October 1956.

On July 1, 1957 the wing was transferred from the deactivated 8th Air Division to Eastern Air Defense Force. Also on this date it became the base unit at Otis, thus assuming the task of giving support to some 57 units and 19,000 people.

Source: The 1957 year book of the 551st AEW&C Wing at Otis Air Force Base, Massachusetts

NOTE: The above article describes the 551ST AEW&C Wing and its mission utilizing the RC-121D Super Constellation. The Wing flew the RC-121D model Super Constellations until approximately the early part of 1963 when they were replaced by the EC-121H model. The three aircraft from the 551st Wing that later ditched in the Atlantic were the EC-121H model.

PHOTOGRAPH PROVIDED VIA GEORGE RUNKLE
http://members.tripod.com/~CldWarHist/ArbnEW.html

PHOTOGRAPH OF LOCKHEED'S SUPER CONSTELLATION OR "CONNIE" AIRCRAFT WHICH PROVIDED AROUND THE CLOCK AIRBORNE RADAR SURVEILLANCE OF THE COASTS OF THE UNITED STATES.

NOTE: To learn more about the "Connie" visit the web site at:

http://www.dean-boys.com/ec-121.htm

LOCKHEED EC-121 - WARNING STAR

Manufacturer: The Lockheed Aerospace Company
Airframe: Modified Lockheed Constellation
Power plant: Four Wright R-3350s.
Power: 3,400 Horsepower each engine.
Length: 116 ft. 2 in.
Wingspan: 126 ft. 2 in.
Height: 27 ft. 0 in.
Radar: Search Radar: AN/APS-20 (original) AN/APS-95 (upgrade)
Height finder: AN/APS-45 (original) AN/APS-103 (upgrade)
Nicknames: Warning Star (Official), Super Connie, Connie
Primary function: Airborne Early Warning
Delivery: 1953
Maximum fuel weight: 145,000 pounds
Maximum speed: 290 mph.
Aircraft Ceiling: 18,000 feet
Operating Altitude: 18,000 feet
Endurance: Official endurance is currently unknown. Longest mission reported by crew member is [**17:35**] hours [1/Lt Joseph L. H. Guenet, Navigator, 551st AEW&C Wing, Otis AFB, MA -December 24, 1965 in EC-121H number 55-5262]
Range: 4,000 miles
Radar range: AN/APS-95 - 250 NM
AN/APS-45 - 120 NM
AN/APS-20 - Unknown.
Armament: None.
Crew size: Varies, but a typical crew consisted of 6 Officers and 11 Enlisted.
Officers: 2 Pilots
2 Navigators
2 Weapons Controllers
Enlisted: 2 Flight Engineers
1 Radio Operator
6 Radar Operators
2 Radar Technicians

Sources: Janes: All the World's Aircraft, EC-121 Crew member: Jim Lawler jclawler@iu.net
By: Bill Richards wildbill@aewa.org
http://www.aewa.org/Library/ec121-info.html
Airborne Early Warning Association
Permission for use granted by Bill Richard

FLYING WITH THE 551ST AEW&C WING
August 1955 - November 1959

A. J. NORTHRUP

On August 16, 1955, immediately after completing the Airborne Radio Operators Course, I was assigned to the 551st Airborne Early Warning and Control Wing (AEW&C), 961st Airborne Early Warning and Control Squadron, Otis Air Force Base, Massachusetts.

After undergoing all the in-processing and survival training, along with the many aspects of squadron training, I made my first flight as a radio operator on the RC-121 "Super Constellation" on October 9, 1955 for 7:45 hours. I was soon routinely assigned to fly missions over the North Atlantic approximately every third day.

I recall that take-off times were scheduled for all hours of the day and night since several aircraft and their crews were manning different airborne stations at the same time over the North Atlantic. Those crews who had been on station for many hours anxiously awaited being relieved by other crews and aircraft.

The schedule basically required me to fly, get some time off for a little rest, train, fly, and repeat this cycle forever. I soon got used to eating breakfast at the time I normally would eat the evening meal, dinner at the time I normally would eat breakfast and so on. Generally, the time off after a flight was really not time off since it seemed they always found something for us to do.

Time spent preparing for a typical flight would require me to arrive at the squadrons' operations briefing room at least three hours before take-off time. There were crew briefings, weather briefings, administrative reminders from the squadron. There was the checking out, fitting and inspection of the survival equipment by the individual crew members, and crews' inspection by the aircraft commander. The radio operator conducted a walk around inspection of the exterior portions of the aircraft where radio antennae, static dischargers, etc., were located, as well as inspecting and testing each of the pieces of the communications equipment to make sure it was operational. If there were problems with the equipment, arrangements were made for it to be replaced or repaired rather quickly. Sometimes the crew had to seek out another aircraft when problems dealing directly with the aircraft, its radar, or its communications and navigation equipment were extensive or not immediately repairable. When that occurred, all the crew members had to transfer their personal equipment to another aircraft, and the inspection and pre-flight process of the new aircraft began all over again.

Each of the approximate 20 member crews (pilot, copilot, navigator radio operator, radar maintenance technicians, radar operators, radar observers) had his own inspections of his equipment and work area as well as operations tests of the equipment he used prior to take off.

The radio operators obtained the Air Traffic Control (ATC) flight clearance, and the aircraft commander requested take-off clearance from the tower. Take-offs on the flights I made were relatively uneventful, although at times there was a lot of anxiety when the plane, with such a heavy load of fuel, seemed to take up a lot of runway or when there was excessive unfamiliar engine noise or what seemed like a lot of flames coming out of the exhaust of the engines.

Once we were in the air we relaxed somewhat, en route to the assigned station area over the North Atlantic where we were to meet and relieve another crew and aircraft or assume the station which had not been manned for one reason or another.

However, there were times when emergencies occurred soon after take-off which required the dumping of excess fuel to get the aircraft's tonnage down to an acceptable landing weight. The fuel dumps became routine, but dangerous nonetheless, since all electronics had to be turned off except for the minimum emergency radios, and no transmissions were allowed during the actual dumping. One commercial airline using the Super Constellation reportedly caught fire and crashed after dumping fuel upon approach to an airport in New York. I doubt that Nantucket ever has cleaned up all the fuel that was dumped over and near there during those years.

Once the aircraft arrived on station and began flying its race track pattern, our task soon became routine and boring. The weather over the North Atlantic normally was not good, and commercial aircraft were assigned preferred altitudes where the weather was not so rough--leaving the military aircraft to be assigned to the rougher altitudes.

A lot of the flights were rough and bumpy, and we soon learned that it was best to stay buckled up in our safety belts at all times. We learned to drink coffee from paper cups without spilling it while experiencing alternating negative and positive G-forces.

Many of the missions were aborted for mechanical or electrical problems with the aircraft and its tons of electronic equipment. We regularly trained for emergencies and, normally, sometime during each flight, usually when en route or on the return from the station, there would be an unannounced emergency to which the crew had to respond and be ready for ditching at sea. One never knew when the alarm bell first sounded whether it was a practice or not, particularly when part of the crew were on break and in deep sleep in the bunks. It was surprising how fast I could recover from deep sleep and respond to the emergency drill. I'm thankful they were only drills as we knew what the possibilities of survival were if we had to ditch in the North Atlantic, particularly during the winter months.

A lot of things happened. Ice would build up on the aircraft due to the weather in which we flew. Engines had problems and were shut down, and the propellers feathered. There were many equipment failures, some lightning strikes, etc. But most of the time the missions were boring, tiresome, long and noisy (particularly for me, the radio operator, sitting next to the left inboard number 2 engine).

I recall that sometimes pilots from the Pentagon who were trying to accumulate flying time were assigned missions with us. On one such occasion, I recall taking a cup of coffee to the cockpit for the aircraft commander (a routine task the radio operators gladly performed) and found the Pentagon pilot fast asleep in the cockpit and the plane on the autopilot. The aircraft commander had sought a short period of rest and had left the aircraft in control of the Pentagon pilot. Both the pilot and copilot could not be expected to maintain alertness, without some rest, when the actual flight time of the missions averaged more than twelve hours duration. The situation of the sleeping pilot wasn't the best, but there were other crew members who also were monitoring the aircraft's altitude, position, heading, etc.

After our aircraft was relieved on station by another aircraft and crew, we headed home. The relief aircraft did not always come for various reasons and sometimes to maintain coverage of the station we were required to fly longer missions than we wanted to. An entry in my Form 5A (Individual Flight Record) reflects that on May 22, 1958 I flew on one mission for a total of 17:05 hours. It was not all that unusual to fly missions of 13, 14, and 15 hours.

Upon landing there were approximately two hours involved in returning the survival gear, writing up malfunctioning equipment, meeting with maintenance people about problems with the aircraft and equipment, attending the post-flight briefing, etc. These two hours added to the time we flew, plus the earlier three hour pre-flight duties, made it a very long day. In numerous instances there were not enough radio operators for two to be assigned to each mission, and that really made it a long day for one person. Crew members were supposed to get a rest period after the flight, but that didn't happen commensurately with the total time spent on a particular mission. And soon afterwards one was back to training, flying, crew rest, and "time off."

My time with the 961st Squadron was a memorable one, and I never forgot the men, my friends, the crew members (both officers and airmen) who had placed so much trust in each other.

I salute the fifty crew members who lost their lives and those four crew members who survived when three EC-121H aircraft (55-0136 - July 11, 1965) (55-5262 - November 11, 1966) (53-0549 - April 25, 1967) were lost at sea. I remember having flown with one of the Flight Engineers who did not survive the ditching of 53-0549, MSgt Frank W. Garner, Jr.

A. J. NORTHRUP - SMSGT USAF - RETIRED

NOTE: I left Otis AFB in 1959 for a three-year tour in Germany. I returned to Otis and to the 961st in January 1963 where I flew just a few more missions before receiving a special assignment to the Air Force Office of Special Investigations (OSI). I remained at Otis with the OSI until February 1968.

ROBERT A. BOSTICK LT. COL. USAF - RETIRED

Forty-three years ago I (A. J. Northrup) was assigned as an airborne radio operator to the 961st AEW&C Squadron at Otis AFB, MA. This was in August 1955 and I was four months shy of my nineteenth birthday. Major Robert A. Bostick was one of the many fine officers I met and flew with in the squadron over the next four years. I still remember many of the other officers and the enlisted crew members but I remember Major Bostick probably best of all. Perhaps it was his personality, how he treated me, his being both an officer and a gentleman. Particularly he was someone I could look up to with admiration and trust. He was someone who always was willing to talk with me. I am glad that I was able to locate him after all that time, and at my request he, as many others did, took time out of their routine to contribute something to this book.

Major Bostick arrived in the 961st just prior to me on June 14, 1955, and except for a 1-1/2 year stint as 551st AEW&C Wing Chief of Current Operations he stayed with the 961st until August 31, 1961.

I remember Major Bostick as a Command Pilot, as an Aircraft Commander, as "A" Flight Commander, and as a fantastic person. Major Bostick served as a 961st Flight Commander four times, as the Operations Officer for the 961st on three occasions, and was the Squadron Commander of the 961st for two periods of time. In May 1961 Major Bostick completed 10,000 hours of flying.

His military career began in 1936 as a machine gunner in the Texas National Guard. Following this tour he enlisted in the Army Air Corp and went through aircraft mechanics school. He was a crew chief on AT-6s when his flight training orders were received. His flight training was attended in the grade of Sergeant with training title of aviation student. He was graduated in class 42-J as a flight officer. Enlisted pilots were to graduate as Staff Sergeants, but that all changed the night before he graduated. He was up all night receiving his appointment as Flight Officer and being discharged. In 1944, while in the China-Burma-India theater, he flew 156 combat missions over the hump. Each mission was a flight through enemy air space to China. He logged 550 combat hours in the C-46. Major Bostick flew the Berlin airlift and flew twenty-eight transport support missions from Japan to Korea in the C-54. He later served as an Instructor Pilot in a Transport Training Unit and later as a Pilot with MATS [Military Air Transport Service]. Prior to his assignment at Otis, Major Bostick served as Liaison Officer to the Royal Thailand Air Force, attached to the 315th Air Division, Tachikawa, Japan. Some of his military awards include the Distinguished Flying Cross, Air Medal with one Oak Leaf Cluster, Air Force Commendation Medal, and Command Pilot Wings.

After retirement from the Air Force in 1961, he continued to fly until October 1982, accruing 40 years as a rated pilot and 21,000 total flying hours, all accident free.

The following aircraft are a few of those he flew as a civilian: 1649 Super Constellation for one year; B-25, B-26, C-320, C-310, C-411, Aero Commander, C-210, C-45, Melen II, Melen III, Beech King Air 210, C-47, C model Super Constellation, CE-500. He holds Airline Transport Pilot Certification No. 1371350. His total RC-121s flight time is 3175.

NOTES FROM LT. COLONEL ROBERT A. BOSTICK - RETIRED

I arrived at Otis AFB with a total of 7152 hours of which 3325 were four engine time. My RC-121 flight training at Otis started August 10, 1955 with final check out on October 3, 1955. I must say that the best, most thorough instructor pilot I ever took instructions from was Captain Jack C. Voliker. Captain Voliker was very well qualified for his position. When I completed flight training, I felt ready and qualified for RC-121 operations. Prior to my training in the RC-121, it had been almost like, "If you can start it, fly it."

It seems there always was a shortage of crew members at one position or another. At one point about 20 navigators were assigned at one time. I did not assign them to crews because of a shortage of aircraft commanders. The rude awakening occurred when 90 days passed and crew assignments took place. I found 20 effectiveness reports were due almost overnight. A lot of midnight time was spent to get the reports prepared in time.

As the 961st Squadron Operations Officer I was responsible to the Squadron Commander to furnish a mission qualified crew for each mission ready aircraft presented to the squadron for flight. Additionally, as the Operations Officer, I was also responsible for the aircrew flying records, training records, and local and mission check rides. I also was responsible for briefing material logs, clearances and military training. I also served seven years as a US Customs Officer at Otis.

Several sections were housed in the Operations Training Section at the 961st. There were training offices for all crew positions, flight commanders' offices (A, B, & C), chief pilots' offices, the clearance section, and records. The operations staff were very professional, qualified, and were mission oriented. All in all they made my job easy.

I recall one mission where my crew had an afternoon departure. Things went normal until we arrived on station, at which time we had a lightning strike. The lightening came through the cockpit and out of the Loran coupler. The navigator attached a jumper cable from the Loran set bypassing the Loran coupler. Within about 30 minutes lightning strike number two came in the same route. The jumper cable burnt and fell on the navigator's table. This strike also knocked out the Loran set and all repeat compass indicators and we discovered that the standby compass was not reliable. I called an adjacent station requesting our heading and got a reply, "We do not know, you are erratic." A climb was requested and approved. We broke out on top at about 17,000 feet and promptly headed into the setting sun, planning on hitting the East Coast. After about 45 minutes to one hour later, all the remote compass indicators slaved back in. We did not feel like following them at first. The rest of the aborted mission was uneventful.

The above event brought to my attention that the navigator was not sure of his ability to navigate taking sun lines for reference. I set up a navigator refresher course and required the navigator on each mission to do one plot by celestial means.

Disregarding enemy action, flying to me is safer than driving a car. The hazards to aviation are, in my opinion, all weather related. Ice in all forms confronts wings, propellers and windshields. Then there are high winds, lightning and so forth.

Now a couple of flights that went wrong. In early 1961 I took a "C" model Connie trip to Bergstrom AFB in Austin, TX. I was told not to land at Kelly AFB, but before we were ready for departure a Major from the 962nd Squadron asked if he could ride with us. A family member had passed away, and he wanted to go to San Antonio. I said, "Come on, let's go." When over Austin, I changed my flight plan, with the destination still being Bergstrom but adding a 10 minute passenger stop at Kelly AFB.

We landed at Kelly and after our landing roll was complete, the crew compartment door was opened. The sounds were not good. An exhaust pipe had come loose at a cylinder on #3 engine. Several parts were burned, buffet planes, cylinder fins, exhaust pipe, cylinder hold down studs, etc.

We were told repairs would be made in two weeks after parts had been manufactured by Wright [the engine manufacturer]. After about three weeks we were on our way back to Otis AFB with 3 large boxes of burned parts for the Wing Operations Officer. When the parts were set on the Director of Operations' desk, the question was asked, "What salvage yard did they come from?" I then was told that the only place I could go until retirement was out to station and back.

With retirement around the corner, less than 60 days, a Master Sergeant asked if he could visit in my office at operations in the 961st. We visited a few minutes, and the he asked if I was taking my airplane with me. I said , "Sergeant, I don't have an airplane." The Sergeant said, "I beg your pardon sir. I thought 843 was yours since you kept it in San Antonio so long."

My last flight from Otis was four hours local. Inasmuch as retirement was near we chose to enjoy a flight with no currency requirements to meet. Major Bill Wilner was the Commander of Texas Tower #2, so I flew out to pay a visit. I made several circles around the tower at about tower deck level. We had a nice visit via radio. When I departed tower #2, we climbed to about 6500 feet and headed for Otis. We had not been at 6500 feet long when two fighter aircraft gave the Air Defense Command Warning System "A Tally Ho - It's an RC-121."

I had caused the big bell to ring all the way to Air Defense Command Headquarters. The Commanding General of NORAD (North American Air Defense Command) telephoned Colonel Ernest J. White, the 551st Wing Commander, to ask him what he planned to do with that pilot. Colonel White's reply was that when the early warning system is checked, all levels of command are told in advance that there will be an alert between now and some date or hour down the road. Colonel White also said, "This pilot checked our alert system, causing a full alert, and was intercepted prior to reaching the East Coast, and our system works. Besides he is retiring next month." No action was taken against me.

In my opinion, my Otis tour of duty was with the best that the Air Force had, both officers and enlisted. In my five and one-half years in the 961st the percentage of missions accomplished was met on time. Only two missions were not accomplished in a manner to the good of the 961st. In one case the aircraft commander was given additional training. In the other case I inspected the aircraft concerned and told the aircraft commander that I would take the mission. He said "Okay. I get to go home." I told him that he would be my co-pilot, at which time he took the mission, as the aircraft commander, to its completion without any problems.

NOTE: The Texas Towers were located in the Atlantic Ocean about 75 miles from shore to extend the radar coverage of the East Coast seaward. The towers rose 65 feet above the sea and were serviced by helicopter and boat. Texas Tower #4 collapsed on January 15, 1961, killing 14 airmen and 14 civilian maintenance men. The other two towers #2 and #3 were decommissioned. Texas Tower #1 never was built.

MAJOR ROBERT A. BOSTICK, "A" FLIGHT COMMANDER OF THE 961ST AEW&C SQUADRON AT OTIS AFB, MA., RECEIVES HIS COMMAND PILOTS WINGS FROM SQUADRON COMMANDER LT. COLONEL ALFRED W. BARRETT, JR.

PHOTOGRAPH APPEARED IN THE 1957 YEAR BOOK OF THE 551ST AEW&C WING AT OTIS AFB.

DUTIES OF THE TECHNICIANS ON THE EC-121
BY
FORMER SENIOR RADAR TECHNICIAN DEAN BOYS

The Technicians (Radar, Airborne Data Processor (ADP), and Navigation) were assigned to the 551st Electronics Maintenance Squadron (EMS) and attached to a crew in one of the three Operations Squadrons for flying. They also performed Organizational Maintenance (repairing electronics equipment on the aircraft on the Flight Line) when not flying. The Technicians were commonly referred to as "Techs" and more specifically as Radar Techs, ADP Techs, and Nav Techs.

A Tech's duty day, when flying, would consist of reporting to the 551 EMS operations 2 ½ hours prior to takeoff. There one would pick up all necessary test equipment, classified Technical Orders (TO's), logbooks, and tools. The Technician would read all required bulletins and memoranda. The Senior Ranking Technician who was in charge of all the Techs would make sure all this was done. The Navigation Tech (Nav Tech) also picked up the Inertial Reference System (a black box) which always was plugged into a power source inside to keep it warm. They then proceeded to the respective Squadron Operations building for crew briefing. After the general briefing the Flight Engineers and Techs were released to start the preflight inspection of the aircraft's systems and electronics equipment, and the rest of the crew continued with the briefing. The Techs would check their equipment to see it was secure and if it was operational. This was done by first checking the aircraft forms (781s) for any writeups, then visually inspecting the equipment. Then the equipment was turned on and operationally checked. The Radar Tech also checked the cargo holds and the lower radome for leaking fluids and fumes. The Nav Tech also checked the radios and intercom systems. The Technicians then received and checked out their Personal Equipment (survival equipment) and prepared for takeoff. After takeoff they got all the equipment operational and then turned it over to the radar crew. During the flight the Techs monitored and repaired the equipment as necessary and wrote up in the aircraft maintenance form 781A any problems with the electronics equipment they could not fix. After landing, the Techs went to both the maintenance and operational debriefings. All this made about a 20-hour work day.

DUTIES OF THE RADAR CREW ON THE EC-121H
BY
JOHN N. PUOPOLO

The radar crew on an EC-121H Super Constellation flying an Active Air Defense Mission was comprised of the radar crew chief, one assistant radar crew chief, and two radar operators.

Prior to a flight the radar crew chief reported to the squadron operations building approximately one-half hour before the assigned briefing time. The crew chief would sign for the radar crew chief's flight briefcase, which consisted mostly of forms and manuals. Additionally, the crew chief read all recent technical order changes, bulletins, and squadron memoranda.

At the briefing an aircraft would be assigned to the crew. The crew would receive a weather briefing over a speaker system and a short briefing from the aircraft commander. After the briefing one radar operator would be assigned to pick up the inflight meals, and the other operator would help the navigator pick up the survival gear for the crew. The survival gear consisted of survival suits and life preservers for each of the aircrew members on the flight plus a flare gun and flares.

While that was going on the radar crew chief and assistant crew chief would proceed to the assigned aircraft to perform preflight operational checks of the equipment. The crew chief's first duty was to test the radios in the radar compartment, and any problems with the radios were reported to the navigation technician. The crew chief monitored the radar compartment, worked closely with the radar technicians, and advised the aircraft commander and the wing operations center of the status of the radar and related equipment. If problems were encountered the crew chief would try to obtain realistic estimates of the time it would take to correct them. Usually, as a rule of thumb, a flight was canceled if you couldn't get the aircraft into the air within six hours from reporting time.

Prior to takeoff the assistant crew chief was in charge of the rear of the aircraft, that area behind the radar compartment. He was responsible for securing all personal baggage and checking the emergency light in front of the rear door. Then he would close and secure the door. He then would inform the pilot or co-pilot that the rear of the aircraft was secured.

The assigned seat for the assistant crew chief for takeoffs and landings, as well as for ditching, always was at radar console #2. His official title was "jump-master", but since we didn't have parachutes aboard, I could never figure out who he "jump-mastered."*

After takeoff, the crew chief would receive the flight plan to the assigned flight station from the navigator. We were assigned to one of four flight stations. They were stations 2, 4, 6, and 8. I could never figure why they weren't numbered stations 1, 2, 3, and 4.**

The crew chief then would contact the ground radar station that was in control of the flight station and give them a verbal copy of the flight plan so they could prepare for our arrival on station. If the assigned ground station was too far away for radio contact, he would call the nearest ground station and ask them to pass on the information to the assigned ground station.

Upon arriving at the designated flight station, contact would be made with the controlling ground station, and the radar technicians would begin testing data transmissions. If there were no problems in sending the radar data, the crew chief would accept control of the flight station and notify the pilot, navigator, and radio operator that the radar tie-in was successful and normal operations were in progress. The crew chief then would designate one radar operator to monitor radar scope #1. Next he would assign times for the assistant crew chief and second radar operator to relieve them. This alternating schedule would usually be two hours on and two hours off.

Since all radar data on missions utilizing the EC-121H was being transmitted electronically, it was not necessary for anyone to manually call in radar sightings as was done on the previous RC-121D models. You basically monitored the radar scopes for emergency signals, the radio channel for distress calls, and maintained communications with the ground control station. At the conclusion of the mission there wasn't much to do except enjoy the ride home.

At the conclusion of the mission, the crew chief would once again receive a flight plan from the navigator for the ride home. He would call the flight plan to the assigned ground control station.

Upon landing after the mission, one radar operator would gather the survival gear and help the navigator return it to the supply squadron. Everyone else would gather his personal belongings and return to the squadron operations building for debriefing. Afterwards, everyone would be dismissed, and the radar crew chief would return the radar crew chief's briefcase with the reports from the just completed mission to squadron operations.

The average time from reporting prior to the briefing until you were dismissed made for a long 17 - 18 hour day.

NOTE: John Puopolo had flown numerous missions on both the RC-121D and the EC-121H models Super Constellation aircraft as a radar operator, assistant radar crew chief, and as a crew chief. He was one of three of the 19 member crew who survived the ditching of 55-0136 in the Atlantic on the night of July 11, 1965.

*The term "jump-master" may have been a holdover from earlier times when crews of the RC-121D models were issued parachutes. The EC-121H carried a sea rescue kit which could be dropped to aid rescue of others at sea, and the jump-master was responsible for deploying it. Also, the jump-master took a head count before take off and was responsible for opening the rear door and counting crew members exiting the aircraft in the event of a emergency ground evacuation.

** Dean Boys, previously mentioned, explained that the even-numbered stations 2, 4, 6, and 8 were assigned to the East Coast and were manned by planes and crews from the 551st Wing at Otis AFB, Massachusetts. The odd-numbered stations 1, 3, 5, and 7 were manned by planes and crews from the 552nd Wing at McClellan AFB, California. Station 10 was manned by planes and crews flying out of McCoy AFB in Orlando, Florida.

ITS HARD FOR ME TO BELIEVE ITS BEEN THIRTY-TWO YEARS NOW!

BY
JOE BROSNAN

In May 1966, the 551st AEW&C Wing was in a state of shock, having sustained a fatal crash following a perfect ten year flying record. I had applied for and received an emergency retirement to move the Air Force Sergeants Association (AFSA) Headquarters back to Washington, D.C. and help it recover from its dire financial state.

Colonel Raymond K. Gallagher, the Wing Commander, shook my hand and wished me well on my new risky venture. Senior Master Sergeant Bob Mulherne offered words of support, and I remember him saying, "Good luck, I guess you know you are taking an awfully big bite."

During a visit back to Otis Air Force Base following my May 1966 retirement, I had met the new Wing Commander, Colonel James P. Lyle.

I and others were deeply moved when we later learned of the crash of Colonel Lyle's aircraft on April 25, 1967. Senior Master Sergeant Bob Mulherne and Master Sergeant Frank Garner were the Flight Engineers. They, along with Colonel Lyle and 12 others, lost their lives - one survived. I also knew all of the other members of Colonel Lyle's crew and had flown with them at different times. Many of his enlisted crew were members of the AFSA. Master Sergeant Frank Garner and I were on the AFSA Executive Council.

The missions flown by the 551st Wing had been so well-handled and safe that we would sometimes joke, ironically, during an early morning pre-flight, maybe up to our ankles in slush, that we were "safer out on station than home tucked in bed." All one had to do was look at the remarkable safety record to attest to that.

A typical 2 AM winter departure usually went something like this. The aircraft was finally "UP" the radar was "UP" and the mission was "GO" after freezing on the ramp for sometimes up to 3 or 4 hours. Maintenance personnel were fixing all the last minute discrepancies that crop up on nights like that while Chief Master Sergeant Walden Bock was barking orders from one end of the flight line to the other and doing a terrific job of coordinating all the fixing going on. It was all together and we would soon be on our way.

De-icing trucks with powerful flood lights and powerful sprays from booms, which leaned out over the plane and wet her down with a steaming hot pink glycol mixture, raised huge clouds of reddish steam. Under the flood lights it looked like a scene from Dante's Inferno.

Then it was crank up the engines for immediate taxi out for runup and take off. The freezing rain or melting snow would soon wash off the glycol and allow a new layer of ice to form on the wings. Once airborne, the Connie had its own systems for handling ice, but on the ground it was defenseless against the elements.

Then the take off. As the big ship gathered speed you could feel rather than hear large gobs of slush and ice banging off the flaps and huge lower radome.

This was a very critical time in the cockpit. The flight engineer advances throttles to max power, scanning and analyzing the fourteen thousand horses thundering forward across the wing. Along with monitoring and controlling all of the many aircraft systems which come up to speed with the advance of power. Hydraulics, fuel system, AC and DC electrical systems emerge as the bird comes alive. The pop of an insignificant looking circuit breaker, one among hundreds, low engine torque, oil pressure, fuel pressure - all must be evaluated and either accepted or rejected during the few seconds until the take off decision speed is reached.

The Aircraft Commander has called for "Max Power," throttles advanced and we are rolling forward. The First Pilot (Co-Pilot) calls out runway markers and airspeeds, "one thousand - 24 knots", "two thousand - 47 knots", "three thousand - 63 knots", etc. The decision speed and the accelerate and stop distance should be reached together, such as "five thousand - 96 knots -- its a go". After that there is no turning back. Before this point the Aircraft Commander calls out "Engineers Report", and if he hears "Power in the green", will continue the take off run.

Tonight the slush is acting like a semi solid set of chocks in front of the wheels, and the speed at each runway marker is a few knots lower than calculated even with a 3% slush factor the engineer added to the roll. This will make the decision point much more critical with the Aircraft

Commander knowing that an "Abort!!" call from the engine room will cause a slithering, sliding, full power reversal attempt to stop the huge machine before it reaches the end of the runway. It happens; but its always a hair raiser, even on a sunny afternoon.

Tonight we are off, climbing and turning to the east. The pilots execute the "After Take Off" checklist together. "Gear up", calls the Aircraft Commander when he sees a visible indication of climb on his altimeter. "Gear up and locked" is the reply, then "Meto Power" to the Engineer, who then reduces from Max Power to Max Except Take Off (METO).

The Aircraft Commander then calls for "Flaps Up", and the First Pilot nurses up the flaps as the air speed builds up, and calls "After Take Off Checklist complete". The next call is for "Climb Checklist". The pilots clean up cockpit items, and the engineer brings in pressurization and air conditioning, sets power for climb, and logs the instrument readings from the take off.

When climb is established, weather permitting, the Aircraft Commander turns off the seat belt sign and informs the radar crew that they can start up their equipment.

An off duty member of the crew will usually bring up steaming cups of coffee for the cockpit crew, and the night's work is underway.

Now, at a point a piercing claxon horn rang out loud and clear over engine noise and through padded headsets. "Engineers Report" comes clearly through the intercom from the Aircraft Commander. "Fire, number three engine" is the engineers reply.

"Execute Engine Shutdown" is next from the Aircraft Commander, and the engineer executes a ten point checklist which he has memorized and drilled over and over in the flight simulator and often during local training flights.

The last item is to discharge the fire extinguisher, which contains a highly effective chemical which smothers the fire and cools hot metal.

This time the fire did not go out!!

A turn and straight line descent toward land. A dive for the nearest runway -- in this case Nantucket. Get on the ground and evacuate the aircraft. This April day they didn't reach the ground. Who knows the reason. A mile too far? A thousand feet too high?

Whatever the reason, the Sentinel fell in the line of duty and deserves our undying gratitude. Each member of that crew and of the crews of the other two downed aircraft was in himself a Sentinel, standing in defense of our country, and deserves the highest appropriate recognition for his sacrifice.

Joe Brosnan   [Flight engineer]
Master Sergeant USAF - Retired
December 1998

NOTE: In April 1967, the day after his friend Sergeant Garner lost his life in the ditching of 53-0549, Joe Brosnan wrote the poem **"A SENTINEL SLEEPS"**, which appears in the section covering the loss of 53-0549.

> Joseph "Joe" Brosnan, was born in New York City on August 13, 1921. He is a veteran of WWII, Korea, numerous brush fires, and Viet Nam. He is a retired reservist, having held various ranks and grades in two services during five recalls. He accumulated over 20 years of active duty.
>
> He holds a degree in Aviation Sciences from U.S.N.Y. and is a graduate of Delehanty Aviation Institute and the Academy of Aeronautics in NY. He attended specialized engineering courses at the University of Illinois, Wright Aeronautical Corporation, Sperry Gyroscope Company, Consolidated Aircraft, and the Norden Company. He first soloed in 1937.
>
> Having accrued over 23,000 flying hours, he is an FAA Licensed Commercial, Multi Engine, instrument rated pilot; a Reciprocating Engine Rated Flight Engineer; holds an Aircraft and Powerplant mechanics license and an FCC General Radio Operators License. Today he owns and flies his own private aircraft, preferring flight to hazardous interstate highway travel. In April 1967 he had retired and was National Executive Director of the Air Force Sergeants Association in Washington, DC.
>
> For his participation in planning and executing a three engine take off of a fully loaded KB50 refueling tanker from Midway Island for the rescue of a single F100 fighter plane low on fuel and out of range of any land, he was cited for the award of the Air Medal but was awarded the Air Force Commendation Medal instead.

EC-121H "WARNING STAR" RADAR PATROL PLANE (SUPER CONSTELLATION) MANUFACTURED BY LOCKHEED AEROSPACE CORPORATION.

AIRCRAFT PICTURED IS OVER THE CAPE COD CANAL NEAR OTIS AIR FORCE BASE, MASSACHUSETTS.

USAF PHOTOGRAPH FURNISHED BY DEAN BOYS

RECOLLECTIONS OF THE 961ST AIRBORNE EARLY WARNING AND CONTROL SQUADRON OCTOBER 1962 - OCTOBER 1965

BY
Art Kerr

The 961st AEW&C Squadron was my first assignment after pilot training in October 1962. When I PCSd from the squadron, the commander was Lt. Col. Robert V. Mitchell, who took over sometime in 1964. Bob Mitchell was a wonderful man - everything you could want in a commander. We were an Air Defense Command (ADC) unit, part of the 551st Airborne Early Warning and Control Wing, at Otis AFB, Cape Cod, Massachusetts. The wing call sign was "Homey." The wing had three flying squadrons and was equipped with RC-121s, TC-121s and EC-121Hs. At the time, the Air Force seemed to be in the process of changing the designation of the Connie from RC to EC-121.

The 551st Wing's mission was to maintain "continuous random" airborne coverage of at least one "station" off the US East Coast. There were four stations located about 150 miles or so off shore, in or just outside of the ADIZ, the Air Defense Identification Zone, where aircraft were required to have ADC clearance to operate. Unknowns in or near the ADIZ were scrambled on by ADC F-101 or F-102 interceptors, a number of which were kept on five minute alert at numerous bases up and down the coast.

(Otis also had an F-101 squadron and an "alert barn" with four alert stalls.) What the continuous "random manning" airborne coverage mission meant was that at least one EC-121H had to be airborne and operational on one or more of the four stations. At higher DEFCONs, increasing numbers of stations would be manned. The stations were basically 100 mile long racetrack patterns, running north-south or NE-SW. They were identified as Station 2, Station 4, Station 6 and Station 8. Station 2 was east of Cape Cod, 4 east of New Jersey, 6 east of Virginia and Station 8 was off of Charleston, SC. Operating altitude was 15,000 feet. (More about that later.) This was the mission during my three year tour with the 961st, and for some time thereafter as I understand it. The wing schedule to maintain this coverage had one aircraft launching every four hours, starting at 0200, then 0600, etc. The six launches a day were allocated among the three squadrons (960th, 961st and 962nd). Every couple of weeks, the schedule would change between squadrons so that each squadron would get their "fair share" of the 0200 launches! If a Connie on station had a problem (radar, data link, in-flight emergency, etc.) typically the next scheduled mission would be moved up for an ASAP takeoff; sometimes there was an alert aircraft to fill in as needed. Also, at increased states of alert, increasing numbers of stations needed to be covered.

When I arrived at Otis, the Cuban Missile Crisis was well under way, so the training program was last priority. All crew training was done at Otis by the wing and the squadrons. We also had an ATC Field Training Detachment there for ground school. And we had a Flight Simulator - a static "box on the floor," no visual system other than a choice of light or dark outside the opaque cockpit windows; but it did everything we needed. Since I wasn't mission ready, I got only a few Connie rides until the "Crisis" scheduling system got sorted out. So in the meantime I flew C-47s with some Lt Cols in base flight, who seemed to me at the time to be really aged. They were excellent pilots, mainly, and I learned a lot about flying from them. The Gooney Bird was a fun plane to fly and I got to know her pretty well. Turned out that the C-47 was the first USAF bird that I flew as an aircraft commander, and I kept flying the Goon all the while after I checked out in the Connie.

Air Defense of the Continental US was a major national concern during this time frame. The Connie missions and the interceptor flights were known as Active Air Defense Missions, commonly referred to as AAD missions. There was virtually total ADC radar coverage of the Continental US, certainly the entire perimeter of the US had coverage, mostly with overlapping radar sites should there be an outage at one radar site. Also, there was the DEW Line of radar sites across the top of North America, the Mid-Canada Line and the Pine Tree Line near the U.S.-Canada border. And then there were also the Navy radar picket ships, and the USAF "Texas Towers," which I've heard was delightful duty. (One of them blew over and sunk in a storm - many people drowned.) Texas Towers were similar to off-shore oil rig platforms with a radar site mounted on them.

Air Defense Exercises were a major part of the Connie operation. The general scenario was: an increasing of DEFCONS levels, recall of maintenance and flight crews, generating AAD mission aircraft, pre-flighting, cocking aircraft and going on alert - we had trailers, with bunks, alongside the squadron ops building. At certain states of alert we would go out to the airplanes and sit alert in the planes. The Big Event was launching the fleet! I mean everything that was flyable would launch! Looking at it many years retrospectively -- this was an absolutely unbelievable operation. At the required state of exercise DEFCONS -- everyone started engines that could start engines, and taxied out on their own command, falling in one behind the other as they got out to the taxiway. Usually, by the time a couple of airplanes got to the end of the runway, you could expect that we had "incoming" so it was time to "FLUSH" the fleet! The trigger for this was the exercise words, "BIG NOISE, APPLE JACK, DELTA." In other words, a red alert as in the movies: Missiles on the way.

This was exciting. The entire wing gets cleared for takeoff and cleared to proceed out to STOPs or "strategic orbit points" to sit out the missile raid. Takeoff was at 15 second intervals. The first one off gets the highest altitude at the STOP, next one 500 feet lower, etc. The STOP was out on the 060 radial. Of course the FAA didn't want anything to do with this wild operation so they just gave us a whole block of sky and we cleared ourselves. One of these FLUSH drills was particularly exciting for me; we were about number four or five in the stream of airplanes and just after breaking ground on runway 31 the turbulence from the previous aircraft rolled us off to the right while the gear was still down. Full left aileron didn't hack it, other than to stop the roll - there we were, tooling along with about 20 degrees of bank with the wing tip pretty close to the ground - the folks on the ground said it took their breath away. They weren't the only ones. Didn't think we were going to make it. But eventually we drifted a little off to the right and got out of the turbulence, leveled the wings and climbed out. More fun - the weather was IFR and we had a bunch of airplanes all climbing out in the same general direction. We started calling out our TACAN positions to each other in order to try to keep some spacing. I remember two of us calling the same radial and DME while trudging along in the murk. One of us was a few hundred feet higher than the other so we increased that altitude separation. I guess our altimeters were inaccurate - or could it have been just the "big sky" theory at work? Eventually, after getting to the STOP, each airplane got a real ATC IFR clearance and got out of there. Each airplane individually went back to land somewhere or proceeded on to an AAD mission. That was the last one of those drills I remember doing! Somebody may have rethought the whole thing.

For the early morning "0-dark hundred" show times, we could go to the in-flight kitchen and get a great home cooked breakfast. I recall that the price was right - only 22 cents for whatever you wanted. But remember, this was at the time when second lieutenant's base pay was $222.30 a month! Flight pay was about $100, quarters allowance less than that. Seemed to pay all the bills - times do change. The in-flight kitchen at Otis was important to Connie crews - they put together some pretty good hot meals that we cooked in two airliner type ovens in the mid-ship EC-121 galley. Kept them in the fridge till ready to cook - the protocol was to check around and make sure anybody who wanted to eat got one in the oven if you were going to turn it on. The galley ranked in importance right up there with the bunks!

The EC-121H Connie crew consisted of the flight crew, radar techs, radio operators and height finder operator. I remember the crew to be about 12 to 15 people - enough of each crew position to allow everyone to get periodic breaks; there were lots of bunks - six to nine in the tail section and three up front (one on the left side that folded down from the head liner, and a bench with three seat belts on the right just behind the door to the flight deck that had a back which folded up to make the top bunk of two bunks.) Bunks were assigned by crew position. Most of the mission activity was in the over-wing area - the navigator's station was on the right (the Nav had a portable stool to sit on in the middle of the aisle - the sextant port was right there too). The radio operator was across from the navigator. Most of the RO's traffic while on station was via HF CW, i.e.., Morse code! Mounted on the RO's table was a Morse code key made by Samuel F.B. Morse himself I'm sure. At the wing command post we had a "radio shack" (actually a little shed to keep the noise out) for the CP radio types to copy and send Morse code, and talk on sideband if they were lucky. The radar techs' jobs were to keep the radar going - apparently this meant having bits and pieces of the radar set spread out, up and down the aisle of the airplane, all lashed together somehow, and all lit up and operating. We were always trouble-shooting something while on station. There were no weapons controllers or anything like a "mission crew." The surveillance mission, scramble authority and weapons control functions were all done at the SAGE Centers or back-up sites. All the EC-121H radar data was digitized and transmitted to ground sites (one ground site for each airborne radar station). From the ground sites, data went via land line, mainly, to the SAGE centers. That's Semi Automatic Ground Environment - and there were a lot of those too. This data link system was known as Airborne Long Range Input (ALRI). Most of the 551st Connies were EC-121H ALRI airplanes. This was a relatively new program and the conversion was ongoing and almost complete when I arrived in 1962. The typical mission seemed to be about nine hours - could be longer if mission requirements dictated - or shorter in the event of an emergency (seemed to be lots of those). (The 552nd on the west coast didn't have ALRI, I think their stations were farther out, beyond line of sight to land. So they had full mission crews.)

Weather wasn't the best at Cape Cod in the winter so we had lots of mission recovery diverts. A favorite place to go for a weather alternate was Kindley Field, Bermuda. There were lots of excuses to divert to Bermuda. Kindley was also one of our dispersal bases for hurricane evacuation. We rode motor bikes around the island and gave the Navy Class VI store a lot of business.

About in-flight emergencies - engine failures of one sort or another, and hydraulic problems, were not at all uncommon occurrences. I believe a lot of this was related to the 15,000 foot on-station operating altitude. (This altitude was required in order to have line-of-sight ALRI radar data link radio coverage with the ground sites for each of the four stations.) Our Connies were always "max'd out" for take off on these AAD missions - about 142,000 pounds - we carried the maximum amount of gas to fly as long a mission as possible. Actually, this weight was pushing the basic design limit of the Connie. Whatever runway there was available, we seemed to use all of it in takeoff performance planning. The flight engineer would keep his foot positioned next to the fuel dump lever on the bulkhead behind the pilots' seats so as to be able to kick the lever to start dumping fuel right after takeoff (or during takeoff!) in the event of an engine problem. Being new to the game right out of pilot training, I naturally took this as just part of the job and happily accepted it as a challenge. The ex-B-17 pilots didn't seem to mind too much either - at least there was no flack and no ME-109s to contend with. (We had several captains that were command pilots who learned how to "really" fly in the "big one.") Once we got airborne, there was the long climb out to 15,000 feet. This, I believe, put a lot of strain on the R-3350 turbo-compound engines, because we usually operated at METO power during the entire climb, and sometimes for up to a half hour after leveling-off. METO power (maximum except take off) was the first power reduction after maximum power for take off. It took about 45 minutes to get up to 15,000 feet. At about 10,000 feet we'd level-off briefly to build up speed for the "blower shift" which entailed throttling back the inboard engines, shifting them to high blower (supercharger), throttle back up, and then do the same with the outboards and continue the climb. These large power changes would tend to wake up any new crew members who hit the bunks early. The latter part of the climb out is where a lot of the engine problems occurred, fires, spark plug breakdowns (shorted secondaries) and turbine failures. The R-3350 had three power recovery turbines (PRTs) on each engine. PRTs are like the turbine on a jet engine. Engine exhaust from six of the eighteen cylinders was collected in a common manifold and routed through one of the three PRTs, which were about a foot in diameter. The three PRT turbine shafts were geared to the engine crankshaft and contributed a significant proportion of the total power of the R-3350. Frequently, turbine blades would separate from PRTs causing power loss and necessitating engine shut down to preclude further damage. Sometimes the turbine blades would punch through the PRT casing and exhaust would then exit though the holes in the casing - a cause of engine fires more than just occasionally. Every Connie crew has lots of stories about three engine operations and engine fires etc.

We always carried several gallons of extra hydraulic fluid (stored in gallon cans in a compartment in the forward latrine). It was routine to have to replenish the system several times during flight. This was done via a port connecting to the hydraulic system in the cockpit - we would punch a hole in the can, stick in a metal tube on the end of a hose which we connected to the port, and an aspirator sucked in the quart of hydraulic fluid. There were two separate hydraulic systems with a crossover for backup - had to be careful not to crossover if a leak in one side wasn't isolated or you could lose the whole thing - both systems. Leaks were commonplace. I remember one where the entire forward lower bay was sprayed with hydraulic fluid leaking under pressure; had to shut down most of the electrics (because of the flammable hydraulic fluid) - major problem. Sometimes, depending on where the leak was, you could recover the system. Manual backups included a long hand crank to wind down the flaps; this took a long time to do. We'd usually just put out a small amount of flaps and let it go at that. Emergency landing gear extension was a real feat. The copilot had a hand pump on the right sidewall. One day in 1965, flying with George Textor, we had such an actual experience (George and I later went to survival school together at Stead AFB, Nevada and eventually ended up together at Pleiku, Vietnam in '66). Well, George got to pump down the gear -- it took several hundred strokes, hard work. Especially the last part of pumping to get the landing gear down locks engaged. Had to relax for a while at the club after that.

Once in 65, George and I flew a Connie at LAX on a boondoggle with a minimum crew. Landed at LAX with a bad engine, the flight engineers and us couldn't fix it or find anybody else around there who we could talk into helping out. But we determined that it was a major internal problem requiring an engine change. The wing folks didn't want to bring an engine to LAX (I guess they didn't want to have get into explaining why we were at LAX) so we decided to go to McClellan and work the problem there. Since we didn't want to draw attention to our three-engine situation, we started up the bad engine prior to takeoff and ran it at a very low power setting during takeoff, being prepared to use as much power as we could get out of it if we needed it, and then we feathered it after cleaning up the airplane after takeoff. The 552nd maintenance folks at McClellan were good enough to give us a replacement engine while we enjoyed Sacramento and San Francisco.

Maintenance was a large operation, needless to say. Engines and radar were the major items requiring constant attention. Not sure what to say about oil leaks; I guess they had to be really big oil leaks before anything was done - there was no need to paint parking spots on the ramp - there were four large engine oil marks permanently soaked into the ramp marking every Connie parking spot. Probably still there today. For every launch, chances were 50-50 that you would have to get something fixed either before or after engine start and run-up. Engine run-up prior to takeoff was a large drill in itself - it took 20 to 30 minutes depending on how things looked and on the engineers proficiency and/or state of nervousness. To run-up, first you put the aircraft on the step; (the main landing gear sort of rotated 10 to 15 degrees back and forth around their main hinge axis in the wheel well.) The idea of getting on the step was to smoothly ease on the brakes while increasing power to keep the gear rotated back so that the airplane wouldn't jerk back and forth onto and off "the step" with power changes during the engine run-up.) It sounds strange now but that was just part of the routine. While on the step, we would check mags, props, blowers and take a look at every spark plug on the engine analyzer (a CRT that displayed a distinctive trace for each spark plug and secondary coil as it fired; malfunctions also had their own distinctive traces.) After run-up, you took it "off the step," easing off the brakes as you reduced power, then reset the brakes. If all was okay, then you checked lots more things, got your ATC clearance, and takeoff clearance.

There were lots of "bag drags" out to the airplane - and back - for maintenance delays. The maintenance guys on the ramp worked their hearts out to get birds launched. In addition to flight line maintenance, I remember two maintenance squadrons, FMS and EMS - Field Maintenance and Electronic Maintenance. Depot level work was done by Lockheed Air Service, Inc. (LASI) at Idlewild Airport in New York City. So we had lots of ferry flights into and out of Idlewild - now known as JFK International - with both Connies and the C-47. It seemed like there were always about six Connies in the LASI hangar.

Maybe one of the more unusual situations that I recall, I wasn't involved in personally, was a prop falling off a Connie on final approach to runway 05 at Otis. Steve Hamer was the AC on that flight. No other aircraft damage; the prop dropped onto somebody's property near Falmouth, a nice Cape Cod town south of the field. (By the way, there was a more serious prop separation accident at McClellan - a 552nd Connie had a prop come off and come through the fuselage - several crew members seriously injured.)

On 11 July 1965, the 961st lost a Connie [55-0136] at sea off Nantucket Island. Lieutenants Fred Ambrosia and Tom Fiedler were the pilots. Tech Sergeants Gene Schreivogel and Gil Armstrong were the flight engineers. There was a full crew on board as well as some ROTC instructors who were at Otis for ROTC summer camp; they were getting some EC-121 mission familiarization. There were three survivors but most of the crew were lost, some bodies were recovered. Miscellaneous parts of the aircraft and crew equipment were picked up. Found Tom's flight jacket - had his keys in the pocket. Made it easy to get his car started - Jim Goodman drove Tom's car back to the mid-west to give it to Tom's parents. (Jim was later shot down in Vietnam in an AC-47 - entire crew KIA.)

The stories told by the survivors were amazing. It was a large fire - number three engine. About at the time of level-off, the emergency occurred. It was a pitch black night and they were in the weather. The sea had swells but was not rough, at least the water wasn't as cold as in the winter. Visibility was "zero zero" at the surface. The crew shut down and feathered number three. They discharged fire extinguishers but the fire persisted. Talk among the Connie folks at Otis at the time was that the fire continued and burned back into the nacelle and maybe even into the wing, and that there was smoke in the fuselage. There may have been another engine problem too. I've since learned that survivors said they didn't see any smoke in the cabin and that while descending, they removed the overwing hatches and had thrown at least the right overwing-hatch overboard through the hatch opening. Number three prop was seen to be definitely feathered. The crew very professionally went about their ditching procedures. Fred decided to put it down in the water. A B-52 in the area heard their radio calls. A ship was in the area (I vaguely remember this as a German Navy destroyer). The crew made a rapid descent from 15,000 feet down to about a thousand feet and then set up a steady slow rate of descent, nose up, on a heading aligned parallel to the swells. When the Connie contacted the water, it broke up fore and aft of the wing into essentially three large sections. The nose section sank immediately. Most of the crew had gotten into survival suits and LPUs. I don't think the rafts got deployed. (The rafts were permanently stowed in compartments on the top surfaces of each wing; deployed by pulling a handle in each over wing emergency exit.) The search and rescue continued for several days. At the accident board, I remember listening to Fred's voice on a recording of some radio transmissions. One thing they wanted me to do was identify his voice -- I had flown with Fred more than anyone else. His were the only radio transmissions heard. His father was also in the Air Force, a Lieutenant Colonel assigned to Burma as an Air Attache. I met with Fred's father and mother to tell them about Fred's time in the 961st.

Lieutenant Fred Ambrosia was posthumously recommended for the award of the Distinguished Flying Cross. Such a high recommendation for an award was almost unheard of at the time - truly a most significant acknowledgment of Fred's amazing feat of airmanship. Only through his skill were there any survivors at all. There were many other awards recommended for other crew members. At the Otis memorial service for the 16 crew members who lost their lives, we had a missing man flyby at about 300 feet - five EC-121Hs in a six-ship close formation, with the number two slot open symbolizing the lost Connie. There is a monument at Otis ANG Base memorializing the crew. There was an individual ceremony for Fred Ambrosia at Arlington National Cemetery. This was arranged by Fred's parents. A plane load of 961st people flew to Andrews [Air Force Base] for the event. A minimum flight crew stayed with the Connie at Andrews while most of us went to Arlington. This was a few weeks after the accident. Following a service in the Chapel, we went to a section of the cemetery reserved for markers when there are no remains to be interred, and a memorial marker was dedicated for Lt. Ambrosia. The crew that had stayed with our Otis Connie made a fly-by during the dedication.

After I left the 961st AEW&C Squadron, I had heard about another 551st Connie [55-5262] being lost at sea under some not too dissimilar circumstances. Then a new wing commander was apparently brought in to get things straightened out and a third Connie [53-0549] was lost near Nantucket; new wing commander was one of the pilots on that flight - I'm not sure, but I heard that the entire crew was lost.

One of the last things that happened to me before I left Otis was an out-of-the-ordinary sort of in-flight emergency that occurred on 31 August 1965. In looking for old stuff about the 961st, I came across some write-ups about it. The aileron cable broke on short final while practicing a flight control hydraulic boost out landing. The control wheel snapped out of our hands, rotating fully to the 90 degree right position -- and it was jammed fully displaced to the right -- the wheel was stuck in a position straight up and down -- no lateral control. We used differential power to keep the wings level and make turns; got around on a very wide traffic pattern and lined up on a very long final approach. One thing that's not in the write-ups that seemed sort of humorous to me at the time was my checking on the crew to see if they were ready for landing when we were out on long final for runway 23, flying level at about a thousand feet: I happened to look back down the aisle and noticed that most everybody was putting on parachutes and some were already heading for the door (which was on the left side, aft). Had to make a PA announcement to convince everyone to stick with the bird - the final approach looked to be fairly stable and the winds weren't too bad. Turned out okay; at maintenance debrief we wrote up the aileron control as being inop - it took a while for folks to understand what we were talking about. And then there was some strange criticism from some wing weenies who thought we should have tooled around out over Cape Cod Bay while they foamed the runway (?) and got more fire trucks from around the local area! It looked to me like it was time to get the bird on the ground and get the crew to the club!!

[Art Kerr was awarded the Air Force Commendation Medal for landing the aircraft safely. See also *http://members.tripod.com/dboys/961/intercept.htm* for an article from the Air Defense Command Interceptor Magazine where he was selected for the We Point With Pride Award].

Well, that's about it. I had a great going away party (that's another thing about the 961st - we had lots of super parties). The squadron gave me the standard pewter mug with glass bottom, engraved with the dates of arrival and PCS departure. While thinking about my early operational flying experiences in the C-121 Connie and writing this tome, I was sipping beer from my 961st mug. There's a lot more that occasionally pops up out of deep memory from time-to-time. Great squadron. Magnificent airplane, loved every minute of it - beautiful machine, that Connie.

Copyright 1997 Art Kerr
adkerr@hitl.washington.edu

****

Art Kerr flew Connies at Otis AFB, Massachusetts and McCoy AFB, Florida. He logged more than 10,000 flying hours in many different airplanes. At the age of 14, he started learning to fly while working as a "dock boy" and apprentice mechanic at the Dobbs Ferry Seaplane Base on the Hudson River, in New York, where he earned his private pilot license. He grew up in Yonkers, New York, where he was born.

Art is a member of the Class of 1961, United States Air Force Academy. Before going to the Air Force Academy, he was a Naval ROTC midshipman at Columbia University for one year. Art was conferred an MBA degree at the Harvard University Graduate School of Business Administration. He was selected as the US Air Force representative on the 1982 course at the Royal College of Defence Studies in London.

After USAF pilot training at Reese AFB, Texas, Art's Air Force assignments took him to a number of stateside locations as well as Vietnam, where he flew the AC-47 gun ship, affectionately known as "Spooky." He was also a staff officer and taught on the faculty of the Air Force Academy. He had a lengthy assignment with the E-3A Airborne Warning and Control System Joint Test Force at the Boeing Company plant in Seattle, followed by an operational AWACS tour at Tinker AFB, Oklahoma.

Art has held several command assignments in different locations. His last military assignments were with the Office of Military Cooperation at the American Embassy in Cairo, Egypt, and the US European Command at RAF Mildenhall, England. He retired at Mildenhall in 1991 as a colonel after 30 years in the United States Air Force.

ARTHUR D. KERR

Unit Patch Courtesy of Art Kerr & Dean Boys

EMBLEM OF THE 961ST AIRBORNE EARLY WARNING AND CONTROL SQUADRON.

The bat, peering out over the water, signifies the radar capability of the 961st. The binoculars, around his neck, and the telescope, under his wing, represents the devices used by the squadron in fulfilling its mission. The lightning bolt signifies the all weather capability of the 961st. The background (red) honors the squadron's valor and its steadfastness to duty. This emblem was designed for the 961st by Walt Disney, the world famous animator.

NOTE: Go to the following web site to view the patch in color and visit with the 961st:

http://members.tripod.com/dboys/961/961.htm

Recollections of the 551st AEW&C Wing and Cape Cod
January 1962 through August 1969
by
DEAN BOYS

Fresh out of Airborne Radar school at Keesler Air Force Base, Biloxi, MS., I arrived at Boston's South Station. Saw Celtics' basketball player Bill Russell drive by. That was the location of the old Boston Garden. I caught the bus to Otis from the Alameda Bus Station. Arrived at the main gate which was located on a traffic circle. This was also called the Buzzards Bay gate.

Otis was a huge base, as I found out when I arrived there. It was about two miles from the gate before I saw any buildings. It was big enough so the Army could bring in 155MM self-propelled guns on rail flat cars to fire on the range. The Army was very busy during the late 60s. The Army portion of the base was called Camp Edwards. Troops came from Fort Devens, MA., to train there. One interesting bit of information was that the 18-year-old could drink beer at Devens, but since Otis was state property (USAF leased the base) they had to be 21 years old to drink on Otis.

Otis was an active base during WWII and housed a lot of prisoners of war. Many of the old wooden buildings from that era were being torn down while I was there. It was about a mile and one-half from the barracks to the flight line. There was a large wooden hospital complex near Camp Edwards which I will talk about later.

I was assigned to the 551st Electronic Maintenance Squadron. I was in the in-flight section and flew with one of the three operational squadrons. I worked maintenance on the flight line between flights, which took the place of crew training. The first airplane I flew on was the EC-121D. They were testing the EC-121H when I got there. Soon all the airplanes were converted to H models except for five. Those five were there for about a year after, being used as trainers for flight crews. We cannibalized them for parts all the time. When they were sent to the 552nd AEW&C Wing at McClellan AFB, CA., they said they were in bad shape -- I wonder why.

The base had a Strategic Air Command (SAC) unit there, the 19th Aerial Refueling Squadron (ARS), which flew the KC-97. The flight line was secure with guards, locked doors and gates. After the 19th deactivated they did away with the security. In fact they removed the gate guards. The SAC area had what was called the Mole Hole, where alert crews stay while pulling alert duty. The Kennedys, Jackie, Ethel and kids, spent time in the Mole Hole during a hurricane alert. Ethel decided she would like to go swimming and had the indoor base pool opened for a midnight swim during the stay. They had to get the pool manager out of bed to open up the building. Heard that Caroline put all the billiard balls in the toilet, don't know if that is true or not. They built a special suite at the base hospital for Mrs. Kennedy to use. She was pregnant at the time and they said that it was very unlikely that she would use it. It was for emergency use only. Well, she used it and sadly the infant [Patrick] died of a lung ailment.

The 60th Fighter Interceptor Squadron (FIS) was also at Otis. They flew the F-101 Voodoo which sometimes carried nuclear weapons. That meant that we were having practice "Broken Arrow" nuclear accident exercises quite often. This was bad when you got off work and the roads were closed for a couple hours and one could not get home. There was also the 26th Missile Squadron with BOMARC (Boeing Michigan Aeronautical Research Center) missiles with nuclear war heads. I did not know much about them. Before they had storage for these devices, Otis had a fleet of C-123 cargo aircraft to shuttle them back and forth. This was before my time at Otis.

The Texas Towers [offshore radar installations which resembled offshore oil rigs] were still operational when I arrived at Otis. Tower Four had collapsed [January 1961] before I arrived. [Fourteen airmen and 14 civilian workers were killed in its collapse with only two bodies being recovered]. The other towers were closed afterwards and lots of the tower personnel were assigned to the wing.

Summer time on Cape Cod was great. It started Memorial Day and ended Labor Day. They uncovered the parking meters a few days before Memorial Day, as I found out. I was having a cold one in the Falmouth Hotel bar when the meter maid came in and said, "Whoever owns the green MG had better put some money in the meter or I will write a ticket." The traffic was really bad in the summer when you got near Falmouth, but I got so I knew the back roads, and could get to down town really easily. I ate a lot of lobster, fried clams and stuffed quahogs. Quahogs were a type of clam that were chopped up and mixed with bread and spices, then baked in the shell. They were really good. A lot of people from the base went clamming. I learned to eat little necks and cherry stones on the half shell. A lot of college students came down to the Cape in the summer, why I don't know. The beaches were terrible (rocky) and the water cold. A lot of the towns had beaches that were restricted to town residents only. I don't know if that was to keep GIs or the tourists out. The only beach I went to was Johns Pond on base. More information about Johns Pond later on.

The locals didn't like the tourists much, but their money was okay. They liked the GIs okay. A few years earlier they enacted some laws because of the tourists. No sleeping on the beaches and no loud noises that could be heard fifty feet away were allowed after a certain hour, 10:00 P.M., I think. One year about a dozen of my comrades from the squadron got arrested for disturbing the peace. They were having a party at the house that a group of them was renting. The Commander had to come and bail them out. It cost him fifty dollars apiece, a lot of money back at that time. He was really upset, not at the troops, but at the town. A few days later some of the same people took a tape measure and measured a chalk marked box fifty feet away from a local night club and stood in it and hollered for the police to make an arrest. The police just laughed them off.

There were the islands off the Cape, Nantucket and Martha's Vineyard. A couple of people from my squadron were floating on inner tubes in the ocean with Chianti wine jugs tied to the tube. When they were picked up by the Coast Guard, they said they were headed for Nantucket.

Woods Hole Oceanographic Institute was located near Falmouth. They had the deep water submergible named ALVIN there. Several members of the squadron worked there. Some also got jobs in the winter as caretakers for some of the expensive summer houses.

There were lots of clubs on the Cape, and they had summer liquor licenses. During the winter they closed and the owners moved to Florida for the winter. You could rent a house in the winter for almost nothing, but come summer the rent went sky high. The Kennedys had their summer home there on the Cape at Hyannis Port. One had to have a sticker on the car to even drive in the neighborhood. The Kennedys were not as popular there as one might suspect. A lot of the old timers remember the Kennedy boys as spoiled brats.

I spent most of my time in Buzzards Bay and Wareham. I think the people there were friendlier. You could have moved to the Cape and lived there thirty years, but be considered a "newcomer."

Earlier I spoke of Johns Pond, which was partially located on the base. They had a nice beach, boats for rent and a beer concession. The beer concession was put to good use several times. My Aircraft Commander, Captain Kelly Hoffer, had several post-mission debriefing sessions there. You know it did not take too many cold ones to put you out after flying a 14-hour mission. Another favorite watering hole was the Ranch, which some people thought was the Non Commissioned Officer (NCO) stag bar, which it was not. It was operated by the NCO club but was open to all ranks.

During my time there were several aircraft accidents. These involved the F-101, EC-121H and EC-121R. The EC-121R landed short of runway 14 in the small scrub trees. It traveled a good way before the nose gear collapsed and was forced through the floor of the cockpit. The flight crew had to leave the aircraft via the cockpit windows. No one was seriously hurt. The 60th FIS lost a bunch of F-101s. One time our ground safety NCO put up a monthly safety tip: "Watch out for falling Voodoos." This was quickly removed as in bad taste.

The 551st Wing lost three EC-121Hs, 55-0136 [July 11, 1965], 55-5262 [November 11, 1966] and 53-0549 [April 25, 1967]. I was part of a flight crew from the 961st AEW&C Squadron and the first two airplanes that were lost were flown by the 961st. On each occasion I was on the next crew to take off after those first two were lost. When I reported for my flights I learned that 55-0136 had ditched and that there had been no radio contact with 55-5262 for over an hour. I was not flying when 53-0549 went down but I remember seeing a couple of the radar technicians leave a softball game we were watching to go flying. After the game I went into the barracks, turned on the tv and saw the news flash: "A radar picket ship was observed in flames passing over Nantucket and crashing into the sea." That one had my flight supervisor and close friend on it, T/Sgt Gordon O. Hamman, who was killed along with fourteen other members of the crew. One survived. In November 1966 I went to the memorial service for the victims of 55-5262 and the first person I meet that I knew was Airman David Surles, who was one of three survivors of 55-0136 which had ditched in July 1965. I remember him looking at me shaking his head and saying, "I just can't believe it." There were a lot of TV cameras there and I think they recognized Surles as they were pointed at us and began running toward us. I remember how sad I felt as I watched Colonel James P. Lyle, the Commander of the 551st AEW&C Wing, presenting flags to the next of kin seated up front in a row. Little could I have known he would be next. He died five months later while piloting 53-0549 on April 25, 1967 when it caught fire and crashed into the ocean at Nantucket Island.

There were consequences to pay after 53-0549 was lost. The Wing and Base had two operational readiness inspections. The EC-121H aircraft were grounded for a good while after the last loss. In about two months time they had only flown a couple of days. After 45 days a crew member was non-current and required a ride with an instructor. I was the only Instructor Radar Technician on base who was current when they started flying again regularly. I was quite busy for a while. During this time a SAC wing trouble shooter named Colonel Max "the axe" Rogers was assigned as the new Commander of the 551st AEW&C Wing. He brought a broom with him and most of the commanders and staffs were reassigned within hours of his arrival. They refurbished the airplanes one at a time and finally got them all back to flying. This took many days. The main reason for this happening was there was such an outcry from the local community, local Representatives and Senator Ted Kennedy. They said they were tired of losing all their friends and neighbors and wanted the wing investigated.

About life in the barracks. Most of the barracks, were brick, two-story buildings with rooms. They were located near a mess hall, cafeteria, and NCO club. There was this time when some guys thought the small blue spruce trees around the barracks weren't blue enough. They spray-painted them blue. Then there was this captain who was being released from the Air Force in a reduction of force (RIF) move and he had decided to make life miserable for the troops in the barracks before he departed. He restricted the people to the base and to the barracks. He had them cleaning for about three days. The captain had an office in one of the barracks from which he discharged his duties as duty officer. After about three days the people had enough and a fire extinguisher with a note came through the office window. It had a simple message, "shape up or die." We had no problems after that. I have no idea who did it. I think the captain talked to the commanders, who ordered him to ease up. He departed Otis shortly afterwards.

My duty schedule for a week was: work the flight line, fly a mission, crew rest, work the flight line, fly, crew rest, off. A lot of times I ended up working on the airplane I flew. For a while we were assigned to an airplane as the radar crew chief. That meant that we were responsible for the repair of the radar and we were to fly with it as the first radar tech. I was on leave when this started. When I returned and was informed about the system, I asked which was my airplane. I was informed that 402 was my airplane and there are the parts. They pointed to a pile of radar equipment. The plane had been cannibalized and the parts had been repaired and were ready to be installed. It looked like most of the radar equipment had been removed. The APS-95 transmitter and receiver had been removed and that must have totaled 1000 to 1500 pounds. I had it all installed and working fine in four days.

That lasted about four or five months. We then were assigned to a hard crew with the operational squadrons. I was assigned to the 961st with Capt. Hoffer and then Major Mirick as aircraft commanders. One interesting fact about aircraft 402 was an entry in the 781k section (deferred writeups) bullet hole in number 6 fuel tank. Number six tank had been deactivated on all EC-121s after aircraft 55-0123 burned, so there were no problems. **[See note at end]**

As a crew we deployed on TDY (temporary duty) together. I deployed many times on Apache Yell missions to Iceland, to help the US Navy keep an eye on Russian aircraft and the Soviet naval fleet. One time we discovered the Soviet fleet in an area. No one knew they were there. We were flying what was known as a gap filler mission. A gap filler mission is one where the radar site is inoperable and the Connie would provide coverage. That unexpected detection of the Soviet fleet made our mission there permanent to this day. The main job was to keep track of the Soviet aircraft (mainly Bear Bombers) that flew around Norway and down the Greenland straits. I understood that they passed messages to the submarines. The Navy had P-3s stationed at Keflavik Naval Air Station involved in Anti Submarine Warfare. They were always complaining about being interrogated by mode 4 IFF (Identification Friend or Foe) while they were on station. Duty in Iceland involved alert duty. The USSR had to fly north of Norway on their way to Cuba and could be picked up by long range radar. We would get the word they were headed our way. We would then flush and go meet them. The way it worked was, we would preflight and cock the airplane and go on 24 hours alert duty. If we did not scramble, we would fly a mission after our relief crew had cocked their airplane. Our alternate landing fields were Norway, Spain and Scotland. One mission we were following a Soviet Bear Bomber and we got into severe icing which used our fuel reserve for alternates. Sure enough Iceland was socked in zero-zero. We made a Ground Controlled Approach landing, the pilot said he finally saw the runway at about 25 feet. We had circled the island for a couple of hours. He said before landing, "Hang on, crew, we may have a rough one." About 15 minutes after landing the weather cleared up. I found out later the ground crew was about to have a "cow" over us. The detachment commander went to the GCA shack and watched us come in. Another interesting event was during a taxi in a white out [fog, rain, snow, or sleet rendering visibility to a few feet]. The pilot would go a few feet stop, wait a little while and try again. I heard him say, "If I did not know better I would say we were flying at 15,000 feet." You could not see the ground in front of you. He finally called for a tug to come out and tow us back to the ramp. During this time the national airline of Iceland landed a plane. Nothing stopped them.

In the middle of 1969, just before I left, Colonel Rogers decided that the people in Standardization Evaluation (Stan Eval) section at the Wing Headquarters had been there too long. So I was to be the second radar tech to go there. They did one at a time so they would have a smooth transition. The first radar tech that went got to give his former supervisor a check ride and failed him. He told me he was going to do it. He was right to fail him, as he was not up to standards. A Stan Eval man said he had slid by long enough. Thank God I left before I had to go up there. I liked Otis but was glad to leave after seven years. Some of the radar techs had been there 15 years.

One more item about Colonel Rogers. Some computer techs made his day when they stole a full-sized fiber glass figure of a fisherman wearing a slicker and holding a lantern -- smuggled it past the gate guard and ran it up the flag pole in front of Base Headquarters. Somehow the <u>Boston Globe</u> got wind of it and ran a front page story titled "Who was that lady hanging from the flag pole at Otis AFB."

DEAN BOYS retired from the Air Force in 1978 as a Master Sergeant. You may contact him at:

dboys@dean-boys.com

NOTE: A. J. Northrup, who then was a member of the Air Force Office of Special Investigations (AFOSI), investigated the shooting of the aircraft. The "sabotage" investigation did not determine who had shot into the aircraft. The projectile, an armor piercing bullet, was recovered, but even with the help of the FBI laboratory it only was determined that the projectile could have been fired upward into the aircraft from land or from a boat as the aircraft flew its mission(s). The caliber of the projectile was similar to several of the type used by military rifles manufactured by many countries. There always was a suspicion that a crew member on one of the many Russian fishing trawlers, which frequented the areas flown by the Connies, possibly could have fired the shot. The time and place of the shooting could not be determined as the flight crew was unaware that the plane had been fired upon. Likewise, it could have been fired upon by anyone possessing a military-type rifle and armor piercing ammunition.

DEAN BOYS

Dean Boys, Air Force Master Sergeant Retired, who as a Radar Technician, flew on the Connies for many years ended up flying AWACS missions as a crew member on the E-3 (modified version of the Boeing 707 jet aircraft) prior to his retirement.

He accumulated a total of 5714 hours flying in the Super Connies and in the E-3. He flew a total of 104 hours on combat missions and 265 hours in support of combat missions.

He was stationed at Otis Air Force Base and knew some of the crew members who perished on the EC-121H aircraft which was lost from there. Dean has a vast knowledge about the Constellation aircraft (most all versions) and has compiled a detailed history about the Constellations, its missions, and the history of the Airborne Early Warning and Control units who flew them. He has compiled a historical record upon which research can be done by way of the internet.

Dean established and maintains the numerous web sites at his own expense. If after you visit the sites you appreciate what he has done, please let him know. His E-Mail address is:

dboys@dean-boys.com

Following are some of the web sites maintained by Dean Boys:

[Aircraft 53-0549]	http://members.tripod.com/dboys/lost/ac549.htm
[Aircraft 55-0136]	http://members.tripod.com/dboys/lost/136.htm
[Aircraft 55-5262]	http://members.tripod.com/dboys/lost/ac-262.htm
[551st AEW&C Wing]	http://www.dean-boys.com/551aew/551stwg.htm
[961st AEW&C Sqdn]	http://members.tripod.com/dboys/961/961.htm
[Super Constellations]	http://www.dean-boys.com/ec-121.htm
[EC-121H]	http://members.tripod.com/dboys/hmodel.htm
[Lost Connies]	http://www.dean-boys.com/lconnie/lconnie.htm
[552nd AEW&C Wing]	http://www.dean-boys.com/552/552ndwg.htm
[Deans Air Force Home Page]	http://www.dean-boys.com

Following are the awards and decorations DEAN BOYS received during his Air Force Career:

AIR MEDAL
ARMY GOOD CONDUCT MEDAL
AIR FORCE GOOD CONDUCT MEDAL(5)
AIR FORCE COMMENDATION MEDAL
AIR FORCE OUTSTANDING UNIT AWARD WITH V DEVICE AND 4 OAK LEAF CLUSTERS
SENIOR AIR CREW MEMBER WINGS
COMBAT READINESS MEDAL
NATIONAL DEFENSE SERVICE MEDAL
ARMED FORCES EXPEDITIONARY MEDAL
VIETNAM SERVICE MEDAL WITH 1 BRONZE STAR
AIR FORCE LONGEVITY SERVICE RIBBON WITH 4 OAK LEAF CLUSTERS
SMALL ARMS EXPERT MARKSMANSHIP RIBBON
REPUBLIC OF VIETNAM GALLANTRY CROSS WITH PALM DEVICE

Dean entered the Air Force in June 1956, went through basic training at Parks AFB, CA. In September 1956 he was assigned to Scott AFB, IL., where he completed basic training and the Heavy Ground Radio School. He next was assigned to the 1961st AACS at Iwo Jima in February 1957. In April he was reassigned to the 1958th AACS Guam Receiver Site near Anderson AFB, Guam. In March 1958 he returned from overseas to the 28th Bomb Wing at Ellsworth AFB, SD., and in June 1960 was discharged.

In April 1962 Dean again enlisted in the Air Force and was assigned to Keesler AFB, MS., where he attended the Airborne Early Warning & Control School and received an assignment to the 551st AEW&C Wing at Otis AFB, MA., upon completion of the school in January 1963. Dean remained at Otis until September 1969, at which time he was assigned to the 552nd AEW&C Wing at McClelland AFB, CA. In June 1971 he attended a school (classified) at Lowery AFB, CO., and in January 1972 assigned to Detachment 333 (classified). In October 1973 he was again assigned to the 552nd AEW&C Wing and in June 1976 received an assignment to the 552nd AWACS, where he remained until his retirement as Master Sergeant in November 1978. During his career flying on the Connies, Dean was assigned on many temporary duty (TDY) assignments, i.e. College Eye, Korea, and Iceland.

551ST ELECTRONICS MAINTENANCE SQUADRON PATCH.

FEB 1999 - DEAN BOYS

1ST MISHAP
THE LOSS OF 55-0136
JULY 11, 1965

CONSOLIDATED NEWS ARTICLES 55-0136

Nantucket, Mass., July 12 [1965] (UPI) - Ships of two nations searched the North Atlantic late today after 16 crewmen were reported dead or missing in the crash of an Air Force radar plane with 19 aboard. Three men were rescued after nearly 12 hours in the water in life-jackets.

THREE PICKET PLANE SURVIVORS SPEND NIGHT IN SEA

9:30 P.M. (Sunday) Plane with 19 crewmen takes off from Otis Air Force Base on routine surveillance mission.

9:58 P.M. Pilot reports he has reached his station and is proceeding at 15,000 feet.

10:13 P.M. Naval Air Station Brunswick, Me., notified Coast Guard Search and Rescue Headquarters Boston, a radar picket plane was experiencing difficulties.

10:15 P.M. Picket plane pilot radios he has feathered No. 2 (left, inboard) engine.

10:17 P.M. Pilot reports his No. 3 (right, inboard) engine is afire, and he has advised the crew to prepare for ditching.

10:18 P.M. Pilot switches on emergency MAYDAY signal.

10:19 P.M. MAYDAY distress received at Brunswick. Following disaster procedures, the signal is automatically relayed to Coast Guard Headquarters, Boston. All Navy, commercial and fishing vessels in the area are notified of the emergency.

10:21 P.M. Pilot reports the plane is at 200 feet and he is ditching. Then complete silence.

10:21 P.M. Coast Guard Cutter General Greene, off Provincetown, Cutter Snohomish, and Cutter Cape Cross, five miles east of Isle of Shoals, off New Hampshire, are sent to the scene.

10:21 P.M. Ditching scene is pinpointed in area 100 miles on a bearing of 080 degrees east of Nantucket. Forty-four footer is dispatched from Nantucket, but recalled because it is considered too small for the task. Cutters Vigilant and Bibb in Boston are placed on alert status.

10:35 P.M. Pan American World Airways pilot reports sighting flash from general area where MAYDAY signal originated.

10:45 P.M. Brunswick Naval Air Station informed Naval Forces headed by Carrier Wasp are proceeding to vicinity of downed plane. Wasp relays message it has aircraft and helicopters available for search. (Three U.S. and three German Destroyers are with the carrier on NATO exercise.)

11:04 P.M. An amphibious plane from Salem Coast Guard Air Station takes off for search area.

11:07 P.M. Another Salem amphibian is sent to Otis Air Force Base to remain on standby status.

11:15 P.M. Otis amphibian takes off for search.

12:33 A.M. (Monday) Carrier Wasp launched four Grumman Tracker Anti-Submarine planes for the search.

12:40 A.M. Wasp dispatches plane to Logan Airport to pick up Lt. Cmdr. Robert Russell, a pilot from the Salem base to fly him back to the carrier and serve as search co-ordinator.

1:00 A.M. Cutter Vigilant sent to the scene.

2:55 A.M. Zero to one mile visibility reported at the search area.

3:28 A.M. Coast Guard plane reported low on fuel and forced to return with negative results. Plane reports numerous cloud formations and a squall line hampering the search. Few holes in clouds reported as not adequate for a search effort.

5:00 A.M. Visual search resumed at first rays of daylight.

5:55 A.M. Air Force received six S.O.S. signals on a frequency used by life raft radio equipment.

6:00 A.M. Air Force plane spotted flare, dye markers and much debris. Position obtained.

6:56 A.M. Carrier Wasp advised survivors sighted.

7:30 A.M. Four men sighted in water. They were wearing Mae West life preservers apparently tied together to prevent the quartet from being separated. Two of the forms were limp. The other two men were gesturing to circling aircraft to inform they were alive.

7:48 A.M. U.S. Destroyer Barry reported eight miles from survivors.

7:50 A.M. Coast Guard plane confirms sighting of survivors.

8:30 A.M. First of the downed aircraft's crew picked up by one of the German destroyers.

9:00 A.M. Five more of the downed crewmen put aboard Wasp by helicopters.

9:54 A.M. Destroyer Barry picked up three more men.

11:30 A.M. Coast Guard advised Otis Air Force Base there were 10 survivors and eight dead men picked up. One man still unaccounted for.

11:32 A.M. Plane reports flares sighted.

11:32 A.M. Visibility reported from 50 to 100 yards in search area.

2:30 P.M. Six bodies reported on German destroyer, which also has three survivors. Three bodies reported on Destroyer Barry.

HUGE SEA SEARCH UNDERWAY
PLANE DOWN OFF CAPE 19 ARE ABOARD
WASP IN HUNT - HOPE IN SIGNALS
Record American July 12, 1965

NANTUCKET - A huge Air Force radar picket plane with 19 crewmen aboard crashed in the Atlantic Ocean about 100 miles northeast of here last night after one of its four engines caught fire. The fate of the crewmen was unknown. Search planes dispatched to the scene in the Georges Bank area reported picking up a homing signal believed from life raft equipment normally carried by the radar-domed aircraft that took off earlier from Otis Air Force Base on a routine radar surveillance mission. Air Force officials said it was raining in the crash area and visibility was zero because of heavy fog. A commercial jetliner and two military craft near the scene at the time of the crash were unable to locate any wreckage or survivors. The plane crashed ten minutes after its pilot sent out a "may day" distress signal that was picked up by the Brunswick, Me., Naval Air Station.

Officials said the pilot first reported one engine was on fire. A short time later, another message was received that a second engine had to be stopped and the propeller "feathered." The pilot said he was attempting to reach Nantucket Island but seconds later gave his position and said he had to ditch the plane. A full scale air and sea rescue alert was broadcast and planes and ships left immediately for the scene.

CARRIER ON WAY - The Aircraft Carrier USS Wasp, on a training mission about 150 miles from the crash, was directed to the scene along with Coast Guard cutters Gen. Green, Cape Cross, Vigilant and Snobomish. A Coast Guard spokesman said aircraft from the Wasp and stations along the coastline will leave for the crash scene at daybreak. They said about 40 aircraft will take part in the search. Officials said a 10-mile-wide air corridor from here to the scene will be established. The planes will cris cross to cover a 50-mile circle in the crash area. Radio messages also were dispatched to all fishing vessels in the area along with commercial craft. The Coast Guard said there should be a "lot of vessels in the area." The FAA Traffic Control Center at Nashua, N.H., said the $2.5 million aircraft crashed shortly after leaving Otis Air Force Base. However, an Air Force spokesman said the plane was on a normal 12-hour radar surveillance mission and had completed about half of its duties when the engine caught fire. Equipped with sensitive radar, the plane was part of the nation's airborne "Early Warning" system against enemy attacks. It was the military version of a Super G Constellation and was assigned to the 551st Airborne and Early Warning and Control Wing at Otis.

The Air Force spokesman said the radar planes take off every two hours from the Cape Cod base to carry out the around-the-clock surveillance. The crash was the first of the NORAD mission in the last 10 years.

HAVE LIFE RAFTS - Normally, the spokesmen said, the planes are not equipped with parachutes but do have life rafts. He said the 19 men aboard was the regular complement. Officials said the first plane at the scene after the crash was a Pan American flight bound for Europe from New York. The pilot of the commercial liner reported he saw a "flash of light" but nothing after that. The Pan American airliner circled the area until Navy planes arrived from Brunswick Air Base. Two F-105 fighter planes and an Albatross rescue seaplane joined the Navy Planes in the search, and will remain hovering over the crash scene until daybreak, when the other craft will arrive. Weather Bureau officials reported visibility will be a problem in the search. They said there was low cloudiness, haze and fog in the area. Identification of the crew members was withheld by Air Force officials pending the results of the search and rescue mission. In Washington, Air Force officials said the plane had a range of about 4000 miles and is capable of staying aloft almost 12 hours. They said radar equipment in the plane weighed about five and a half tons. The gear includes five radar scopes and three radar domes. The downed craft was one of about 38 assigned to Otis Air Force Base, that provides a protective screen from Newfoundland to Norfolk, VA., and checks the location of surface vessels as well as other aircraft. Each plane carried radar specialists in addition to normal flight crews.

RADIO SOS GIVES HOPE - A slim beacon of hope for the 19 servicemen who ditched 100 miles off Nantucket Island last night in an EC-121H radar picket plane came from a radio signal picked up by one of the search planes. It may be from a life raft. The signal which was not repeated, was heard by a jet fighter about 90 minutes after the Otis Air Force-based plane went into the fog shrouded Atlantic at 10:30 p.m.

8 CREWMEN DIE, 11 SAVED BY ARMADA AS OTIS PLANE DITCHES IN ATLANTIC
CAPE COD STANDARD-TIMES JULY 12, 1965

OTIS AIR FORCE BASE, July 12 - Eight crew members died when an Otis-based EC-121H Super-Constellation ditched last night in the Atlantic Ocean 100 miles northeast of Nantucket. They were confirmed as dead by base officials shortly before noon today. Latest word received at the base at noon was that 11 of the original crew members survived the crash and were picked up by a German destroyer operating in the area. Four of the 11, base officials said, were reported to be in good condition. Conditions of the other survivors were not available at press time today.

BELIEVED TRANSFERRED - The survivors were believed to have been transferred to the U.S. carrier Wasp which was on a training mission with five German destroyers in the general area where the Super-Constellation ditched. Base information service officials said at noon that a helicopter was bringing some of the survivors back to Otis. First word of the fatalities was received here from a Salem-based Coast Guard rescue plane, one of several aircraft flying over the scene of the ditching. Names of those who lost their lives have been withheld pending identification and notification of next of kin. Also withheld from publication at noon is the name of the aircraft commander.

TO ARRIVE - Brigadier-General Von R. Shores, commander of the 26th Air Division, was expected to arrive at Otis early this afternoon for a briefing on the disaster and to hold a press conference when he has sufficient facts. Bodies of the eight crew members killed in the ditching were believed to have been recovered in the water. There were conflicting reports on the number of survivors with some early reports saying that there were 10 survivors and one missing. A rescue flotilla of helicopters, planes, and ships of two nations picked up the dead and living airmen bobbing in life jackets in three to five foot swells. The Coast Guard said seven of the survivors were put aboard a German destroyer on maneuvers in the area and that three others were on the U.S. destroyer Barry. The West German warship was one of three on maneuvers with the carrier Wasp. All were diverted to participate in the rescue. The life and death drama unfolded at daybreak when rescue craft saw flares, dye markers, an oil slick and plane debris. Planes circling overhead spotted the survivors floating fairly close together in inflated vests. A dozen ships converged on the area including the Wasp and three destroyers of the West German Navy. The German destroyer Blotter, a former U.S. destroyer, was the first to pick up survivors. The massive air-sea search was launched shortly after the plane plunged into the ocean last night with one of its four engines aflame. The pilot had feathered or cut the power on a second apparently disabled engine six minutes before the crash.

PICKED UP SOS - Shortly after the crash at 10:20 p.m. a search plane picked up SOS calls on a frequency used by emergency radio transmitters in life rafts. First word that the plane was in trouble was reported by Federal Aviation Agency (FAA) air traffic control tower at Nashua, N.H. The pilot reported to the tower one engine out and another on fire. Thunderstorms lashed the area about the time the plane went down in fog of almost zero visibility. It was not known whether the plane was hit by lightning.

HAMPER SEARCH - The weather worsened during the night, hampering search operations, but improved by mid-morning. The plane went into the water on Georges Banks, a commercial fishing ground used by Russian as well as American fishermen. Air Force Captain Theodore Shaffer of Tiltonbille, Ohio, pilot of one of the search planes, said the first four men sighted were bobbing close together in life jackets. Shaffer's crew relayed messages from low flying search planes to the mainland but did not actually sight any survivors. Captain Shaffer said debris and an oil slick were sighted at the same time four men were seen in the water. One of the search planes dropped a life raft, he said. The first airman was pulled from the water by the German destroyer at 4:15 a.m. about eight hours after the ditching, Captain Shaffer said. One Air Force plane taking part in the search reported receiving six SOS calls on a frequency used by emergency radio transmitters found in life rafts. The patrol plane ditched about 95 miles northeast of Nantucket. The $2,500,000 plane crammed with 5 tons of sensitive radar gear crash landed last night. The pilot reported that one of its four engines was afire. He feathered another apparently disabled engine six minutes before the plane hit the water. Thunderstorms lashed the area about the time the plane went down in fog in almost zero visibility. It was not known whether the plane was hit by lightning. At least 10 ships including the Boston - based aircraft carrier Wasp sailed for the crash scene. Scores of planes circled overhead. The air-sea search was concentrated on a part of Georges Banks, a commercial fishing ground used by the Russians as well as Americans. Many Soviet fishing vessels were reported in the area recently. The weather worsened during the night, hampering search operations, but was expected to improve by mid-morning. Sea swells were five to six feet high. After the plane went down at 10:20 last night, one of the search planes picked up a radio signal that might have come from a life raft. However, the signal was not repeated. Federal Aviation Agency air traffic control at Nashua, N.H. said the pilot reported one engine out and another on fire six minutes before the craft hit the water. The ditching was the first for a North American Radar Air Defense (NORAD) plane in 10 years. Normally such a plane does not carry parachutes. The plane with a range of 4,000 miles and the ability of staying aloft eight to 12 hours was assigned to the 551st Airborne Early Warning and Control Wing at Otis. It was part of a group whose protective screen ranged from Newfoundland to Norfolk, Va. Shortly after the plane hit the water, a Pan American World Airways jetliner en route to Europe from Kennedy Airport was diverted to the scene of the ditching. The Pan Am captain said he could find no trace of wreckage or survivors. He said visibility was poor. The radio signal was picked up by a jet fighter about 1 hour after the crash. It was believed the homing signal came from life raft equipment normally carried by the plane, the Air Force said.

AIR FORCE LISTS CREW OF DOWNED AIRPLANE

Cape Cod Standard-Times July 12, 1965

OTIS AIR FORCE BASE, July 12 - The Air Force today Identified 18 of the 19 crewmen aboard the EC-121H Radar picket plane that ditched last night in the Atlantic Ocean off Nantucket. The names of the 19th crewman, identified only as a pilot, was withheld pending notification of next of kin. Listed were:

1. Captain Murray J. Brody, New York City, the pilot, lives at Otis.

2. 1st Lieutenant Thomas Fiedler, Davenport, Iowa, the co-pilot, lives at Otis.

3. 1st Lieutenant Bruce E. Witcher, Reading, Cal., the navigator, lives at Otis.

4. 2nd Lieutenant Ira J. Husik, Philadelphia, navigator, lives in North Falmouth.

5. Captain Edward N. Anaka, an Air Force Reserve Officer Training Corps (AFROTC) instructor at Davis and Elkins College in Elkins, West, Va.

6. Captain Michael R. Barbolla, an AFROTC instructor at Manhattan College in New York City (The Air Force said Captains Anaka and Barbolla were not members of the planes crew but were on the flight as observers.)

7. Technical Sergeant Gilbert L, Duncan, S.C., flight engineer, lives at Otis.

8. Staff Sergeant Raymond M. Washam, Wilmington, Del., radio operator, lives at Otis.

9. Staff Sergeant Francis J. Griffin, Toronto, Canada; radio operator, lives at Otis.

10. Staff Sergeant John L. Howard, Sanford, Fla., radar technician, lives in Buzzards Bay.

11. Airman 1st Class George R. West, Grand Rapids, Mich., radar technician, lives at Otis.

12. Airman 1st Class Charles K. Sawyer, Anderson, S.C., radar technician, lives in Pocasset.

13. Airman 1st Class John N. Puopolo, Roslindale, radar technician, lives in Sagamore.

14. Airman 2nd Class William E. Howe, North Augusta, S.C., radar technician, lives at Onset.

15. Airman 2nd Class David A. Surles, Raleigh, N.C., radar technician, lives in Falmouth.

16. Airman Charles H. Williams, Worcester, radar technician, lives at Otis.

17. Airman 3rd Class Charles J. Podiaski, Evergreen, Ill., radar technician, lives at Otis.

18. Technical Sergeant Eugene J. Schreivogel, Springfield, Colo., flight engineer.

[19. NOTE The pilot who was the Aircraft Commander subsequently was identified as l/Lt Frederick H. Ambrosia of New York City].

BAD COMMUNICATIONS, WEATHER ARE BLAMED
Cape Cod Standard-Times July 13, 1965

By United Press International BOSTON, July 13 - Communications problems and bad weather created confusion in reporting the fate of 19 airmen who ditched their patrol plane at sea, the Coast Guard said today. The four-engine plane from Otis Air Force Base crashed some 100 miles off the Massachusetts coast Sunday night because of engine trouble. During the next 14 hours the reported number of survivors ranged from four to 11. Three men actually survived, nine were killed, and seven are missing and feared lost. The Coast Guard said crews aboard rescue ships misinterpreted messages from other surface [ships] and aircraft in the area. One report said a German destroyer had taken aboard nine survivors. Actually, six of the airmen on the warship were dead. In addition, stormy weather in the search area hampered radio communications and poor visibility increased the possibility of duplications in reports of those seen in the water.

HOPE WANES FOR 7 CREWMEN
BOARD OF INQUIRY WILL SIT
By PAUL W. KEMPRECOS and KEN ILG Cape Cod Standard-Times Staff Writers July 13, 1965

OTIS AIR FORCE BASE, July 13 - Hope waned today for seven crewmen of an Air Force Radar picket Constellation that crashed off Nantucket Sunday night with only three survivors. Even as an armada of Naval and Coast Guard ships continued today to search the waters and a sister plane of the downed craft circled overhead, her crew scanning the sea for a flare or other signal, the wheels began to turn in the long and tedious process of investigation. A board of inquiry was scheduled to arrive at Otis today from Washington to question the three survivors of the 19-man crew of the craft. The crewmen were at the base hospital today recuperating from their ordeal. None was in critical condition. First Lieutenant Bruce Witcher of Redding, Cal., and Airman John Puopolo of Sagamore and Roslindale and David S. Surles of Raleigh, N.C., arrived at Otis shortly before 11, last night. They had spent more than 10 hours in the water. The first account of the crash from a survivor was relayed at 3 a.m. today by Colonel Raymond K. Gallagher, wing commander of the 551st Flight Group, who talked with two of the three survivors shortly after they were flown to the base from the deck of the aircraft carrier Wasp.

He said the surviving crewmen told him the crash of the plane was like hitting a brick wall at 100 miles an hour. The plane, crammed with radar and electronic gear, crashed after losing two engines. Nine men were killed in the crash or died in the water and seven others are missing. Colonel Gallagher said that he talked with Lieutenant

Witcher and Airman Surles early today at the hospital, but they would not be available for a press conference before 2 p.m. today and even that time would depend on the approval of the flight surgeon.

WERE PICKED UP - The survivors were picked up shortly after dawn yesterday by a West German destroyer participating in NATO maneuvers in the North Atlantic with the Wasp and U.S. destroyers. They had spent the night bobbing in their life-jackets. They were then flown to Otis from the Wasp. A van met them at the landing strip and carried them directly to the hospital. Two of the airmen walked into the hospital, unassisted while Airman Puopolo, who suffered deep shin cuts, abrasions and water immersion, was carried in a stretcher. The board of inquiry will be from the Air Defense Command, 26th Air Division, Colonel Gallagher said. It will convene at Otis today and as a probable first step in its investigation, will talk to the three survivors. Physical evidence on the cause of the crash will require more time and effort. Colonel Gallagher said it would be necessary to recover the planes engines before the cause of the disaster could be determined. He said the water at the crash site was 50 to 150 feet deep and Navy divers would be asked to help locate the wreckage and if possible to raise the engines. Moments before the plane ditched, the pilot radioed that one engine was afire and another had been feathered because of a malfunction. The plane was a modified version of the Lockheed Constellation and was part of the Early Defense Warning System. It was one of 36 such aircraft based here as part of the 551st Group. After talking with Lieutenant Witcher and Airman Surles, Colonel Gallagher said "We had already pieced together something of what happened." They seemed to verify that things happened fast and that an engine was afire. They told us they got the announcement from the pilot that they were going to ditch while the plane was still at 15,000 feet.

UNUSUALLY RAPID - The boys estimated they made an unusually rapid descent. The best they could figure it was five to 10 minutes. In other words, they were trying to get down and ditch as fast at they could, the colonel said. He explained that this was not a normal ditching procedure, when a shallow glide is made. The life rafts were stored in the wings, but both wings were torn away in the impact, he said, and the survivors thought the plane broke up into two or three pieces. The plane sank only a few minutes after hitting the water. The colonel said that Airman Surles told him he managed to get to a small piece of the wing which was floating in the water. Also clinging to the wing was Lieutenant Witcher. Airman Surles told him, the colonel said, that there were one or two persons also clinging to the wing but he could not identify them in the darkness. A few waves washed over the section and they disappeared, he related. Colonel Gallagher said Airmen Surles and the other survivors first saw a Coast Guard amphibious craft at daybreak and then sighted a Constellation from Otis. This plane, the colonel said, was flying a low search pattern and relaying communications to another Constellation at 15,000 feet. The German destroyer then picked them up. The colonel said that this was the first serious mishap in more than 400,000 hours flying time logged by the Constellations which have traveled a total of 2,200,000,000 miles since they were first used in a radar picket capacity.

PILOT TOLD - Colonel Gallagher said that the commander of the plane was 1st Lieutenant Frederick H. Ambrosia, who, with the pilot, Captain Murray J. Brody, were among the dead or missing. Both were from New York City. Lieutenant Ambrosia, the colonel said, had been checked out in June as an aircraft commander of the Constellation and this was his fifth flight in this position. He explained that poor communications from the search and rescue armada was responsible for the confused, exaggerated accounts of the number of survivors. Searchers kept counting the same survivors repeatedly, he said. The condition of the seas at the time of the crash hindered the search. Water temperature was 58 degrees, and rain and fog were intermittent. The first statements to be released had 11 men surviving with 8 lost.

NOT FOR SOME TIME - Officials at Otis said today that a list of the dead and missing airmen in the plane will not be available for some time, pending positive medical identification of the six bodies recovered. Weather conditions were reported as good in the area as an intensive search was still underway for the seven other crew members. The wind was blowing at 10 knots and seas were from one to three feet. The 90-square mile search area has been divided into five sections. Coast Guard units from Salem and from Quonset Point, R.I.., have one section each; planes from Otis patrolled two sections, and the Wasp has charge of the fifth sector. Coast Guard Search and Rescue headquarters in Boston said that there was at least one ship and one plane in each sector. The Wasp had 13 helicopters aloft.

IT WAS HORRIBLE 20 HOURS, SAYS WIFE

By CATHARINE A. BAKER Cape Cod Standard-Times Reporter July 13, 1965

EAST FALMOUTH, July 13 - "It was the most horrible 20 hours of my life and I hope I never have to go through anything like this again," Mrs. David A. Surles, wife of one of the three survivors said today. In a telephone interview with this reporter, Mrs. Surles described her hours of anguish. "I have a habit of sleeping through the late news broadcasts and so I missed the first report at 11 p.m. Sunday but received a call from Otis at about 11:45," Mrs. Surles said. "From that time until 7:30 last night I had heard nothing when the news of his survival was telephoned to me."

WAS AT HOSPITAL - The anxious wife was at the base hospital when airman 2d Class David A. Surles was brought in at 2 a.m. today. "We had a brief visit," Mrs. Surles said. "And he seemed fine. I just received another call from the hospital telling me I could visit him again this morning for a brief period. This is perhaps one incident where overweight was a help rather than a hindrance. My husband doesn't have a scratch on him," Mrs. Surles continued. "In fact, he has been a little over-weight by 10 or 15 pounds. This gave him an excess roll around the middle which may even have saved his life. He seems to be in excellent physical condition," Mrs. Surles said, "and in very good spirits. I do not know much of what happened out there for it is highly technical and even if I did I would not be permitted to tell."

NOT WAIT ALONE - Her waiting hours were spent with one of the wives whose husband did not return and with neighbors and friends. "One of the rules at the base is that none of us were to wait alone." Mrs. Surles' happy news was dampened a great deal, she said, by the sad tidings brought to her waiting companion. "I had definite mixed emotions, she said. I couldn't be completely happy myself when I felt so sorry for her. I really didn't know how to cope with it." Airman Surles is not an Air Force career man. In fact, he and Mrs. Surles are career government employees, according to Mrs. Surles. Mr. Surles has been in the service since November, 1962 and this is his first experience with a plane crash. Mrs. Surles is from Illinois and he from Raleigh, N.C., but they will make their home near Washington, upon completion of his Air Force enlistment. Mrs. Surles is employed at the Bureau of Commercial Fisheries in Woods Hole.

RESPECT FOR OCEAN - Perhaps another contributing factor in Airman Surles survival is his respect for the ocean, as his wife termed it. "He is very fond of the ocean and spends a lot of time at the beach but he has a very healthy respect for it. He often has given me instructions in the Dos and Don'ts of swimming in the ocean". There were no tell-tale signs of her ordeal in Mrs. Surles voice today. She sounded like an extremely happy wife on her way to see her husband.

LIKE HITTING A BRICK WALL
Cape Cod Standard-Times July 13, 1965

By United Press International OTIS AIR FORCE BASE, July 13 - Crewmen who survived the ditching of their crippled Air Force patrol plane in the Atlantic Ocean Sunday night said today the crash was like hitting a brick wall at 100 miles an hour. Two of the three survivors were interviewed by Colonel Raymond K. Gallagher, Wing Commander of the 551st AEW&C Wing, after they were flown here from the deck of the aircraft carrier Wasp. Nine men were killed in the crash or perished later in the ocean. Seven others were missing and feared lost. An extensive air-sea search continued for them. The huge four-engine patrol plane, bristling with radio and radar gear, ditched about 100 miles off the Massachusetts coast after one malfunctioning engine was shut down and another caught fire. The 90-square-mile area was divided into five sections. Coast Guard units from Salem, and Quonset Point, R.I., had one section each; planes from Otis Air Force Base Patrolled two sections; and the Wasp had charge of the fifth sector. Coast Guard Search and Rescue Headquarters in Boston said there was at least one ship and one plane in each sector. The Wasp had 13 helicopters aloft. Weather in the area was good. The wind was blowing at about 10 knots and the sea was running about one to three feet.

WERE PICKED UP - The survivors, a navigator and two technicians, were picked up nearly 10 hours after the crash by a West German destroyer which had been participating in NATO maneuvers in the North Atlantic along with the Wasp and U.S. destroyers. Colonel Gallagher talked with two of the men, 1st Lieutenant Bruce E. Witcher of Redding, Cal., and Airman 2d David A. Surles of Raleigh, N.C., early today in the hospital at this Cape Cod base. After talking with them, Colonel Gallagher said, "We had already pieced together something of what happened. They seemed to verify that things happened fast, that an engine was afire. They told us they got the announcement from the pilot that they were going to ditch while the plane was still at 15,000 feet. The boys estimated they made an unusually rapid descent. The best they could figure it was five to 10 minutes. In other words, they were trying to get down and ditch as fast as they could," Colonel Gallagher said.

SANK IN MINUTES - The plane sank only a few minutes after hitting the water. Life rafts are stored in the wings but both wings were torn away from the fuselage by the impact. Colonel Gallagher said they told him the $2,500,000 plane hit the water at a steep angle, broke apart and sank within a few minutes. Several crewmen escaped before the plane went down, Colonel Gallagher said, but apparently some of them drowned and others died of exposure or shock. Colonel Gallagher said Lieutenant Witcher was hurled into the water when the plane crashed but swam to a piece of the wing and clung there until he was rescued. He said two other men clinging to the wing were washed away by a big wave. Airman Surles told Colonel Gallagher he climbed through a hole in the plane and managed to stay afloat through the night. He said a fog bank rolled in at dawn and the German destroyer that rescued him nearly ran him down because visibility was so poor. Both Lieutenant Witcher and Airman Surles walked into the hospital unassisted. The third survivor, Airman 1st Class John N. Puopolo of Sagamore, was carried in on a stretcher. Colonel Gallagher said he had severe leg cuts. "At first there were voices shouting and calling. But then as time went on the voices faded away and there was only silence on the ocean", Airman Surles told Colonel Gallagher. "It appeared to me," Surles said, "that the ship broke into two or three pieces and the nose dug under. I climbed out through a break in the fuselage." Colonel Gallagher said Airman Surles' survival suit, a watertight rubber cover-all, somehow became ripped. It was full of water, he said. Lieutenant Witcher said he and a few others held on to a piece of one wing in three to five foot waves. " And suddenly one of them swept us and two of the men slipped away and were lost," Lieutenant Witcher told Colonel

Gallagher. "The other man hung on and I tried to encourage him. But I looked at him once and saw his eyes were getting glassy and he lost his grip and slipped under the water."

THIRD OF WISH IS REALIZED
Cape Cod Standard-Times July 13, 1965

OTIS AIR FORCE BASE, July 13 - Young Airman 2nd Class Thomas Burman of Saginaw, Mich, climbed into the front seat of the car that stopped for him at the main entrance to Otis Air Force Base. "Thanks," he said. He lighted a cigarette. "Pretty bad about that crash," he said. "I went through tech school with three of them. I roomed with one." He looked out the window. Must have been cold out there. The young airman was silent for a moment. "I used to fly with them. Now I work on the flight line. I'm sure they're all right." Airman Burman got one third of his wish. Airman 2nd Class David A. Surles, his roommate at Electronics Maintenance School at Keesler Air Force Base, Miss., was one of three survivors. His other two friends are among the victims. The two unidentified Air Force men stood with newspapermen outside the base hospital. They were hoping for some word about a friend, Staff Sergeant John L. Howard, who lived with his family in Buzzards Bay. "He was going to get out, had a job to go to," one said. "But he made staff sergeant in his second hitch and decided to stay in." Sergeant Howard, his waiting friends said, re-enlisted about the end of May. The sergeant was one of the crash victims.

TIME LIKE THIS I WISH WE WERE CIVILIANS
Cape Cod Standard-Times July 13, 1965
By TILSON S. DENAHM Cape Cod Standard-Times Staff Writer

OTIS AIR FORCE BASE, July 13 - Yesterday afternoon before the grim word that only three airmen survived the crash, activities at Otis appeared, on the surface, to be nearly normal. Only at base operations did the strain become apparent. A group of officers clustered about a desk, sweating it out. They were constrained, but polite to a reporter who asked if any relatives of the crewmen of the fated Connie were available for interview. One officer said, "Civilians? Why you're the only civilian that's been in here. I guess a lot of us wish we were civilians after a day like this."

WAS DIRECTED - The reporter was directed to the wing commander's headquarters where the press had gathered. Captain Wayne Barrows, in charge of information on the crash, had just issued word that there were only three survivors. The knot of newsmen and photographers were silent, wondering if this communication were accurate. Previous word had been that 11 men had been rescued. There were no civilians, other than the press. A helicopter flew in to refuel. Presently word come back from the pilot that heavy mist covered the scene of rescue operations and the visibility was so poor the search was nearly static. Some suggested the relatives of the crewmen might be in the hospital area. Someone else said the area was closed. It was not closed.

LAY SPRAWLED - The hospital sprawled in the hot sunshine. The only sign of activity was a group of children at play awaiting their mother's return from a visit with a patient. One or two nurses, looking cool in their white uniforms, waited at the bus stop. No hint of the tragedy appeared on the surface of things, just down below the surface. The effect of the news on the Town of Bourne was widespread. Nearly everyone exchanged the latest information. Many of the airmen stationed at Otis live in the town.

ONE OF THE THREE SURVIVORS, Airman 1st Class John N. Puopolo, with his wife Nina and their 16-month old daughter, Karen, live on Meeting House Lane, North Sagamore. Another, Technical Sergeant, Gilbert L. Armstrong, was listed as dead. He was well-known in Bourne, having worked with a local building contractor. His wife, 8 months pregnant, had to be taken to Otis Air Force Base Hospital. Another woman, who withheld her name, reported her brother was scheduled to make the ill-fated patrol. He prevailed on a fellow airman to take his place because he had to take his children to a doctor. "Thank God, Thank God, our boy is safe." This was the reaction of Rocco and Esther Puopolo of Roslindale Monday night, when they received word that their son, Airman Puopolo, survived the crash. The 66-year old couple slumped against their kitchen table and sobbed yesterday when they heard that their only child was aboard the downed plane. "Oh my God, bring back our child," Mr. Rocco cried. Down on Cape Cod, Mr. and Mrs. Joseph Scuderi had rushed to the Sagamore home where John's wife, Nina, and the 16-month-old baby, Karen, awaited news of the fate of their loved one. A doctor gave Nina a sedative and she mercifully slept for part of the day. "Pray God we have good news before she wakes up," Mr. Scuderi said. His prayers were answered. She awoke to the joyous shouts of her parents, who told her the good news.

SURVIVORS TELL STORY OF PLANE CRASH
Cape Cod Standard-Times July 14, 1965

OTIS AIR FORCE BASE, July 14 - Two of the three survivors of the first ditching crash of an OTIS Air Force based EC-121H radar patrol plane Sunday night 80 miles off Nantucket in which 16 other officers and airmen were drowned or are missing, told how they bobbed in the chilly waters for more than eight hours and watched fellow crew members slowly drift away. Airman 2nd Class David A. Surles, 24, of Pinecrest Drive, Falmouth and Raleigh, N.C., and 1st Lieutenant

Bruce E. Witcher, 27, of Redding, Cal., were released from the Otis 551st Base Hospital for a short time yesterday afternoon to appear at a long-awaited news conference. The third survivor, Airman 1st Class John N. Puopolo of Roslindale and Sagamore, is still a bed patient at the hospital with deep cuts on both legs. The flight surgeon's office described Puopolo's condition as fair to good and the condition of Surles and Witcher as excellent, despite their long ordeal.

SEARCH CONTINUED - Meanwhile, a Coast Guard cutter, one helicopter and two Air Force planes made a final effort today to find seven crewmen still missing after the crash. A Coast Guard spokesman said the search for the missing men will be called off at the end of the day. An Air Force board of inquiry convened yesterday to investigate the accident and examined maintenance records of the aircraft for its last five missions in an attempt to determine why the two engines failed. Air Force officers indicated last night they believe the bodies of the missing crewmen may be trapped in the $2,500,000 plane. Wing Commander Raymond K. Gallagher said he asked the Navy for assistance in attempting to salvage the sunken sections of the aircraft.

POSITION GIVEN - The broken pieces of the plane were thought to be under 50 to 100 feet of water. Authorities said one of the three survivors of the crash, Lieutenant Witcher, was the navigator and gave them an accurate position on the point of the crash. Surles, in the Air Force for two years, told newsmen that he managed to escape from his radar post in the aft section of the huge electronic-crammed aircraft after the ditching. "It was my job to activate the 20-man life rafts in the wing sections, but they were under water and I got out and swam from the plane. I didn't want to get sucked under," Surles said. Both airmen said the aircraft hit the water very hard and must have broken up in two or three sections. "There were several of us in the water together at first," Surles said. "I heard Puopolo calling out and managed to get to him. We held onto each other for 10 hours and 40 minutes until the destroyer sighted us and sent over a whale boat." Neither airmen commented as to how the remainder of the crew were lost.

DRIFTED AWAY - "There were several of our buddies with us for a while, but then they just drifted away," Surles continued. The two said they did not try to hang onto any wreckage as they both feared their rubber suits or life jackets would be torn. Lieutenant Witcher described the first minutes after the initial ditching alarm as very fuzzy. "I took a navigational fix to determine our position and relayed it to the nearest station," he said. Witcher added that when the plane struck the water, his section was under water and that he remembered getting out of his seat and going to the surface. "After I reached the surface, I heard others calling. One was Surles; we tried to stay together the whole time, but I wasn't sure it was him until we were aboard the rescue boat," Witcher said. He remembers climbing onto a small piece of wing section with two or three other crewmen. "A few waves broke over the section and when I looked up they were gone," he said. Both airmen said that the water was really cold and that our teeth didn't stop chattering until about noon.

8 IDENTIFIED-The Air Force today identified four more of the nine crewmen known dead in the crash. They brought to eight the number of dead crewmen identified. Listed as dead were:

Captain Murray J. Brody, 28 of New York City, husband of Claire Brody, Otis Air Force Base. The Air Force listed his father as Irving Brody of 304 West 92nd Street, New York City, and his mother as Mrs. Marcia Reinstein of 735 Bryant Avenue, New York City.

Staff Sergeant Francis J. Griffin, husband of Doris Griffin, Otis Air Force Base. The Air Force said he listed his home town as Toronto, Canada, and his parents were deceased.

Staff Sergeant John L. Howard, husband of Shirley Howard, Buzzards Bay. The Air Force said he listed his hometown as Sanford, Fla., but no information was available on his parents.

Airman 1st Class George R. West, husband of Dorothy West, 21 Wilson Street, Lewiston, Me., and son of Mr. and Mrs. George S. West, 4165 Ovile Street, Wyoming, Mich.

Airman 2nd Class William Ernest Howe Jr., husband of Cynthia Howe, Onset, and son of Mr. and Mrs. William E. Howe of 115 North Woodlawn Avenue, North Augusta, S.C.

Airman 3rd Class Charles J. Podjaski, son of Mr. and Mrs. Charles Podjaski, 9613 South Troy Street, Evergreen Park, Ill.

Airman 2nd Class Charles H. Williams, son of Mr. and Mrs. John A. Williams, 11 Nixon Avenue, Worcester.

Airman 1st Class Charles K. Sawyer, husband of Mabel Sawyer,

Pocasset, the son of Mr. and Mrs. Charles L. Sawyer, 205 Peach Tree Street, Anderson, S.C.

SPECIAL FLY-OVER RITE PLANNED AT OTIS BASE
Cape Cod Standard Times July 15, 1965

OTIS AIR FORCE BASE, July 15 - Five huge four-engine Constellations will roar over Otis Air Force Base tomorrow in tribute to 16 airmen dead or missing in the crash of an Otis radar plane Sunday off Nantucket. The planes, sister ships to the one that crashed, will pass over the base as its military and civilian personnel attend an inter-faith memorial service in a transient alert hangar. The radar picket planes will fly a missing airman formation as a final farewell to the lost crewmen.

WERE SAVED - Only three of the 19 crewmen aboard the Air Force patrol plane survived Sunday night's crash. Nine bodies have been recovered and seven crewmen are still listed officially as missing. Hope waned for the rescue of the missing crewmen Wednesday when fog which obscured the crash scene the night of the crash rolled back over the ocean area. There also was speculation that the missing crewmen may have gone down with the plane, which sank within minutes of hitting the water. A lone Coast Guard cutter roamed the area in the Atlantic today, however, searching for a sign of the missing men. The Coast Guard said the cutter Vigilant would remain on the scene about 100 miles off Nantucket until tomorrow at the request of the Air Force.

HEAD BACK - Search planes were ready to head back into the area when the fog lifted but all other surface vessels have abandoned the search. The Air Force has asked the Navy to try to recover the wreckage of the plane which is believed to be in about 150 feet of water. Officials want to raise the plane because of the possibility of the bodies still missing and to aid the board of inquiry in determining the cause of the crash. The Air Force has released the last of the names of the nine airmen who died in the ditching of the plane. The last dead man identified was Captain Edward Anaka of Akron, N.Y., an instructor of military science at Davis and Elkins College in West Virginia.

LIST THE DEAD - The Air Force previously listed as officially dead:

Airman 2nd Class William Ernest Howe, Jr., husband of Cynthia Howe, Onset and son of Mr. and Mrs. William E. Howe, 115 North Woodlawn Avenue, North Augusta, S.C.

Airman 3rd Class Charles J. Podjaski, son of Mr. and Mrs. Charles Podjaski, 9613 South Troy Street, Evergreen Park, Ill.

Airman 2nd Class Charles H. Williams, son of Mr. and Mrs. John A. Williams, 11 Nixon Avenue, Worcester.

Airman 1st Class Charles K. Sawyer, husband of Mabel Sawyer, Pocasset, and son of Mr. and Mrs. Charles L. Sawyer, 205 Peach Tree Street, Anderson, S.C.

The wife of Airman 1st Class George R. West said the Air Force had notified her that Airman West also was among the dead. Mrs. West, an expectant mother, resides at 21 Wilson Street, Lewiston, Me. Airman West is the son of Mr. and Mrs. George S. West, 4165 Ovile Street, Wyoming, Mich.

Eleven other airmen dead or missing in the crash have been identified, but the Air Force has not said which bodies were recovered.

BIG AF PLANE IN OCEAN OFF CAPE
Record American July 12, 1965
BULLETIN

NANTUCKET(UPI)--An Air Force EC-121H with 19 persons aboard ditched in the Atlantic Ocean some 125 miles east of here last night.

The Federal Aviation Agency (FAA) air traffic control center at Nashua, N.H., said the four-engine plane ditched shortly after taking off from Otis Air Force Base on Cape Cod. The fate of the airmen aboard was not known. The Coast Guard said a Pan American World Airways jetliner en route to Europe from New York was circling the area. The FAA air traffic control center said the plane reported at 10:15 p.m. that it had "one engine out and another on fire." The control center said the pilot of the plane reported six minutes later that he was going to ditch the craft.

'WARNING STAR' IS FLYING RADAR SHIELD FOR U.S.
Record American July 13, 1965 By GEORGE NEARY

The downed plane out of Otis AF Base was a segment of the Air Defense Command's flying radar stations, a part of the protective screen for the East Coast from Norfolk, Va., to Newfoundland. Due to its new airborne electronics system, known as ALRI (Airborne Long Range Input), it was a significant factor in the AF decision in 1963 to deactivate the Texas Tower radar stations off the coast with no loss in adequate air defense radar surveillance. Its function is to detect and attack intruders as it sweeps the horizon in all directions at all flight altitudes, down to water level. The ditched radar picket craft was one of 36 attached to the 551st Airborne and Early Warning Control Wing at Otis.

RADAR POTENCY - Approximately 5000 officers and men are assigned around the clock to support the activities of the $2.5 million aircraft. Powered by Wright turbo compound engines, the EC-121H is the military counterpart to the commercial Super G Constellation.

It carries six tons of highly technical equipment, cruises up to 330-miles-an-hour and has a range of 4000 miles. The plane normally can stay aloft up to 14 hours on an average mission. The EC-121H is no beauty as airplane designing goes, but what it lacks in aerodynamic good looks it makes up for in the reach of its long-range radar potency. Every few hours one of the planes of the wing, with a normal complement of 16, takes off from Otis for its sweep somewhere far out over the ocean. Because the plane searches out, tracks and alerts the U.S. about approaching aircraft, it has been dubbed the "Warning Star." The flying radar stations send out electronic beams to pick up approaching aircraft. As soon as contact is made ALRI goes to work immediately.

The information is flashed into data processors, then relayed to SAGE (Semi-Automatic Ground Environment) Center, Continental Air Defense System.

MY SWEETIE IS ALIVE
Record American July 13, 1965 by Jack Kendall

EAST FALMOUTH--"All I know is that my sweetie is alive," declared Mrs. Jane Surles, 24, of 191 Pinecrest Dr., wife of Airman David Surles, 24, one of the survivors of the radar picket plane crash in the Atlantic. And Mrs. Surles, in the true fashion of a military man's wife, said any future decision by him to keep flying "is up to him. It's his life," she said. "I had expected the worst when I heard of the accident," Mrs. Surles said.

HOSPITAL VISIT - Mrs. Surles visited her husband at the Otis Air Force Base Hospital. "We didn't say very much at that time. We were just rejoicing at his being safe. Then he called me Tuesday morning. Again we had little conversation," she continued. "He is in pretty good condition," Mrs. Surles said. Airman Surles, a technician, is from Raleigh, N.C. His wife calls the Washington, D.C. area her home although she is originally from Illinois.

SAD FOR VICTIMS - "Of course, we feel terribly about the other men and their families," Mrs. Surles said. "Now, I'm on my way to the hospital to see him again." Mrs. Caroline Witcher, wife of 1st Lt. Bruce E. Witcher, another of the three survivors, was too shocked by the tragic crash to discuss her husband's brush with death.

MOTHER AWAITING VISIT FROM SON
Record American July 13, 1965

WILMINGTON, Del. (AP) - Mrs. Mattie Washam said Monday she was planning for a visit by her son and his family when she was informed that he was one of a crew of an EC121 radar picket plane that ditched in the Atlantic ocean about 100 miles northeast of Nantucket. Mrs. Washam, of suburban Belvidere, said her son, S/Sgt Raymond M. Washam, 34, radio operator on the EC-121, telephoned her about a week ago, and said he and his family were coming to visit her as soon as he got leave "in about a week." Mrs. Washam said her son's wife and two children, a daughter, 4, and son, seven months, are living at Otis Air Force Base.

SISTER PLANE IS ALOFT AS FLYING RELAY POST
Record American July 13, 1965 By JOHN McGINN

OTIS AIR FORCE BASE - The crewmen of an Air Force picket plane that spent more than eight hours circling over the area where a sister plane went down in the Atlantic told Monday how they served as a flying relay station sending messages from rescue craft to shore stations. For most of the time they were flying in a huge arc at 15,000 feet, said Capt. Theodore Shaffer, the pilot, the visibility was zero, ice was forming on the wings and, until daybreak, they did not know whether the crew of the downed craft was alive or dead. Then, he said, a dye marker was spotted and a few minutes later, a rescue plane saw four men bobbing in the water. Shaffer was ordered back to Otis when his fuel ran low. As soon as he landed, he sent most of his exhausted 17-man crew to bed but asked five to join him at a press briefing. They were Lt. Joseph B. Taylor of Willows, Cal., co-pilot; Capt.

George Williams of Port Malabar, Fla., navigator; Sgt Glendon Jackson of Gardiner, Me., radio operator; SSgt William Jordan, Green Lake, West VA., assistant crew chief, and TSgt Joseph G. Ondish, of Swayesville, Pa., radar crew chief.

Shaffer said they were leaving Otis at 9:30 p.m. Sunday to patrol off the Virginia coast when the flash that another picket plane was down came in and they were sent instead to Area Two - east of Nantucket. When they arrived, he said, they were ordered to circle at 15,000 feet, relaying radio messages from search planes flying at lower altitudes to the Stage and Direction Center, a communications complex at Otis. "We were in weather all the time out there," he said. "It was raining and there was heavy icing. We could see absolutely nothing, visibility was zero." Then at dawn, a rescue craft reported seeing a flare and later corrected it to say it was a dye marker. At about 6:30 another plane saw debris and oil slicks and a little after that four men were seen in the water. They were wearing "Mae West" life jackets and they were close to each other, probably tied together. A Coast Guard plane dropped a raft to them. Shaffer said the picket planes are equipped with rafts stowed in the wings and he said it was possible that the downed airmen were unable to break them out when the aircraft ditched because the impact jammed them.

SEA SURVIVAL PROBLEMATIC
Record American July 13, 1965

Man's survival in the water is dependent on many variables, including his physical condition, the clothing he wears and the temperature of the

water. These were the conditions to be considered in the case of the 19 crewmen of the Air Force radar picket plane forced down off Cape Cod. Initial reports failed to list what had caused the deaths of some crew members, whether they had been injured in the water landing, or had died from exposure. But water temperatures in the area of Georges Banks were estimated at between 55 and 58 degrees.

Survival charts indicate a man dressed in a flight suit such as the crewmen would have worn during the mission could only live between two and four hours in such temperatures. If he were wearing an exposure suit--the equipment designed to protect the human body from the rigors of frigid water--the immersed man might live more than twice that length of time.

BIRTHDAY FETE BEFORE CRASH
BAY STATE KIN WAIT WORD
Record American July 13, 1965 By MARY X. SULLIVAN

Less than 24 hours before the ill-fated Air Force picket plane left Otis, one of the two Massachusetts crewmen aboard shared his 25th birthday with his wife and baby daughter in their home in Sagamore. Airman First Class John N. Puopolo of Roslindale and Sagamore and Airman Charles H. (Chickie) Williams, 21, of Worcester, were the two local airmen aboard the plane when she soared seaward Sunday. The Puopolos - John, his wife Nina and their 16-month old daughter, Karen, had a birthday cake in an otherwise quiet observance. Mrs. Puopolo, from Schenectady, first learned of the plane ditching when the base called her early Monday. "Since then I haven't heard a word from them about John," she said. "I am hoping and praying that he will come through all right. He's been in the Air Force seven years. I listened briefly to the news about the crash over television after hearing from the base, but I haven't turned on TV or radio since." The parents of Airman Puopolo, Mr. and Mrs. Rocco Puopolo of 69 Wellesmere Rd., Roslindale, stayed up all night waiting to hear the fate of their only son. Their home was filled with relatives and neighbors as word of the crash spread. The mother was on the verge of collapse and the family physician administered a sedative. He matriculated at Northeastern "but after three months came home with a paper for us to sign," the father said. "He wanted to join the Air Force although he was only 17. We signed permission although we wanted him to remain in college." Airman John Puopolo served in Korea and Germany before being shipped to Otis and his family has been living in a year-round house on the Cape.

Airman Williams, single, is the son of Mr. and Mrs. John Williams of 11 Nixon Ave., Worcester. He joined the AF three years ago after graduating from South High School in Worcester. His folks were told of the crash Sunday night and they have been depending on broadcasts for further news. Mrs. Williams said she "thought I heard his name mentioned as one of two boys who were rescued but we were so excited hearing his name that we weren't sure what went before that news. We are worried but we feel confident that he is all right."

MISSING AIRMEN SEARCH IS ENDED

OTIS AIR FORCE BASE, July 20, 1965 - Boston Coast Guard Search and Rescue officials have discontinued the search for 7 airmen missing in the crash of an Otis Based Air Force Radar aircraft July 11 off Nantucket. Coast Guard officials announced today, "the search operations were secured at sundown on Friday pending further developments." Officials added that "all ships operating in the shipping lane area are still being alerted to keep a sharp watch out for bodies and any wreckage of the ill-fated electronics-laden Constellation."

TO RECOVER WRECKAGE - The Air Force has asked the Navy to try to recover the wreckage of the aircraft, believed to be in about 100 to 150 feet of water. A special Air Force general officer board of inquiry is still in progress at Otis, to determine the cause of the first crash of an Otis based Early Warning aircraft in more than 10 years of operational flights along the Eastern Seaboard. On Friday more than 1,400 persons attended an interfaith, memorial service for the lost flyers at the base. The service concluded with a "missing airman" flyover by 5 radar aircraft. Nine bodies have been recovered. 7 are missing, and three men were rescued.

TOLD OF RESCUE - At Boston, the captain of a West German destroyer yesterday told how his ship knifed through dense fog to pick up survivors and dead crewmen of a downed radar picket plane. Captain Jurgen Goetschke, skipper of the destroyer Z1, brought his vessel to Boston Monday for a five-day courtesy call after completing joint NATO maneuvers in the North Atlantic. Two other German destroyers which took part in the operations also arrived for the visit.

Two of the three survivors of the plane ditching July 11 were on hand when the destroyers entered Boston Harbor with the traditional fireboat escort. Sixteen airmen died in the downing of the aircraft. "The sea was calm and flat, but heavy fog prevented us from seeing more than 100 to 150 yards," Captain Goetschke said in recounting the search operation.

SPOTTED JACKETS - "We first spotted a life jacket then debris from the plane and finally members of the crew. They were picked up in a whale boat within an hour of first being sighted by a helicopter," he said. Lieutenant Bruce E. Witcher of Reading, Cal., navigator of the ill-fated plane, and Airman 2nd Class David A. Surles, radar technician of Raleigh, N.C. , greeted Captain Goetschke and the crew of the Z1 when it docked there. The third survivor, Airman 1st Class John

Puopolo of Sagamore, was unable to attend because of foot injuries suffered in the ditching. Air Force Lieutenant Colonel Robert V. Mitchell and Major Edward Fredericks presented a plaque to the German skipper and his crew on behalf of the survivors.

> Record American Articles [Reprinted with permission of Boston Herald]
> Cape Cod Times articles [Reprinted Courtesy of Cape Cod Times]

HISTORY OF FLIGHT - 55-0136

At 1830 EDST, 11 July 1965, the Aircraft Commander of crew #27 briefed an aircrew of 19 for an Active Air Defense mission to Air 1 station #2. Homey 63, an EC-121H, Serial number 55-0136 was assigned by Wing Operations Center. Fuel load was 6,600 gallons. The DD Form 175 filed by the Aircraft Commander listed 11:30 hours fuel on board, estimated time en route 9:20 and 7:45 on station #2 at FL 150.

Briefing and pre-flight were normal except for minor problems with the AN/ARN-14 which was replaced. The aircraft blocked at 11/2045 EDST, and take-off was made from runway 23 at 11/2133 EDST.

(Unreadable)... weather at take-off was thin obscurement, measured 300 feet broken 900 feet overcast, visibility two miles in light rain and fog, wind 170 degrees at three knots, ceiling ragged.

The flight was cleared for cross-rip departure 21 to Nantucket then, Control Extension 1 144 to Cod Intersection, direct station #2, climb to and maintain 15,000 feet. The route was flown as cleared and Homey 63 reported its position through Andrews Airways as over Cod Intersection at 2149 EDST, FL 150, estimating station #2 at 2157 EDST.

During the climb between Nantucket and Cod Intersection, the engine superchargers were selected to high blower at approximately 11,000 feet. Number two engine failed to shift into high blower and they continued the mission with engine number one, three and four in high blower and number two in low blower.

Homey 63 completed radar tie-in with BOADS on Station #2 at 2207 EDST. At approximately 2210 EDST, BOADS received a call to the effect that number three engine was on fire and that an emergency was being declared. The rest of the transmission was not clear, but seemed to indicate they were clearing BOADS frequency. At 2212 EDST, Brunswick and Otis Approach Controls simultaneously received a Mayday call on Guard channel from Homey 63. Later, transmissions were received from Homey 63 by Friar II, a KC-135, and Brunswick Approach Control to the effect that Honey 63 had lost number two engine and that number three was feathered and on fire.

The aircraft's position was reported as about 125 NM (nautical miles) from Nantucket Tacan on the 090 degree radial and clearance was requested to Nantucket. At approximately 2213 EDST, the pilot reported, "preparing for ditching, we have number three engine on fire, and number two is not so good". The pilot took up a heading of 270 degrees magnetic to the nearest land. The wind aloft was 230 degrees at 40 knots. At 2215 EDST, Friar II advised Boston Center that he had copied a Mayday call from Homey 63 with a request to land at Nantucket. Boston Center cleared Homey 63 to Nantucket as requested. At 2219 EDST, Homey 81 (on station #4) heard the transmission, "Ditching in two minutes". Friar II reported that at 2221 EDST, Homey 63 stated twice: "200 feet over the water and ditching". Friar II replied, "Okay buddy, good luck" or words to that effect and relayed the call to Boston. At 2222 EDST, the transmission "30 seconds to ditching," and then an emergency squawk believed to be Homey 63 faded from their radar scopes.

Homey 63 ditched at 2222 EDST within two miles either side of a line formed by the graphical coordinates of 41 degrees 45 minutes north - 67 degrees 37 minutes west and 41 degrees 43 minutes north - 67 degrees 41 minutes west. Touchdown on the water was very hard.

At approximately 0900 the next morning, three survivors and the bodies of nine other men, were picked up by whale boats from German Navy Destroyer "Blotter" and US Destroyer "Barry" at 41 degrees 40 minutes north, 67 degrees 37 minutes west. The remaining seven men are still missing and presumed dead.

Aircraft damage: The aircraft broke in two places on the fuselage with at least partial wing separation. Forward break was in the latrine/galley area (station area 592) and the rear break was in the APS 103 area (station area 962).

All available aircraft maintenance records were analyzed and no maintenance actions or parts replacements were noted. It was noted that the 24th Phase Inspection was completed on 4 July 1965 and a functional check flight was performed. Complete engine conditioning of # 1, # 3, and #4 engines was accomplished during the 24th Phase Inspection. This includes cylinder compression check, valve clearance check and spark plug replacement. Conditioning was not accomplished on #2 engine since it was not required. During the flight a fire had occurred in the accessory area of the #3 engine. The only additional deficiencies indicated was the inability of the flight engineer to obtain high blower operation on the #2 engine. However, recorded radio transmissions from the aircraft reported, "loss of power" or "lost number three engine."

Checks of records revealed all primary crew members to be well trained, current, and proficient in their crew specialty. Investigation did not reveal any unusual physical or psychological factors that would have impaired their crew efficiency prior to the flight.

SOURCE: Department of the Air Force, Headquarters Safety Center Kirtland Air Force Base, NM

BOARD OF INQUIRY 55-0136

On 15 July 1965 Headquarters 26th Air Division, Stewart Air Force Base, New York, issued orders appointing members of a board for the purpose of investigating "major aircraft accident" which occurred on July 11, 1965 involving an EC-121H aircraft Nr. 55-0136 assigned to the 551st AEW&C Wing at Otis AFB, Massachusetts.

The President, who headed the Coordinating Staff, was Brigadier General Oris B. Johnson (WAADS). His staff consisted of Major Orrie Merrill, 38884A, 964th AEW&C Squadron, McClellan AFB, California, who was the Investigative Officer. Lieutenant Colonel Howard A. Olson, 12754A, 551st AEW&C Wing Otis AFB the Flight Safety Advisor; and First Lieutenant Frederick D. Ralstep, AO3137268, of the 551st Combat Support Group at Otis AFB, the Recorder.

The Maintenance Group included Lieutenant Colonel Charles R. Hartwell, AO799016, Headquarters 26th Air Division, who served as the Maintenance Chief. Others in that group were Captain Gerald C. Krupowicz, AO3006986, 552nd AEW&C Wing, McClellan AFB, Maintenance Advisor; Senior Master Sergeant Christor C. Bezdaris, AF13113369, 551st Organizational Maintenance Squadron at Otis AFB, the Engine Specialist, and Senior Master Sergeant Linwood E. Doane, AF12252965, 551st AEW&C Wing, Otis AFB, the Records Specialist.

The Life Sciences Group consisted of Lieutenant Colonel David A. Beyer, 20546A, 551st USAF Hospital, Otis AFB, the Team chief; Captain David S. Russell, AO3165411, 551st USAF Hospital, Flight Surgeon; Captain Carol R. Coolet, 47182A, 551st Support Group, Otis AFB; and Life Support member Lieutenant Colonel Thurman Parker, AO2100523, Headquarters 26th Air Division.

The Operations Group Chief was Lieutenant Colonel James E. McCall, 35011A, 960th AEW&C Squadron, Otis AFB. Captain Morgan M. Reuter, 72302A, of the 962nd AEW&C Squadron, Otis AFB, was the Flight Member, while First Lieutenant Bruce W. Turner, 72451A, of the 960th AEW&C Squadron, Otis AFB, was the Pilot Member. The completed investigative report was to be submitted to the Headquarter's 26th Air Division.

[NOTE] Ms. Deborah Brody, the daughter of Captain Murray J. Brody, who was killed in the crash of 55-0136 on July 11, 1965, sought copies under the Freedom of Information Act from the Air Force Safety Center of the findings of the investigative board. Although she was provided some documents pertaining to that accident, similar to the documents I was furnished when I made requests for the two other crashes of 55-5262 on November 11, 1966 and 53-0549 on April 25, 1967, neither of us received the findings of the boards of inquiry. Even after she and I submitted separate appeals to the Secretary of the Air Force and to our Senators, the Air Force asserts that the analysis, findings, and recommendations of the investigative boards are "exempt from disclosure."

CREW MEMBERS OF 55-0136
CRASHED JULY 11, 1965

OFFICER - SURVIVOR

1/LT BRUCE E. WITCHER
72954A
NAVIGATOR

OFFICERS - DECEASED

CAPTAIN MURRAY J. BRODY
71909A
PILOT

1/LT FREDERICK H. AMBROSIA
70494A
AIRCRAFT COMMANDER

1/LT THOMAS FIEDLER
69998A
CO-PILOT

2/LT IRA J. HUSIK
AO3147737
NAVIGATOR

CAPTAIN EDWARD N. ANAKA
74134A
AFROTC - OBSERVER

CAPTAIN MICHAEL R. BARBOLLA
58086A
AFROTC - OBSERVER

SURVIVORS - ENLISTED

A1C JOHN N. PUOPOLO
AF11346448
SURVEILLANCE TECHNICIAN

A2C DAVID A. SURLES
AF13784150
RADAR TECHNICIAN

ENLISTED - DECEASED

TSGT GILBERT L. ARMSTRONG
AF31339667
FLIGHT ENGINEER

TSGT EUGENE J. SCHREIVOGEL AF17240566 FLIGHT ENGINEER	
SSGT RAYMOND M. WASHAM AF13316653 RADIO OPERATOR	
SSGT FRANCIS J. GRIFFIN AF10602510 RADIO OPERATOR	
SSGT JOHN L. HOWARD AF14602848 ADP TECHNICIAN	
A1C GEORGE R. WEST AF16728130 SURVEILLANCE TECHNICIAN	
A1C CHARLES K. SAWYER AF14666776 SURVEILLANCE TECHNICIAN	
A2C WILLIAM E. HOWE AF14792536 RADAR TECHNICIAN	
A3C CHARLES J. PODIASKI AF16810785 SURVEILLANCE TECHNICIAN	
A2C CHARLES H. WILLIAMS AF11413043 NAVIGATION TECHNICIAN	

PHOTOGRAPHS IN THE RECORD AMERICAN ON JULY 11 & 13, 1965

1/LT FREDERICK H. AMBROSIA - AIRCRAFT COMMANDER

1/LT THOMAS J. FIEDLER CO-PILOT

A2C CHARLES H. WILLIAMS - NAVIGATION TECHNICIAN

A1C JOHN N. PUOPOLO SURVEILLANCE TECH [SURVIVED CRASH AND WAS AWARDED THE *AIRMAN'S MEDAL*].

CAPTAIN MURRAY J. BRODY - PILOT

PHOTOGRAPHS IN THE <u>RECORD AMERICAN</u> ON JULY 13, 1965

**1/LT BRUCE E. WITCHER
NAVIGATOR
[SURVIVOR]
AWARDED** *AIR FORCE COMMENDATION MEDAL*

**A2C WILLIAM E. HOWE
RADAR TECHNICIAN**

2/LT IRA J. HUSIK
NAVIGATOR

CAPTAIN EDWARD N. ANAKA [AFROTC - OBSERVER]

CAPTAIN MICHAEL R. BARBOLLA [AFROTC - OBSERVER]

PHOTOGRAPHS IN THE RECORD AMERICAN ON JULY 13, 1965

COLONEL RAYMOND K. GALLAGHER, 551ST AIRBORNE EARLY WARNING AND CONTROL WING COMMANDER AT OTIS AIR FORCE BASE HOLDS MODEL OF CONSTELLATION RADAR PICKET PLANE THAT CRASHED OFF THE CAPE SUNDAY NIGHT JULY 11, 1965.

PHOTO BY CARROLL MYETT - RECORD AMERICAN

RETURN FROM SEA SEARCH - CAPTAIN THEODORE SHAFFER, (STANDING) WITH HIS CREW AFTER THEY RETURNED TO OTIS AIR FORCE BASE, CAPE COD. SHAFFER SAID HIS AIRCRAFT WAS USED AS A RADIO RELAY STATION BETWEEN OTHER PLANES AND SURFACE SHIPS SEARCHING FOR SURVIVORS OF ILL-FATED AIR FORCE PICKET PLANE THAT DITCHED IN FOG-SHROUDED SEAS 100 MILES OFF NANTUCKET. SHAFFER INDICATED ON MAP TO REPORTERS WHERE THREE OF 19 CREWMEN WERE PICKED UP ALIVE. OTHERS ARE SEATED (L. TO R.), LT. JOSEPH TAYLOR, CAPT. GEORGE WILLIAMS, JR., SGT. GLENWOOD JACKSON, SGT. W.L. JORDAN, SGT. JOSEPH ONDISH.

PHOTOGRAPHS IN <u>BOSTON TRAVELER</u> ON JULY 13, 1965

UPI TELEPHOTO

PLANE CRASH SURVIVOR - 1/LT BRUCE E. WITCHER, ONE OF THE THREE RESCUED FROM AIR FORCE RADAR PLANE WHICH DITCHED IN THE ATLANTIC OCEAN OFF NANTUCKET SUNDAY NIGHT, ARRIVES AT OTIS AIR FORCE BASE HOSPITAL.

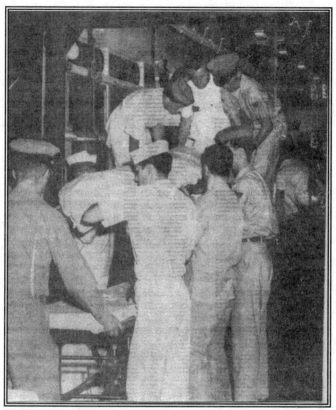

TRAVELER STAFF PHOTO BY CLIFF JONES

BODY OF AIRMAN, ONE OF 16 CASUALTIES OF CRASH AT SEA OFF NANTUCKET IS LIFTED FROM AIR FORCE BUS-AMBULANCE AT CHELSEA NAVAL HOSPITAL. CRASH VICTIMS WERE FLOWN FROM AIRCRAFT CARRIER WASP TO OTIS AIR FORCE BASE, AND TRANSPORTED TO THE HOSPITAL IN CHELSEA.

RECORD AMERICAN PHOTO - JOHN MURPHY

"I WAS HERE" - A2C DAVID SURLES, OF RALEIGH, N.C., WITH POINTER, INDICATES WHERE HE WAS WHEN AIR FORCE RADAR PICKET PLANE DITCHED INTO ATLANTIC. ONLY THREE OF 19 ABOARD LIVED. FIRST LT. BRUCE WITCHER, OF REDDING, CA., CENTER, AND AIRMAN JOHN PUOPOLO OF ROSLINDALE, MA [NOT PRESENT IN PHOTO], WERE OTHER SURVIVORS. TO THE RIGHT IS COLONEL ROBERT V. MITCHELL, COMMANDER OF THE 961ST AIRBORNE EARLY WARNING AND CONTROL SQUADRON AT OTIS AIR FORCE BASE, MA.

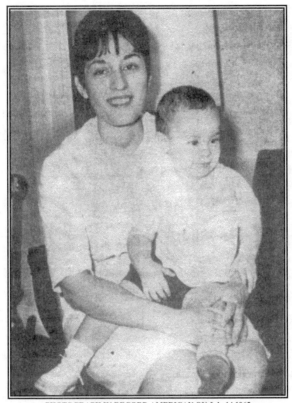

PHOTOGRAPH IN <u>RECORD AMERICAN</u> ON July 14, 1965

AN OVERJOYED MRS. NINA PUOPOLO, HOLDING HER 16-MONTH-OLD DAUGHTER, KAREN.

HAPPY PARENTS OF AIRMAN JOHN PUOPOLO BEAM WITH RELIEF IN THE LIVING ROOM OF THEIR ROSLINDALE HOME AFTER THEY WERE NOTIFIED THEIR SON WAS SAFE. MR. AND MRS. ROCCO PUOPOLO WERE NOTIFIED BY THEIR DAUGHTER-IN-LAW NINA.

PHOTOGRAPH BY CARROLL MYETT FROM RECORD AMERICAN
JULY 13, 1965

MRS. DORIS GRIFFIN PHONES OTIS AIR FORCE BASE FOR NEWS OF THE RESCUE. DAUGHTERS, OLIVIA, 6; MARY 11, LOOK ON. HER HUSBAND SSGT FRANCIS J. GRIFFIN, RADIO OPERATOR ON 55-0136 WHICH CRASHED ON JULY 11, 1965 DID NOT SURVIVE THE ORDEAL.

PHOTOGRAPH BY CARROLL MYETT FROM RECORD AMERICAN ON JULY 13, 1965

MRS. JEAN SCHREIVOGEL WITH TINA, 7: DEBORAH, 5; GREG, 12. HER HUSBAND TSGT EUGENE J. SCHREIVOGEL WAS THE FLIGHT ENGINEER ON 55-0136 WHICH CRASHED AT SEA ON JULY 11, 1965. TSGT SCHREIVOGEL DID NOT SURVIVE THE ORDEAL BUT SUBSEQUENTLY WAS AWARDED THE *AIRMAN'S MEDAL* (POSTHUMOUSLY).

PHOTOGRAPH FROM BOSTON GLOBE JULY 12, 1965

RADAR CREW CHIEF, AIRMAN FIRST CLASS JOHN N. PUOPOLO, 25, A SEVEN-YEAR VETERAN OF THE AIR FORCE, SHOWN IN AN EARLIER PHOTOGRAPH MANNING ONE OF THE EC-121H RADAR DISPLAYS. PUOPOLO WAS ONE OF THREE SURVIVORS OF THE CRASH OF 55-0136 ON JULY 11 1965.

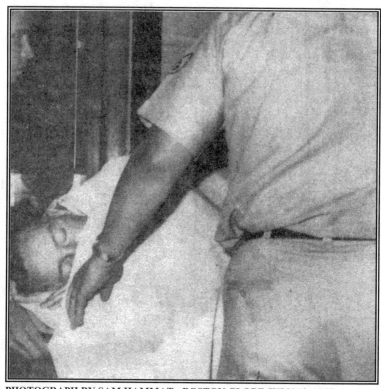

PHOTOGRAPH BY SAM HAMMAT - <u>BOSTON GLOBE</u> JULY 13, 1965

AIRMAN JOHN N. PUOPOLO, ONE OF THREE SURVIVORS OF THE CRASH OF 55-0136 OF JULY 11, 1965 IS CARRIED INTO THE HOSPITAL AT OTIS AIR FORCE BASE, MA.

RECORD AMERICAN - JULY 14, 1965

SURVIVOR, 1/LT BRUCE E. WITCHER, NAVIGATOR

SURVIVOR, A2C DAVID A. SURLES, RADAR TECHNICIAN WAS AWARDED THE *AIRMAN'S MEDAL*

AP WIRE PHOTO FROM RECORD AMERICAN JULY 13, 1965

U.S. NAVY PICKET DESTROYER *VESOLE* AND AN AIR FORCE RADAR PICKET PLANE, SAME TYPE AS DOWNED AIRCRAFT, SEARCH THE ATLANTIC FOR MISSING CREW MEMBERS OF 55-0136 WHICH DITCHED JULY 11, 1965.

JOHN N. PUOPOLO AND HIS WIFE NINA - MAY 1997

MAY 1997 [LEFT TO RIGHT] - JOHN N. PUOPOLO, DAUGHTER KRISTINE, SON STEVEN, DAUGHTER KAREN [WHO WAS 16 MONTHS OF AGE AT THE TIME OF THE DITCHING], WIFE NINA, AND DAUGHTER KATHLEEN

PHOTOGRAPH FURNISHED VIA ART KERR/DEAN BOYS

MISSING MAN FORMATION FLYOVER ON JULY 16, 1965 AT THE MEMORIAL SERVICES FOR THE CREW OF 55-0136

MEMORIAL SERVICE PROGRAM FOR THOSE CREW MEMBERS WHO LOST THEIR LIVES ON 55-0136 ON JULY 11, 1965

THE MEMORIAL SERVICE

INVOCATION
Lieutenant Colonel Earl Mack
Base Chaplain, Otis Air Force Base

A READING FROM THE HOLY SCRIPTURES
Rabbi Ronald M. Yates
Auxiliary Jewish Chaplain, Otis Air Force Base

THE AIR FORCE HYMN
Chapel One Choir

MEMORIAL ADDRESS
Colonel Roland C Remy
Staff Chaplain, 26th Air Division

MEMORIAL PRESENTATIONS TO THE NEXT OF KIN
Colonel Raymond K. Gallagher
Commander, 551st AEW&Con Wing

Lieutenant Colonel Robert V. Mitchell
Commander, 961st AEW&Con Squadron

Lieutenant Colonel Earl E. Putnam
Commander, AFROTC Field Training Detachment

Major Edward Fredericks
Commander, 551st Electronic Maintenance Squadron

BENEDICTION

Captain Norman C. Leger
Catholic Chaplain, Otis Air Force Base

(The audience is requested to leave the
building at this time and gather outside
for the concluding ceremonies)

"Taps"

AERIAL SALUTE
THE MISSING MAN FORMATION

DEDICATED TO THE HONOR AND

MEMORY OF OUR COMRADES

United States Air Force ROTC Field Training Unit

Captain Edward Nicholas Anaka
Captain Michael Richard Barbolla*

961st Airborne Early Warning & Control Squadron

Captain Murray J Brody
First Lieutenant Frederick H. Ambrosia*
First Lieutenant Thomas John Fiedler*
Second Lieutenant Ira Jay Husik*
Technical Sergeant Gilbert Leno Armstrong*
Technical Sergeant Eugene Jake Schreivogel*
Staff Sergeant Francis John Griffin
Staff Sergeant Raymond Michael Washam*
Airman First Class George Raymond West
Airman First Class Charles Keith Sawyer
Airman Third Class Charles James Podjaski

551st Electronic Maintenance Squadron

Staff Sergeant John Lawrence Howard
Airman Second Class Charles Henry Williams
Airman Second Class William Ernest Howe Jr.

(*Missing)

Memorial Program Provided Courtesy of Dean Boys

REMEMBERING CAPTAIN EDWARD N. ANAKA

NOTE: Captain Edward N. Anaka lost his life in the crash of 55-0136 on July 11, 1965. During my research I located his wife, and she contributed the following:

Captain Anaka was born on 1/22/34 in Pennsylvania. He spent his childhood and most of his life living outside Buffalo, NY. After graduating from the University of Buffalo he was commissioned a 2/Lt in the USAF on February 1956. He completed pilots training in 1957 and became proficient in B-25s. He subsequently became proficient in piloting the C-119, C-97, and C-130 aircraft. His military assignments included Kinstron Air Base in NC; Ellington AFB in Houston, TX., Travis AFB, CA.; and Everux-Fauville AFB in France. He next was assigned as an instructor in the AFROTC at Davis Elkins College, in Elkins, WV. Captain Anaka was required to fly a minimum number of hours monthly to maintain his flying status as a pilot. Captain Anaka was at Otis AFB, MA., for the College ROTC student requirements when he was killed while flying aboard one of the Super Constellation radar patrol aircraft as an observer.

On July 11, 1965, at about 2:00 am, I received a phone call from the information officer at Otis Air Force Base that his plane was down. Earlier that day I had talked with Ed, and he stated he was flying that night, to complete his flying requirements. He was then planning to drive to his mother's where I was with our children for a vacation.

July 11th was the longest day in my life. His mother, brother, my family and I all awaited word but none came. The staff at Otis never contacted me with follow up reports until it came time to return his remains back home. Most of the information we received was from the media. Late that evening I received word from his commanding officer in the ROTC. He advised Ed did not survive, but that they did recover his body. I was advised not to do anything until I received the all important telegram. This was received late on the night of July 12, 1965.

I do not know the cause of death, but I assumed he had drowned. We were able to have a open viewing. His upper body and face showed no signs of injury, just

swelling. It took until that Friday, July 15, 1965 for them to return his remains. It was explained to me that none of the remains would be released until all were ready. This was a very difficult week for myself and my family.

Not living in that area for the last 9 years, I had to rely on my father for much guidance on making arrangements. We decided to have the interment at a local cemetery in Kenmore, NY., where Captain Anaka's father was interred. I would have preferred Arlington, Virginia, but we had many things to consider. His funeral was that Saturday with full military honors provided by Niagara Falls Air Force Base.

It is now 33 years since all this has happened. If I did not have my faith and family, it would have been very difficult to survive this ordeal.

The only medal Captain Anaka received was the Air Force Commendation Medal, awarded posthumously in September 1965, for his work in the ROTC.

At the time of Captain Anaka's death we had four children - Karen Lee who then was 7; Kristen Elizabeth who then was 5, Kathleen Marie who then was 3, and Edward Nicholas Anaka, Jr., who then was 18 months.

In November 1967 I was remarried to James H. Wallingford, a widower with 3 boys. Later we had a boy and a girl, making us a nine-member family. And with God's help we came through raising all 9 children.

JUDITH C. WALLINGFORD

THE FOLLOWING PHOTOGRAPHS WERE FURNISHED BY MRS. JUDITH C. WALLINGFORD

CAPTAIN EDWARD N. ANAKA

SEPT 1965 - POSTHUMOUS AWARD OF THE AIR FORCE COMMENDATION MEDAL TO CAPTAIN ANAKA. ACCEPTING ARE HIS WIFE JUDITH AND MOTHER ELIZABETH. AWARD WAS FOR CAPTAIN ANAKA'S AFROTC ACHIEVEMENTS.

CAPTAIN ANAKA'S CHILDREN - PHOTO TAKEN CHRISTMAS 1964 - SIX MONTHS PRIOR TO CAPTAIN ANAKA'S DEATH ON JULY 11, 1965.

PHOTOGRAPH CHRISTMAS CARD SENT TO THE ANAKA FAMILY IN 1966 FROM THE WIFE AND SON [DIANE AND EDWARD] OF CAPTAIN MICHAEL R. BARBOLLA. CAPTAIN BARBOLLA, ALSO AN AFROTC INSTRUCTOR, WAS KILLED ON JULY 11, 1965 IN THE CRASH OF 55-0136. AT THE TIME OF THE CRASH CAPTAIN BARBOLLA WAS UNAWARE THAT HIS WIFE WAS PREGNANT. ANDREW WAS BORN IN MARCH 1966.

REMEMBRANCES OF
CAPTAIN MICHAEL RICHARD BARBOLLA
AUGUST 21, 1933 - JULY 11, 1965
BY
DIANE E. BARBOLLA

I begin this essay struck by the thought that our son, Andrew, is now the same age as his father was when he died. Thirty-two. And now thirty-two years later, I am reconstructing, rereading, reliving, and trying to write a clear account of what I remember. It is not easy. A lot of what I had planned to remember and preserve gets formally visited on Memorial Day when Andy and I look at photos, letters, and weep together. So, selective memory as it be, here goes....

Mike was stationed at Sembach Air Base in Germany when we met. I was a senior in High School, Kaiserslautern American High School, and my dad was the base school principal. I did not want to spend my senior year in Germany 1963, but as a 17 year old, I did not get to vote in family decisions. Actually, it turned out to be an exciting turn in my life. I hated the K-Town High School guys, but I loved the chance to pretend to be an adult and the chances to travel. Mike said that he noticed me eating lunch one day and thought that I was one of the new base teachers. I was infatuated right away. Mike was not pleased by my age, but I acted "older." My parents really liked him, as a friend, and so did the Sembach family. As a civilian daughter, I was not a legitimate "brat," and the little cultural island of American military was foreign to me. I did not know that protocol made me an outsider. But I sure had fun anyway!

I graduated from K-town, my parents went to Bitburg, and I went to Munich for the first two years of college at the University of Maryland's McGraw Kaserne. Somewhere in this time period, Mike and I started to date, mostly by phone and letter. Mike was a great writer. He was a CPA, but not by choice. In those days, one could qualify as a CPA if you had "connections." He had them, as I would learn when I met his family. But mostly, Mike was a writer, and he expected to write a novel or two. I was a dorm prefect. I had some status, and late night phone calls, even visits, were permitted or at least overlooked.

As "occupying forces" in the early 1960's, Americans in Germany got to travel, enjoy resorts, and generally have a good time. We enjoyed Garmisch, St. Moritz, Augsburg, and other areas in Austria, Italy, Switzerland, and Germany. Mike accompanied me and girlfriends to Paris, ski areas, and various resorts. As long as girlfriends came along, my parents were agreeable. Besides, they were often included as well.

Mike was good friends with my younger brother, Steve. Mike had a black convertible Chevy Impala that barely navigated narrow German roads, and my brother was impressed. Mike said little about his family, but one day we visited Dachau. He told me that his mother was Jewish and his father Italian, Sicilian actually. He expressed some mixed feelings about ethnic loyalty, but was a Catholic by choice. He was baptized, as an adult, in Germany. I was a lapsed Lutheran, so his faith was never an issue for me.

The world, for me, was on a wild ride from 1962 - 1965. JFK died while I was at Munich. The dorm girls were to be hosted at a dance for German cadets. On the bus, on route, the dance was canceled because the President was "ershossen," shot dead. I think that we knew he was dead before others did. I was accepted at Georgetown University. Mike asked for a stateside assignment so that I could finish college and we could be together. Vietnam was a sort of "non-war" in 1963 and 1964, but campus protests were starting. I was told to stay out of "politics," not to "pat" him on the butt when he was in uniform, and that he wanted to go to Vietnam because as a "regular" Air Force type, he felt that he was supposed to go. We spent many weekends together while I was at Georgetown, and I finally met his family.

Mike's family was unlike any I had met. I came from a

147

Norwegian/WASP family who were quiet and formal; even stuffy and elitist. His family was funny, warm, welcoming, noisy, loving, and a crazy mix of Jewish and Italian energy. They thought I was too thin, too conservative, and too monochromatic because I mostly wore black. Actually, I was mostly monochromic.

Mike's mom, Sylvia, was a great cook. I was loaded with so many "care packages" that I got testy about his eating my dinners and his mom's dinners. Mike tried to do both, mostly not too successfully. Sylvia had a big family. Six sisters and one brother who were involved in lots of businesses. One of which was Carter's baby stuff. When Andy was born, I was swamped with baby clothes. Mike's dad, Rocco, was a very good looking man. He had a sister, Angie, who was married to a guy who was a driver for some Mafia type. Mike said that his CPA license came via this connection. The Italian side were also great cooks. Basically, during my year at Georgetown, I learned to cook Jewish and Italian food. But mostly I learned to heat leftovers!

Mike and I had an engagement party and were married February, 1965. We went to Stowe, Vermont for our honeymoon. We moved into an apartment in Riverdale, New York. Mike was an instructor at Manhattan College, ROTC program, and I was a Junior at NYU, Washington Square Campus. The months between January and July were spent getting familiar with marriage, a new home, relatives, co-workers, and the New York subway system between the Bronx and Washington Square. One of Mike's colleagues was Joe Trochta and his wife Charlene. Joe was an Air Force Colonel, Charlene was a teacher, and they really were helpful allies for the new Air Force bride. I remember that as a gift, they organized my kitchen, bathroom, and closets. I still use the systems they introduced, and continue to fold towels Charlene's way.

In late June [1965], Mike and his ROTC cadets were to go to Otis AFB for a Field Training Unit internship. The session was to last for six weeks. I guess it was an assignment required of *the ROTC he taught at Manhattan College. I was enrolled in some summer classes at NYU, so six weeks did not seem difficult to manage. Mike called frequently, and in one of those calls, I told him that we might be "pregnant." He was so happy! I warned that the final tests were still pending, but he was certain that we would be parents in March. We talked about names, worried that it was a false alarm, and eagerly expected our reunion. Mike said that he needed to get some "flight time," and would be going out on an Early Warning flight in July. He never called again.*

I don't remember exactly who called me, came to the door, but I think it was Joe Trochta. Mike was in a crash. He was missing. The plane went down. There were survivors. Mike was not one of them. The missing status lasted for several days, and then the word came that his body was not recovered. His father was devastated. He kept asking why there was no body to bury. I just floated in and out of reality. The confirmation of our pregnancy came at about the same time. I tried to finish my classes at NYU. My dad arrived. He and I were often at odds, but his being there helped. My grandmother died (mom's mom) at about the same time. My world was in chaos, and I was in some very weird widow zone.

Lots of mail came: from the Commander of the ROTC Field Training Unit at Otis; from the Commander of the Combat Support Group at Otis AFB; from General Lindley of the Air University; President Lyndon Johnson and his wife sent a letter, as did Brother Gregory at Manhattan College and General Blanchard, Vice Chief of Staff. Mike received a Commendation Medal, and I received letters and poems from friends. I tried to not be bitter at "feel free to call on me at any time" comments, but I was. The two questions I had - what happened and why didn't they find his body - were never answered. I never knew that two other "Connies" crashed in addition to the one Mike was on. I think that Colonel Joe Trochta saved my sanity; maybe even my life. He was my "casualty assistance officer" and he was my lifeline. He probably knows more about what happened during those several days than I do. He covered the financial issues, got me out of an Encyclopedia membership, and made sure that the life insurance was paid, even though "in flight" deaths brought minimal funds to pilots killed in the line of duty. I bless him to this day. There was a memorial service, I received a flag, and a headstone was placed at Arlington National Cemetery.

New York was not my home. I left in the car Mike bought for us, a Pontiac Le Mans, and drove alone to Los Angeles. Mom made me call daily. I felt that I was not alone on the trip. Andy, our son, within me, was good company.

As a postscript:

Andrew is a writer, published author, and poet. He teaches English at the School for Creative and Performing Arts in San Diego where he is Chair of the Department. I finished my Ph.D. in Anthropology at UC Riverside and am Professor of Anthropology at San Diego Mesa College and Chair of the Department of Behavioral Sciences.

I think Mike would be proud of both of us.

                Diane E. Barbolla
                8183 Via Mallorca
                La Jolla, CA. 92037
                    January 1999

PHOTOGRAPH FURNISHED COURTESY OF DIANE BARBOLLA

ANDY BARBOLLA - LEFT - SON OF CAPTAIN MICHAEL R. BARBOLLA.

DIANE BARBOLLA -FAR RIGHT - WIFE OF CAPTAIN MICHAEL R. BARBOLLA.

NEXT TO DIANE IS HER MOTHER AND NEXT TO HER MOTHER IS HER MOTHER'S BEST FRIEND.

SECOND FROM LEFT IS DIANE BARBOLLA'S BROTHER ANDY.

Photograph is dated December 1998

TO A LOST AVIATOR

They came to tell us that your flight was done
and sadly guessed its far and fatal end,
and mourned the passing of the gallant one
but I could neither weep nor grief pretend,
for I who knew you best can never think
that you are lost to skyways and to me;
love long has been the only gentle link
that drew you back to earth repeatedly.

The sullen swamp may claim the earthly part
but all your bird like spirit lives above
and some where you are free to bank and dart
through pale, wide reaches of the sky you love;
and one day you will circle low and call --
believing this, I shall not grieve at all.

DIANE BARBOLLA

OUR WORLD AND CAPTAIN BARBOLLA

The following appeared in the September 27, 1965 Manhattan College Religious Bulletin as a prelude to a Requiem Mass for Captain Barbolla on October 1, 1965.

On July eleventh an Air Force C-121 radar patrol plane plunged into the Atlantic some 100 miles from Nantucket. On board as a crew member was Capt. Michael R. Barbolla, Assistant Professor of Aerospace Studies and friend to many of the men in the R. O. T. C. at Manhattan. Stark reality, not romanticism, suggests that his death in the line of duty involving American's system of vigilance was a death in defense of us all. The tragedy brought shock and consternation to the campus. To his wife, Diane, and his parents it brought irreparable loss.

The air crash faded from the headlines to be replaced by stories of death and wounding in Viet Nam; of accidents on military training missions; of explosions at missile sites. All over this land there were pockets of sorrow-- sad reminders of the troubled world in which we live, and of America's commitment to keep the peace even at the price of force.

Since the ending of World War II and the emergence of the United States as the key power in the Western World, we have been uneasy and uncertain in our new role. We were ambivalent about Korea -- some wanting to pull out; some urging atomic bombing beyond the Yalu. We are by no means unanimous about the U. N. organization. Adlai Stevenson could be labeled, alternately, "traitor" and "saint." We are uneasy in our relationships with the emerging nations, and resent any display of ingratitude, suspecting what it really is, a fear on their part to show dependence.

The responsibility to be our brother's keeper has been thrust upon us and we find it difficult to bear that weight and the inevitable misunderstanding gracefully. Some of us are even a little guilty now about legitimate patriotic concern for ourselves. The salute to the flag and the pledge of allegiance are slovenly done, and at more than one college commencement last spring, the commissioning of R.O.T.C was hooted and booed.

World responsibility can be staggering. Uncertainty and confusion can breed anxiety. Unexplained suffering can be crushing. The age-

old problem of evil grows more complex in our time. But there is a positive force greater than evil, more powerful than death, and Diane Barbolla, in the midst of sorrow, drew from it meaning, resignation and courage. In her simple note of thanks to Brother Gregory, we discover her own and surely her deceased husband's faith, sturdy patriotism and undying love.

Amidst temptations to be discouraged, bewildered or cynical, we can take strength from this young widow's words:

> "Dear Brother Gregory,
>
> It was very kind of you to write me and offer such well received words of consolation. I know that my husband enjoyed the time he spent at Manhattan College, and being able to tell other young men of the life he found in the Air Force must have made him proud of all servicemen.
>
> I shall always miss my husband to the very depth of my being, but I shall always be comforted by the knowledge that his religion gave him strength and courage, as surely as the Air Force gave him an obligation to his country. To each other we gave love. This knowledge will comfort me.
>
> Please thank the Brothers for their prayers and for the Masses. I'm sure that the Lord will and always has blessed us all."
>
> Sincerely,

Diane Barbolla

REFLECTIONS ON CAPTAIN MURRAY J. BRODY
By
Deborah A. Brody

I will not forget you; I have held you in the palm of my hand.
Isaiah 49:15

I had just passed my three-year birthday when my father, Captain Murray J. Brody, was killed in the July 11, 1965 "Connie" airplane crash off the Coast of Nantucket Island. He was twenty-eight-years old. My sister, Karen, was five; my brother, Paul, nine months; my mother, Claire, twenty-five. My sister was born in Biloxi, MS; I was born in West Point, NY (because it was near Stewart AFB), and my brother was born in Enid, Oklahoma. My parents had been married for about six years.

Because I was so young, I don't have any memories of my father or of this time. My first memory is of my fourth birthday party the next summer when we had been living in Yonkers, NY for about nine months close to where both of my parents grew up. Shortly thereafter, I remember being at Otis AFB for a ceremony. I didn't know what it was about, but I knew it was serious. A pleasant man wearing a uniform looked after me as I fell asleep in the sun on the warm metal chair: This was the dedication of the Otis Airmen's Memorial, which I did not see again until I was thirty-five years old.

Everything that I will relate I have learned in bits and pieces over the years. Even after thirty-three years, it is difficult for my family to discuss my father. My sister remembers the night the plane crashed: She is sitting on the stairs in our house at Otis; my brother and I are asleep in the bedroom. My mother is on the telephone to my Uncle Louie. "Murray's plane went down."

Upon learning of my father's death, my mother was hospitalized, apparently in shock. My sister and I were at a neighbor's house wearing boys underwear because we didn't have our clothes with us. An airman, at some point, returned my father's car to our house: It was a little blue sports car Murray had recently purchased. Karen, seeing the car, ran outside screaming, "Daddy's home!" But, of course, he wasn't. We had only been at Otis for about three months, so no one at the Base knew my father very well. Murray had not wanted to go to Otis and had made several requests to the Air Force to go to a base in Florida. He volunteered to fly these long surveillance missions to log as many flight hours as possible and advance his career.

The funeral was difficult even beyond the enormity of my father's untimely death. My mother is from a large Italian-Catholic family, and my father was Jewish. Although he converted to Catholicism before he married, his family never accepted it. My father's mother and sister wore black to the wedding to show that they were in mourning. Ironically, a few years later they would truly be mourning for him.

Murray had listed his father as one of his next-of-kin on his Air Force enlistment form. So my grandfather came to Massachusetts and, in all likelihood, identified my father's body. He tried to persuade the Air Force to release the body to him, so it could have a Jewish burial. My mother was in the hospital and not able to respond, so the funeral was delayed until she could state her wishes. Ironically, Murray's father, Irving, had never played much of a role in his son's life. Irving, in fact, had opted out of service in World War II and had very little interest in his son's military career. Eventually, my father had a Catholic burial in Gates of Heaven Cemetery in Hawthorne, NY.

In September of 1965, we moved to Yonkers, NY to the top floor of an apartment building my Uncle Louie owned. We lived there for the next six years. The highlight of each summer was our vacation. We drove to Lake George, NY the first year. The next summer we took the train (because my mother was afraid to fly) to visit some of my father's relatives in Florida. I remember that we flew home to New York from Florida because the train ride was so long. My mother did surprisingly well and remarked that the flight was so smooth she could pretend she was on a bus or train. The next year we went to California and the following year Colorado Springs, Albuquerque, and Phoenix.

My mother liked Colorado Springs, so a year later, we packed our belongings and drove West. We stayed for a year and then drove back East. Upon arriving in New York, my mother realized that Colorado had become home after all. After one day, we drove back to Colorado Springs. I have fond memories of living in the Motel 6 and eating dinner at Shakey's Pizza until my mother rented an apartment near the Air Force Academy. One year later, she bought the house in which she still lives. And so we grew up.

My sister is married and a lawyer in Denver, and my brother works in the computer industry in Silicon Valley. I live in Arlington, VA and work at a nonprofit health association in Washington, D.C. In 1982, my mother married Major Leon S. Kirk, retired Air Force.

We still know relatively little about my father and about the cause of the plane crash. The Air Force has not been very helpful or forthcoming in providing information. It seems the Air Force is exempt from releasing the crash investigation findings under the Freedom of Information Act --even after thirty-three years!

At an early age, my father had always had an obsession with flying. He elected to go to Manhattan's Aviation High School and led his Civil Air Patrol squadron. AHS sent me copies of my father's school records, which have been invaluable in helping me get to know him. He was an excellent student, class president, and outstanding in shop class. My brother started his career as a mechanical engineer and seems to have inherited many of my father's aptitudes. My sister and I were both our respective class presidents at Air Academy High School. After graduating, Murray worked for Pan American Airlines and spent some time in Iceland. From there he wrote my mother letters and sent pictures. Soon thereafter, he began his Air Force career. My mother once described a day when Murray took her flying: Being above the clouds like that can make one really believe that God exists.

Children who lose a parent at such a young age also lose their innocence and the belief that the world is a safe place. While other children were playing ball with their fathers, we were visiting his grave. It is a polished brown granite stone in a lovely cemetery. We would visit on Sundays and feed the ducks at a nearby pond. Although what I lost is immeasurable, I have gained an understanding of the fine line between life and death and the depth and perspective that comes from loss. My father will always be a young, handsome, and perfect Air Force Captain to me, and part of me, for better or for worse, will always be a three-year-old little girl waiting for him to come home. With thanks and appreciation to A.J. Northrup, Dean Boys, Art Kerr, Jim Walsh, John Puopolo, and all the others who have been so helpful to me in reconstructing this event, listening to my story, and sharing theirs.

September 30, 1998

PHOTOGRAPH COURTESY OF DEBORAH BRODY

THIS PHOTOGRAPH OF HAPPIER TIMES IS THAT OF THE BRODY FAMILY. DEBORAH BRODY IS SITTING IN HER MOTHER CLAIRE'S LAP. DEBORAH'S BROTHER PAUL, JUST SEVERAL MONTHS OLD, IS BEING HELD BY HIS FATHER, CAPTAIN MURRAY J. BRODY, PILOT, WHO WAS KILLED IN THE CRASH OF 55-0136 ON JULY 11, 1965. SITTING BETWEEN HER MOTHER AND FATHER IS DEBORAH'S OLDER SISTER KAREN.

A SURVIVOR'S STORY
BY
JOHN N. PUOPOLO

I was born on July 10, 1940 in Boston, Massachusetts, the only child of Rocco and Esther Puopolo. My family moved to Roslindale Massachusetts in 1948. In 1957 at age 16, I graduated from Roslindale High School. I then enrolled at Northeastern University. In February, 1958, I withdrew from Northeastern University and enlisted in the US Air Force on March 3, 1958.

I completed my basic training at Lackland AFB, San Antonio, Texas. I was then assigned to Radar Operators' School at Keesler AFB, Biloxi, Mississippi. From there I was assigned to the 6123rd Aircraft Control and Warning Squadron in South Korea. I had several other assignments in South Korea before being assigned to the 26th Air Division (NORAD) at Hancock Field, Syracuse, New York. While there I met Nina Scuderi, whom I married on May 11, 1963. In August 1962, I received a three-year assignment to Freising AFS, Freising Germany. In November, 1962, my father had a serious heart attack. Being the only child, I received a humanitarian reassignment to the 551st Airborne Early Warning and Control Wing at Otis AFB, Falmouth, Massachusetts, so I could be close to my family who still resided in Roslindale. Upon arriving at Otis, I was assigned to the 961st Airborne Early Warning and Control Squadron. While at Otis, I flew initially as a radar operator and later on as a radar crew chief aboard the RC-121D and EC-121H Super Constellation, performing radar surveillance missions over the Atlantic Ocean.

On February 29, 1964, Nina and I had our first child, Karen Marie. She was our leap year surprise.

On July 10, 1965, my wife, daughter and I drove to my parents' home in Roslindale to celebrate my 25th birthday.

The following day, July 11, 1965, I reported at 6:30 PM to my unit, the 961st AEW&C Squadron, for a briefing for a flight that night. I was the Assistant Radar Crew Chief. Although I was senior to Airman First Class Charles Sawyer, the Crew Chief, he had *qualified for Crew Chief before me. The scheduler probably thought he was senior, so he made him the Crew Chief. I didn't know it at the time, but this turned out to have great ramifications further on in the evening. I will explain later.*

The flight briefing was normal. At this point in my career, I had accumulated approximately 1200 hours flight time in the RC-121D/EC-121H aircraft. We were assigned to patrol Station #2, an area approximately 150 miles east of New England. We received a weather briefing and were told to expect thunderstorms on station. We were further advised that it would not be a smooth flight. Usually when we were scheduled for a night flight, most of us would be up all day with our families. We would try to get some sleep between shifts on the aircraft.

There were seventeen of us assigned to the aircraft (55-0136) that evening. When we had our flight briefing at the squadron operations building, we found out that there were four Air Force Reserve Officer Corps instructors who were at Otis on training who wished to fly with us in order to fulfill their flying time requirements. Two of the four ROTC instructors were assigned to our flight: Captains Edward N. Anaka and Michael R. Barbolla. The other two ROTC instructors were scheduled on a later flight that evening.

The pre-flight by the crew was normal, and take-off was at 9:30 PM.

This crew was the fifth crew I had been assigned to, and it was fairly new for me. I had come from Crew #36, the same crew that would fatally crash on November 11, 1966. When I became qualified as a Crew Chief on Crew #36, they didn't have a vacancy for me. When a vacancy opened on Crew #27, I was reassigned to them. I had flown with most everyone on Crew #27 a few times, but I didn't know them well. The two I probably knew best were the co-pilot, First Lieutenant Thomas Fiedler, a graduate of the Air Force Academy and probably one of the finest officers that the Air Force has ever seen, and Technical Sergeant Gilbert Armstrong, one of the two flight engineers. Sergeant Armstrong and I had flown together for quite some time on Crew #36. At the time of the crash, he was less than six months from retiring.

There was nobody on this plane I would call a really close friend.

The one I probably liked the most was First Lieutenant Thomas Fiedler, a native of Davenport, Iowa. We had many interesting conversations. I cannot say enough good things about him. The pilot, Lieutenant Ambrosia, was another fine young man, a real gentleman with a very positive attitude. You could not find two finer people or more qualified pilots than Lts. Ambrosia and Fiedler.

We proceeded to Station #2 and leveled off at 15,000 feet. Charles Sawyer, the Crew Chief, was in charge of the radar compartment. He took the initial action of getting the radar set up, working with the Radar Technicians and co-ordinating the radar mission via voice and electronic communications with the Syracuse Air Defense Sector at Hancock Field, Syracuse, New York. I went to the forward part of the aircraft and sat in the airline-type seats. I wanted to get some sleep before I relieved Airman Sawyer in about three hours.

I tried to sleep, but we ran into turbulence and thunderstorms and I was unable to sleep. I stayed in my seat, and a few minutes later Lt. Fiedler came by and sat in a seat across the aisle from me. We started to chat, and soon afterwards the pilot announced that we were having problems with number two engine. They were going to feather it, abort the mission and return to Otis AFB. I later learned that number two engine was feathered because it would not shift into high blower. By not shifting, the engine was operating at a reduced power level. We feathered engines often, and flying on three engines was no problem. I checked with Sawyer in the radar compartment. He didn't need any help, so I returned to my seat in the forward part of the aircraft for the ride back to Otis.

Shortly afterwards, there was an explosion in the number three engine. Being in the clouds, the explosion caused a very bright flash which illuminated off them. Lieutenant Fiedler said, "What the heck was that?" There was a window in the front of the galley where you could view engines #3 and #4. There was another window just past the navigator's work station where you could also view the engines. Someone yelled out, "number three is on fire." Very shortly thereafter, the Aircraft Commander, Lt. Ambrosia, announced over the loudspeaker, "We have feathered number two and number three is on fire -- prepare to ditch".

I never saw the actual fire. I saw the flash from my seat just forward of the galley, and although I was asked many times during the Board of Inquiry interview about the fire, I could not answer specific questions about it. All the crew members had assigned duties in the event of an emergency, and I proceeded to do my assigned duties and stay out of other people's way. Even though I did go by the window near engine #3 on my way to the radar compartment, I did not stop to look out as others were already there assessing the situation. I proceeded to the very rear of the aircraft and turned on a portable light mounted over the rear exit door. I also checked the bunk beds in the rear of the aircraft. There I found the two Air Force ROTC officers sleeping. I woke them to tell them that we were preparing to ditch and for them to don their survival suits and life vests. One of them was really sound asleep and his face showed disbelief when I woke him to tell him we were preparing to ditch. Their ditching positions were in the front of the aircraft in the airline-type seats. The radar technicians secured all of their electrical equipment. Airman Sawyer, the Radar Crew Chief, called our position to Syracuse, and the rest of us donned our yellow, rubber survival suits and life vests and took our ditching positions.

Being the Assistant Radar Crew Chief on this mission, my position for ditching was at radar console #2. There were two consoles, and I was at the one farthest to the rear of the aircraft. The ditching positions for most of the crew had them facing the rear of the aircraft on impact.

Airman Sawyer, the Crew Chief, had to sit in a seat which was only mounted to the floor by a couple of metal runners and was located just off the middle of the aisle. The seat had nothing around it to absorb the impact of a ditching. It was probably the worst ditching position on the aircraft with the exception of the cockpit.

Our descent from 15,000 feet to the ocean surface took approximately ten minutes. On the way down, there was not much communication, if any, that I can remember. Everyone was preparing for the ditching, and once the rear of the aircraft was readied and the crew members had donned their survival equipment, it was just a matter of waiting. I was sitting at my console for approximately five or six minutes, and a lot went through my mind.

Your life sort of passes in front of you. I am a Roman Catholic and active in the church. The first thing I did was say the Act of Contrition in the event I did not survive. When I was much younger, I had made the Nine First Fridays. This required going to Mass and receiving Holy Communion on nine consecutive First Fridays of the month. By doing this, the belief is that you will see a priest and confess your sins before you die. Somehow or other, I really believed I was going to survive. I could not see myself dead. However, I was still scared; there were no two ways about it. The thought did cross my mind that I was not going to make it, that I would end up drowning. I really had faith that I was going to get out of this thing because of the First Fridays. When you are only 25, you figure that you are too young to die.

There was absolutely no panic aboard the aircraft. Everybody was a professional and carried out their assignment to the letter. Everybody had passed their "check-ride" examination. There were no students among the crew. Airman Third Class Charles J. Podiaski, a radar operator, was fairly new. However, he was still able to get out of the plane. From where he was sitting, I believe he may have been the first to find the crack in the fuselage and get into the water.

Part of our survival drill for ditching was that the pilot would give a series of rings on the alarm bell thirty seconds prior to ditching. Even in practice, the alarm bell noise is quite discomforting. Lt. Ambrosia chose to announce over the loudspeaker that we were thirty seconds from ditching. This was a more personal touch and less scary. That is the kind of crew we had up there in the cockpit.

The conditions just prior to ditching were extremely poor. There were thunderstorms in the area, a low ceiling, some fog, and the seas had six foot swells. Impact with the water was severe. We lost all lights. The electronic equipment did not hold and was all over the place. If the battery-operated light over the rear door that I turned on was still lit, I couldn't tell. The only light in the aircraft came from the crack in the fuselage. It didn't help much, but it was better than nothing. The two other survivors, Airman Surles, a Radar Technician, and Lt. Witcher, the Navigator, subsequently described the plane's impact at the news conference as "like hitting a brick wall at one hundred miles an hour." I would say that is an accurate description. It was a very, very difficult landing.

I was very fortunate to have the ditching position assigned to the Assistant Crew Chief, in front of radar console #2. The back of my chair rested against radar console #1. My ditching position was the farthest from the front of the plane. Upon impact, radar console #1 cushioned some of the shock. However, my seat broke and I ended up lying on the floor, still strapped to my seat. The only bad break that I got was when radar console #2, which I faced, broke loose from its mounts on the floor and landed on my right foot and leg. Immediately water began coming into the aircraft and was sloshing around my head as I lay in the aisle. It was very dark and you could barely see. Someone yelled out that there was a hole in the fuselage wall. I don't know who exited before me, but it took me some time to pull my right foot loose from under the radar console that came to rest on my right leg. The injuries to my right foot and leg were the only injuries I sustained. I received severe lacerations, but nothing was broken. After freeing myself, I went forward toward the break in the fuselage, exiting the aircraft through the right side. The break was located just past the rear of the right wing. I believe there was a similar break on the left side also.

As I tried to exit the plane, my survival suit got caught on the plane's aluminum covering which had been torn and was very sharp. I was somewhat stuck trying to get through the opening. I finally just lunged through the opening into the ocean. In doing so, I ripped my survival suit on both sides. However, I previously ripped it when I freed my leg from the radar console.

I landed in the water and realized I was not alone, as I heard voices. I could not see anyone because of the very choppy water. I looked for the right wing because it held a 20-man life raft. I could not find the wing and could not see any other parts of the aircraft other than the fuselage from the rear of where the wing normally would have been, to the tail section. The plane had broken into at least two pieces, probably three. I never saw any evidence that the right wing section or the forward part of the aircraft was afloat. I don't know if the right wing got sheared off or was just under water. I looked around for someone but could see no one. There was an awful smell of aviation fuel on the surface of the water. It was by the grace of God that we did not have an explosion when the aircraft hit the water with the engine ablaze and all that fuel. I don't believe that we dumped any fuel on descent because of the engine fire. We probably still had 6000 of the original 6600 gallons that we had on takeoff.

I had been in the water for a couple of minutes when I started to get dizzy. I felt like I was spinning around. I knew that I was probably going into shock. I closed my eyes, and that helped somewhat. When I opened my eyes, the spinning stopped. It was then that I realized that I had never activated my life preserver. Although my survival suit was torn on both legs, the air trapped in the top half of the suit was keeping me afloat. I then pulled on both activation cords at the same time and the "Mae West" instantly inflated. As a matter of fact, it inflated so quickly and powerfully that both chambers came up and hit me in the face. It was like taking two jabs to my head. Anyway, I realized that it was working properly for which I was very thankful. Seconds later three airmen floated by me. They were Airman Second Class David A. Surles, Staff Sergeant John Howard, and Airman Second Class William E. Howe. The three of them were radar technicians. The four of us joined together and held onto each other. My best guess is that most of the other crew members who got out exited through the left side of the fuselage where number one and two engines were located. It was pretty dark in the water, and the only thing visible was the tail section of the aircraft, which sank within ten minutes or so. There were still thunderstorms in the area. The water was very choppy, with swells varying from a minimum of four feet to six feet. The sky was heavily overcast, and any hope of being seen by a rescue aircraft was very remote.

Lt. Bruce Witcher, the navigator who was sitting in the forward section of the aircraft, was able to exit the aircraft and was one of the three who ultimately survived. Lt. Witcher later said that he did not know how he got out of the aircraft. One minute he was under water, and then he somehow floated to the surface. He spent the night alone until his rescue.

I really did not know just how bad the ocean was until I was in it. Considering the thunderstorms, the rough sea, the foggy, dark, overcast conditions, the type of aircraft, its weight with an almost full fuel load, along with the large lower radome and radar antenna protruding from the bottom, the pilots and flight engineers accomplished a miracle landing. I feel that Lts. Ambrosia and Fiedler and Sgt. Armstrong are most deserving of the Distinguished

Flying Cross for their demonstrated skills in landing the aircraft. The three survivors owe their lives to the skills of these three men. It is criminal that they have never been recognized.

I recall that Airman Howe had hurt his leg in the crash. He was having trouble in the water putting his leg down and was more comfortable with his leg in an "L" shape position, perpendicular to his body. Airman Howe was facing me at the twelve o'clock position in the circle. I was at six o'clock and the other two at three and nine o'clock. He lifted his legs and put them around me and was much more comfortable in that position. His legs helped steady me and I seemed to ride the waves better. The big ones still buried me but the intermediate ones were more tolerable. He also had a problem with his life preserver. One part of it was fully inflated, and the other side was only partially inflated. We all did out best to manually inflate the side which was partially inflated, but we found it very difficult under the conditions present. You had to blow into a tube while pushing down on some kind of a valve. You also had to time it so no air escaped while you held the valve down. This was extremely difficult since your hands were very cold and inside of a rubber suit filled with water, while bouncing between waves.

During the course of the night, the four of us got colder and colder.

According to the personnel on the German Destroyer who rescued us, the water temperature dropped to 51 degrees. Most of us were very tired from not having slept prior to the evening flight. We knew we were drifting quite rapidly because before the tail section sank, we were surprised on how fast we were floating away from it. Once the tail section sank, it gave us a lonely feeling. At least with the tail visible, you had a feeling where you were. It sank like something from a World War II movie. It made a bunch of cracking noises, rose straight up perpendicular to the water, and slid straight down. Once the tail section sank, the vastness of the sea overtook us.

After the first few minutes in the water, we all said the Lord's Prayer. Within an hour or so, we could hear planes searching for us. There were jet aircraft overhead, but there was no way they could see us with the overcast skies and darkness. I do not recall us having a flashlight to signal them. We all had flashlights on the aircraft, but I lost mine upon impact. We knew they were looking for us because we got distress calls off prior to the descent. After the initial planes flew over and then flew away, we realized that we would probably not be rescued until daylight at the earliest. Nothing was going to happen during the night, so we were more or less prepared to spend a minimum of eight hours in the water. During the course of the night, the four of us stayed together and did not see anyone else. Initially we yelled to some other crew members and asked if anyone had a raft. Someone replied in the negative. We did not make any effort to get together with anyone else for several reasons. Mainly, you couldn't see anything between the waves, and we tried to conserve as much energy as possible. Your lower body tends to grow numb from hanging in a life preserver. It is like someone holding you up by your armpits. Every now and then, someone would kick their legs to relieve the pressure from "hanging." This was not a problem unless they kicked you. You would then wonder whether it was one of your crew members or a hungry fish. Although nobody would talk about it, we all felt that only a dumb shark would swim in such cold waters.

The night became colder and colder, and I was lapsing in and out of consciousness. I don't know when I lost consciousness initially, but I remember waking up one time to find Airman Surles and I were the only ones alive. Sergeant Howard and Airman Howe were still floating with us but their heads were mostly underwater and I knew they were dead. We still held on to the two bodies and waited. Finally around 6:00 AM, an amphibious US Coast Guard plane flew over but elected not to land. Evidently the pilot felt the water was too rough for a landing. If Lts. Ambrosia or Fiedler were at the controls, that plane would have been on the water and we would have been safely inside. A few minutes later, an Air Force EC-121H like the one we lost flew over and the pilot dipped the plane's wings several times as he flew over us. This was an acknowledgment that we had been seen. We waved back to him. We continued to wait for a rescue craft as the planes continued to fly over us. Meanwhile, I lost consciousness again. Somehow or other during the night, I managed to lock my arms together under my life preserver and keep part of my face on the preserver and out of the water. I still managed to swallow a great amount of sea water. By the time we were rescued, we had been in the water for almost eleven hours.

I do not remember my rescue, but I was told that the German

Destroyer, Z-1, came near, saw us, launched a small boat and removed us from the water. The destroyer also picked up several bodies, including those of Sgt. Howard and Airman Howe. The destroyer was on maneuvers with the US Navy Aircraft Carrier Wasp.

I subsequently awoke naked in bed, covered with warm towels and blankets. They were trying to raise my body temperature back to normal. There were several people around my bed speaking in a foreign language. I immediately thought it was Russian and that I was aboard a Russian trawler. On a recent mission to the same area where we ditched, I had reported a large number of trawlers. Most trawlers in this area were Russian. I had even hoped that night in the sea that a trawler would find us. Soon a US Navy officer came to see me and explained to me who my rescuers were. The officer was aboard the German destroyer during the maneuvers with the Carrier Wasp.

Once I began to feel better, I was taken to another room on the destroyer. There I met Airman Surles and Lt. Witcher. I was given warm clothes, a warm drink and cookies. I began asking who the survivors were and soon learned that the three of us were the only ones. I was told that they had recovered nine bodies which were also aboard, but no names were disclosed.

Several hours later we were told that the officials at Otis AFB wanted us returned as soon as possible to talk to us. We bid our German friends "goodbye" and thanked them for everything, including saving our lives. We were placed in a small boat and transferred to the Carrier Wasp. This was a real experience. The Wasp lowered a winch driven platform, and I was put on it. It was then raised from sea level to the deck. It seemed like 200 feet. I just closed my eyes and prayed. While on the Wasp, I became very sick. The food I ate plus the sea water I swallowed didn't mix well. I vomited for quite a while. By now it was early evening. They asked me "if I had a problem with flying back to Otis AFB?" I told them I was concerned about flying again so soon and asked if they would be kind enough to just bring the ship in with me. They said it would not be possible to do that, and they gave me an injection that was some kind of a sedative to calm me for the flight. I was placed aboard a small plane with Airman Surles and Lt. Witcher and experienced my first Carrier takeoff. By the time we landed at Otis AFB, it was about 11:00 PM. I was on a stretcher and subsequently placed in an ambulance and taken to the base hospital where I was examined. I fell asleep around midnight. My wife and her father, Joseph Scuderi, came to visit me during the night. We exchanged a few words but I had a hard time staying awake.

I woke up the next morning with my stomach much improved. I asked if there were more survivors and was told there were none. I felt pretty bad about that. Most of the crew was so young. It was tough realizing that they were dead, especially Lt. Fiedler. He was a special person who was always very nice to me and treated me with dignity and respect.

At the base hospital, Lieutenant Colonel Robert V. Mitchell, Sr., my Squadron Commander of the 961st AEW&C Squadron, came to visit me. Colonel Mitchell was pretty broken up. You could see he had taken the loss of his men very hard. He was a fine man, an excellent officer, and a good Commander. I knew he had not been to bed since he received word that the plane had ditched. He had the families of the dead and missing to deal with, and that certainly was not an easy task.

The chef at the hospital came to see me and asked what I wanted to eat. Since I had trouble eating, I asked for a fruit cup. Soon they brought me a tray with what looked like half of the citrus from the State of Florida on it. I was treated very well at the base hospital.

I was unable to attend the memorial service for those lost on 55-0136 as I was confined to the hospital, where I remained for ten days. I was only able to walk with crutches. I was also unable to travel to Boston when the German Destroyer Z-1, which rescued us, docked there. Airman Surles and Lt. Witcher did go there to visit our German friends.

The Air Force Board of Inquiry was headed by General Johnson from McGuire AFB, New Jersey. He was a real gentleman. At the Board of Inquiry, I was asked a lot of technical questions that I was unable to answer. It appeared to me that some of the officers on the Board were quite upset with my lack of knowledge and information. Even though I was in the front of the aircraft and did see the flash from the engine explosion, I never saw the actual engine fire even though I passed by the two windows being used to evaluate the engine fire. This was not my job. People who had to make life and death decisions were at these windows evaluating the problem. We had been trained to do our assigned job in the event of an emergency, and that is what I did. They asked: "Did you hear this noise, or did you hear the hydraulics, or did you listen for landing gear deployment, etc?" I explained to them that after I completed my ditching duties and donned my survival suit and life jacket, I looked around the radar compartment and saw nothing but fellow airmen in big, yellow, rubber suits. For some reason, this scene really scared me. I guess it was time for a realization check. The first time I was able to do some thinking about the pending situation was when I sat down at my console. At this time I thought of my family and what this was going to do to them. The last thing on my mind was hydraulics, engines, and strange noises. Anyway, General Johnson sensed that there was frustration on my part for not being able to answer so many redundant questions, and he got the officers to back off me. He ran a good Board of Inquiry and treated me well.

Upon discharge from the hospital, I was given a ninety-day deferral from flying. I was still able to draw my flight pay during this time. The hospital administrator told me that I would be given thirty days of administrative leave upon discharge. Somehow or other, my squadron got this changed to fifteen days. So much for sympathy! It took me over a month, using a cane, to be able to walk without limping. After I was able to discard the cane, I still had problems with my ankle swelling. This became a serious problem between the Air Force and me. Towards the end of my enlistment, the Air Force wanted to discharge me under honorable conditions with no compensation for my injuries. I told them of my foot problems and although I didn't ask for a permanent disability, I felt that I was entitled to a temporary disability until I was able to walk correctly without discomfort. The outcome was that I received an honorable discharge without any disability on March 29, 1966, eight months after being injured. So much for loyalty!

At the time of the ditching, Nina and our daughter Karen lived off base. The communications between the Air Force and my wife immediately after the ditching left something to be desired. From the time the plane ditched until I landed at Otis AFB, there were only two communications between the Air Force and Nina. Shortly after the plane ditched, the Air Force called her and said that "my plane was having a problem". At 5:30 PM on July 12, 1965, two officers came to our house and said that I was one of the survivors. It seems that they could have tried a little harder to provide some support during this difficult time. She called the squadron several times during the day, but any information they had was treated like it was "top secret." Even after the first call, she called back and asked what kind of a problem is the plane having. They refused to respond. Out of desperation, she called our friend, Airman First Class Sam Baber, and asked him to find out what was happening. He called a friend in squadron operations and got the details about the ditching. He called my wife back to bring her up to date. Meanwhile, he had sent his wife over to stay with Nina so she wouldn't be alone.

Several weeks later, Airman Surles and I were awarded the Airman's Medal and Lieutenant Witcher received the Air Force Commendation Medal. I don't know who recommended us for this honor. I found out later that Technical Sergeant Eugene J. Schreivogel was awarded the Airman's Medal posthumously for his actions. Sergeant Schreivogel was extremely busy preparing for the ditching. A lot of his time was spent evaluating the fire. He also helped some crew members with their survival gear. He never made it to his ditching position because of his concern for others. He richly deserved the Airman's Medal for his heroism.

I believe that one of the all time greatest injustices that occurred was that of Lts. Ambrosia and Fiedler, the Aircraft Commander and Co-Pilot, respectively, not receiving a medal. They took the plane from 15,000 feet to the water with only two engines. Of the remaining two, one was feathered and the other was feathered and on fire. The visibility was terrible. It was dark, foggy, and thickly overcast. There were thunderstorms with severe lightning. The sea was rough, with constant six foot swells. During the height of the thunderstorms, the sea swells increased to eight feet. All these figures were later supplied by the Navy. The plane was heavy with electronic gear and over 6000 gallons of fuel that couldn't be dumped. The three of us who survived owe our lives to the skills of the pilots and engineers. Sergeant Armstrong should have received the Air Force Commendation Medal at a minimum. Lts. Ambrosia and Fiedler should have received the Distinguished Flying Cross. I feel as strongly about this today as I did thirty-three years ago on July 12,

1965 when I was aboard the German destroyer discussing the miracle landing that these men performed. I would be willing to offer testimony to anyone as to why these medals should be awarded. In 1995, an AWACS plane crashed on takeoff from Anchorage, Alaska. The entire crew was killed and all crew members received the Meritorious Service Medal. The crew members of 55-0136, 55-5262 and 53-0549 were no less heroic and deserve to be recognized.

While I was in the hospital recovering from my injuries, my wife received confirmation that she was pregnant. We found this out two or three days after the crash. In October, 1965, I was cleared to resume flying status, but having only five months to go before my discharge, I told my Commander, Lt. Colonel Mitchell, that I wanted to resign from flying. I was then assigned to Squadron Base Operations. I drove a truck that serviced the planes until my discharge.

I left the Air Force with eight years, twenty-seven days of active service. My main reason for leaving was the lack of opportunity for promotion. I was an Airman First Class with five years' time in grade for promotion to Staff Sergeant. However, my career field was frozen for promotion. Several months before, the Air Force took away our "proficiency pay" of thirty dollars per month. They ruled that our career field was no longer deserving of it. I was married with one child and was not making much money. I felt I had a lot to offer and could provide my family with a higher standard of living as a civilian. Although I reenlisted when I was single, I found that being married in the service was not the life I was seeking. My decision to leave the service was a good one. My wife, children, and I have been very happy and successful as civilians.

In November, 1965, while visiting Nina's parents in Syracuse, New York, my wife lost the boy she was carrying. Michael was born prematurely at seven months. He only lived about sixteen hours and had lung problems. I believe the aircraft accident and its aftermath had placed a lot of stress on Nina and certainly didn't help her pregnancy.

I think that by 1965 the EC-121Hs had seen their better days and probably were fast approaching the end of their life cycle. I was not aware of any poor maintenance being performed on them, but I had no way of knowing that. I do know that after flying around the clock *for ten years with no loss of aircraft, there was pressure on the pilots to keep the planes in the air and get as much flying time as possible logged for the Squadron and the Wing. It was rumored that if the pilots didn't give their "all," they would end up on ground duty. This may have been a rumor. I don't know. It seemed like we didn't take every precaution available to us when we flew. When there was a problem, the first question was, "How serious is it, and can we keep flying?" I felt that all problems were serious at 15,000 feet. There was definitely some laxity in order to stay in the air and accumulate more hours. One practice that was detested by everyone was "dropping your alternate." You were required to return to Otis AFB with one and one-half hours of fuel in your tanks plus enough fuel to fly to an alternate base in case Otis was closed due to weather. Most often we used Westover AFB as our alternate. This required forty minutes of fuel. If you were flying on station and the weather at Otis was forecasted to be good, you could use up the forty minutes of fuel and stay on station. Nobody minded this because we were providing an additional forty minutes of radar surveillance. This is what we were paid to do. However, when the weather was marginal at Otis, some pilots wold return to Otis, drop their alternate landing site, and use up the forty minutes of fuel by flying circles around Otis. No radar data was being provided. This was nothing but a waste of fuel and a lot of needless wear and tear on the aircraft.*

Everybody has their favorite horror story. I guess mine was the night we were rolling down the runway for takeoff when we got a fire warning light in one of the engines. The pilot aborted the takeoff and we returned to the parking area to have the engine checked. No problem was found, so we tried it for the second time. Same result. We returned again and, once again, no problem was found. We tried it for the third time. Same result. We returned again, and for the third time they couldn't identify the problem. The maintenance sergeant, who would never be confused with a brain surgeon, told us to "take off and disregard the fire warning light because it was obviously malfunctioning." The flight engineer offered to let the dummy fly in his place, but he refused. The flight was eventually canceled. Unfortunately, this type of thinking was becoming more prevalent. It only changed when the planes started dropping out of the sky.

Another decision regarding safety should have been questioned. Until recently, I never knew that at one time each crew member had his own one-man life raft and parachute. Although I don't advocate bailing out of an aircraft over the ocean, especially at night, I do believe that if we had one-man life rafts on 55-0136, we could have had as many as twelve survivors. There is an excellent chance that some or all of the nine bodies recovered would have survived. I don't know when the decision to remove the one-man life rafts was made, but it was an extremely poor decision.

I had been discharged for seven and one-half months when 55-5262 crashed on November 11, 1966. It was Crew 36, the crew I was on before being reassigned to Crew 27. I knew most of the crew. All nineteen were killed. They must have had a major power loss because they never got off a distress call. A fishing boat said that the plane was intact when it hit the water. I had an excellent relationship with the navigator, First Lt. Richard K. Hoppe. He was outstanding. He was cut along the mold of Lt. Fiedler, a very friendly and professional gentleman.

Lt. Hoppe was given much of the credit for finding us in the ocean. When the Connie came to look for us after we ditched, Lt. Hoppe was the navigator on it. He practically brought the Connie which spotted us on top of us. A lot of people told me afterward that one of the reasons we were spotted in the vastness of the ocean was Lieutenant Hoppes great job of "dead reckoning". He accurately estimated our point of impact, the ocean current, and the position of his aircraft. When we were found, we had drifted over 25 miles.

The only person I knew on 53-0549, which crashed just off of Nantucket Island on April 25, 1967, was Airman First Class Richard D. Gravely. He was a country boy from West Virginia and one of the nicest guys you could be with on the plane. I had previously flown with him when we both flew for the 961st. He left Otis and spent a year in Labrador. He then was reassigned to Otis. Rich's plane was also on fire and tried to land on the runway at Nantucket Island. The pilot either overshot the runway or tried to avoid the homes around the runway. He ditched the plane in the ocean just off the Island, and it exploded on impact. There was only one survivor out of sixteen.

After my discharge, I went to work for Carrier Corporation for four months. I left Carrier on July 30, 1966 and started a new career as *a Distribution Clerk with the US Postal Service. It was a very rewarding career. I received six promotions over the years and finally retired on January 3, 1996 as the Manager of the Teall Station Post Office in Syracuse, New York. Nina and I now spend six months of the year in Syracuse, New York and the other six months in Punta Gorda, Florida. Nina and I have four children. Karen was the sixteen month old when my plane ditched. She was valedictorian of Liverpool High School, received a degree in physics from Yale University, received her MD/PHD from Tufts Medical School, and today is a neonatologist at Children's Hospital in Boston, Massachusetts. She is married and has a son and daughter.*

Kathleen graduated from Bryant and Stratton Business School and is now the Postmaster of Windham, New Hampshire. She is married and has a daughter.

Kristine was also valedictorian of Liverpool High School, received a degree in English from Harvard University, and is now an editor at Penguin Putnam in New York City.

Steven received a degree in Biology from Duke University, and received his MD from the State University of New York at Brooklyn. He is a second year resident in Orthopaedic Surgery at New York University.

The only relatives of the men who died in the crash whom I have maintained contact with are Carl Fiedler and his late wife, Irene. If all goes as planned, Nina and I should meet the Fiedler family in September, 1999. We have exchanged Christmas cards and short notes over the years. Lt. Thomas Fiedler was their only son. I believe that he had three sisters.

Why did I decide to tell my story? It was definitely not easy to do so. I have not been able to discuss this for many years. I have told this story because I would sincerely like to see the fifty deceased officers and enlisted men given the recognition that they so richly deserve. Every one of them should have received the Air Force Commendation Medal at a minimum. Lt. Ambrosia, Lt. Fiedler, and Sgt. Armstrong most definitely deserve the Distinguished Flying Cross. I would willingly travel anywhere to give first hand testimony concerning their heroics. It is also very possible that other crew members on 55-5262 and 53-0549 are deserving of the same award. Finally, I would like the families of the fifty deceased flyers to know that I have faithfully remembered these brave men in my daily prayers since the respective dates of their crashes. May they rest in peace.

John N. Puopolo now resides at 6830 Crystalwood Drive, Liverpool, NY 13088-5902 and is enjoying his retirement.

© ***By John N. Puopolo October 1998***

<u>NOTE</u>: CARL FIEDLER, THE FATHER OF LT. THOMAS FIEDLER, PASSED AWAY ON JANUARY 21, 1999.

A SURVIVOR'S STORY
BY
DAVID A. SURLES

I was born November 10, 1940 in Hartsville, SC, the last of four children, to Beatrice and William Surles. When I was six, we moved to Raleigh, NC. I graduated from Millbrook High School in 1959 and moved to Washington, DC, where I worked for several government agencies. I enlisted in the USAF on November 26, 1962.

I completed my basic training at Lackland AFB, TX, and was assigned to tech school at Keesler AFB, Mississippi. But I almost didn't make it to Keesler. After graduation from high school I got a job working in the fingerprint identification division of the Federal Bureau of Investigation. While at Lackland, the Consolidated Base Personnel Office folks discovered that I knew a lot about fingerprints, and at that time their fingerprint rejection rate was about 30%. The officer in charge of the unit called me one day and asked me if I would consider changing my school and stay at Lackland. I declined his offer. I completed tech school at the end of 1963 and was assigned to the 551st Electronics Maintenance Squadron at Otis AFB, MA. I reported to Otis the first part of 1964. I became eligible for flight status on May 1, 1964.

I remember that on July 11, 1965, it was a cloudy Sunday afternoon when I prepared to leave home. I was scheduled to fly that evening, and the brief was at 1830. The weather outlook was bad, so I told my wife not to worry if I didn't make it back to Otis the next morning. I expected the weather to be down on our return and that we would have to remain over night somewhere.

Shortly before I left home, my wife gave me a small box, which contained her charm bracelet, and asked me to drop it at the base jeweler upon my return on Monday. But then she said, "On second thought, I don't think I trust you with it." Don't worry, I answered, "I will leave it in the glove compartment in case something happens."

I departed my home in East Falmouth at 1645 for the 15 minute drive to the base. After arriving at the Electronics Maintenance Squadron Operations, I was informed that our assigned aircraft was A/C # 136.

I sat down and reviewed the previous mission history. Electronically the previous mission was a good one. At 1730 the other three technicians and I loaded our bags, tool boxes, and other equipment into the truck for the short ride to the aircraft. Our job was to pre-flight the aircraft electronic equipment and have it ready to go when the flight crew arrived.

We were ready when the crew arrived. The aircraft had Visual Omni Range (VOR) problems, but they were soon corrected. We blocked at 2050 and were airborne at 2115 en route to station # 2. At approximately 2145 we started the tie-in test with the ground site. By 2210 we were at 15,000 feet and tied in with the ground site.

About this time one of the pilots told us via the aircraft public address (PA) system that number 3 engine was on fire and to prepare the aircraft for ditching. I quickly went about stowing any and all loose equipment that I could see. I pulled on my exposure suit and life preserver. I helped the other radar tech, Airman Howe, get his life preserver on correctly. Since we were both first radar technicians, I asked Howe where he wanted to sit. He chose the aisle seat, and I took the seat at the height finder. I took one last look out the hatch at the number 3 engine. (Lt. Witcher had already pulled the hatch cover and discarded same.) The prop was feathered, and I saw no signs of fire. I returned to my seat and sat down and braced myself for the crash that was soon to come. The height finder had an altimeter, and as I watched it pass zero feet, we impacted the water. There was no skip. The aircraft impacted the water and stopped. After we impacted the water and the aircraft stopped, I released my seatbelt and tried to go forward and release the starboard (right) life raft that was stored in the right wing. It was impossible to get near the wing exit because that area of the aircraft was under water. For several seconds I thought I was trapped with no place to go. I looked towards the rear of the aircraft and saw that it was still out of the water. I made my way towards the rear of the aircraft with several other airmen. We found a split in the side of the aircraft and dropped into the water.

It was foggy, and the sickening smell of gasoline was all around me. Once in the cold water I worked my way over to where Airman Puopolo was drifting. We were soon joined by Airman Howe and Staff Sergeant Howard. We remained close to what was left of the tail section of the aircraft, but it started to sink. I told the other three airmen that we should get away from the aircraft. I was afraid we might get sucked under as the tail section sank. It wasn't long before the remains of A/C 55-0136 slipped beneath the cold waters.

All night long I could hear aircraft above us, but we had no way to signal them. As if things weren't bad enough, it started to rain. Each time a rain squall would appear the waves would get high and rough. This really didn't help our situation at all. As hard as I tried, I couldn't make myself comfortable hanging in that life preserver. I just got colder and colder. About daybreak Sergeant Howard and Airman Howe died. We held onto them for awhile, but then we just let them go. There was nothing else we could do. That left Airman Puopolo and I. He looked to be in pretty bad shape and was fading fast.

Several times during the night I would call out to see if anyone else was alive and near us. At first I got several responses, but as night turned into morning I got only one response. At that time I didn't know who it was, but I later learned that it was Lt. Witcher.

About 0600 I heard a plane fly over us, but the fog was so bad that spotting us was impossible. Miraculously, the fog lifted, and as he made another pass over the area he spotted us. The plane, a Navy S2F, then made another pass and dropped a smoke marker. Soon there were three planes flying around us: the S2F, an HU-16, and one of our own EC-121Hs.

We were picked up around 0900 Monday morning the 12th of July by a lifeboat crew from the German Destroyer Z1. The Germans were in the area on a NATO exercise with our U.S. Navy. Airman Puopolo had passed out several hours before we were picked up. The German lifeboat crew had to pull him off my back first, and then they pulled me into the boat. I had been supporting Airman Puopolo for several hours because he had slipped into unconsciousness. They also had to cut our exposure suits because they were full of water. Once aboard the German destroyer we were stripped of our wet clothes, wrapped in warm blankets, and tended to by their medical staff. They also gave us hot coffee and warm soup. Later on I asked for and received an egg and some toast. They really treated us good while aboard their ship. The officers gave up their rooms so we each could have a private room. They took excellent care of us. We were transferred by boat from the Destroyer Z1 to the U.S. Navy Carrier Wasp later that evening. While on board the Wasp we were given examinations by the navy doctors. We rested in sick bay for about 1 hour and 45 minutes. At about 2200 the Navy flew us off the carrier direct to Otis, where an ambulance was waiting to take us to the base hospital. I was discharged from the hospital three days later at 1200 on July 15th.

Twenty six hours had passed from the time I had left Otis on July 11th at 2115 until I got back on July 12th at 2315. It sure had been a long and trying day and one that I wouldn't soon forget.

Several days after the accident Lieutenant Colonel Mitchell, Lieutenant Witcher, and I drove to Boston and were reunited with the officers and sailors from the German Destroyer Z1. It was good to finally meet those who pulled us from the cold waters.

I left the USAF at the completion of my enlistment on November 25, 1966. I went to work for Norden Systems on December 1, 1966. I am now starting my 33rd year with the company.

I have heard and read lots about this accident, and most of it comes from those that weren't there. Those that could tell us the facts are no longer with us. I can tell you some of the facts I know for sure. I can't remember if I ever saw a fire coming from the number 3 engine, but I do know that the last time I looked out the hatch opening the prop was feathered and I saw no signs of fire. There was never any smoke in the cabin. There was one announcement over the aircraft PA system that we are going to ditch, and that was at the very beginning of the emergency. There was nothing after the initial announcement. There was no panic in the aircraft that I was aware of. I know for a fact that there was no panic in the rear of the aircraft. Prepare to ditch was done in about as orderly a manner as could be expected.

Bruce Witcher and I remained in contact with one another for years. We even lived near each other in southern California for several years. I lost contact with him up until a short time ago. It was good to hear from him again. I have never heard from or had any contact with Airman Puopolo.

© By David A. Surles - December 1998

David A. Surles
December 24, 1998

Photograph provided courtesy of David A. Surles

The West German Destroyer - Known as the "Z1" [formerly the US Destroyer "Blotter"] rescued the three survivors from 55-0136 [1/Lt. Bruce Witcher, A/1C John N. Puopolo, and A/2C David A. Surles]

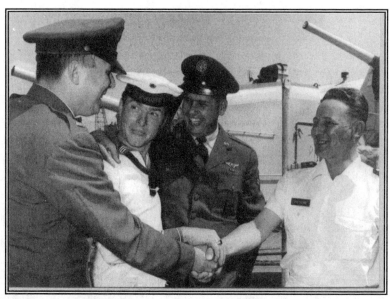

Photograph provided courtesy of David A. Surles

THE RESCUERS GREET TWO OF THOSE RESCUED - The Skipper of the Z1, Captain Jurgen Goetschke, and an unidentified sailor from the Z1 greets 1/Lt Bruce E. Witcher [left] and A/2C David A. Surles. The sailor is the man who pulled the three survivors [Witcher, Puopolo and Surles] from the frigid North Atlantic. Puopolo, the only other survivor, was unable to attend the ceremony aboard the ZI in the Boston Harbor since he still was hospitalized at Otis Air Force Base from injuries he received in the ditching of 55-0136.

Photograph provided courtesy of David A. Surles

[Left to Right] 1/Lt Bruce E. Witcher [survivor]; Captain Jurgen Goetschke, skipper of the Z1; the unidentified sailor who pulled the survivors from the ditching of 55-0136 from the frigid North Atlantic; A/2C David A. Surles [survivor] and an unidentified West German Naval officer aboard the Z1 in Boston Harbor.

Photograph provided courtesy of David A. Surles

[Left to Right] West German Counselor [name unknown]; 1/Lt Bruce E. Witcher; A/2C David A. Surles and Lt. Colonel Robert V. Mitchell, Sr. Colonel Mitchell was the Commander of the 961st AEW&C Squadron. Thirteen members of the crew of 55-0136 were assigned to the 961st.

David Surles, one of the three survivors, was assigned to the 551st Electronics Maintenance Squadron (EMS) as a Radar Technician. Three other technicians from the 551st EMS perished.

Two of the 16 who perished were AFROTC Officers who were flying as Observers.

For views of the above photographs on the internet go to:

http://members.tripod.com/dboys/crash/crash.htm

WHY, FOR A PERIOD OF TIME, WERE THERE NO MA-1 SURVIVAL KITS [INDIVIDUAL LIFE RAFTS] FOR CREW MEMBERS OF THE RADAR PATROL AIRCRAFT AT OTIS?

THE DOCUMENTS DESCRIBED BELOW WERE PROVIDED BY DEBORAH BRODY. SHE RECEIVED THIS DOCUMENT FROM THE AIR FORCE WHEN SHE REQUESTED INFORMATION ABOUT THE DITCHING OF 55-0136 IN WHICH HER FATHER CAPTAIN MURRAY J. BRODY, A PILOT, WAS KILLED ON JULY 11, 1965.

BELOW, FOR CLARITY, IS A TYPED VERSION OF A COPY OF A MESSAGE THE AIR FORCE FURNISHED MS. DEBORAH BRODY.

FOR OFFICIAL USE ONLY

TO RJEZSNT/26 AIR DIV HANCOCK FLD NY
INFO RJEZDG/551AEW&CON WG OTIS AFB MASS
RJWZAG/SMAMA MCCLELLAN AFB CALIF'
RJESBK/WRAMA ROBINS AFB GA
BT
UNLAS ADOOP-EU 7088D
ACTION FOR 26 AIR DIV
INFO FOR 551ABWCONWG, SMAMA, WRAMA
T.O. COMPLIANCE. RELEASE FROM COMPLIANCE WITH T.O. 1C-121 (R) D-560 TO INSTALL MA-1 SURVIVAL KITS IS GRANTED ON AN INTERIM BASIS. ADC WILL FORWARD NECESSARY DOCUMENTS TO THE PRIME AMA FOR PERMANENT RELEASE.
BT
10/2235L MAY RJWFAL

I certify that this is a true extract from a message received at Otis AFB, Massachusetts.

S/T/ CHARLES R. HARTWELL
    Lt Colonel, USAF
    Maintenance Team Chief
    Aircraft Investigation Board

* * * * *

NOTE: Lieutenant Colonel Charles R. Hartwell, AO799016, 26th Air Division, was assigned as a member of the Air Force Board of Inquiry into the loss of 55-0136.

Upon seeing the message I could not decipher what it meant and I believed that perhaps it permitted the removal of the MA-1 survival kits from the Connies at Otis. In searching for an explanation of that message I located Senior Master Sergeant Frank T. Pilat, now retired from the Air Force, who served as the Life Science Member on the Board of Inquiry investigating the loss of 53-0549 on April 25, 1967. Life Science deals, in part, with the aircrew survival equipment carried aboard Air Force aircraft. We spoke briefly on the telephone and he told me that he had been assigned to the 1st Air Force and had been in charge of Personal Equipment for aircrews at the time of the Connie ditchings at Otis Air Force Base. I asked him if he knew whether or not the crews of the Connies at the 551st AEW&C Wing at Otis Air Force Base were issued the MA-1 survival kits (individual life rafts which were inflatable with a carbon dioxide cylinder). He said the MA-1 inflatable life rafts always were part of the air crews' personal equipment. He said that it was he who caused the message to be sent and it merely meant that a change was in progress in the way the MA-1 survival kits, which are attached to the parachute harness, would be worn in the future. He explained that the aircrews had back-pack parachutes and the MA-1 attached to the harness at the bottom beneath an individual's buttocks. This, he said, was bulky and possibly would prevent a crew member from making an emergency exit from a stricken aircraft through a window or other small opening. A modification, he said, was made to use chest-type parachutes which were attached to the harness at the chest area of the flyer and the MA-1 survival kit was attached to the harness immediately beneath the parachute. This, he said, eliminated some of the bulk and would hopefully permit aircrews to exit more easily through a smaller opening in the event of an emergency. He again assured me that the aircrews at Otis who flew on the Connies always had had the MA-1 survival kits.

I next contacted John Puopolo - one of the three survivors of 55-0136 which ditched in the Atlantic Ocean on the night of July 11, 1965. Puopolo told me that when he and some other crew members went into the ocean from their ditched plane they spent over ten hours in 51 degree water before being rescued. He said the only survival equipment he and other survivors had been issued prior to that flight were the survival suits or anti-exposure suits (R-1A suit) and a Mae West life vest (LPU-2). He said he believes that had the crew members been able to get into a life raft that those who survived the initial impact and exited the aircraft but later died most likely would have lived had they not been exposed to the cold water for so long. He noted that the two 20-man life rafts installed, one in each of the wings of their aircraft, could not be released due to the damage the aircraft had undergone in the ditching.

Puopolo also noted that while he was recuperating at the Otis Air Force Base Hospital from injuries he had received in the ditching he was told by a nurse that she was aware that the injuries sustained by the dead flyers, whose remains had been recovered and autopsies performed, had not died from their injuries but from hypothermia (subnormal temperature of the body).

When asked if the crew members had been issued the MA-1 survival kits (inflatable one-man life rafts) he said the kits were not issued. In fact, he said, he knew nothing about the one-man life rafts and never received survival training instructions in its use. He expressed that had the crew members had the individual life rafts they surely would have used them and perhaps there possibly would have been more survivors.

Puopolo, when asked if the numerous Connie aircraft in which he flew at Otis from early 1963 until July 11, 1965 ever had the MA-1 survival kits stored aboard the aircraft or if those kits were issued to him and the crew members with which he flew - he said "never".

Ms. Brody also received a copy of the receipt regarding the personal equipment issued to the crew of 55-0136 immediately prior to its flight on July 11, 1965. The receipt for the equipment was signed by 2/Lt. Ira J. Husik - one of the sixteen crew members who perished. The receipt reflects a total of 21 LPU-2/F Vests and 21 R-1A Suits and other miscellaneous equipment were received by the 19 member crew. There is no mention of the MA-1 kits.

Retired Master Sergeant Dean Boys, who flew aboard the Connies at Otis Air Force Base as a Radar Technician from 1963 until 1969, stated that during the early part of 1963 through July 1965 the MA-1 survival kits never were issued to the flight crew members, with whom he flew, as part of their personal equipment. Nor, he said, were the MA-1 kits stored aboard those aircraft.

There was one entry on a document also received from Deborah

Brody, reflecting the *"OPEN TECH ORDERS ON AIRCRAFT 55-0136 AS OF JULY 11, 1965"*. The next to last entry on the above listing mentioned the MA-1 Survival Kits as follows:

1 Dec 61   1C-121(R)D-560   INSTALLATION OF MA-1 SURVIVAL EQUIPMENT   ADC WAIVER

Note: Technical Orders (T.O.) are detailed instructions and illustrations covering every aspect of the aircraft, its systems, and related equipment. Technical Orders are revised by Technical Changes to Technical Orders (TCTO). While changes are pending they are referred to as Open Technical Orders.

Retired Senior Master Sergeant Pilat also was asked to explain the significance of the open technical order entry relating to the MA-1 survival kits on aircraft 55-0136. He said that he, at this late date, no longer has access to the Technical Orders mentioned and therefore could not provide an explanation. Sergeant Pilat said that if the MA-1 survival kits were in fact removed or were not being issued to the flight crews on the Connies, as confirmed by a survivor and another flyer, then he cannot understand why. He opined that someone, somewhere, made a decision to not use them, probably because the Connies always carried two 20-man life rafts in the wings.

Sergeant Pilat stated that had the crew of 55-0136 had the MA-1 survival kits he feels that there obviously would have been more survivors. He said the anti-exposure suit the flyers were using would not sufficiently protect anyone for a long period of time in very cold water.

Joseph L. H. Guenet, the only survivor of 53-0549 when it ditched on April 25, 1967, wrote me in response to an e-mail message I sent to him about the MA-1 survival kits. Guenet wrote, **"After the ditching of the second Connie [55-5262 on November 11, 1966] the Air Defense Command directed the Wing to add parachutes and one man life rafts to the survival gear carried on the missions. On 53-0549 we were each equipped with an exposure suit, an LPU life preserver, a chest or back pack parachute, depending upon seat style, and a one man life raft in an MA-1 kit. In addition, the aircraft had two twenty-man life rafts, one in each wing."**

NOTE: Survivor Puopolo reported that the personnel of the German ship that rescued him told him the temperature of the ocean water at that time was 51 degrees. The three who survived had been in the water more than 10 hours when rescued. Nine other crew members who apparently survived the initial ditching and were in the water with the three ultimate survivors died while awaiting rescue.

I (the author) recall that while I was assigned to the 551st AEW&C Wing, from Aug 1955 until November 1959, all crew members received a back-pack parachute, an inflatable life vest, an anti-exposure suit, and a one-man life raft (MA-1 Kit) as their personal equipment issue prior to each flight. Each crew member received survival training, at regular intervals, in the use of each piece of his personal equipment. The "wet ditching" training was most significant since all the radar patrol missions flown by the 551st AEW&C Wing were over the North Atlantic. The missions were flown around the clock 365 days a year.

As a member of the flight crew, I always believed that I would survive the ditching of my aircraft since I was well trained and confident in water survival techniques. Also, instilled in each of us was the theory that the ditching of the radar version of the Super Constellation would not be a problem -- that the huge lower radome and the radar antenna inside the radome would shear off and the aircraft would come to a reasonably smooth stop after skipping and gliding on top of the ocean surface. I recall that we were assured that everyone would be able to exit the aircraft through the two over-wing exits onto the wings and get into the two 20-man life rafts.

One only has to read the stories of the few survivors of the ditching of the Connies lost at Otis AFB to realize that crew members were flying under false impressions. It appears to be obvious that the speculative theory on the ditching of the aircraft was not tested with a series of events and adverse elements that those crews and aircraft were expected to experience in real life. Attempting to obtain more information regarding the placement or removal of the individual life rafts (MA-1 Kits) on the Connies, I made a Freedom of Information Act (FOIA) request on October 5, 1998 to Headquarters Air Force Safety Center which had furnished Ms. Deborah Brody copies of the documents shown above. On October 13, 1998, The Safety Center advised that they have no other information available regarding the survival kits and had forwarded my request to the Air Force Pentagon (11 CS/SCSR). I subsequently was informed that no information pertinent to my request could be located.

I had furnished the Air Force all the information shown above regarding the MA-1 Survival Kits. I asked for documents, an explanation, or any information pertaining to the MA-1 Survival Kits at Otis AFB, as follows:

Were the MA-1 survival kits issued to crew members of the EC-121H prior to July 11, 1965?

If so, during what dates were they issued?

If the issuance of the MA-1 kits were discontinued at some point, when did this occur, why did it occur, and by whose or what authority was the issuance stopped?

Were the MA-1 kits again issued after July 11, 1965 to crew members of the EC-121H aircraft?

If so when did the re-issuance of them begin again?

PAGE 1
THESE NEXT FIVE PAGES HAVE BEEN LEFT BLANK FOR YOUR PERSONAL PHOTOGRAPHS, MEMORABILIA, AND NOTES

PAGE 3

PAGE 5

195

2ND MISHAP
THE LOSS OF 55-5262
NOVEMBER 11, 1966

CONSOLIDATED NEWS ARTICLES 55-5262

IT WAS TO BE AN ORDINARY NIGHT FLIGHT
The Boston Globe - November 12, 1966 by EDWARD A. JENNER - Staff Reporter

OTIS AFB--Aircraft No. 262, an EC-121H Lockheed Super Constellation, roared off the runway here at 12:35 a.m. Friday enroute to patrol Station 2, a 175-mile stretch of ocean and coastline off Georges Bank. Aboard was a crew of 19 settling in for what was a normal and monotonous 13-hour flight. The "bird" call signal "Homey 64" was known in the wing as one of the better aircraft. There had been no problems with it, and it handled exceptionally well. In flight, the crew had nothing much to do, since all systems are fully automated. Some slept; some read; and chow was the same for all, a TV lunch wrapped in foil and heated aboard. Flight crews on the patrol missions are the best in the business. All pilots and flight engineers put in six to eight hours a month "flying" the simulator, a fully equipped cockpit permanently grounded. Lovingly named the "stimulator" and "panic palace," its instruments give the crews every emergency situation that could be encountered in actual flight, but haven't until now. Crews have [in the simulator] ditched planes, coped with all four engines on fire, severe icing and the rigors of an Atlantic storm, where the lightning flashes light up the cockpit and the thunder's roar is deafening.

Before takeoff the flight crew begins briefing as much as three hours in advance. They find out which bird they'll fly, check out its maintenance records and find out everything about it since it came off the assembly line. Radio and electronics specialists also get the records on their equipment and know it as well as if they were with it from its construction before going aloft.

A normal flight crew on patrol missions consists of a commander, co-pilot, two navigators, two flight engineers, [radio operator], radar men and electronics specialists. Occasionally, a second pilot is aboard to assist the commander.

The birds have been flying out of Otis for 10 years, in all kinds of weather, around the clock. Their mission--to scan the coast and feed back data to a ground station, which in turns tracks, identifies and, if necessary, vectors in jet fighters or missiles on incoming "unfriendly" aircraft. Not until the crew are on the ground and in debriefing do they know what they came across.

The 551st began operating out of Otis 12 years ago February and went 10 years without a fatal accident.

[Sixteen months earlier] this bird's predecessor, Homey 63, also attached to the 961st, set out on routine patrol of the same Station 2. It crashed into the sea with 19 men aboard. There were three survivors.

THEY WERE ALWAYS AFRAID IT MIGHT HAPPEN
Boston Globe November 12, 1966 By RICHARD A. POWERS - Staff Reporter

It was something they worried about each time one of the huge planes took off from Otis Air Force Base. They didn't talk about it, though, and each prayed it wouldn't happen. Friday morning, the thing they dreaded the most happened 19 times in home towns near the base--a knock on the door. At Otis it is the custom to have the base chaplain accompanied by close friends of the family break the news of a tragedy. Beverly Ann Kay was asleep in her apartment at 73 Everett St., Middleboro. In the next room was her cousin Loretta. The two and their husbands, A2C Larry L. Stoner, 20, and A2C Robert P. Kay, 21, had spent Thursday night at the apartment for a get-together before the airmen left for the base and routine patrol duty.

At the base Maj. Robert A. Baird, 44, tucked his eight children into bed before leaving for a 9:30 p.m. briefing. He had spent the day supervising the construction of a chapel outside the base. He was Cape Cod President of the Church of Jesus Christ, Latter Day Saints.

For Mrs. Adamick, it was [to be] a happy occasion. It was one of the last flights her husband, A1C Joseph Adamick, 26, would be making. He was due to be discharged in two weeks.

The knock on Mrs. Kay's apartment door woke her and Loretta Stoner. They opened the door to find the chaplain and friends--Mr. and Mrs. Kenneth Lord. The chaplain told them the plane was missing. "Pray to God they return safely," he said before bowing his head in prayer. Mrs. Kay sat on a sofa in her mother's home at 114 Wareham St., hugging a pillow and crying softly. Kay and Stoner had been friends since the early days of basic training in Mississippi. The Thursday night flight was their first together since their marriages to the cousins. Mrs. Kay had met her husband at a dance in Wareham shortly after he was assigned to Otis about a year ago. They have been married nine months and Mrs. Kay is expecting their first child.

Months ago, Mr. and Mrs. Kay introduced her cousin Loretta to Stoner. They were married four months ago, and Mrs. Stoner is also expecting. Clutching the pillow, Mrs. Kay told reporters, "Bob was taking a course in accounting and bookkeeping. We planned to return to his home town, Niagara Falls, N.Y., where he hoped to get a job doing that type of work." She said her husband joined the Air Force in September, 1964, and after training in Mississippi and a follow-up base, he was transferred to Otis, where he had been stationed for the last year. Kay did not plan to reenlist when his hitch was up in September, 1968. His flight duty on the patrolling aircraft was not always the same but the young couple managed to sit and talk quietly after his [flight] was over. "Several times he mentioned how unequipped the planes were. They were not up to par, and he told me they had to land early several times because of engine failure." "They were forever having trouble with them," Mrs. Kay said.

PLANE HUNT PUSHED BUT HOPE SEEN DIM
Boston Globe November 12, 1966

With hope virtually abandoned, Coast Guard cutters and aircraft continued to search today for survivors of the four-engine Constellation which plunged into the ocean Friday 125 miles east of Nantucket. Nineteen airmen were aboard the Otis Air Force Base craft when it mysteriously crashed and exploded in view of a passing fishing trawler. While the Coast Guard cutters Yakutat and Acushnet scoured the crash area and planes flew overhead, a crack team of Air Force investigators launched a probe of the crash. Col. John H. Pease, Vice Commander of the 37th Air Division at Goose Bay, Labrador, flew in to head the official investigation. He termed the crash a complete mystery. The New Bedford fishing boat Stephen R. reported seeing the plane flying low in fog and rain squalls. It banked steeply to the right, and plunged cartwheeling into the water with a fiery explosion at 1:30 a.m. The modified Lockheed Constellation was on patrol over the Atlantic, part of the nation's radar defense network that operates 24 hours a day. On July 11, 1965, another picket Constellation crashed in thick fog in the general area--the

southern end of Georges Banks fishing grounds--with 19 men

aboard. Three men survived. Aside from these two tragic crashes, the Air Defense Command has piled up an outstanding record of safety and service during the past 10 years.

LIST OF 19 OTIS CRASH VICTIMS
Boston Globe November 12, 1966

The following crew members were identified as having been aboard the military aircraft which crashed Friday 125 miles east of Nantucket Island:

BAIRD, Maj. Robert A., 44, husband of Lolita T. Baird, 5767 Kelly St., Otis Air Force Base, aircraft commander.

RUCKER, 1st Lt Larry D., 25, husband of Alice Rucker, 5406D Yeager Cir., Otis AFB, copilot.

HOPPE, 1st Lt Richard K., 26, husband of Caroline Monette Hoppe, 5360A Carpenter St., Otis AFB.

TAYLOR, 1st Lt Edward W., 25, husband of Elaine C. Taylor, 5373B Ogle Cir., Otis AFB.

NEROLICH, MSgt John J., 45, husband of Margaret Nerolich, 5540B Tibbetts St., Otis AFB.

DiBONAVENTURA, MSgt Armand H., 45, husband of Julia F. DiBonaventura, 5606B Patrick Rd., Otis AFB.

SIMMONS, SSgt Robert J., 36, husband of Anneliesse Simmons, 5662 Luffberry Cir., Otis AFB.

LAMBERTl, TSgt Albert J., 34, husband of Louise Delia Lambert, 5542A LeMay Ave., Otis AFB.

McNEILL, SSgt Lawrence E., 31, husband of Sharon A. McNeill, Bath, Me.

KAY, A2C Robert P., 21, husband of Beverly Ann Kay, 73 Everette St., Middleboro.

STONER, A2C Larry L., 20, husband of Loretta A. Stoner, Box 326, Wareham St., Middleboro.

PATER, SSGT James R., 37, husband of Shirley L. Pater, 358 Lakehurst St., Freeport, La.

HENDRICKSON, MSgt Clarence L., 39, husband of Elizabeth N. Hendrickson, 5657B Vincent Cir., Otis AFB.

SPARKS, SSGT Robert, 34, husband of Marie Sparks, 873 Pleasant St., New Bedford.

ROGERS, A/1C James D., 24, husband of Mary Ann Rogers, 11474 76th Ave., North Largo, Fla.

BAILEY, A2C David N., 20, husband of Beverly Carol Bailey, 211 Wareham Rd., Marion.

ADAMICK, A/1C Joseph E., 26, husband of Margaret R. Adamick, 23 Cahoon Ct., Falmouth.

THIBODEAU, MSgt Robert A., 41, husband of Joyce T. Thibodeau, 5583C Hunter Av., Otis AFB.

WILBUR, A2C James D., 21, son of David B. Wilbur, Sidney, N.Y.

SEARCH ENDS FOR FLIERS
Boston Globe November 13, 1966

The Coast Guard called off the active search Saturday night for possible survivors of an Air Force radar picket plane that crashed in the Atlantic Friday. Nineteen airmen were aboard the Otis Air Force Base plane when it plunged into the ocean 125 miles east of Nantucket. Coast Guard aircraft and the cutters Yakutat and Acushnet searched the area throughout the day Saturday, but they left the scene with the coming of darkness. Meanwhile, a team of Air Force investigators were conducting an investigation into the tragedy. A spokesman said wreckage recovered at the scene late Friday had been "Positively identified" as having come from the missing four-engine Constellation. Col. John H. Pease, Vice Commander of the 37th Air Division at Goose Bay, Labrador, flew in to head the inquiry. He termed the crash a complete mystery. The plane crashed and exploded in full view of the New Bedford trawler

Stephen R. Crewmen reported seeing the plane flying low in fog and rain squalls, then banking sharply to the right and plunging into the water with a fiery explosion at 1:30 a.m.

The plane was on routine patrol over the Atlantic as part of the nation's 24-hour-a-day radar defense system. In July 1965, another radar picket plane of the same type crashed in the same general area with 19 men aboard. Three of the crew survived. Despite the two crashes, the Air Defense Command has compiled a record of safe operations during the past 10 years.

Concerning the possibility of engine failure, Col. James Lyle, Commander of the 551st Early Warning and Control Wing, to which the lost plane was attached, said Saturday: "The EC-121H aircraft used at Otis are well maintained and adequately equipped for the type missions being flown. The engine used on this aircraft has a dependable record. Engine shutdowns in flight--due either to actual failure or as a precautionary measure--are not excessive."

[NOTE] *Colonel James P. Lyle, some six months later, while commanding an EC-121H, number 53-0549, is killed along with 15 other members of his crew in a crash at Nantucket Island. His aircraft caught afire and upon his attempting to ditch it in the Atlantic just off Nantucket it explodes. There was one survivor.*

OTIS BASE RADAR PICKET PLANE CRASHES, EXPLODES; 19 CREWMEN BELIEVED DEAD
By PAUL N. ANDERSON Cape Cod Standard-Times Staff Writer - November 12, 1966

OTIS AIR FORCE BASE. Nov. 12 - The entire crew of an Otis Base EC-121H radar Constellation was feared killed early Friday when a huge aircraft believed to be the missing Connie was seen plunging and exploding into the Atlantic Ocean some 125 miles east of Nantucket.

The crew of the Lockheed Warning Star included a full complement of 19 officers and airmen. Names and addresses of all were released shortly after noon yesterday by Colonel James P. Lyle, Commander of the 551st Airborne Early Warning and Control Wing at Otis.

NOTIFY KIN - Colonel Lyle had withheld the names pending notification of next of kin. Shortly before 5:30 p.m., Colonel Lyle announced the flight plan of Aircraft 262, identified as the missing Constellation, had expired and the aircraft was presumed to have ditched in the ocean. He said the aircraft had been en route to Station 2 some 125 miles off Nantucket. There were no reports of survivors, he added, and the cause of the crash continues undetermined. The crew of 19 included 18 married men with 40 children. Three wives are pregnant. Board of inquiry appointed from the 1st Air Force of ADC includes Colonel John H. Pease, Chairman; Lieutenant Colonel Emil V. Busch, Maintenance Officer; Major Robert A. White, Investigating Officer; Major William R. Willner, Pilot-member; Major Morgan G. Childs, Jr., Otis Safety Officer; Captain Norman J. Harris, Flight Surgeon and Chief Warrant Officer Eulalio B. Labato of Otis, Board Recorder.

The EC-121H was powered by four 18-cylinder turbo-compound engines. Its fuel capacity was 40,000 pounds of high-test fuel. The mammoth radar plane was crammed with $5,000,000 worth of supersensitive equipment for its role in the nation's air defense network. It may have used 5,000 pounds in attaining 15,000 feet altitude for its patrol, Colonel Lyle said. An explosion with that much fuel remaining--about 35,000 pounds--wouldn't leave much more than bits and pieces.

3RD TRAGEDY - This was the third Otis-connected tragedy with heavy loss of life in five years. On January 15, 1961, the ill-fated Texas Tower 4 collapsed 80 miles off the New Jersey coastline during a fierce storm with the loss of 28 lives. Just 16 months ago to the day 16 crew members of another Otis Constellation crew lost their lives when their EC-121 was lost at sea off Nantucket on July 11, 1965. Ironically, the crew of the Veteran's Day tragedy was stationed in Lieutenant Colonel Jack January Jr's., 961st AEW&C Squadron as was the crew of the 1965 crash. Yesterday's tragedy also took place in nearly the same location. Three survived last year's ditching. First bulletins of the crash were released by Otis information officials shortly before 5 a.m.

HAD DITCHED - They said it was suspected an EC-121H radar Constellation of the 551st AEW& C Wing had ditched into the sea approximately 125 miles east of Nantucket. The aircraft departed Otis at 12:35 a.m. on a routine air defense mission with 19 crew members aboard. Radio contact was last made with the $7,225,000 plane at1:22 a.m. with the weather reported fairly clear and visibility at 10 miles. The aircraft at that point was flying at an altitude of

15,000 feet. The quoted radio message from the ill-fated craft was "All Normal . . . No Problems." At the same time, the aircraft was reporting in on its tracking station through radar with ground sites. After that, Otis officials continued, radio and radar contact was lost and no further word was heard. At 1:30 a.m., the 70-foot New Bedford fishing dragger Steven R. reported seeing an aircraft ditch into the ocean and added that it exploded as it entered the water. The Steven R. and several other fishing vessels in the area were said to have picked up debris. Gene R. Connors, skipper of the Stephen R. reported watching the plane soar over the vessel with a stream trailing it. He could not tell if it was a fire or jet trail. The plane rolled over about two miles past the vessel, nosed into the water and burst into flames on impact, he reported. The weather was good and seas were fairly calm. Debris located during the day long raking of the area included a plane seat and cushion, three life jackets and parts of the plane. Although Otis officials could not positively identify the fragments as parts of the missing plane, they said information at their disposal would appear to be sufficient to indicate the ditched plane was from Otis. A large-scale search of the area near Georges Banks continued throughout Veteran's Day with ships and planes of the Coast Guard and Air Force participating as well as commercial fishermen. Included in the massive search were the Coast Guard cutter Acushnet out of Portland, Me., a Coast Guard HU-16 aircraft from Quonset Coast Guard Air Detachment, another Otis Base EC-121H, C-130 transport planes with paramedics from Goose Bay Air Force Base, Labrador and Kindley Air Force Base, Bermuda, the cutter Yakutat out of New Bedford and the Navy rescue vessel, the U.S.S. Sunbird.

FREIGHTERS AIDED - Also taking part were two freighters, the S.S. Atlantic (American), and the British motor vessel, Phyllis Bowater, two other fishing vessels, the Terra Nova and the Fern and Isabel and another British ship, the Alaunia. The Otis Information Office was flooded with telephone calls throughout the early morning after the crash from anxious families of airmen stationed at Otis. The office also served as headquarters for at least 23 members of the press, radio and television covering the disaster. First of several press conferences throughout the day was conducted by Colonel Lyle at the wing command post at 7:50 a.m. He confirmed the message received in the last radio contact and that several items of debris had been found but these could not be confirmed as part of the missing aircraft. He said the debris would be brought to Otis. Colonel Lyle said the Air Force had used the EC-121H since 1954 and had experienced just two crashes during missions - Friday's and one exactly 16 months earlier in almost the same spot which killed 16 crewmen. There also was a crash within two weeks after the planes went into service but that was strictly pilot error, he added. There was nothing wrong with the plane. The big unanswered question here is why there was no radio contact between 1:22 a.m. and when the fishing vessel reported seeing a plane go down. It's ridiculous to think they had no communications because the plane is loaded with back up radios for just such an emergency. Colonel Pease said the investigation may not turn up anything more than what we have now - an unidentified plane crashed in the Atlantic for an unidentified reason.

NOT TO CONTACT - Families of the crew members had been told a plane was down but its Otis identification couldn't be confirmed, Colonel Lyle said. He urged members of the news media not to contact families once the names of the crew were released. Also cause for temporary concern was an Otis-based RC-121 aircraft, an earlier model of the missing plane, which departed Otis for the Azores at midnight, a half hour before the ill-fated Constellation took off. It is due back on Sunday. At 10:50 a.m., Lieutenant Commander Albert Tingley of the Quonset Coast Guard Air Detachment, pilot of the Grumman HU-16, held a press conference to announce he had been in contact with the Steven R. He said the detachment received word of the mishap at 1:45 a.m. and arrived at the scene of the ditching at 3:15 a.m. The Coast Guard officer said crewmen of the fishing vessel reported sighting a low-flying aircraft about two miles away . . . rolling to its right, overturning and then diving into the ocean and exploding.

SIGHTED DEBRIS - Commander Tingley said he too sighted debris but could not identify it. The battery of press and radio television newsmen discussed the tragedy in hushed undertones as they awaited further word. Another press conference was called by Colonel Lyle at 1:05 p.m. to release the names of 18 of the 19 crewmen and to announce a board of inquiry will conduct an immediate investigation. He said items found at the scene included a seat with a cushion, three life preservers and sundry small fragmentary pieces of debris. It is pure speculation as to what happened, Colonel Lyle told the gathering. He mentioned the aircraft's fuel consumption and certain items of debris as giving rise to the probability the aircraft was from Otis. Bulletins were released intermittently as developments occurred throughout the day and into the late hours Friday. When last radio contact was made with the ill-fated aircraft, the destination was North. This was at 1:22 a.m. Further contact was not to be made. Otis radar tracked the plane then proceeding South. An attempt for contact proved futile. It was speculated a power failure may have developed in the aircraft and the crew may have attempted to head back for Otis. There was an eight minute differential between the last voice contact with the plane and the time it crashed. Search by air and sea continued Saturday for any sign of survivors or additional debris. Captain Paul Downey, a 551st AEW&C maintenance officer aboard the Coast Guard cutter Yakutat identified the fragments of debris found Friday as belonging to an EC-121 aircraft although he could not pinpoint this debris as part of Aircraft 262. Otis officials said none of the debris will be brought back to Otis until the search is discontinued. Meanwhile, non-Otis members of the board of inquiry are expected at Otis later today and their intensive investigation will begin.

BRIEFING BEFORE FATAL FLIGHT CALLED ROUTINE
Cape Cod Standard-Times November 12, 1966

OTIS AIR FORCE BASE. Nov 12 - Major Robert A. Baird, commander of ill-fated aircraft 262, conducted what was to be his final briefing in the 961st Airborne Early Warning and Control Squadron operations center shortly before midnight. The crewmen appeared to be in good spirits as Major Baird outlined the weather forecast for the flight and pertinent aspects of what seemingly would be a routine surveillance mission over the Atlantic. There was the usual chit-chat and a few jokes. Then the crew, equipped with flight gear, went out onto the runway to their bird for a last-minute check of the Warning Stars' readiness. There was a brisk breeze blowing and an occasional drop of rain foretold showers which were to follow. The routine checks the flight and radar crew had made time and time again prior to many other such missions were carried out on radio sets, radar sets, oil pressure and other mechanical phases of the plane's operation. The four engines were warmed up and Major Baird taxied 262 down the runway. Take-off was on schedule at 12:30 a.m. Airman 1st Class Richard Lussier, the proud crew chief of 262 had done his work and his aircraft was on her way. Only last month Lussier had received the Crew Chief of the Month award in the 551st Wing for the second consecutive time. Less than an hour later, the clear voice of Major Baird came through the radio . . . "All normal.. . no problems." It was the last word received from the huge plane. Moments later, aircraft 262 plunged into the Atlantic and exploded.

OTIS SURE DEBRIS FROM LOST PLANE
Cape Cod Standard-Times November 13, 1966

OTIS AIR FORCE BASE. Nov 12 - Additional equipment picked up today at the scene of the Veteran's Day Otis Radar Constellation disaster has been positively identified as having come from the missing 551st Airborne Early Warning and Control Wing aircraft. Air-sea search and rescue operations for the downed plane, called off at dusk Friday night, resumed at daybreak today. Two Coast Guard cutters, the Acushnet out of Portland, Me., and the Yakutat out of New Bedford, remained at the scene during the day along with an HU-16 Coast Guard aircraft from Salem Air Station. Both the Yakutat and Acushnet crewmen have debris aboard. Captain Paul Downey, an Otis-based maintenance officer aboard the Yakutat, has identified debris found Friday and early Saturday as EC-121H Warning Star Constellation material. Later on Saturday, other equipment had been picked up and positively identified as having come from the missing aircraft which apparently exploded at sea, 125 miles from Nantucket. There were still no reports of sightings of survivors or bodies. There were 19 crewmen aboard the ill-fated plane. All members of the board of inquiry appointed by First Air Force in the Air Defense Command have arrived at Otis and an intense investigation into the cause of the disaster is in progress. The board is headed by Colonel John H. Pease, Chairman. Recorder is Chief Warrant Officer Eulalio B. Labato of Otis. Colonel Pease, Vice Commander of the 37th Air Division at Goose Bay, Labrador, flew to Otis to head the official investigation. The New Bedford fishing vessel Stephen R. reported the crash. It said the EC-121H banked steeply to the right and plunged into the water. The modified Lockheed four-engine Constellation was on patrol over the Atlantic as part of the nation's radar defense network.

On July 11, 1965, another picket Constellation went down in thick fog in the same general area with 19 men aboard. Three survived.

By TILSON S. DENHAM Cape Cod Standard-Times Staff Writer - November 12, 1966

BUZZARDS BAY. Nov 12 - There will be a vacant chair when officers of Major General Leonard Wood American Legion Post take their places at their next meeting. That chair belonged to Major Robert A. Baird, commander of the aircraft which went down in the Atlantic yesterday while on a routine patrol from Otis Air Force Base.

Major Baird was Chaplain of the American Legion Post and was scheduled to have been installed for a second term in a ceremony at the NCO Club at Otis Air Force Base last night. That ceremony was postponed when news of the disaster became known. "The Major was known and loved by all members of the post," John Holland, Post Commander, said. "We are all heartbroken. Major Baird was rated as an excellent pilot by members of his squadron. He was described as a serious man and a fine fellow when you got to know him. He was active in the Mormon church and was president of the group, which is building a church in Cataumet," Commander Holland said. "We will have a quiet installation later with no fanfare. No other chaplain will be chosen. His chair will remain vacant for a year with only his Legion hat on it. At the end of the year, when a new chaplain is installed, the hat will be presented to his widow." The Legion commander said he had called Major Baird Thursday night to invite him and Mrs. Baird to a dinner. He said Major Baird told him, "John, I am sorry my wife and I can't be there because I'm leaving for a briefing right now." Commander Holland said, "I wished him God speed and those were the last words I spoke to him." He continued, "Speaking for all members of our post, I must say all of us are better men for having known him."

OTIS PLAQUE HONORS DEAD OF 1ST CRASH
By United Press International Cape Cod Standard-Times November 12, 1966

OTIS AIR FORCE BASE, Nov. 12 - A wooden plaque hangs on a wall at Otis Air Force Base headquarters, bearing the names of 16 airmen. The men died last year when their Constellation radar picket plane [55-0136] went down in the Atlantic on a routine mission. "Died in valor in the performance of an active defense mission," reads the inscription. The dead were attached to the 551st Airborne Early Warning and Control Wing. On Friday, the 16-month anniversary of the fateful flight, another 551st Constellation [55-5262] on a routine mission crashed at almost the same spot, 125 miles east of Nantucket. Its 19-man crew were feared dead.

The following article appeared in the Air Force Sergeants Association Magazine November-December 1966 Issue:

MEN LOST IN PLANE CRASH FROM OTIS AIR FORCE BASE

It is with deep regret that we have to announce in our Christmas issue of AFSA Magazine the loss of five members of Chapter 202 at Otis AFB, Mass. The entire crew of an Otis Base EC-121H radar Constellation was killed November 11, when an aircraft plunged and exploded into the Atlantic Ocean some 125 miles east of Nantucket. The crew of the Lockheed "Warning Star" included a full complement of 19 officers and airmen. Names and addresses of all were released by Colonel James P. Lyle, Commander of the 551st Airborne Early Warning and Control Wing at Otis. Colonel Lyle said the aircraft had been en route to Station 2 some 125 miles off Nantucket. There were no reports of survivors, he added, and cause of the crash continues undetermined. . . . .

Boston Globe articles [Reprinted Courtesy of The Boston Globe]
Cape Cod Times articles [Reprinted Courtesy of Cape Cod Times]

HISTORY OF FLIGHT - 55-5262

At 2130 EST, 10 November 1966, Major Baird, the Aircraft Commander assigned to the 961st Airborne Early Warning and Control Squadron, Otis AFB, Massachusetts, briefed an air crew totaling 19 for an active air defense mission to airborne long-range input (ALRI) station # 2. Homey 64, an EC-121H, serial number 55-5262, was assigned by the 551st AEW&C Wing operations center. Fuel load was 7330 gallons of 115/145 aviation gasoline. The DD Form 175 flight plan filed by the Aircraft Commander listed 12+00 hours of fuel on board, estimated time en route 9 hours plus 50 minutes and 8 hours plus 5 minutes on station # 2 at fifteen thousand feet (FL150).

Briefing and pre-flight were normal

The aircraft blocked on 10 Nov at 2310 EST. At 2338 EST, the aircraft taxied back to the maintenance ramp reporting malfunctions on #1 engine #1 cylinder and #2 engine #1 Power Recovery Turbine (PRT). The spark plugs, coils and leads were changed on #1 cylinder #1 engine, and the clamps were tightened on #1 PRT, #2 engine. Engines were again started at 11/0020 EST and the aircraft blocked the second time at 11/0025 EST. Take off was made from runway 23 at 11/0037 EST. Otis AFB weather at take-off was 6000 feet scattered clouds, 8000 feet overcast, 7 miles visibility, light rain-showers, surface winds 210 degrees at 22 miles per hour, gusts to 30 miles per hour.

The flight was cleared to station # 2 by Otis AFB departure Cross Rip #1 to Nantucket VOR, control eleven forty four COD intersection, direct to station # 2, to maintain fifteen thousand feet altitude. Immediately after take-off, a transmission from Homey 64 was made to Homey Control on company frequency (channel 9) "still have flames coming from PRT #2 engine". However the aircraft continued on its mission. DELETED---------------------------------------
-

The aircraft accomplished departure instructions as cleared. Homey 64 contacted Boston Center on UHF radio enroute to Nantucket VOR. He last reported his position as over COD intersection at 0114

EST passing through thirteen thousand four hundred feet and climbing to flight level 150. This same information was passed to Andrews Airways Military Relay facility by high frequency (HF) radio terminating his report about 0117 EST.

UHF radio contact was established with the 35th Air Division surveillance section by the Homey 64 Combat Information Center Officer (CICO) at 0040 EST. Three of four UHF radios were checked and reported to be loud and clear (#3 UHF was not installed for this flight). Homey 64 was tracked by radar throughout the flight by the 35th Air Division. The Homey 64 CICO reported at 0110 EST that he would be ready for his Airborne Long Range Inputs (ALRI) pre-tie-in tests about 0115 EST. Radar shows Homey 64 reached station # 2 at 0123 EST and turned south on track. At this time Homey 64 had not completed the tie-in with SAGE or provided further radio transmissions. Inspection of SAGE radar printouts show that at 0122 EST operations were normal aboard Homey 64 as the radio operator positioned his Selective Identification Equipment (SIF) mode selector switch from mode 3 Code 1100, to Mode 3 Code 0000 the normal code for station operation. At 0124 EST, the SAGE printout shows Homey 64 position to be on track center line of station # 2 approximately 7 NM south of center stabilization point, still transmitting Mode 3 Code 0000. At 0125 EST, the 35th Air Division Radar Input Counter Measure Officer (RICMO) lost all radar contact with Homey 64. He attempted emergency radio contact and requested North Truro radar site to increase their gain control on the radar. Radio and radar contacts were unsuccessful. At this time, Boston Center called the 35th Air Division RICMO to inquire whether they had contact with Homey 64. The 35th Air Division RICMO indicated negative. Boston Center advised they had a report of an aircraft down near COD intersection. At approximately 0126 EST, an aircraft later identified as Homey 64 DELETED---- by the 1st mate of the fishing vessel "Stephen R" passing overhead at approximately 200 feet going in a northeast by due north direction. The aircraft appeared to be in level flight navigation lights on and emitting a smoke or vapor trail. Two miles beyond the "Stephen R" the aircraft passed directly over the fishing vessel "Terra Nova" at an estimated altitude of 150 feet, wings level, red and green navigation lights on, and engine or engines back-firing. DELETED------------------------------ engine noise to be minimum which gave them the impression that the aircraft was small in size. DELETED--
----

The aircraft continued past the "Terra Nova" for approximately 3/4 to 1 mile and struck the water at approximately 0127 EST. An Explosion and fire resulted. DELETED----------------------------------

------------ Weather at time of impact was clear, visibility 4 to 6 miles, winds from the south at 10 to 18 knots, and the seas running 1 to 3 feet from the south-southwest, water temperature was +48 F. Immediately after the impact, and during the period that fire persisted, the fishing vessels "Terra Nova", and "Fern" and "Isabel" and "Stephen R" retrieved their fishing nets and proceeded to the crash scene. The fishing vessels "Terra Nova", "Stephen R" and "Fern" and "Isabel" were within three-miles radius of where the aircraft crashed, exploded, and burned. The position taken at that time was Loran Fix of 1H4 6262 and 1H3 2762. This information was relayed to the Woods Hole Coast Guard by the "Terra Nova". First call to the Coast Guard informing them of the crash was sent by the "Stephen R" at 0129 EST, approximately two minutes after the aircraft crashed. The aircraft crashed ½ mile east of station track 5-1/2 south of station center point, and 1-1/2 miles north of last radar position plotted at 0124. Water depth at this point is listed on the most recent Coast and Geodetic Survey chart dated 5/9/66 as being 174 feet to 200 feet. The fishing vessels proceeded to the crash site after hauling in their fishing nets, arriving from 10 to 15 minutes after the crash. They crossed back and forth sweeping the area with their search lights trying to locate survivors or bodies. None have been recovered to date. Recovered parts of the aircraft indicate that it contacted the water extremely hard in a nose up, slight bank attitude. DELETED---

SOURCE: Department of the Air Force, Headquarters Air Force Safety Center, Kirkland AFB, NM

[NOTE] *The deleted or redacted portions of the History Of Flight had been marked through in black by the custodian of the document prior to its receipt under a Freedom of Information Act request.*

[COMMENT] *The crew from the "Stephen R" a 70 foot fishing vessel out of New Bedford, Massachusetts witnessed 55-5262 crash on November 11, 1966 approximately 125 miles from Nantucket Island. This fishing vessel also was nearby when 53-0549 crashed on April 25, 1967 approximately one-mile off Nantucket Island and the crew recovered one of the two bodies found soon after the crash.*

BOARD OF INQUIRY - 55-5262

The Board of Inquiry into the loss of 55-5262 and its 19 crewmen was Chaired by Colonel John H. Pease, Vice Commander of the 37th Air Division at Goose Bay, Labrador. Some other members were Lieutenant Colonel Emil V. Bush, Maintenance Officer; Major Robert A. White, Investigating Officer; Major William R. Willner, Pilot-Member; Major Morgan G. Childs, Jr., Otis Safety Officer; Captain Norman J. Harris, Flight Surgeon, and Chief Warrant Officer Eulalio B. Labato of Otis, who served as the Board's Recorder.

****

In trying to find out what happened to 55-5262 I learned that Lieutenant Colonel Emil V. Bush and Major Morgan G. Childs, Jr., are deceased.

Eulalio B. Labato, who was a Chief Warrant Officer and who served as the Recorder for the Board now resides in Colorado. When I wrote to him explaining that I was seeking information about the loss of 55-5262 my letter went unanswered.

I located Major William R. Willner, the Pilot-Member of the Board and spoke with him by telephone. Major Willner, who has been retired from the Air Force since the early 70's, was a pilot with the 961st AEW&C Squadron and flew missions on the EC-121H radar patrol planes. He now resides near Otis Air Force Base from which the ill-fated plane and crew had departed on its last mission.

Major Willner said the Board of Inquiry never determined the reason why 55-5262 was lost. He noted that from the testimony of the men on the fishing boats who observed the aircraft when it passed over them that "it appeared to be under control by the crew." The noise heard by the men on the fishing boats, he opined, possibly was the cutting back of power to the engines in preparation for the ditching. He said the aircraft was not recovered. However, he noted, that a commercial firm had been retained to provide underwater camera coverage at the crash site and there were several hours of pictures which the Board reviewed. The aircraft had broken into pieces and was scattered, he said.

When I asked him about there being no communications from the crew during the descent of the plane from its last reported altitude and it having been lost from radar coverage for seven minutes he said he had no explanation.

When asked if I could send him a package of material pertaining to 55-5262 he said he did not want to receive it.

NOTE: I had flown with Major Morgan G. Childs Jr., a Pilot in the 961st AEW&C Squadron at Otis Air Force Base.

CREW MEMBERS OF AIRCRAFT 55-5262
CRASHED ON NOVEMBER 11, 1966

OFFICER - DECEASED

MAJOR ROBERT ABNER BAIRD
FV682603
AIRCRAFT COMMANDER

1/LT RICHARD K. HOPPE
FV3139354
NAVIGATOR

1/LT LARRY DENNING RUCKER
FR79991
PILOT

1/LT EDWARD WILLIAM TAYLOR
FR75727
NAVIGATOR

ENLISTED - DECEASED

MSGT ARMAND HENRY DiBONAVENTURA
AF11166476
FLIGHT ENGINEER

MSGT CLARENCE DAVID HENDRICKSON
AF37806596
RADAR OPERATOR

MSGT JOHN JOSEPH NEROLICH
AF33260111
FLIGHT ENGINEER

MSGT ROBERT ALLEN THIBODEAU
AF13105504
RADIO OPERATOR

TSGT ARTHUR JOSEPH LAMBERT
AF1119334
RADAR SUPERVISOR

SSGT LAWRENCE ELTON McNEILL
AF11266991
RADAR OPERATOR

SSGT JAMES ROBERT PATER
AF16234964
RADAR OPERATOR

SSGT ROBERT JAMES SIMMONS
AF12358174
RADIO OPERATOR

SSGT ROBERT SPARKS
AF15449495
RADAR TECHNICIAN

A1C JOSEPH FRANK ADAMICK, JR.
AF21279785
AUTOMATIC DATA PROCESSOR TECHNICIAN

A1C JAMES DWIGHT RODGERS
AF14743876
RADAR TECHNICIAN

A2C DAVID NORMAN BAILEY
AF13844241
NAVIGATION MAINTENANCE TECHNICIAN

A2C ROGER PAUL KAY
AF12719058
RADAR OPERATOR

A2C LARRY LEE STONER
AF13826950
RADAR OPERATOR

A2C JAMES DAVID WILBUR   [NOTE]
AF12709949
AUTOMATIC DATA PROCESSOR TECHNICIAN

NOTE: This was the first mission on which A2C JAMES DAVID WILBUR had flown

PHOTOGRAPH PROVIDED COURTESY OF DEAN BOYS

PHOTOGRAPH OF EC-121H SUPER CONSTELLATION 55-5262 IN EARLIER TIMES. THIS AIRCRAFT WAS LOST IN THE NORTH ATLANTIC OCEAN WITH ITS CREW OF 19 MEN ON NOVEMBER 11, 1966. NONE OF THE CREW MEMBERS WERE FOUND AND ONLY PARTS OF THE AIRCRAFT WERE RAISED FROM A DEPTH OF APPROXIMATELY 200 FEET.

PHOTOGRAPH BY ED JENNER OF THE BOSTON GLOBE ON NOVEMBER 12, 1966

PHOTOGRAPH IS OF COLONEL JAMES P. LYLE, COMMANDER OF THE 551ST AIRBORNE EARLY WARNING AND CONTROL WING AT OTIS AFB, MA. THE CAPTION OF THE PHOTOGRAPH READS "WING COMMANDER IS STUNNED BY LOSS". AIRCRAFT 55-5262 HAD JUST CRASHED AT SEA ON NOVEMBER 11, 1966 WITH ALL ITS 19 MEMBER CREW KILLED.

FIVE MONTHS LATER ON APRIL 25, 1967 COLONEL LYLE AND 14 MEMBERS OF HIS CREW WERE KILLED, ONE SURVIVED, WHEN HE DITCHED AN EC-121H (53-0549) IN THE ATLANTIC AT NANTUCKET ISLAND AFTER EXPERIENCING AN IN-FLIGHT FIRE.

MAJOR ROBERT ABNER BAIRD - AIRCRAFT COMMANDER

2/LT RICHARD K. HOPPE - NAVIGATOR

NAVIGATOR   PILOT

USAF PHOTOGRAPHS WHICH APPEARED IN THE <u>BOSTON GLOBE</u> ON NOVEMBER 12, 1966. IN ADDITION TO THE DEATH OF THESE FOUR OFFICERS THERE WERE 15 OTHER CREW MEMBERS WHO ALSO DIED IN THE CRASH OF 55-5262 ON NOVEMBER 11, 1966.

A/2C ROGER KAY AND WIFE ANN. AIRMAN KAY WAS LOST IN THE DITCHING OF 55-5262 ON NOVEMBER 11, 1966.

AIRMAN LARRY STONER AND WIFE LORETTA. AIRMAN STONER WAS LOST IN THE DITCHING OF 55-5262 ON NOVEMBER 11, 1966.

PHOTOGRAPHS FROM THE <u>RECORD AMERICAN</u> NOVEMBER 12, 1966

COL JOHN H. PEASE
... to investigate crash

PHOTOGRAPH APPEARED IN THE <u>BOSTON GLOBE</u> ON NOVEMBER 12, 1966.

COLONEL JOHN H. PEASE HEADED THE AIR FORCE BOARD OF INQUIRY INTO THE DITCHING OF 55-5262 AND THE LOSS OF ITS ENTIRE CREW OF 19 OFFICERS AND AIRMEN ON NOVEMBER 11, 1966.

THIRTY-TWO YEARS LATER COLONEL PEASE WROTE THE *FOREWORD* FOR "*FIFTY FALLEN STARS*".

MEMORIAL SERVICE PROGRAM FOR THE NINETEEN MEMBER CREW OF 55-5262 WHO LOST THEIR LIVES ON NOVEMBER 11, 1966

Memorial Service Program Provided Courtesy of Dean Boys

DEDICATED TO THE HONOR AND MEMORY OF OUR COMRADES

961st Airborne Early Warning & Control Squadron

Major Robert Abner Baird
First Lieutenant Richard K. Hoppe
First Lieutenant Larry Denning Rucker
First Lieutenant Edward William Taylor
Master Sergeant Armand Henry DiBonaventura
Master Sergeant David Hendrickson
Master Sergeant John Joseph Nerolich
Master Sergeant Robert Allan Thibodeau
Technical Sergeant Arthur Joseph Lambert
Staff Sergeant Lawrence Elton McNeill
Staff Sergeant James Robert Pater
Staff Sergeant Robert James Simmons
Airman Second Class Roger Paul Kay
Airman Second Class Larry Lee Stoner

551st Electronics Maintenance Squadron

Staff Sergeant Robert Sparks
Airman First Class Joseph Frank Adamick, Jr
Airman First Class James Dwight Rogers
Airman Second Class David Norman Bailey
Airman Second Class James David Wilbur

THE MEMORIAL SERVICE

INVOCATION
Lieutenant Colonel Earl A. Mack
Base Chaplain, Otis Air Force Base

A READING FROM THE HOLY SCRIPTURES
Major George R. Connelly
Catholic Chaplain, Otis Air Force Base

THE AIR FORCE HYMN
Chapel One Choir

MESSAGE OF CONDOLENCE
Colonel Thomas M. Groome, Jr.
Staff Chaplain, First Air Force

MEMORIAL ADDRESS
Colonel Roy M. Terry
Staff Chaplain, Air Defense Command

MEMORIAL PRESENTATIONS TO THE NEXT-OF-KIN
Colonel James P. Lyle
Commander, 551st AEW&Con Wing

Lieutenant Colonel Jack January, Jr.
Commander, 961st AEW&Con
Squadron

Major Butler Redd, Jr.
Commander, 551st Electronics Maintenance
Squadron

BENEDICTION
Major George R. Connelly
Catholic Chaplain, Otis Air Force
Base

"TAPS"

TWENTY-ONE GUN SALUTE

WHAT HAPPENED TO 55-5262
A. J. NORTHRUP

On August 16, 1955, after completing the Airborne Radio Operators Course, I was assigned to the 551st AEW&C Wing, 961st AEW&C Squadron, Otis AFB, Mass. I made my first flight on the RC-121 on October 9, 1955 and during the next four years accumulated more than 2000 hours in the various model Super Constellations on active ADC radar surveillance missions.

I retired from the Air Force in August 1975. After my retirement I never forgot having been a crew member on those aircraft, nor did I forget the really wonderful people, both officers and airmen, with whom I had been fortunate enough to have flown. It is an experience for which I am thankful and which I always will remember with kind thoughts -- although I am aware that some 50 officers and airmen lost their lives in the loss of three of the aircraft stationed at Otis AFB when they crashed in the North Atlantic. I also am very thankful that four crew members did survive the ordeal.

The aircraft from Otis which were lost at sea are:

Aircraft Nr. 55-0136 - lost July 11, 1965 - with the loss of 16 officers and airmen - with three survivors

Aircraft Nr. 55-5262 - lost November 11, 1966 - with the loss of 19 officers and airmen (the entire crew)

Aircraft Nr. 53-0549 - lost April 25, 1967 - with the loss of 15 officers and airmen - with one survivor

Although thirty years had passed since the last mishap noted above occurred, I remembered the accidents and in 1997 I began doing some research regarding their loss.

I began by writing to then Chief of Staff of the Air Force, General Ronald R. Fogleman, requesting under the Freedom of Information Act for information about all EC-121 mishaps of aircraft assigned to Otis AFB.

I subsequently received a letter dated 24 March 1997 from the

Deputy Director, Headquarters Air Force Safety Center, Kirtland AFB, NM, transmitting the releasable portions of the mishap report of an EC-121H aircraft [55-5262] which was lost at sea on 11 November 1966. The Air Force stated that this is the only incident of this type aircraft from Otis AFB that could be found.

I later identified another loss -- that of aircraft 53-0549 and made the same request and received the releasable portions of that mishap report.

I further identified another loss -- that of aircraft 55-0136 but did not make a request for documents regarding that aircraft loss as by then I knew the limited information the Air Force would release.

By that time I also had found information on the internet at web sites maintained by USAF Retired Master Sergeant Dean Boys relating to the three accidents and was able to learn that the basic cause of two of the three aircraft ditching at sea had been fire. There had been three survivors from one and one survivor from another accident from whom I could get information. Some eye witnesses reports had been reported by the press and I turned to this source for additional information. However there was no information available on the internet or in information furnished by the Air Force that disclosed what caused 55-5262 to be lost at sea.

I did receive some information from the Air Force regarding the loss of 55-5262 and 53-0549. However, I did not receive a copy of the investigating boards' *analysis*, *findings*, and *recommendations* regarding the mishaps. The Deputy Director, Headquarters Air Force Safety Center, wrote that they are *exempt from disclosure* under the United States Code, Title 5, Section 552(b)(5), and Air Force Instructions (AFI) 37-131, paragraph 10.5. The Deputy Director wrote in part:

Release of this information would have a stifling effect on the free and frank expression of ideas and opinions of Air Force officials...and Release of these portions of the safety report, even though the report is old, would jeopardize a significant government interest by inhibiting its ability to conduct future safety investigations of Air Force aircraft mishaps. Disclosure of this information would be contrary to the promises of confidentiality extended to witnesses and investigators. There was not a time limit placed on this promise, and such a disclosure could set a precedent that would result in a weakening of the process whereby the Air Force gathers and evaluates safety information in future aircraft mishaps. The decreased ability of the Air Force to gather and evaluate safety information would result in the increased loss of aircraft and crew members and ultimately have a detrimental effect on national security.

Additionally I was informed that:

The statements of witnesses giving unsworn testimony before the safety investigating board, as well as any direct or implied references to such testimony, are exempt from disclosure under the United States Code, Title 5, Section 552(b)(5), and AFI 37-131, paragraph 10.5. In order to promote full disclosure, witnesses are promised by the mishap investigation board that their testimony will be used solely for mishap prevention and for no other purpose. This promise of confidentiality is made in order to encourage witnesses to disclose to the investigating board everything they know about the mishap even though the statements they make may be against their personal interest or possibly incriminating.

Information from the Life Sciences Report is exempt from release under the United States Code, Title 5, Sections 552(b)(5) and (6), and AFI 37-131, paragraphs 10.5 and 10.6. Disclosure of this information would result in an unwarranted invasion of personal privacy.

In April 1997 I submitted an appeal to the Secretary of the Air Force requesting that the decision not to release the safety investigating boards analysis, findings, and recommendations regarding the loss of 55-5262 be reconsidered. I based my appeal on the following points:

The length of time since the incident (thirty years).

The type aircraft involved in the mishaps have long since been withdrawn from service.

The early warning radar missions previously flown by that type aircraft were not covert in nature.

The cold war has subsided and our former foes no longer are the focus of the threat we guarded so diligently against by flying the early warning radar missions.

A good percentage of the individuals from whom the investigating board may have taken testimony and a good percentage of the members of the investigating board of inquiry probably are now deceased.

All the officers and airmen aboard aircraft 55-5262 lost their lives and a mystery remains how the loss could have happened.

The families and descendants of the men who lost their lives need to know what caused the loss.

Communications indicating that the aircraft was in trouble never were received.

As a former crew member on those type aircraft I am aware that the radio operator had the responsibility for setting the Selective Identification Equipment (SIF) for radar identification of the aircraft to ground radar stations tracking it. This setting also could readily and immediately be changed to reflect emergency conditions existed, yet this did not occur.

The radio operator had access to several Ultra High Frequency (UHF), Single Side-Band (SSB), and High Frequency (HF) radios as well as an automatic keying toggle switch which was within reach and which, when thrown, would automatically transmit an emergency message.

The radio operator was required to maintain constant communications with the radio ground stations by HF radio.

The radar crew maintained constant communications with radar ground stations by UHF radios.

The pilot and co-pilot had access to several radios.

The aircraft was constantly under radar surveillance by the 35th Air Division's radar. The crew positions named above were located in different sections throughout the aircraft, and radios worked on different aircraft electrical systems.

Altimeters were located at different crew positions throughout the aircraft, and individual crew members could have detected unannounced changes in altitude had a pilot fallen asleep at the controls and the aircraft descended into the ocean. This obviously did not occur as the last radio message received from the aircraft was that it had just reached its assigned altitude and arrived on station when it was lost from radar.

All crews flying those type aircraft were well and regularly trained in emergency radio transmission procedures pertaining to in-flight emergencies and ditching at sea.

Emergency communications would have been expected and should have occurred had there been trouble of any kind. Emergency messages would have been transmitted had there not have been something happened so quickly and perhaps violently from an internal or external source that immediately incapacitated all of the nineteen crew members or caused a total power failure.

The following chronology of time on 11 November 1966 was extracted from the History Of Flight (furnished by the Air Force under the Freedom of Information Act). Eastern Standard Time (EST) is shown when radar and/or radio communications were made with or by aircraft 55-5262, as well as when visual sightings were made immediately prior to the aircraft impacting into the ocean.

0037 The aircraft takes off from Otis AFB en route to Station # 2.

0040 The aircraft establishes UHF radio contact with the 35th Air Division and radar tracking of the aircraft commences. Radio checks with the Air Division were conducted on three UHF radios.

0114 The aircraft makes a radio report by UHF radio to Boston Center reporting it is passing through 13,400 feet climbing to 15,000, the flight level it was cleared to fly and maintain.

0117 The radio operator aboard the aircraft reported to Andrews

Airways Military Relay Facility by High Frequency radio the same information.

0122 The 35th Air Division radar tracked the aircraft and showed it had reached Station # 2 at that time. Operations aboard the aircraft were determined to have been normal as the radar showed that the radio operator had positioned his Selective Identification Equipment (SIF) switch from Mode 3, code 1100 to Mode 3, Code 0000, the normal code for Station operation.

0124 The 35th Air Division Radar showed the aircraft to be on track center-line of Station # 2 still transmitting Mode 3, Code 0000.

0125 The 35th Air Division Radar Input Countermeasures Officer lost all radar contact with the aircraft. Attempts to make radar and radio contacts with the aircraft were unsuccessful.

0126 A crew member from a fishing vessel, the Stephen R reported an aircraft passed overhead at approximately 200 feet going in a northeast by due north direction. The aircraft appeared to be in level flight, navigation lights on, and emitting a smoke or vapor trail.

Two miles beyond the Stephen R the aircraft passed directly over the fishing vessel Terra Nova at an estimated altitude of 150 feet, wings level, red and green navigation lights on, and an engine or engines back-firing.

0127 The aircraft struck the water approximately 3/4 to 1 mile past the Terra Nova and an explosion and fire resulted.

I appealed to the Secretary that the release of the information would not in any way decrease the ability of the Air Force to gather and evaluate safety information, as alleged, release of the information would not in anyway result in the increased loss of aircraft and crew members, as alleged, and release of the information would not have a detrimental effect on national security, as alleged.

Although I later wrote the Air Force Chief of Staff and the Secretary of Defense, a final decision subsequently was made by the Air Force regarding my appeal.

The Air Force, following time-tested procedures, does not release the causes of aircraft crashes.

NOTE: In March 1998 I made a request to the Central Intelligence Agency (CIA) under the Freedom of Information ACT (FIOA) for information that Agency may have pertaining to the loss of a United States Air Force aircraft, Lockheed Super Constellation, Radar Patrol plane EC-121H, Number 55-5262, on November 11, 1966.

On September 10, 1998, I received notice from the CIA that my request (F-1998-00629) had been processed and "No records responsive to your request were located".

During my research I located Colonel John H. Pease, USAF Retired, who headed the Board of Inquiry regarding the loss of 55-5262. He wrote:

> *I have scanned the materials you have forwarded on the various EC-121 accidents. Unfortunately time has about erased all memory and I can't be very helpful. The official accident reports, which may be difficult to obtain from the USAF, are the only specific facts available. As I recall, the Inquiry Boards had access to all aircraft and engine records as well as experts from the manufacturers concerned. No discernible pattern could be determined at that time other than what was normally expected from similar tactical operations. Thus, in my inquiry, the cause of the accident remained unknown. Years later, I heard that a problem with the Power Recovery Turbines (PRT) was ascertained. The PRTs could rupture from fatigue causing shrapnel to penetrate the wing's leading edge where the main fuel lines to the engines were. This could cause a catastrophic fire and accident. Undoubtedly this was the cause of some accidents. Sorry I can't be more helpful.*
>
> John H. Pease
> Colonel USAF - Retired

A. J. NORTHRUP - SMSGT - USAF Retired
IF YOU HAVE INFORMATION PLEASE CONTACT ME AT: (850)514-7441   (850)514-7416 [FAX]
north.north@worldnet.att.net   [E-Mail]

EC-121H ELECTRICAL SYSTEM

In discussing a **theory** of what may have happened to cause the loss of 55-5262 without emergency radio communications having been received, Art Kerr, a former Instructor Pilot who flew the Super Constellation with the 551st AEW&C Wing, and Dean Boys, retired Master Sergeant who flew on them as a Radar Technician, the following data pertaining to the electrical system on the EC-121H model aircraft was developed.

The electrical system consisted of six 28 volt direct current (DC) generators. One DC *generator* was on engines number 1 and 4, and two each were on engines number 2 and 3. There were two alternating current (AC) generators on engines 1 and 4. There was one instrument *inverter* with a spare and an emergency inverter for the flight instruments only - which ran off 28 volts DC. The instrument inverter was powered from the main DC *bus*. The navigational lights also ran off the 28 volt DC system. If all DC generators were tripped the emergency inverter would be powered by the aircraft's batteries.

If the instrument inverters were lost, some of the equipment which would still operate from the emergency inverter were the AC flight instruments, engine and systems AC instruments, some navigational aids, and the public address system. All other AC supplied powered equipment would not be operational.

With the AC generators and inverters inoperable, there would be no high frequency (HF) radios, no identification friend or foe (IFF) and no ultra high frequency radios (UHF).

The discussion concluded that most likely there were no communications because all the electrics were shut down except for the emergency DC bus and the emergency inverter.

The emergency checklist for cabin or electrical fire included, in part, these steps:

2. AC Control Switch - Inverter
4. AC Generators - Tripped
5. Radio Call - Crew and Ground Station Notified (Co-Pilot)

9. All DC Generators Tripped.

Art Kerr said a crew would not make an emergency descent unless it was their only way to possibly survive an extreme emergency.

Art concluded by saying he recalled from a listing that the navigational lights were certainly on the emergency DC bus, as was the instrument inverter for flight instruments. But it was a very minimal list - just barely enough systems to get you back on the ground and only if you didn't take too much time getting there. He said communications were not a consideration, apparently, when they designed the "last ditch" emergency power system.

Bus - A point in a circuit which collects, carries, and distributes electrical currents

Generator - A device that converts mechanical energy into electrical energy

Inverter - A device that converts direct current (DC) into alternating current (AC)

COLONEL JACK JANUARY, JR., RECALLS

Dear A. J.:

I have carefully reviewed the information you sent me concerning the loss of Aircraft #55-5262 on November 11, 1966. In addition I have scratched my head to recall those events and have reviewed what few pertinent records I still possess. The total result does not provide a meaningful chapter to your book, but I will submit my random thoughts on the subject.

> 1. No one on this Planet was more concerned about what caused the Connie accidents than the Commanders and men who flew repeated missions on these aircraft. (4,300 of my 10,800 military flying hours were in the Connie.)
>
> Causes of aircraft accidents are generally determined by physical evidence at the crash site, a record of radio transmissions received from the aircraft before the crash, survivor accounts of events leading up to the crash, and eyewitness reports. In the case of 55-5262, the only conclusion that could be reached after a review of all factors was that the aircraft did crash and that there were no survivors. Any other conjecture is pure guesswork, and that includes my input.
>
> 3. My guesswork is influenced by two incidents that I experienced.
>
>> A. On a day when the ocean was as smooth as glass, I was the pilot at the controls of a C-47 when a series of unthinkable material failures forced a ditching with 13 folks aboard. As the aircraft entered the water, the passengers could see a fine spray over the wing surface and then an abrupt stop. Speed dropped from 100 MPH to 0 MPH in an instant. (One aircraft manual I remember said, "An aircraft hitting a brick wall will bounce and will lose speed with each additional bounce. An aircraft hitting

the water will stop in an instant.") True, in this case with ideal conditions, no injuries were experienced.

B. On a bright sunny day when there wasn't a cloud in the sky, I was the Aircraft Commander of a Recon Connie in Southeast Asia when the unthinkable happened again: All four engine propellers went to the full feather position, resulting in no generated electrical power and no hydraulic boost for flight controls in addition to the obvious----no stay aloft power. (With the loss of hydraulic boost, the flight controls are virtually frozen until action is taken to by-pass the hydraulic system.) After about 40 minutes or so of button pushing and nail biting, we landed safely with 19 uninjured but shaken crew members aboard. (Daytime, ideal weather.) After weeks of investigation by a team of Lockheed Technical Representatives, the results were: No reason found to explain why all four engine propellers suddenly went to full feather. No record at Lockheed of this ever happening before. The next several pages elaborated on what caused some normal and emergency systems to malfunction once the unexpected and unexplained did, in fact, happen. Crew member mistakes were made but did not affect the happy outcome.

It is written that crashes of airborne aircraft are generally the result of a combination of worsening conditions and not just the result of one terrible event (pre-terrorism).

Before the first Connie ditching at Otis, no one had ever attempted to ditch one. The airlines had used Connies for years. The curved-down nose always appeared to present a "dig in" ditching problem, but who knows? No tests were ever performed on a Connie.

5. *Guesswork:* Now let's just return to the night of Nov. 11, 1966. This particular Connie was loaded with

complex electronics gear and enough fuel to last most aircraft for a flight halfway around the world. Experience total electrical generator/alternator failure, unexpected but not impossible as proven on my Southeast Asia experience, and all but a few emergency lights and instruments work. You are surrounded by total darkness. The flight crew is concentrating on keeping the aircraft airborne. Crew members have nothing but their flashlights (if they can find them). There is no radio contact. With your headphones on, you can hear your mike key, but no transmissions reach anyone. In the darkness and excitement, some switches may have been turned off or on that should not have been. Other problems develop: control may have been lost, the aircraft may have stalled and valuable altitude lost in seconds. Well---perhaps, but then again, perhaps not. We have nothing to indicate what catastrophic events took place aboard that aircraft.

I believe they did experience complete generator/alternator failure. (My Southeast Asia experience occurred after the loss of 55-5262. This hindsight and years of reasoning was not available to the crew.) I believe they did attempt to ditch the aircraft after they had regained enough control, but ditching a big heavy aircraft at night with sea swells would be very difficult. (Remember the sudden stop.)

My guesswork may be right, but then again, it may be wrong. The facts are probably a little of each. We will never know.

6. So much for 55-5262. Now, I would [like] to tell you a bit about me and my desires for this submission. I am almost never politically correct and I have been known to be brutally honest. I like to deal in facts. In the case of 55-5262, there isn't much in the way of facts, so I have clearly identified my guesswork. I submit this to you for your information in the hope that it will assist you in your endeavor.

I now want to comment on my most precious award. This award was not a medal, not a written citation, but a statement I overheard while turning off the runway after the Southeast Asia experience. I will never know which crew member bestowed this honor on me, but I will never forget his words: 'Thank God for Col January.'

Jack January, Jr.
December 27, 1998

Jack January, Jr.
Colonel USAF - Retired
179 Ramada Lane, Aptos, CA 95003

NOTE: Colonel Jack January was the Commander of the 961st AEW&C Squadron at Otis AFB when 55-5262 was lost with its entire crew of 19 men on November 11, 1966. Fourteen of the crew members were assigned to the 961st and 5 were assigned to the 551st Electronic Maintenance Squadron.

Colonel January commanded the 961st from June 1966 - April 1968.

Korat AB in Thailand is where Colonel January departed from on a reconnaissance mission along the Vietnam border when he experienced the feathering of all four engines of the Connie. He flew the aircraft for approximately one hour and landed it at DaNang AB in South Vietnam. For his flying skill and extraordinary effort in landing the plane safely he received the Distinguished Flying Cross.

3ᴿᴰ MISHAP
THE LOSS OF 53-0549
APRIL 25, 1967

CONSOLIDATED NEWS ARTICLES 53-0549
HERO PILOT HAD LONG RECORD OF BRAVERY

Boston Traveler, April 26, 1967

FALMOUTH--Colonel James Perkins Lyle, the hero pilot who kept his radar plane from crashing onto Nantucket Island yesterday, plunging into the sea instead, was a veteran of two wars and has received numerous decorations for bravery.

The Colonel, ironically, was the officer who briefed newsmen here November 11, 1966 during another such tragedy when 19 airmen died in a plane crash 120 miles off Nantucket.

Colonel Lyle was Wing Commander of the 551st Early Warning and Control Wing at Otis Air Force Base, Falmouth, Massachusetts. A spokesman said Lyle took the flight in order to fulfill Air Force requirements of a wing commander. His normal duties entail directing ocean hops from his base headquarters.

Colonel Lyle was born in Springtown, Texas, 47 years ago. He had been in the Air Force for 26 years.

A year after he graduated from North Texas State College, Denton, Texas, in 1939, Lyle entered the Aviation Cadet Program.

He graduated from flying school and navigation school and also the B-24 transition training.

In March of 1944, Colonel Lyle was reassigned to the Mediterranean Theater as commander of the 827th Bomb Squadron in Italy. While in that country, he flew 35 combat missions and had a total of 246 combat hours.

His next major assignment came in 1948 when he was sent to Itazuke Air Base, Japan, as inspector-general of the 315th Air Division.

In 1950 he was made wing inspector-general for the 8th Fighter Bomber Wing, Far East Air Force.

During the Korean War, Colonel Lyle flew 12 combat missions and 37 combat hours.

In 1954, he served as Acting Chief, Flight Branch, in the Flight Division of Headquarters USAF, in Washington, D.C.

Colonel Lyle completed a course in Spanish and was next assigned to the Republic of Honduras in 1957 as Assistant Chief of the USAF Mission there.

In 1961, he became Deputy Commander of the 522nd Airborne Early Warning and Control Wing at McClellan AFB, California. He became commander of the wing a year later.

In 1964 he was assigned to Air Defense Command Headquarters, Ent AFB, Colorado, as Director of Officer Personnel. He held that post until his assignment to the 551st Airborne Early Warning and Control Wing at Otis on July 22, 1966.

Among his decorations are, Distinguished Flying Cross; Air Medal with three oak leaf clusters; Bronze Star; Air Force Commendation Medal; Army Commendation Medal; Presidential Unit Citation with one oak leaf cluster; Korean Presidential Unit Citation, and the French Croix de Guerre with one palm.

The Colonel is married to Juanita (Musgrave) Lyle. He has two children, James L. 22, and Jana, 15.

Today, newsmen who were present during last November's crash, recalled how visibly shaken Colonel Lyle was during a news briefing.

Colonel Lyle was one of those who worked for the establishment of a memorial park at the base in tribute to the 19 who lost their lives in 1966 and the 16 other airmen who died in another crash on July 11, 1965. During memorial services for the victims of the 1966 crash, Colonel Lyle presented each next of kin with a flag.

ENGINE DISINTEGRATING - HOLE IN WING
Witnesses Watch In Horror
BOSTON TRAVELER

NANTUCKET------Two fishermen and a veteran flight instructor who had just taken off with a student witnessed the death throes of thegiant Air Force radar plane. Maxwell Ryder of West Creek Road and Ralph Handy of Somerset Rd. were fishing at 7 p.m. from the shore near Madaket Harbor. "We saw a plane with one engine disintegrating heading right for us," they both said. "When I looked up," Handy said, "I could see a hole in the wing, the pilot was trying to gun the engines to avoid hitting the houses, It seemed that he cleared them by about 200 feet. Then we saw a terrific explosion." The fishermen's wives, who were driving to the beach to pick them up, spotted the plane heading into the area where they knew their husbands were fishing.

SEES FIREBALL SKIM WATER FOR 4,000 FEET

Another eyewitness, R. Arthur Orleans of Monomoy, a flight instructor and pilot for 34 years, took off from Nantucket Airport at 6:56 p.m. in a Cessna 150. With him was a student flyer, Lyle Rickard. "Suddenly the tower ordered us to divert from the flight pattern for an emergency," Orleans said. "I pulled up, fearing that Michael Lamb, another pilot coming in for a landing, might be in trouble." Lamb, a Nantucket carpenter-contractor, was flying in from Westchester County, NY, in his Mooney single-engine plane. Then at 1,000 feet, Orleans said. "I saw this fire, obviously an aircraft fire at about 5,000 to 6,000 feet and about eight miles from the airport. At first it was small, then the smoke and fire increased. Then there was a fireball explosion. It was a tremendous thing."

"It looked to me as though at least one, possibly two, of the engines dropped off the aircraft right after the burst. And it looked like parts of the structure dropped away. Suddenly, the flame was snuffed out. The pilot turned about 90 degrees left and headed a little south of west. He went along the north shore, turning slowly and descending slowly over Madaket, the north point. He kept turning along the shore and reached the south shore of the island and appeared to be in control." About a half mile offshore he began what seemed to be a ditching attempt. "The instant he contacted water there was a tremendous burst of flame, one of the biggest things I've seen. It was just a fireball skidding about 4,000 feet along the water parallel to shore. At the end of the skid she disappeared. You couldn't see a thing. You knew she was gone."

3RD PICKET PLANE CRASH PROBED
GRIM SEARCH INTENSIFIES OFF NANTUCKET

Boston Traveler Wednesday April 26, 1967 - By DICK LAMERE and DAVE BEATON

NANTUCKET-Five Coast Guard cutters and several helicopters swept the waters off this island resort today in a grim search for a giant Air Force radar picket plane which crashed in a ball of fire last night, killing 15 of the 16 men aboard. The wreckage of the $7 million craft was believed to be about a quarter-mile off Madaket Beach in approximately 50 feet of water. An oil slick spotted at dawn today was ringed with flares. Officials reported that several pieces of debris believed to be from the plane had washed up on the beach.

By mid morning, only two bodies had been recovered. The sole survivor of the fiery crash, First Lieutenant **Joseph L.H. Guenet, 29,** the navigator, was reported in good condition at Nantucket Cottage Hospital. He was expected to be transferred to the Otis Air Force Base Hospital later today. As the search continued, a special investigation board was meeting at Otis to probe the third crash of a picket plane.

SURVIVOR WEARING EMERSION SUIT

Survivor Guenet was wearing a rubber emersion suit when he was plucked from the water. Air Force officials said crew members don the suits only in time of emergency. There had been some reports of some crew members manning individual life rafts for the ditched landing, but Air Force officials doubted anyone could have survived the flames. Had anyone escaped, he could have survived only 45 minutes in the chill 41-degree water without an emersion suit, or several hours with the suit. One of the bodies was pulled from the water by fishermen aboard the trawler Stephen R. out of New Bedford and transferred to the cutter Cape George, which earlier had picked up the other body. The two previous picket plane crashes occurred last November, when 19 men were lost, and in July of 1965, when 16 men died. Only recently, plans were announced for a memorial park for those victims at the air base.

Colonel Lyle, 47, had assumed command of the 551st Early Warning and Control Wing at Otis last July. He was a veteran of World War II and the Korean War, and was reported to be "one of the best-liked men on the base." During the two wars he compiled 283 combat hours as a pilot.

The plane, an EC-121 Constellation, was carrying six tons of electronic equipment and was embarked on an 18-hour mission at the time of the crash. The mission was called a "routine, active air defense" one, an Air Force spokesman said. He also said that Colonel Lyle was putting in normal flight time to maintain his accreditation as a pilot. "As commander," the spokesman said, "Colonel Lyle could schedule himself for any flight he wished."

NAMES OF CREW MEMBERS ABOARD PLANE
Boston Traveler April 26, 1967

Members of the crew, listed as missing, are:

Colonel. James P. Lyle, 47, aircraft commander, 5377 Lindbergh Ave., Otis AFB; wife, Juanita, and children, James L., 21, and Jana, 14. Hometown, Springtown, Tex.

Maj. Howard N. Franklyn, 44, first pilot, 21 Maple St., Buzzards Bay; wife Marjorie, daughter, Sandra, 20. Hometown, Medford.

Capt. Frank R. Ferguson II, 27, navigator, 5317D Arnold Ave., Otis AFB; wife, Diane, children, Daryn, 3, and Todd, three months. Hometown, Newport News, VA.

Senior M/Sgt Robert E. Mulhern, 42, flight engineer, Briarwood Ave., Hyannis; wife, Margaret. Hometown, Ft. Walton Beach, Fla.

M/Sgt Frank W. Garner Jr., 38, flight engineer, 5610A Patrick Rd., Otis AFB; wife, Shirley, daughters, Betsy, 12, and Jean 10. Hometown, Springfield, IL.

T/Sgt Gordon O. Hamman, 36, radar technician, 457 Main St., West Yarmouth; wife, Anita; children, Tina, 11; Michell, 7; and Bennie, no age. Hometown, Altoona, Pa.

S/Sgt Richard D. Bearden, 34, radar crew chief, 5547B Gibson St., Otis AFB; wife, Pauline; children, Randall, 10, and Thelma, 9. Hometown, Douglasville, Ga.

Airman 1st Class Robert J. Clapper, 25, airborne data process technician, 5615D Randolph St., Otis AFB; wife, Janice; children, Kevin, 3; Deborah, 2. Hometown, Glen Aubrey, N.Y.

Airman 1st Class Theodore E. LaPointe Jr., 25, radio operator, 163 Clifford St., New Bedford; wife, Marie; children, Theodore, 4; and Michael, 2. Hometown, Pittsfield.

Airman 1st Class William M. Walsh, 34, radar operator, 53 Carte

Real Ave., Falmouth; wife, Joan; children, James 8; Denis, 7; Ruth Ann, 5, and Kevin, 3. Hometown, Providence.

Airman 1st Class Richard D. Gravely, 26, radar operator, 108 Lock Wood Ave., Onset; wife, Louelle, son David 1. Hometown, Mabscott, W.Va.

Airman 2nd Class Dennis E. Boyle, 20, navigation technician, stationed at Otis AFB, single, from Brooklyn.

Airman 2nd Class Danny R. Burden, 22, radar technician, stationed at Otis AFB, single, from Lexington, Ky.

Airman 2nd Class William M. Cook, 20, radar operator, stationed at Otis AFB, single, from Amherst.

Airman 3rd Class Dennis R. Cole, 19, student radar operator, stationed at Otis AFB, single, from Westboro.

Rescued a short time after the crash was **1st Lieutenant Joseph L.H. Guenet**, 29, navigator, 5421C Tinker St., Otis AFB, wife, Anna Jane. Hometown, Montreal.

BLAST SAVED PLANE SURVIVOR
FOUGHT THROUGH FLAMES AS 15 AIRMEN DIED
By DICK LAMERE and DAVE BEATON

NANTUCKET-- "All I can remember is being thrown out of the plane, getting under the flames on top of the water, and then coming up, kicking like hell and shouting to the helicopter overhead." Those were the words of Lt. Joseph L. H. Guenet, only survivor of the fiery crash of an Air Force radar picket plane off the coast here last night. Fifteen of Guenet's fellow crew members apparently were trapped in the wreckage in 50 feet of water a quarter of a mile from land. Guenet told two Air Force officers he recalled "clutching a piece of wreckage right in the middle of the flames and kicking like hell." He said he could remember nothing else about the crash.

Only two bodies have been recovered from the frigid waters, and a pending storm may seal the fate of the others forever. Search vessels pushed their efforts to the limit today in an effort to locate the wreckage before the storm strikes tonight. The giant plane plunged into the ocean in a ball of fire shortly after 7 last night. Residents and eyewitnesses credited the pilot with ditching the plane in an heroic effort to avoid slamming into homes on the summer colony. The wreckage of the $7 million craft was believed to be about a quarter-mile off Madaket Beach in approximately 50 feet of water. An oil slick spotted at dawn today was ringed with flares. Officials reported that several pieces of debris believed to be from the plane had washed up on the beach. By mid-morning, only two bodies had been recovered.

As the search continued, a special investigation board was meeting at Otis to probe the third crash of a picket plane from Otis in less than two years. The two previous crashes, in waters on the other side of Nantucket, claimed 35 lives. The investigative team is being headed up by Col. Albert Evans of the 21st Air Division, McGuire Air Force Base, N.J. Last night's crash occurred at 7:05, less than 10 minutes after the huge, expensively-equipped plane had taken off from Otis. Two minutes before the crash, the pilot, Wing Commander Colonel James P. Lyle, reported fire in his number three engine, and radioed the base he would attempt a landing at Nantucket airport.

Eyewitnesses said the plane belching flames, was in "steep descent position," heading for runway six at that airport, when it suddenly veered 180 degrees and headed for open water. Air Force officials speculated Col. Lyle realized than any attempt to land at the airport could endanger scores of homes in the area, and that he decided to ditch the plane at sea.

One eyewitness, Rene A. Orleans, said the plane "skidded along the water for about 4,000 feet and when it hit there was this huge burst of fire and a big red fire-ball." Both Orleans and another pilot, Michael Lamb, were airborne at the time of the crash. Lamb said he followed the plane and saw it "descend rapidly amid a glare of fire in the water". "There was a ball of flame and fire that spread out for 200 yards," Lamb said. "You could see the flames silhouette the plane on the water. It stayed on top for no more than a minute."

Albert L. Manning, another pilot, witnessed the crash from the kitchen of his home. "I am convinced that this boy fought desperately to get the plane into the water to avoid this summer colony," Manning said. He said he heard a roar over his home about 7 p.m. and when he looked out, he saw the plane was on fire and the engines were revved up to full speed. "I followed it and watched it drop in the water. It exploded about a quarter of a mile off shore. The roar of the engines shook my entire house. Plates rattled."

Guenet was pulled from the frigid waters by a helicopter about 20 minutes after the crash. He was clinging to debris. He was treated at the Nantucket Hospital for burns on the right side of his face, cuts, bruises and shock. Survivor Guenet was wearing a rubber emersion suit when he was picked from the water. Air Force officials said crew members don the suits only in time of emergency. There had been some reports of some crew members manning individual life rafts for the ditched landing, but Air Force officials doubted anyone could have survived the flames. Had anyone escaped, he could have survived only 45 minutes in the chill, 41-degree water without an emersion suit, or several hours with the suit.

One of the bodies was pulled from the water by fishermen aboard the trawler Stephen R. out of New Bedford, and transferred to the cutter Cape George, which earlier had picked up the other body.

The two previous picket plane crashes occurred last November when 19 men were lost, and in July 1965, when 16 men died. Only recently, plans were announced for a memorial park for those victims at the air base. Col. Lyle, 47, had assumed command of the 551st Early Warning and Control Wing at Otis last July. He was a veteran of World War II and the Korean War, and was reported to be "one of the best-liked men on the base."

AIR SURVEY SHOWS NO SIGN OF PLANE
Boston Traveler April 26, 1967 By DICK LAMERE

NANTUCKET--Hundreds of feet below our single-engine plane bright yellow markers billowing grey smoke showed the approximate position where the radar picket plane from Otis Air Force exploded in a deadly nightmare that took 15 lives last night. As we passed over the scene of the disaster, I had hopes that the stricken giant Constellation might be seen in 50 feet of water--an estimated quarter of a mile off the westerly tip of the famed summer resort. No such luck. Instead, the green colored choppy waters completely hid the exact location of the ill-fated plane. In the air with us were several Air Force, Navy and Coast Guard helicopters and patrol planes, cris-crossing a 10-mile stretch along the coast as they searched for the bodies of the 13 victims still missing.

Our plane was at least 800 feet in the air above the search scene at all times, leaving the lower altitudes to the helicopter crews to skim the surface in their attempts to pinpoint the disaster. As the hours passed, it was apparent that the majority of the crew members in the downed plane were still trapped inside the wreckage lying on the ocean's floor. The only survivor, the plane's navigator, apparently was catapulted out of the plane as it burst open during an explosion as it hit the water. The bodies of two of the victims were found floating in the icy cold water. "The explosion sounded like a plane breaking the sound barrier with tremendous force," noted a companion, Capt. Parker Gray, USNR (Ret.) an old-timer who flew some 26,000 hours with the Navy and now resides on Nantucket.

A Coast Guard buoy tender directly below our plane apparently was directing the search mission which was pressed to the hilt as the weatherman reported rain and possible snow as a forecast for tomorrow. Foggy, overcast conditions tomorrow, it was feared, might hamper the search. From our vantage point, it was evident that the search teams wished to bring their grim mission to a speedy conclusion. Our plane joined the search while in the disaster area--all hands straining their eyes as they gazed down on a beautiful stretch of coastal water, hoping for a quick, pinpoint location.

PLANE BIG BALL OF FIRE BEFORE IT DISAPPEARED

Boston Traveler April 26, 1967 - [Michael Lamb, 35, of Hummock Pond Rd., Nantucket, a carpenter - a contractor, was returning home from Westchester County, N.Y., in his Mooney single engine plane about 7 last night. He told this story to Traveler Reporter Dick Lamere.]

I saw something that looked like a bright light about 2,000 feet in the air. It seemed peculiar but I didn't realize it was a plane in distress. I called the tower at Nantucket Airport and they advised me of an emergency. They advised me to keep the plane in sight and I followed it.

It made one turn about five miles from Nantucket and then proceeded northerly. Then it made a 180 degree turn and proceeded southerly to the west end of Nantucket. Just before hitting the water off Long Pond, there was an explosion in the plane and it plunged into the water and sank. I couldn't see any signs of survivors. All I can remember is that big ball of flame and seeing it sink.

RUBBER SUITS COULD SAVE MEN IN WATER
Boston Traveler April 26, 1967

OTIS AFB--What are the chances for survival in the water off Nantucket? Colonel John M. Konosky, Vice Wing Commander at Otis Air Force Base, said that without special apparel a man can live only 45 minutes in that particular water. However, he said that with the rubber suits issued crew members a man could survive several hours in the chill water. The colonel said the indications were that crew members of the crashed plane had time to don their survival suits before going into the water. They usually are kept at the feet of the crew members during flight.

WRECKAGE DEBRIS PLACED UNDER GUARD

NANTUCKET--A military guard was assigned to keep watch of the wreckage from the radar plane which crashed into the sea yesterday a mile off this island's coast. The guard was mounted by the Air Force pending today's arrival of an Air Force team assigned to investigate the crash. The wreckage consists of pieces of debris plucked from the chill waters off Nantucket by Coast Guard crews, and some pieces found strewn along the coast for a distance of a mile and a half. The wreckage had been stored in a building at Nantucket Airport.

EVERY WIFE KNEW AND HAD TO WAIT
Boston Traveler April 26, 1967-By Paul Sawin

OTIS AFB--At five minutes after seven last night, most of the Air Force wives who live here or nearby were washing the supper dishes. Their children were doing homework or watching TV. It was a typical Tuesday night. Somewhere over the Atlantic, approximately 64 Air Force men were flying missions in radar picket planes. Most of them had wives and children at home. It is possible that manymore men from Otis were flying at five minutes after seven. On each mission, four planes are always in the air. Four planes could be starting missions as four others are finishing up. Each plane on an average carries 16 men. And wives always know in advance when their husbands are on missions. But at 7:05 p.m., the wives and children here knew nothing of the disaster off Nantucket. It was almost 8:15 p.m. when the bulletins started coming over TV and radio. Then the wait began. Every wife who knew her husband was flying had to wait. They had to pray and hope that the phone would not ring, that a chaplain or a friend would not come to the door. In the base headquarters, about the same time, two squadron commanders, Lt. Col. Earl E. Putnam and Maj. Butler Reed Jr., six chaplains and a number of other officers were meeting. They were deciding how to tell 15 families about sudden death. Twelve of the crewmen were married. One survived and 11 died. The four single men aboard were dead, too.

At least three officers were assigned to notify in person each family. It took some time to do this. The last personal notification could not be made until 2:30 this morning. That was because the family lived some distance from the base. This is the way, most of the time, that wives and parents of Air Force men are told about death.

Last November 11, however, one man, took it upon himself to notify all the families of the 19 men who died when another radar picket plane crashed off Nantucket. That man was Colonel James P. Lyle, the 47-year-old commander of the 551st Early Warning and Control Wing.

Last night, some other officers had to go to the colonel's house and tell his wife, Juanita, that her husband, the father of her children, James 21, and Jana, 14, was dead.

CRASH SPURS DRIVE FOR MEMORIAL PARK
Boston Traveler April 26, 1967

FALMOUTH - Air Force personnel at Otis Air Force Base, who started a fund drive recently, had an added incentive to spur their efforts today. When announced originally, the drive was for $24,000 to establish a memorial park on the base for 35 airmen lost in crashes of early warning planes in July 1965, and November 1966. Last night the fiery crash of still another Air Force radar plane off Nantucket Island added possibly 15 more names to the memorial roster. Plans for the park include setting aside and developing a 15-acre tract between the bachelor officers' quarters and the base housing area and adjacent to Osborne Pond as a recreation area for base personnel. Dedication of the memorial is scheduled for July 4.

WEATHER IS IDEAL AS SEARCH CONTINUES
Cape Cod Standard-Times April 26, 1967

WOODS HOLE - Weather conditions at the site of the tragic crash were ideal as an armada of surface vessels and aircraft combed the Atlantic Ocean for survivors and traces of wreckage from the plane. Coast Guardsmen at the scene reported unlimited visibility, a 15 knot southwest wind with waves of between three and five feet high. Temperature was a nippy 43 while the water temperature was listed at 41 degrees - an ominous threat to any of the possible survivors who might not have had time to don their exposure suits before hitting the water. "The search is being concentrated in an area five miles in diameter." Coast Guard Lieutenant Maurice R. Dumas told newsmen who remained on vigil throughout the night at the base public information office. Lieutenant Dumas drove from Boston early last night to act as a liaison man with the Air Force officials who huddled behind closed doors in the base command center. He said seven Coast Guard cutters, a fixed-wing aircraft and seven Coast Guard and Navy helicopters "are conducting an intensive search of the area. The site of the search area may be increased as the hunt continues," he admitted. Lieutenant Dumas said the 210-foot cutter Active of Newcastle, N.H., was directing the operation. Captain of this vessel is Commander W. G. Dick. Queried as to what the planes and ships were using to illuminate the off-shore waters, he said "parachute flares dropped from the helicopters and amphibious aircraft."

Lieutenant Dumas was accompanied to Otis by Lieutenant Al Smith, Senior controller of the Coast Guard Search and Rescue Center at Salem. Lieutenant Dumas is assigned to First District Headquarters in Boston. Both men were forced to drive to Otis as all available aircraft had been diverted from the search and rescue center before their departure.

PILOT AVOIDS BEACHFRONT HOMES; HITS SEA IN 'BALL OF FLAME'
Cape Cod Standard-Times April 26, 1967

There were several eye-witnesses to yesterday's fiery Otis-based radar picket aircraft crash off Nantucket. A private flier saw the Warning Star loop away and come back in the air. Residents of Nantucket saw the aircraft steered away from homes on the beachfront and a mother putting her son in bed actually saw the crash a quarter of a mile off shore. Michael O. Lamb, 36, a Nantucket general contractor, has been flying a private plane for 20 years.

SAW BRIGHT LIGHT - Tuesday night, as he was coming in for a landing at Nantucket Airport with two passengers, he noticed a "bright light." The veteran pilot suddenly found himself trying to help out in an emergency situation. The Nantucket airport tower asked Lamb if he could keep an eye on the radar picket plane. Lamb said the Air Force plane flew in a straight line parallel to Nantucket Sound, made a long loop away and from the airport then came back as if to make another approach.

AT THE SAME LEVEL - At this point, Lamb was less than a quarter of a mile from the EC-121H... at the same level. "He was descending rapidly," Lamb said. "He crossed Madaket and headed toward the Atlantic". It was at this point Lamb and his passengers said they saw the glare of the fire in the water. "It hit in a ball of flame and the flames spread out for 200 yards. You could see the flame and the silhouette of the airplane."

AIRCRAFT DISAPPEARED - Lamb said the plane stayed up for less than a minute and then disappeared. He said he flew several passes over the area, some as low as 25 feet, "but all we could see was the burning debris." Rene Orleans, 49, a flight instructor was flying with another man off Dionnes Beach when he saw the plane burst into flames and its engine drop. His wife, who witnessed the crash from her home, said she heard the explosion, saw the fire, and watched the engine and other parts fall. At Cottage Hospital, a score of local men lined up as volunteer blood donors.

PLUCKED FROM SEA - The crewman was plucked out of the water by a helicopter, dropped off at Nantucket Airport, and rushed by ambulance to Cottage Hospital. An emergency landing area was set up at the municipal airport in the event more survivors were brought in.

Albert I. Manning, a member of the Nantucket Airport Commission, lives near the crash scene. He said the pilot made a desperate effort to swing away from homes and in the direction of the airport. "He was following Madaket Road toward the airport and losing altitude rapidly. About a mile from Madaket Beach, the planes' altitude had dropped to 100 feet. The vibration was so great, it shook our house, rattled the dishes and moved the furniture."

RUSHED TO DOOR - Manning rushed to the door and looked up to see the entire right wing in flames. Manning's wife ran to the front door and looked out. "My God," she exclaimed, "It's on fire. . . it's a huge plane."

"It was right at 7 p.m.," said Mrs. Sidney Mancovsky of Madaket. "I was putting my son to bed-and you know how that is-and that's when I heard this tremendous noise, a horrible roar of engines." Mrs. Mancovsky, 29, said she rushed to the nearby window. "Then I ran outside. I saw flames coming out of the bottom of the plane between the wings. I somehow knew it was going to crash and it did."

BURNED FOR 10 MINUTES - "The plane burned for about 10 minutes and then there was nothing but a column of smoke," said George Hamblin, Nantucket's assistant fire chief. He and 200 others kept looking into the darkness for signs of life.

Maxwell Ryder of Nantucket said, "While we were fishing in the Nantucket section we saw this aircraft off the Dionnes Beach coming to the south and we thought, Ralph Hardy was fishing with me, that we saw a flare at first, but then there was this ball of fire that seemed to drop from the plane and down to the ground. The plane kept on coming directly towards us losing altitude all the time and went directly over us. I would say about 400 feet above us and the inboard engine on it, or where the inboard engine was, the fuselage was all exposed and it was all afire. When the plane was directly over us the pilot seemed to 'rev' the engine a little like he was trying to get clear of the Madaket houses. He looked like he might have been trying to put it down on the water there but he started to descend quite rapidly and when he hit the water it exploded on impact. All we could see was about 100 square yard area of nothing but debris and flame on the water."

Mrs. Anthony Ostrowski of Nantucket said - "We were sitting in our living room when we heard the plane coming over and we thought it was going to hit the house, it was so low. We ran out the back door and looked up and the plane was all aflame underneath and then it just circled and went down. We thought it was going to land on the shore but it landed about a mile out in the water. We jumped in the jeep and ran up there to see if there was anything we could do but it was so far out that we just had to sit there and watch the plane burn. It was all lit up from stem to stern and the lights inside showed all windows and there was no one coming out of it."

Art Orleans - a Nantucket flight instructor said: "I had a student and we had been shooting landings and were at the Nantucket Airport. We were ordered to clear the area for an emergency, which we proceeded to do with all dispatch and I was proceeding out on a north-northwest heading about 1,000 feet and I noticed this fire heading over me, maybe six miles to the north. The aircraft obviously was in bad trouble. The fire developed rapidly, and suddenly erupted in a fire ball - tremendous burst of flames and much smoke, parts flying and it looked somewhat like an engine parted company and fell away from the wing. The aircraft proceeded almost in a 180-degree turn, proceeded westward along what we call the north shore of the Island and passed over a section of Nantucket called Madaket. Proceeding west to an easterly-south east heading about a mile off shore and contacted the water which looked like a regular ditching procedure. When the aircraft contacted the water, it burst into flames, tremendous flames and it proceeded along the surface for about 4,000 feet. That was the end of the procedure and we saw nothing of any wreckage that bobbed up out of the water. From the time that we saw the original fireball north of the island at about 6,000 feet and after that big burst of flame and the parts falling, there were no further signs of fire until the aircraft contacted the water."

OTIS PLANE CRASHES AT SEA; 15 FEARED DEAD, ONE SURVIVES
Cape Cod Standard-Times April 26, 1967

An Editorial

THOROUGH INQUIRY URGENT IN WAKE OF 3 CRASHES

The sympathy of the entire Cape Cod Community goes out to Otis Air Force Base and the families of flyers missing in last night's plane crash off Nantucket. The decisiveness of last night's tragedy made the details all the harder to hear. Almost from the moment of the first news from Nantucket of a flaming plane diving into the sea there was little hope for survivors in large numbers. Loss of the third radar plane, coming after a decade of operation without a loss of life from 1955 to 1965, puzzles the public. The planes first came to Otis Air Force Base in 1955 and until July of 1965 operated with the regularity of a night patrolman making his rounds in the Cape town. Then 16 men were killed in a crash July 11, 1965, 19 died in an accident Nov. 11, 1966 and 15 more apparently perished last night. A total of 50 have gone down on the picket planes in less than two years. Not in a spirit of finger-pointing, but with real concern the Cape hopes the cause of the sudden reversal of the safety record will be probed deeply so as to eliminate further accidents, if possible.

If the planes are growing obsolete in service, then it is imperative that upper echelon decisions be made to eliminate the possibility of further decimation of the ranks of the 551st Airborne Early Warning and Control Wing.

Cape Cod is anxious to see a thorough investigation because it has become a matter of losing good neighbors every time the crash alert is sounded. The wing personnel have taken an active part in the life of their community. And loss of a civil leader in a village, the loss of a father of 11 children, yes, the loss of the Wing Commander hits Cape Codders in terrible fashion. It may be well that any investigation should be wide ranging enough to cover all three crashes since that fateful day in July 1965, when the series started in an attempt to access the 10-year accident-free record against that of the last 21 months.

LYLE LAUDED 19 CREWMEN
CONDUCTED SERVICE AFTER '66 DISASTER
Cape Cod Standard-Times April 26, 1967

OTIS AIR FORCE BASE - Colonel James P. Lyle had only assumed his new duties as commander of the 551st Airborne Early Warning and Control Wing for a few months when he was called upon to perform a tragic mission last November. It was with heart-felt emotion that he conducted the memorial service for the 19-member crew downed in the radar picket crash off Nantucket last Veteran's Day. Those who attended the service in the Otis transient alert hangar will never forget his words of quiet understanding, deep compassion and sympathy for each widow of that crew of 19. And now, hardly more than five months later, Colonel Lyle himself is listed as missing in another EC-121H aircraft crash off Nantucket. Stark reality strikes again at Otis Air Force Base and Cape Cod.

FISHING CREW AGAIN ON HAND FOR CRASH
Cape Cod Standard-Times April 26, 1967

OTIS AIR FORCE BASE- A remarkable twist of fate occurred at daybreak today when a second body was reported by base officials to have been picked up approximately one mile south of Nantucket by the fishing vessel Steven R of New Bedford. The 70 foot dragger is the same craft that was an eye witness to the November 11 [1966] Constellation crash that claimed 19 airmen's lives. At that time Gene R. Connors, Captain of the vessel, notified Otis that he saw the stricken Connie "rollover about two miles past the vessel, nose into the water and burst into flames on impact." It was not immediately known if Captain Connors was aboard the dragger last night. Otis officials said the body of the unidentified airman was transferred to the New Bedford-stationed cutter Cape George, which earlier plucked the first body from the Atlantic. In conjunction with the announcement, base officials said search operations at the scene "were being intensified" at dawn today. Participating in the stepped-up hunt were five Coast Guard cutters, two smaller unidentified vessels and three Navy and Coast Guard helicopters.

Bates, Philbin Seen On Committee
HOUSE UNIT TO PROBE NANTUCKET AF PLANE CRASH
Boston Traveler April 27, 1967

A special Congressional subcommittee will be named today to investigate Tuesday's crash of an Air Force radar picket plane in which 16 men were killed. Rep. L. Mendel Rivers (D.-SC), chairman of the House Armed Services Committee, is expected to name Reps. William H. Bates of Salem and Philip J. Philbin of Clinton to handle the probe. The subcommittee, at the request of the Massachusetts Congressional delegation, will seek to determine whether there were any similarities between Tuesday's crash and two earlier picket plane tragedies which claimed 35 lives. One of those demanding the investigation was Rep. Hastings Keith of West Bridgewater, who wants the subcommittee to settle the question whether the Constellation-121s used as radar planes are obsolete. As this probe shaped up, a special Air Force board of inquiry was visiting Nantucket to interview about 15 residents who witnessed the fiery crash. The search for the bodies of 13 men missing since the plane plunged into the Atlantic was called off at dusk last night. Officials at Otis Air Force Base officially declared the men dead after a Coast Guard plane made a final pass over the crash scene in the faint hope of spotting a flare from possible survivors. Nothing was seen. The two bodies that were recovered were identified as those of M/Sgt Frank W. Garner Jr., 38, a flight engineer, of Springfield, and Airman 1/C Theodore E. LaPointe Jr., 25, a radio operator, of Pittsfield. The lone survivor, First Lt. Joseph L.H. Guenet, 29, a navigator, of Island Pond, VT., who was blown from the plane by the explosion, is in good condition at the base hospital at Otis. Guenet was interviewed last night by Col. Albert Evans, who is heading up the board of inquiry. Earlier, Guenet had said his only recollection of the tragedy was that he was hurled into the water, and found himself beneath burning fuel. He was pulled from the water by a helicopter crew.

KEITH, KENNEDY DEMAND PLANE PROBE; AIR FORCE INVESTIGATION UNDER WAY - HOUSE UNIT TO VISIT OTIS
Cape Cod Standard-Times Washington Bureau April 27, 1967

WASHINGTON - Senator Edward M. Kennedy (D.-Mass) and Representative Hastings Keith (R.-Mass) each called on the Air Force Wednesday to determine whether Super Constellation aircraft flying radar missions from Otis Air Force Base should be grounded. The requests came after the crash Tuesday night of a Constellation from Otis which went down off the coast of Nantucket Island killing 15 of the 16 men aboard. It was the third fatal crash of an Otis radar picket plane in the last two years. A special subcommittee of the House Armed Services Committee has been appointed to go to the Cape to look into the circumstances of the crash. Representative Philip Philbin (D.-Mass), ranking Democrat on the committee, said that Chairman Mendel Rivers (D.-S.C.) designated the special investigative panel at the request of Massachusetts lawmakers. Philbin said he did not know who would be making the trip to Otis or when the group would arrive. Philbin also disclosed that the Air Force is preparing a special report on the crash at the request of Air Force Secretary Harold Brown who was said by Philbin to have raised some questions when he heard the news. The exact nature of Brown's inquiries could not be determined but Philbin said he had been promised a copy of the special report when it is submitted to the secretary. Representative Keith mourned the loss of a personal friend, Colonel James P. Lyle, who was piloting the doomed aircraft. "His heroic efforts in turning the plane to sea and avoiding a populated area of Nantucket were in the finest tradition of the U.S. Air Force," Keith said. The Congressman also extended his "heartfelt sympathies" to the families of all the men lost. "Because this is the third crash within two years of an Air Force Constellation-type aircraft flying out of Otis, I am demanding that the Air Force and the House Armed Services Committee investigate not only the cause of this crash but also the question of whether these aircraft are perhaps dangerously obsolete," Keith said.

NOT PHASING OUT - The Congressman noted, "While the commercial airlines are phasing their aging Constellations out of service, the military is still using these planes on a continuous duty basis." He said their use "might be justified by cost analysis at the Pentagon. However, cost analysis is no justification for the use of dangerously obsolete equipment by our Air Force." Senator Kennedy sent a letter to Air Force Secretary Brown, specifically requesting a broad enough inquiry to determine whether the three crashes of Otis aircraft were related. He said the Air Force has this responsibility to the crews flying these planes. An Air Force spokesman would not comment on the safety of the Constellation aircraft while the Tuesday night crash is still under investigation. He did indicate that data from investigations of the previous two accidents, in the Summer of 1965 and the Fall of 1966, would be used in the current probe.

BOARD QUERIES LONE SURVIVOR
Cape Cod Standard-Times April 27, 1967 - By A. Winfield Schley -- Cape Cod Standard-Times Staff Writer

OTIS AIR FORCE BASE - While an Air Force Board of inquiry was questioning the lone survivor of Tuesday night's fiery EC-121H crash the missing 13 members of the crew have been officially declared dead. Air and sea search operations off Nantucket were suspended late last night for the lost airmen. Meanwhile, the two recovered bodies were brought to the Woods Hole Coast Guard Base yesterday afternoon aboard the buoy tender Hornbeam.

They were taken to Otis and later transferred to the Chelsea Naval Hospital where autopsies will be performed to determine the cause of death.

TWO IDENTIFIED - The two men have been identified by Air Force officials as Master Sergeant Frank W. Garner Jr., 38, flight engineer, and Airman 1st Class Theodore E. LaPointe Jr., 25, the radio operator. The official declaration that the missing crewmen are dead brings to 15 the total number of airmen killed in the latest tragedy involving radar planes operated by the 551st Airborne Early Warning and Control Wing. Among those killed Tuesday was Colonel James P. Lyle, 37, wing commander. He was the command pilot aboard the ill-fated craft.

The lone survivor of the engine fire and subsequent explosion that racked the plane in the attempted ditching one mile south of Nantucket was being interviewed this forenoon by the especially appointed investigative board. He is 1st Lieutenant Joseph L. H. Guenet, 29, the aircraft's navigator. The eight-man board, headed by Colonel Albert Evans, Commander of the 21st Air Division at Maguire Air Force Base, New Jersey, hopefully will be able to glean from Guenet the events leading up to the third air disaster to strike the 551st Wing within two years.

50 LOST - A total of 50 airmen now have been lost in the separate crashes. Although results of military investigations are rarely made public, a special subcommittee of the House Armed Services Committee has asked for a full report of the investigation. Otis officials are expected to announce later today whether the press will be able to interview Lieutenant Guenet. The survivor was flown to Otis shortly before noon yesterday from Nantucket Cottage Hospital in a C-47 transport. He was whisked to the base hospital where he was listed in satisfactory condition. Lieutenant Guenet spent Tuesday night in the Nantucket Hospital after he was plucked from the frigid Atlantic waters soon after the crash by a Navy helicopter from Quonset Point, R.I. He apparently was thrown from the huge Connie when it exploded on impact in the attempted ditching. The board of inquiry had hoped to talk with him yesterday, but base officials said he fell asleep soon after arriving at the hospital.

RECORDS IMPOUNDED - Meanwhile, all maintenance and pilot records of the aircraft have been impounded at Otis for use by the investigative body. In other developments, it was announced today that memorial services for the lost 15 airmen will be held at 10 a.m. Saturday. Simultaneous services will be held at Protestant and Catholic Chapels on the base, a spokesman said. At 4 p.m. tomorrow a special retreat ceremony will be held at the memorial rotary circle adjacent to the wing headquarters.

BACKGROUND TOLD -The base public information office also released today the first extensive background information on Lieutenant Guenet. He first entered the Air Force in November, 1955 and served as an enlisted man until January, 1964. He entered officers training school the same month and received his commission on March 31, 1964. Lieutenant Guenet attended navigator training school at James Connally Air Force Base, Texas, and was assigned to Otis in June, 1965. He holds a Bachelor of Science degree in education from Lyndon State College in Vermont. He is a native of Montreal, Que., and makes his home at Otis with his wife, Hannah Jane, and one child.

HOPEFULLY IT PUTS OUT THE FIRE
Cape Cod Standard-Times April 27, 1967

OTIS AIR FORCE BASE- The Air Force major pointed to an illuminated switch, pushed it and remarked with a smile, "this...hopefully...puts out the fire." Major Howard N. Franklyn of Buzzards Bay was demonstrating to a reporter last week with the use of a flight simulator how engine fires in Otis EC-121H aircraft are extinguished. The mock drill became stark reality Tuesday night for Major Franklyn, first pilot, and the 15 other crew members of the downed "Connie" as the plane reported an engine fire prior to crashing. Only one survived who may know whether or not the illuminated switch on the "Connie's" control panel worked Tuesday night. It was not Major Franklyn. He is one of those listed as dead in the crash.

LOST WING COMMANDER OFTEN DEFENDED CONNIES
Cape Cod Standard-Times April 27, 1967

OTIS AIR FORCE BASE - It was his duty as wing commander. He had to do it and there wasn't any question about it. Thus it was a somber, but calm, Colonel James P. Lyle, who slowly read off the names of crew members of the EC-121H that crashed Nov. 11 last year. It seemed rather strange to newsmen Tuesday night that the wing commander wasn't present during the long wait for developments on the crash. It didn't take long to determine the reason. Although base officials wouldn't comment on it at the time, there was only one other place that the skipper would be under the circumstances...and that was on the ill-fated Connie.

CAREER OFFICER - The Texas-born career officer was a stout defender of the EC-121s. Although, in interviews, he anxiously anticipated the arrival of the new radar jets that are to replace the EC-121s, he refuted claims after the last crash that the Connies were over the hill or in bad shape. "They're well-maintained and adequately equipped" for their mission, he said, citing what he called their "defendable record." He admittedly was "a four-engine" man in preference to jet fighter piloting.

James Perkins Lyle was born in Springtown, Texas, Dec. 21, 1919. After obtaining a Bachelor of Science degree from North Texas State College, he entered the aviation cadet program shortly before World War II and later completed training in flying B-24s.

HAD COMMAND IN ITALY - In 1944, he was assigned to the Mediterranean Theater as commander of the 827th Bomb Squadron in

Italy from where he flew 35 combat missions for a total of 246 combat hours.

He was sent to Japan in 1948 where he later became wing inspector general for the 8th Fighter-Bomber Wing. During the Korean War, Colonel Lyle flew 12 combat missions and 37 combat hours.

He served in a variety of duties in the next few years in Washington, Honduras and McClellan Air Force Base, Cal., where he assumed command of the 552nd Airborne Early Warning and Control Wing in October 1963. From there he was assigned to Air Defense Command Headquarters at Ent AFB in Colorado as director of officer personnel.

In June of 1965 he became assistant deputy chief of staff, Personnel, ADC, the position he held until assuming command of the Otis Wing in July of last year.

DECORATIONS LISTED - Colonel Lyle was a command pilot. Among his decorations are the Distinguished Flying Cross, Air Medal with three Oak Leaf Clusters, Bronze Star, Air Force Commendation Medal, Army Commendation Medal, Presidential Unit Citation with one Oak Leaf Cluster, Korean Presidential Unit Citation, and the French Croix de Guerre with one Palm.

Colonel Lyle married Juanita Musgrave of Denton, Texas. They have two children, a son, James L., 21, and a daughter, Jana, 14.

Mrs. Louis Musgrave of Denton, Texas, the wife of Colonel Lyle's brother-in-law, said he had three years to go to retire and hoped to reach a promotion to brigadier general rank before then. He graduated from North Texas State University at the age of 19, went immediately into the Air Force and served so well that he was decorated by the U.S., French and Korean Governments. Although a man of medium stature, Colonel Lyle was an active man unaccustomed to sitting still, Mrs. Musgrave said. "He even helped with services at the churches on Base," she said.

PROBE FOR CAUSE
As We See It - Editorial - Boston Traveler April 28, 1967

The unusual discrepancy between the Air Force safety records on Constellation planes and the series of fatal crashes involving Constellation flights from Otis Air Force Base is ample justification for an official probe. If a pattern exists in the three fatal flights out of Otis, it should be spotted by the special Congressional subcommittee appointed for that purpose. This week's crash off Nantucket, with a loss of 15 lives, means that 50 men have died in similar accidents in the past 21 months. This figure includes the 16 who were killed in a July 1965 crash, and the 19 who died last November. The question of whether the C-121 (Constellation) may be "dangerously obsolete" has been raised by Rep. Hastings R. Keith of Bridgewater. "While commercial airlines are phasing their aging Constellations out of service," he notes, "the military is still using these planes on a continuing basis." But Air Force safety records appear to justify this use. According to the Pentagon, the C-121 has a very low accident rate, and actually shows a better safety performance than any other Air Force cargo plane. Obviously something is wrong in this picture. And since the Air Force uses Constellations 24 hours a day as Atlantic radar picket planes, it is urgent that the investigators isolate the cause (or causes) of the Otis tragedies. With so many lives at stake, this probe calls for the utmost in effort and research.

CONGRESSMEN TO OPEN CRASH PROBE MONDAY
Cape Cod Standard-Times April 28, 1967

OTIS AIR FORCE BASE - A special subcommittee of the House Armed Services Committee will arrive at Otis Air Force Base Monday to investigate the three recent crashes of EC-121H radar Constellations based here. The subcommittee was named soon after Tuesday's fiery crash that killed 15 of the 16 crew members aboard the picket plane that went down in flames a mile south of Nantucket Island. The Air Force's special board of inquiry meanwhile, reconvened today as it pressed its investigation of the tragedy.

TALK TO SURVIVOR - The eight-man board met with the lone survivor of the crash yesterday and later flew to Nantucket where eye-witnesses to the crash were interviewed. Heading the special Congressional subcommittee that will delve into the three separate crashes is Representative Richard Ichord (D. Mo.). The other member is Representative William L. Dickinson (R. Ala.). Representative Mendell Rivers (D. S.C.), Chairman of the House Armed Services Committee, armed the special subcommittee and directed it to report back its findings. Meanwhile, attempts to recover

13 missing bodies and the doomed aircraft itself have been temporarily thwarted by a violent northeast storm. Coast Guard officials at Nantucket reported early today that winds were gusting up to 70 miles an hour with turbulent seas creating waves of up to 15 feet.

SALVAGE TRY EYED - Air Force officials said the Navy Bureau of Salvage has retained a private salvage firm to attempt the salvage and recovery operation. A base spokesman also reported today that contrary to some reports, the Connies of the 551st Airborne Early Warning and Control Wing "are not grounded." This corroborates a statement made early Wednesday morning by Colonel John M. Konosky, wing vice-commander, that the mission of Otis was being carried on despite the crash. Colonel Konosky, who made the announcement shortly after disclosing that Colonel James P. Lyle, wing commander, was the pilot of the downed aircraft, automatically becomes wing commander with Colonel Lyle's death.

INTERVIEW SOUGHT - It still had not been determined as of early today whether the press will be allowed to interview Lieutenant Joseph L.H. Guenet, the plane's navigator and sole survivor of the crash. Lieutenant Guenet miraculously escaped from the plane after it exploded and perhaps holds the key to what caused the engine fire that led up to the explosion. Base officials said yesterday afternoon he was under sedation at the Otis Hospital after being interviewed by the board of inquiry.

It is at the discretion of Colonel Albert Evans, Commander of the 21st Air Division at Maguire Air Force Base, whether the press will be allowed to talk with Guenet. Colonel Evans is the president of the military investigating group.

IS SATISFACTORY - Guenet, meanwhile, is reported in satisfactory condition by Otis officials. Colonel Evans has made no announcements regarding the inquiry and none are expected for some time, a spokesman said. A special retreat ceremony is scheduled at 4 p.m. today for the lost airmen at the Memorial Rotary Circle at Otis. Memorial services will be held at two base chapels at 10 a.m. tomorrow for the 15 men. Cape civilian population will be represented by the Otis Air Force Base Advisory Commission. In Nantucket Thursday; the Chamber of Commerce sent flowers for a memorial service at the Cape Cod air base with a card reading "With humility before your bravery. Our prayers go with you." A chamber spokesman said "It seems a fact as clear as facts ever are" that the pilot tried to avoid the town.

MEMORIAL RITES HELD AT OTIS FOR 15 FLIERS
Boston Traveler April 29, 1967

OTIS AFB--Memorial services were held today for the missing 15 crewmen of an Air Force plane which went down in flames and exploded in the ocean Tuesday night. Protestant and Catholic services were held at two chapels. The plane was from the 551st Airborne Early Warning and Control Wing based here. Memorial services will be held tomorrow on Nantucket by grateful islanders whose lives were spared when Col. James P. Lyle, Commander of the 551st and pilot of the flaming plane, led the craft out to open water rather than try to land it at Nantucket Airport. Services will be held at St. Mary of Our Lady of the Isle, and the Congregational, Episcopal, Baptist and Unitarian churches.

PLANE CRASH SURVIVOR TELLS OF ESCAPE
NAVIGATOR WANTS TO FLY "CONNIE" AGAIN
Cape Cod Standard-Times May 1, 1967 - By A. WINFIELD SCHLEY Cape Cod Standard Times Writer

OTIS AIR FORCE BASE--The lone survivor of the most recent tragedy involving an Otis based EC-121H Warning Star says he has "no compunctions" about flying once again in the radar picket planes or any other aircraft. Lieutenant Joseph L. H. Guenet said that, despite the fact that three of the picket planes have crashed within the last 21 months he believes the Connies "are not obsolete or unsafe." "I feel they are basically a sound aircraft" Lieutenant Guenet told a battery of news men, radio and television cameramen yesterday in his first public appearance since he miraculously escaped from the doomed Connie.

ONLY SURVIVOR - The 29 year old navigator is the only member of the 16 man crew that survived the fire and explosion that wracked the aircraft last Tuesday as it attempted to ditch in the Atlantic one mile south of Nantucket. Asked how he managed to escape with only minor injuries from the fire that engulfed the aircraft, Lieutenant Guenet said, "I don't know. I don't understand how I cleared the aircraft if it exploded." Lieutenant Guenet was remarkably composed at yesterday's press briefing at the Otis Air Force Base Hospital considering the fact that the ordeal he survived was just five days ago. Although his face showed the effects of burns suffered from the fire that ensued after the crash the only other visible sign of his brush with death was his left arm which was in a sling underneath his pajamas and robe.

ROUTINE MISSION - Lieutenant Guenet said it was a routine Air Defense Command mission until the crew felt what appeared to be "a small explosion" as the aircraft was climbing for altitude over Nantucket. "The entire crew immediately assumed their ditching positions and prepared for an emergency landing," he said.

The Canadian-born navigator explained that the plane went into a dive soon after the explosion, but was pulled out of it by the pilot, former commander of the 551st Airborne Early Warning and Control Wing, Colonel James P. Lyle. He revealed that the crew had "between 5 and 10 minutes" warning of the impending crash and that "everyone donned their rubberized exposure suits."

VERY ORDERLY - Questioned as to what those final minutes in the air were like, he firmly said "orderly, very orderly. Captain Frank R. Ferguson 2nd, the other navigator and myself both gave the orders to get to the ditching stations and prepared for a crash. Everyone was helping everyone else, there was no panic or confusion," he said. The lieutenant vividly remembered a new crew member aboard the Connie being helped by three other veteran airmen. "There was smoke in the aircraft that ranged from light to heavy. It considerably slowed down our preparations for the ditching" he stated. Lieutenant Guenet also said he "did not know" if Commander Lyle had purposely avoided an attempted landing on Nantucket so as not to endanger the residents of the island.

NO TIME - "Colonel Lyle had no time to issue any orders as such or converse with the crew. He was too busy flying the aircraft and we were too busy preparing for the ditching to look out the window at the scenery," he averred. Had the fire extinguishing apparatus each engine is equipped with worked when the fire broke out? "I have no idea," Lieutenant Guenet answered. "This procedure is done from the cockpit." Asked if the three recent crashes that claimed 50 lives could be related in any way, he said that if a major problem should occur it logically would come when the Connies are near Nantucket. "The planes are fully-loaded with fuel and working their hardest to attain altitude. This is the most likely time that an emergency will occur," he said.

A COINCIDENCE - Continuing, the lieutenant added, "To lose this number of planes (three in 21 months) does not indicate they are obsolete, I feel it is more of a coincidence." Lieutenant Guenet said, "I remember the plane hitting something" as it attempted the Atlantic ditching. "The next thing I knew, I was swimming below a surface fire in the water. It took me some time to clear the fire," he stated. The two-year veteran of Connie flying said he thinks he was in the water for about 45 minutes before being picked up by a Navy helicopter. "I floated on my back for a while and then climbed on a piece of debris. I could see the lights and antennas on the beach. I was angry at everyone that rowed a boat as nobody was coming to pick me up," he continued.

NO CRIES FOR HELP - At no time while bobbing on the three to five foot swells did Lieutenant Guenet see any portion of the plane floating or hear cries for help from the other crew members. "There was just wreckage and fire," he declared. The only happy moment of the ordeal came when the sling was lowered to Guenet by the helicopter that picked him up. "I remember thanking God at the time," he reflected. As for the present investigation by the Air Force's board of inquiry and a pending Congressional probe, Lieutenant Guenet says he can make no recommendation to suspend or ground the aircraft. "I'm a navigator. I guide, not fly the Connies, but from what I know they are a sound plane."

WILL BE ALL RIGHT - Lieutenant Guenet admitted he still "is a little rough around the edges. However, I'm sure I'll be all right soon," he said. It was obvious the lieutenant meant what he said when he stated earlier he means to return to flying soon. "I like to fly" is the way he summed it up.

"WARNING STARS" INSPECTED
OTIS TAKES PRECAUTIONARY ACTION
Cape Cod Standard-Times May 1, 1967

OTIS AIR FORCE BASE--The vast stretches of Atlantic Ocean of the Eastern Seaboard usually patrolled round-the-clock by Otis Air Force Base's EC-121H radar Constellations are not being left unprotected with the temporary suspension of their flights. Emphasizing this point and clarifying the difference between the terminology "suspension" and "grounding" yesterday was the new commander of the 551st Airborne Early Warning and Control Wing here, Colonel John M. Konosky. "During the interim period, all other

Air Defense Command early warning and control systems throughout the United States still are in operation," he said. "These include land based radars, fighter interceptor squadrons, and Bomarc missiles along the entire East Coast." Colonel Konosky also indicated other classified defense systems he is not at liberty to divulge are in operation. The new wing commander's remarks were made at a hastily-called press conference yesterday at the wing command post. Colonel Konosky said the decision to temporarily suspend the EC-121H flights was made by him after consultation with 1st Air Force officials. "The significant point is that the aircraft are available and ready to fly in a matter of minutes if they are needed. We would not hesitate to fly them if the situation warranted it," Colonel Konosky stated. "However, as a precautionary measure we are thoroughly inspecting each aircraft at the base," he added. The move was made by the Air Force after last Tuesday's Connie crash, the third in the last 21 months. Fifteen men were killed in the mishap. The wing commander said each of the 27 "H" model Connies at Otis are being taken apart one by one by maintenance crews. "We have crews working 24 hours a day," he said, adding "the first plane should be completed today." The over-all project is expected to take "several days" the Colonel explained. "The planes will be placed back on normal flying status as their inspections are satisfactorily completed," Colonel Konosky added. "This is a total inspection of the entire aircraft, more thorough than any periodic maintenance checks they undergo." The suspension of the surveillance flights of the EC-121H aircraft marks the first time since the 551st Wing arrived at Otis 12 years ago the planes have not fulfilled their mission. Not affected by the flight suspension are the TC-121C and C-121G models of the Constellations assigned to Otis. "These aircraft are continuing to meet their flying programs in support of the wing's mission," the colonel explained.

STILL EARLY FOR DECISION ON CAUSES
Cape Cod Standard-Times May 2, 1967 By A. Winfield Schley Cape Cod Standard-Times Staff Writer

OTIS AIR FORCE BASE - The two-man Congressional subcommittee appointed to investigate the three recent crashes at Otis base EC-121H radar Constellations said here yesterday the incidents "warrant serious consideration of both Congress and the military." Although admitting "it's too early to make a determination of the latest crash," Representative Richard H. Ichord (D. Mo.) said the group will "try at all costs to determine its cause. We will follow this matter very closely and hopefully make certain the causes of all three accidents are pin-pointed," the congressman pledged.

AWARE OF BOARD - The Democratic legislator also said his subcommittee "is aware that an Air Force Board of Inquiry has been appointed and we'll follow its progress very closely." Representative Ichord and Representative William L. Dickinson (R. Ala.) make up the specially appointed subcommittee of the House Armed Services Committee that arrived here Monday. The congressmen were directed by representative Mendell Rivers (D. SC.), chairman of the committee, to investigate the three recent crashes--the latest of which claimed 15 lives last Tuesday off Nantucket. The subcommittee has been ordered to report its findings to the House Armed Services Committee.

COUNSEL, LIAISON - Accompanying the two congressmen on their flight to Otis were Ralph Marshall, a staff counsel for the committee, and Air Force Liaison Officer Lieutenant Colonel Burke. In addition to conferring with top level Otis officials, the legislators talked with Colonel Albert Evans, Commander of the 21st Air Division at McGuire Air Force Base, N.J. Colonel Evans is heading the 8-man military board of inquiry which is investigating last week's Connie crash. "The facts speak for themselves as to why we are here," Representative Ichord explained at a press briefing held in the wing command post.

COMMITTEE ALARMED - He indicated the Armed Services Committee is alarmed at the three, rapid-fire tragedies to strike Otis's 551st Airborne Early Warning and Control Wing within 21 months. "When 50 airmen and three airplanes, each valued at some $7,000,000 are lost within such a short period, such conditions warrant the serious consideration of both Congress and the military," Representative Ichord stated.

THE INQUIRER AND MIRROR
NANTUCKET, MASS
April 27, 1967

Crash of Giant Air Force Plane Off Madaket Brings Death to 15 Airmen - An Air Force Super Constellation Radar Picket Plane, out of Otis Air Force Base, roared in from the north side of the island early Tuesday night, its number three engine missing and its under belly and right wing ablaze, and crash-landed in the ocean about a mile off the Madaket shore taking 15 of its 16 crew members to their deaths. Observers saw the plane destroyed in a "ball of fire" and disappear below the surface of the water seconds after it landed.

The lone survivor, Lieutenant Joseph L. H. Guenet, 29, of Montreal, who was the plane's navigator, was plucked from a wing of the plane by a rescue helicopter and was brought into the Nantucket Memorial Airport from where he was rushed by ambulance to the Nantucket Cottage Hospital and was reported in fair condition. Lt. Guenet was transferred by Air Force plane to the Base Hospital at Otis yesterday morning. It was reported that Lt. Guenet said he was thrown out of the plane and into the water by an explosion when the plane crash landed and that he managed to climb onto a wing and hold on until help arrived in the form of the helicopter. He said he had to beat off flames from the fuel that caught fire on the water. He had burns on the face and throat and complained of an injured shoulder.

The plane was the EC121H, attached to the 551st Airborne Early Warning and Control Wing out of Otis and was piloted on the fatal flight by the Wing Commander, Colonel James P. Lyle, 47, a 26-year veteran of Air Force service.

It is the opinion of most of the people, who watched the plane as it crossed the island belching fire and smoke, that Col. Lyle was making a desperate and heroic effort to keep it above the houses in Madaket by revving the three remaining engines to get the last ounce of drive out of them. Observers at Madaket said it appeared that the plane was only about 100 feet above the houses as it headed for the water.

According to officials at Otis, the radar picket plane left the base at 6:58 p.m. on a routine air defense mission. A few minutes after departure, the plane commander, Col. Lyle radioed that his No. 3 engine was afire and he was going to try and land at the Nantucket Memorial Airport. The Control Tower at the airport gave the plane clearance for the emergency landing and kept other aircraft in the area in the air. At 7:05 the plane crashed in the ocean and exploded.

Immediately the FAA Flight Service Station, in charge of Lester Bachman, notified Otis and all units on the island of the disaster. The Navy Base, the Coast Guard, the police and fire departments, the airport crew, the Nantucket Cottage Hospital, and the Civil Defense all sprang into action in the emergency.

Helicopters were dispatched from Otis Air Force Base and the Coast Guard Base at Quonset Point, R.I., and they were joined by the patrol boat "Point Bonita" and the cutter "Cape George" as soon as they could make the long haul by water. Only two bodies were recovered from the sea, one by the "Cape George" and the other by a fishing boat, the new Bedford based "Stephen R." Patrols along the beach front found pieces of the wreckage that washed ashore and turned them over to Air Force officers who flew in here from Otis. Raymond DeCosta found a large section like a portion of the tail assembly and David Watts and James Hastings brought in a section that had a jagged metal edge that looked as if it had been cut with a large can opener.

At the Nantucket Cottage Hospital, Leroy H. True, hospital administrator, put into effect its disaster emergency plan by which all of the doctors, nurses and the staff reported for duty and prepared to take care of any survivors. Blood donors with type O negative blood, which can be administered to anyone, were called on a standby basis. It was heart warming to have so many volunteer blood-donors call in at the hospital and leave their names. After the arrival of the first and, as it turned out, the only survivor, the hospital received a report that any other survivors would be landed by helicopter on the hospital grounds. A ring of cars was placed near the auto parking space with their headlights on to mark it out for the planes which never came. Sergeant Wesley E. Simmons, of the Police Department, had charge of the placing of the vehicles.

There were many eyewitnesses to the plane disaster. One of them was Albert L. Manning, Chairman of the Nantucket Airport Commission, who with his wife, Jane, heard and saw the flaming aircraft as it passed over their home in Madaket.

Mr. Manning said he and his wife were sitting in their kitchen when they heard a loud roar approaching. He ran to the window and looked out and his wife rushed outside. "Oh! Burt, it's a big plane. It's on fire," she shouted.

Mr. Manning said he then left the house and they both watched it pass over about 100 feet above their home headed for the ocean. "We saw it go down and then a big ball of fire shoot into the air. It was all over in a few minutes. When we got to the shore there was nothing to see."

Mr. Manning said that when the plane went over it shook the house and rattled the dishes just like an earthquake. "He came right along over the houses on Tennessee Avenue and he was apparently trying to keep the plane up so it would clear the houses as it kept sounding as though the pilot was revving the engines."

Another eyewitness was Michael O. Lamb of Hummock Pond Road, who was approaching the island in his plane with Albert F. Egan, Jr., and William Yarmy along as passengers. Lamb radioed the Control Tower he was coming in for a landing and was directed to remain aloft as there was an emergency on. He said he saw the radar plane approaching and noticed a bright light on the plane which he soon made out as fire. He informed the tower he had the plane that was in trouble in sight and was asked to keep an eye on it.

Lamb said later that the plane came straight in towards the island then made a loop that carried it near the Jetties and then headed back over land near Dionis as though he was making an approach for a landing. He also said he saw something fall from the plane that he presumed was a part of an engine. "He was descending rapidly as he crossed Madaket and headed for the ocean," Lamb said.

It was at this point that Lamb and his passengers saw the glare of fire rise up from the water. "The plane hit in a ball of flame and then the flames spread out for at least 200 yards around it. You could see the flames and the silhouette of the airplane very clearly. It stayed up for no more than a minute, then disappeared." Lamb stayed in the area circling the spot where the plane went down until the helicopters arrived to take over.

Art Orleans, who was giving flight instructions to Lydel Rickard, was flying off Dionis Beach when he saw the plane burst into flames and its engine drop off into the water. His wife, Merle, who was at their home in Monomoy, looked out the window in time to see the big Constellation trailing smoke as it passed the range lights at Brant Point. Others who reported seeing the plane accident were Mr. and Mrs. Sidney Mancovsky, Douglas Williams, Maxwell Ryder and Ralph Hardy.

The airport had been a very busy place for the past two days with Air Force planes coming and going. Right after the accident a huge Globemaster plane of the Military Airlift Command that was returning to the States from the Azores was directed to land at Nantucket in case their rescue equipment was needed in the emergency.

The beaches and the waters off Madaket as far as Surfside have been combed by shore patrols and surface craft, along with helicopters, in a search for bodies or wreckage. The search was officially called off by the Air Force at 9:15 last night.

A statement was issued today by the Information Office at Otis that said: "Officials of the Otis Air Force Base have announced that the U.S. Navy has begun recovery and salvage operations in the area where an EC121H Radar Constellation crashed on April 25. All efforts are being made to recover bodies and the aircraft itself."

"First Lieutenant Joseph L. H. Guenet, sole survivor of the accident, is still at Otis Air Force Base Hospital under sedation. Lt. Guenet has been interviewed by the Accident Investigation Board but he will not be available for press interviews until further notice."

"The Accident Investigation Board convened yesterday and is presently attempting to determine the cause of the accident. Col. Albert Evans, President of the Board, has made no announcement concerning the investigation and none are expected for some time."

"Otis officials also announced that denominational services for the 15 crew members will be held simultaneously at 10 a.m., Saturday, April 29, in Chapels 1 and 2 at Otis Air Force Base. These services will be held primarily for the next of kin and military personnel. The press will be allowed at the services but no photographs will be permitted."

THE INQUIRER AND MIRROR
Nantucket, Massachusetts - May 4, 1967

Last Tributes Paid Fliers At Otis Base Ceremony - While eight hundred people listened in hushed quiet at the Otis Air Force Base, and planes hovering over the site of the crash off Nantucket dropped floral tributes, the fifteen men who lost their lives when the huge Constellation plunged into the sea were accorded a final tribute on Saturday last. The throng which joined the relatives and friends of the victims overflowed the Chapel at the Otis Air Force Base to participate in the service conducted by Lt. Col. Earl A. Mack, the Chaplain at the Base. The eulogy was delivered by Lt. Col. Deane Shiveley, another chaplain. A requiem Mass was celebrated by the Catholic chaplain, Maj. George Connelly, with about 400 in attendance. As during the Protestant service, there were not enough seats to accommodate all.

"The deceased have already written their chapter in history." Fr. Connelly said of the victims. "The living can look with pride and inspiration at that chapter."

"Who is there who can challenge the value of their worth, spirit of dedication and attitude of unselfishness?" he asked. "The peacemakers of that flight have left their loved ones a great legacy."

Among the floral tributes was a wreath bearing the following card: "With humility before your bravery. Our prayers go with you. The People of Nantucket."

Tuesday morning an Air Force C-119 "Flying Boxcar" came in, taxied over to the maintenance hangar, pivoted about and, putting the props in reverse pitch, backed up to the hangar. Military personnel then loaded various odd pieces, presumably fragments of the wrecked radar Connie, and after an hour the big Fairchild buttoned up its hinged rear end and took off. There has been a continual flow of military traffic through the airport in connection with search and salvage operations, and this will probably go on until the job is done. The wreck was apparently located and buoyed without much trouble once they set out to do that, but any extensive salvage operations will pose more of a problem. Retrieving a large airplane or large sections thereof, from open water presents all the difficulties of hoisting heavy weights in a seaway combined with the handling of low-density objects which offer maximum resistance to current and waves. Complicating it further are the facts that airframe structure must be handled very carefully to avoid further breakage and that jagged sheet metal is very dangerous for divers - or anyone, for that matter - to work around. Any salvage crew will have their work cut out for them.

....

Island Churches Offer Prayers for Lost Fliers - At morning services held Sunday, each of the Nantucket churches offered prayers in solemn memory of the fifteen men who lost their lives in the crash of the Air Force radar plane off Madaket on Tuesday, April 25. The congregations at the several places of worship were led by their ministers in services commemorating the sacrifices brought about by the tragic circumstances of the crash. The solemn character of the occasion brought to mind those times in the past when Island churches were the scene of similar observances, both in periods of war and after shipwrecks on these shores.

By co-incidence, the guest pastor at the Methodist Church was the Rev. Peter Palches, who is also one of the Protestant Chaplains at Otis Air Force Base. He had participated in two previous memorial services at Otis. His presence on Nantucket at this time made his sermon of particular significance, as he led the prayers for those who had met such an untimely ending.

Rev. Arthur Darby, at the Baptist Church, offered prayers for the lost men, and for their wives and children. He reminded that, in the decision to ditch the plane at sea, the pilot had chosen for himself and his companions certain death but by deliberate action had avoided an equal disaster on the Island.

At the Episcopal Church, the Rev. Bradford Johnson, during the course of his sermon remarked: "We find ourselves reminded that consequently the whole community is involved in the tragic catastrophe off our western shore Tuesday night, involved in tragedy and in thanksgiving. For the pilot's decision not to attempt an airport landing doubtless saved us from unimaginable loss and destruction. We cannot estimate our debt and we must not limit our gratitude."

Rev. Fred D. Bennett, of the Congregational Church, during the period of silent prayers by the Congregation at the Old North Vestry, offered: "Let us at this time silently raise up prayer to God, our Father, for those men who have perished in the air and on the seas which surround our small Island during the past week. Let us praise God for these men who, in the service of their country were quietly doing their duty and protecting our shores from possible danger. Let us raise prayers for their families and ask God's help and comfort to them. Let us humbly thank God for the courage which led the pilot to risk his life and those of the companions in order to avoid the great danger to our town had he not so decided."

At the Unitarian church, Rev. William R. Reid, in the course of his sermon, spoke of the sacrifice made by the men in the doomed plane, and of the constant price which must be paid for our freedom.

During services at St. Mary's Catholic Church, the Rev. Father Daniel Carey offered the following to the "Men of the Air Force.": "It appears to be definite that the courageous pilot of the Constellation deliberately avoided a crash landing in a populated area of the Island. God alone knows how many civilian casualties there might have been. None of us should be unaware of the gratitude we owe these men, and the gratitude we owe to God. In all our Masses today we will commemorate their sacrifice and pray to God to grant them eternal rest and peace. We will also have a Requiem Mass for the repose of their souls tomorrow (Monday) afternoon at 4:00 o'clock."

....

Radar Plane Wreckage Now Being Recovered - The submerged wreckage of the giant radar plane, which plunged into the ocean last week, carrying fifteen men to their deaths, was located off Madaket on Monday after extensive dragging operations. It lies 35 feet below the surface, obscured from sighting by the murkiness of the water. "According to reports, the fuselage is pretty well intact," Rep. Richard Ichord, D-Mo., said at a news conference before he flew back to Washington. Ichord was part of a congressional team investigating the crashes which have claimed 50 lives in 21 months.

"When we recover the plane, we have a good chance of determining the cause of the crash," he said.

A huge lighter [barge], with attendant craft, is now at the scene, with divers working steadily and if the weather holds the recovery of the battered and fire-twisted plane's fuselage is expected to be successfully accomplished during the next twelve hours.

....

Investigation of Plane Crash to be Held Here - A congressional probe of the crash of the Air Force Radar Picket plane at Nantucket is now being held. Chairman L. Mendel Rivers (Dem.-S.C.) of the House Armed Services Committee has appointed a sub-committee to make the probe.

The order for the investigation came on the heels of pleas of Senator Edward M. Kennedy (Dem.-Mass.), and Congressman Hastings Keith (Rep.-Mass) and four other members of the Massachusetts delegation in Congress that steps be taken to make sure the four-motored craft are safe for the men who fly them.

As expected, as soon as the committee was named by Chairman Rivers they flew to Otis Air Force Base.

The crash was the third in the past 21 months involving radar picket Constellation planes. A total of 50 men have been killed in the three crashes. The crash here Tuesday night widowed 11 women and left 21 children fatherless.

....

May 11, 1967 - A Life-Saving Boathouse At Madaket - During those first fateful moments, a few weeks ago, when the giant radar plane crashed in flames off Madaket, some of those who raced to the shore were suddenly conscious that there was not a single small boat at the beach available for launching. It was nearly an hour before the only survivor was plucked from the sea by a helicopter. Had there been other men trying to keep afloat in the icy water it is doubtful they could have survived during that crucial time. A difference of five to ten minutes in reaching the scene of a boating accident or a plane crash is the difference between life and death.

ISLANDERS REMEMBER THE FIERY CRASH OF 1967
From the Cape Cod Times June 23, 1996 *by Hobson Woodward*

The afternoon of April 25, 1967, was a quiet one in the hamlet of Madaket on the western tip of Nantucket. There was little hint in the air of the impending disaster that would visit the sleepy village just after 7 p.m. that evening 29 years ago. At 6:45 that night, Air Force Colonel James P. Lyle and 15 crewman boarded a Super Constellation radar picket airplane on the tarmac at Otis Air Force Base. The craft was part of an Airborne Early Warning and Control Wing, and its pilot had 26 years' experience in the cockpit. The flight was expected to be a routine one, but fate would tragically intervene.

The huge aircraft lifted off from the runway at 6:58 p.m. and headed toward Nantucket and the open ocean beyond. Almost immediately, however, the crew knew that something was wrong. Lyle radioed about three minutes out that one of his engines was on fire. He requested and received permission from the Nantucket airport control tower to make an emergency landing at the island's airport. On the ground on Nantucket, emergency crews scrambled to alert. Navy, Coast Guard, police, fire, airport, hospital and civil defense officials prepared for the worst. All eyes were on the sky as the giant airplane came in to view. "The plane came straight in towards the island, then made a loop that carried it near the jetties and then headed back over land near Dionis as though he was making an approach of a landing," the Inquirer and Mirror reported in its next edition.

The pilot of a small private plane watching from the air reported seeing an engine fall from the stricken aircraft. Apparently, the pilot either lost control of the airplane at that point, or made a decision to head for the open ocean to spare Nantucket a fiery crash. One island couple was sitting at their kitchen table when they heard what sounded like the roar of a freight train bearing down on their home. They emerged into their yard in time to see the airplane pass directly over their home, head out to sea, and hit the water about a mile off the island only seven minutes after takeoff.

Fifteen crew members perished when the plane exploded on impact. The lone survivor was the navigator, Lt. Joseph Guenet, 29. Lt. Guenet was thrown from the plane when it hit the water, and managed to swim through flaming aviation fuel to the wing of the aircraft. A Coast Guard helicopter plucked the injured man from the wreck and carried him to Nantucket Cottage Hospital. Islanders created an impromptu helicopter landing pad near the hospital by placing several vehicles in a circle with their headlights ablaze, but an exhaustive search yielded no more survivors.

A memorial service at Otis Air Force Base drew 1,200 mourners. Simultaneously, an airplane dropped memorial wreaths at the ocean site of the crash. One of the wreaths came from islanders thankful for the heroic maneuvers of Col. James P. Lyle."**With humility before your bravery,**" the tribute read. **"Our prayers go with you. The People of Nantucket - 28 April 1967."**

Col. James P. Lyle School is commemorating the heroism of this "Connie" crew on April 28 at 1:00 PM at the Lyle School. The story of the crash, several student readings, and Taps played by the honor guard of the Massachusetts Maritime Academy will be part of the tree planting ceremony in the Lyle School courtyard. This crew gave their lives to save the town of Madaket. We honor their memory.

The following inscription appears on a plaque on the base.

"In memory of the crew of Homey 82 lost in a crash at sea one mile south of Madaket Beach, Nantucket Island on April 25, 1967 during an active air defense mission for the 551st Airborne Early Warning and Control Wing."

June 19, 1997

Col. James P. Lyle	A1/C Robert J Clapper
Maj. Howard N. Franklyn	A1/C Richard D. Gravely
Capt. Frank R. Ferguson II	A1/C Theodore E. LaPointe Jr.
S/MSgt. Robert E. Mulhern	A1/C William M. Walsh
M/Sgt. Frank W. Garner Jr	A2/C Denis E. Boyle
T/Sgt. Gordon O. Hamman Jr.	A2/C Danny R. Burden
S/Sgt. Richard D. Bearden	A2/C William M. Cook
	A3/C Dennis R. Cole

Colonel J. P. Lyle Middle School is located in Bourne, Massachusetts, on Otis Air National Guard Base on Cape Cod.

Lyle Middle School was named after Colonel James P. Lyle who sacrificed his life to spare the island of Nantucket a fiery plane crash.

Bourne Middle School at Lyle
5700 LeMay Avenue

Otis ANG Base, MA 02542
(508)563-5635
(508)564-6170 (fax)

Boston Traveler articles [Reprinted with permission of the Boston Herald]
Cape Cod Times articles [Reprinted Courtesy of Cape Cod Times]
Inquirer and Mirror articles [Reprinted Courtesy of Inquirer and Mirror]

SUMMARY OF CIRCUMSTANCES - 53-0549

At 7:05 p. m. Eastern Standard Time (EST) on April 25, 1967, EC-121H serial number 53-0549 crashed and was destroyed one mile south of the western tip of Nantucket Island, Massachusetts. Of the 16 crew members aboard the aircraft, 15 were fatalities. One of the two navigators aboard survived, sustaining major injuries.

The aircraft and its crew were assigned to the 551st Airborne Early Warning and Control Wing [AEW&C] and were participating in an active air defense mission over the Atlantic Ocean [enroute to ALRI Station # 4]. The aircraft commander for the flight [who also was the 551st AEW&C Wing Commander] briefed the aircrew and completed a normal pre-flight clearance form for the mission. The pre-flight inspection of the aircraft was accomplished and no significant deficiencies were revealed. Following normal engine starts, the aircraft departed the parking ramp at Otis Air Force Base at 6:30 p.m. EST.

Takeoff was made from Runway 23 at 6:30 p.m. EST. Observed weather conditions at the time of takeoff were: four thousand feet scattered visibility nine miles and surface winds from 190 degrees at velocity of four knots. Following takeoff, the aircraft made a left turn and proceeded to Nantucket Range for a radar monitored departure. The crew members were to leave their seats to start up their equipment as the aircraft passed through 2,000 feet in the climb. The aircrew is allowed to activate all necessary equipment after passing 2,000 feet providing operation of the aircraft is normal.

At 6:58 p.m. EST, the pilot of the aircraft reported climbing through 6,000 feet and on a heading of 150 degrees. Following this transmission, he declared that he thought the number three engine was on fire and that the aircraft was returning to Otis Air Force Base. One minute later, he stated the fire was in the right wing root section of the aircraft. Although the pilot made a left turn toward Otis Air Force Base, he then elected to land at Nantucket Airport and continued his turn to a southerly heading. At this time, he was eight miles from Nantucket and 22 miles from Otis Air Force Base.

The aircraft was cleared to land on any runway at Nantucket Airport and the last radio transmission from the pilot was 7:03 p.m. EST when he requested that the runway lights at Nantucket Airport be turned on. The aircraft was observed to fly over the west end of Nantucket Island on a southerly heading and ditch into the ocean one mile south of the west end of the island. The aircraft was seen to impact the water in a flat attitude and immediately burst into flames and travel approximately 1,000 feet before submerging.

Immediately upon receiving notification that the aircraft had crashed Otis Air Force Base officials contacted the U. S. Coast Guard detachment at Quonset Point, Rhode Island. Also alerted were an Air Force and a Navy aircrew that were flying in the nearby area. Air Force and Coast Guard helicopters were dispatched and soon arrived at the crash site. All search efforts were coordinated by a Coast Guard cutter.

The search aircraft dropped flares, as it was getting dark, and also released survival equipment at the scene of the crash. One of the helicopters discovered the surviving air crewman [*1st Lieutenant Joseph L. H. Guenet - Navigator*] and accomplished an immediate rescue. The air crewman was flown to Nantucket Island for medical attention. The bodies of two crew members [*M/Sgt Frank W. Garner Jr., Flight Engineer and A/1C Theodore E. LaPointe Jr., Radio Operator*] were located and recovered by surface vessels. The other crew members were not recovered. [E.S.]

Salvage operations for the recovery of the aircraft wreckage were initiated by the Navy. The primary search area was established at two square miles with a secondary area of eight square miles. The search operations conducted by the Navy utilized nets and divers. SONAR equipment was also used. The main portion of the wreckage was located on May 1 in 50 feet of water, with water visibility of only one foot due to local storm conditions. The search, which continued for 30 days, was often hampered by bad weather or strong winds.

Search and salvage operations were finally discontinued on May 31, 1967, after the majority of the aircraft wreckage had been recovered and no additional aircrew members bodies had been located. [E.S.]

SOURCE: Department of The Air Force, Headquarters Air Force Safety Center, Kirtland AFB, NM

BOARD OF INQUIRY - 53-0549

A Board of Inquiry was formed to look into the loss of 53-0549 and 15 crewmen (one crew member survived). The Board was headed by Colonel Albert Evans Jr., of the 21st Air Division at McGuire Air Force Base, New Jersey. Others on the Board were Lieutenant Colonel Emil V. Bush, Maintenance Officer; Major William R. Willner, Pilot Member; Major Morgan G. Childs, Jr., Safety Advisor; Lieutenant Colonel Frank J. Logwin, Accident Investigating Officer; Captain Thomas L. Kelly, Jr., Medical Officer; Major Robert J. Rossitto, Recorder and SMSgt Frank T. Pilat, Life Sciences Advisor.

****

I learned that Lieutenant Colonel Bush and Major Childs are deceased as is Lieutenant Colonel Logwin.

I did locate Major Willner and spoke with him (see Board Of Inquiry 55-5262).

I was unable to locate the other members listed above.

NOTE: I had flown with Lieutenant Colonel Frank J. Logwin and Major Morgan G. Childs Jr., both of whom were pilots in the 961st AEW&C Squadron at Otis Air Force Base.

CREW MEMBERS ABOARD 53-0549
CRASHED ON APRIL 25, 1967

OFFICER - SURVIVOR

1/LT JOSEPH L. H. GUENET
FR80047
NAVIGATOR

OFFICERS - DECEASED

COLONEL JAMES P. LYLE
FR4846
AIRCRAFT COMMANDER

MAJOR HOWARD N. FRANKLYN
FV820985
FIRST PILOT

CAPTAIN FRANK R. FERGUSON
FR75950
NAVIGATOR

ENLISTED - DECEASED

SMSGT ROBERT E. MULHERN
AF12191742
FLIGHT ENGINEER

MSGT FRANK W. GARNER JR.
AF11214357
FLIGHT ENGINEER

TSGT GORDON O. HAMMAN
AF13257903
RADAR TECHNICIAN

SSGT RICHARD D. BEARDEN
AF 14494389
RADAR CREW CHIEF

A1C ROBERT J. CLAPPER
AF12623437
AIRBORNE DATA PROCESS TECHNICIAN

A1C THEODORE E. LaPOINTE JR.
AF11358214
RADIO OPERATOR

A1C WILLIAM M. WALSH
AF11298681
RADAR OPERATOR

A1C RICHARD D. GRAVELY
AF13603943
RADAR OPERATOR

A2C DENIS E. BOYLE
AF12725223
NAVIGATION TECHNICIAN

A2C DANNY R. BURDEN
AF15707069
RADAR TECHNICIAN

A2C WILLIAM M. COOK
AF11452889
RADAR OPERATOR

A3C DENNIS R. COLE
AF11960224
STUDENT RADAR OPERATOR

Photograph published in the <u>Boston Traveler</u> on April 26, 1967

Colonel John M. Konosky, Vice Wing Commander, 551st Airborne Early Warning and Control Wing, Otis Air Force Base, Massachusetts, displays a photograph of the type of radar picket plane that plunged into the Atlantic off Nantucket. Colonel Konosky became the Commander of the 551st upon the death of Colonel James P. Lyle, 551st Wing Commander, the Aircraft Commander of the ill-fated flight aboard 53-0549.

PHOTOGRAPH FURNISHED BY JAMES WALSH (SON OF WILLIAM WALSH)

TYPICAL "CONNIE" CREW <u>NOT THAT OF 53-0549</u>. WILLIAM WALSH, WHO WAS KILLED IN THE CRASH OF 53-0549 AT NANTUCKET ISLAND, MASSACHUSETTS ON APRIL 25, 1967, IS PICTURED IN BACK ROW - SECOND FROM LEFT.

PHOTOGRAPH COURTESY OF JAMES WALSH (SON OF WILLIAM WALSH)

[ON LEFT] A1C WILLIAM M. WALSH, AF11298681, RADAR OPERATOR WHO WAS KILLED ON 53-0549 ON APRIL 25, 1967.

PREVIOUSLY CONGRATULATING AIRMAN WALSH ON HIS RECENT PROMOTION IS COLONEL ROBERT KALTENBACHER, COMMANDER 551ST COMBAT SUPPORT GROUP, OTIS AIR FORCE BASE, MASSACHUSETTS.

THE PHOTOGRAPH IS DATED AUGUST 1965. THE WRITING ON THE PHOTOGRAPHS READS: *"TO A1C WALSH - MY BEST REGARDS FOR A JOB WELL DONE! I HOPE I AM ON HAND TO PIN ON ANOTHER STRIPE"*.

PHOTOGRAPH FROM <u>RECORD AMERICAN</u> APRIL 27, 1967

MAJOR HOWARD FRANKLYN [DECEASED] - FIRST PILOT ON 53-0549 - WHICH CRASHED ON APRIL 25, 1967

PHOTOGRAPHS FROM RECORD AMERICAN APRIL 27, 1967

TSGT GORDON O. HAMMAN, RADAR TECHNICIAN [DECEASED] ABOARD 53-0549 WHICH CRASHED ON APRIL 25, 1967

THE EIGHT HAMMAN CHILDREN LEFT FATHERLESS UPON TSGT GORDON O. HAMMAN'S DEATH IN 53-0549 ON APRIL 25, 1967

BOSTON TRAVELER PHOTO BY FRANK KELLY - April 26, 1967

Civilian flight instructor R. Arthur Orleans of Nantucket describes crash of Air Force radar plane off the island.

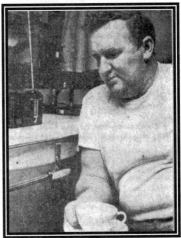

BOSTON TRAVELER PHOTO BY FRANK KELLY - April 26, 1967

Listening on radio to details of search for survivors of plane crash off Nantucket is Michael Lamb of Nantucket. He was one of two private pilots aloft at the time who witnessed the crash.

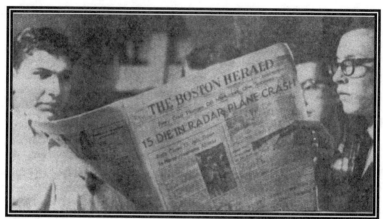

BOSTON TRAVELER PHOTOGRAPH BY JACK CONNOLLY - April 26, 1967

AIRMEN (UNIDENTIFIED) AT OTIS AIR FORCE BASE IN FALMOUTH CLUSTER AROUND NEWSPAPER REPORTING DETAILS OF RADAR PLANE CRASH OFF NANTUCKET THAT KILLED 15 OF THEIR COMRADES. ONE CREWMAN SURVIVED.

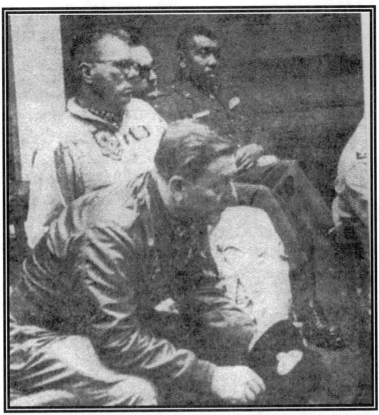

BOSTON TRAVELER PHOTOGRAPH BY JACK CONNOLLY - April 26, 1967

STANDBY PLANE CREW (UNIDENTIFIED) AWAITING ORDERS AT OTIS AIR FORCE BASE FOR POSSIBLE MISSION TO SEARCH FOR SURVIVORS OF PLANE THAT CRASHED OFF NANTUCKET.

THE COMMANDER OF THE 551ST ELECTRONICS MAINTENANCE SQUADRON (EMS) [AT REAR CENTER IN UNIFORM] MAJOR BUTLER REDD, JR., AWAITS WORD ON HIS SQUADRON MEMBERS [TSGT HAMMAN, A/1C CLAPPER AND A/2C BOYLE AND BURDEN] - THEY PERISHED.

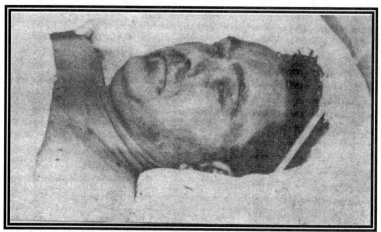

BOSTON TRAVELER PHOTOGRAPH BY FRANK KELLY - April 26, 1967

LONE SURVIVOR OF AIR FORCE PLANE THAT CRASHED OFF NANTUCKET KILLING 15 CREWMEN, LT. JOSEPH L. H. GUENET, 29, IS RECOVERING IN COTTAGE HOSPITAL, NANTUCKET.

MEMORIAL SERVICE PROGRAM FOR THOSE CREW MEMBERS WHO LOST THEIR LIVES ON 53-0549 ON APRIL 25, 1967

Memorial Service Program Provided By Dean Boys

DEDICATED TO THE HONOR AND MEMORY OF OUR COMRADES

COMMANDER, 551ST AIRBORNE EARLY WARNING & CONTROL WING

Colonel James Perkins Lyle

962ND AIRBORNE EARLY WARNING & CONTROL SQUADRON

Major Howard Newell Franklyn
Captain Frank Bailey Ferguson, II
Staff Sergeant Richard Dennis Bearden
Airman First Class Theodore Edward LaPointe, Jr.
Airman First Class William Michael Walsh
Airman First Class Richard David Gravely
Airman Second Class William Mann Cook
Airman Third Class Dennis Richard Cole

553RD RECONNAISSANCE WING

Senior Master Sergeant Robert Edward Mulhern
Master Sergeant Frank Walker Garner, Jr.

551ST ELECTRONICS MAINTENANCE SQUADRON

Technical Sergeant Gordon Oakley Hamman, Jr.
Airman First Class Robert Jeffrey Clapper
Airman Second Class Denis Edward Boyle
Airman Second Class Danny Ray Burden

THE MEMORIAL SERVICE

(As chaplains enter, congregation will please rise and remain standing.)

OPENING SCRIPTURE READING

INVOCATION

(Congregation will be seated.)

RESPONSIVE READING

The Lord is my shepherd. I shall not want.
HE MAKETH ME TO LIE DOWN IN GREEN PASTURES:
He leadeth me beside the still waters.
He restoreth my soul:
HE LEADETH ME IN THE PATHS OF RIGHTEOUSNESS FOR HIS NAME'S SAKE.
Yea, though I walk through the valley of the shadow of death, I will fear no evil.
FOR THOU ART WITH ME; THY ROD AND THY STAFF THEY COMFORT ME.
Thou preparest a table before me in the presence of mine enemies:
THOUGH ANOINTEST MY HEAD WITH OIL; MY CUP RUNNETH OVER.
Surely goodness and mercy shall follow me all the days of my life:
AND I WILL DWELL IN THE HOUSE OF THE LORD FOR EVER.

SELECTED SCRIPTURE READINGS   **PSALMS 130**
JOHN 14
ROMANS 8

SPECIAL MUSIC

MEDITATION

PASTORAL PRAYER

HYMN:					"O God, Our Help In Ages Past"

					No. 154

BENEDICTION

*****

HE IS NOT DEAD

From "Adona La"

Peace, Peace! He is not dead, he doth sleep,
He hath awakened from the dream of Life -
'Tis we who, lost in stormy visions, keep
with phantoms an unprofitable strife.....

We have out soared the shadow our night;
Envy and calumny, and hate and pain.
And that unrest which men miscall delight,
'Can touch him not, and torture not again.....

The one remains, the many change and pass,
Heaven's light forever shine, Earth's shadows fly;
Life, like a dome of many-colored glass,
Stains the white radiance of Eternity.

-Percy Bysshe Shelley

Memorial Service Program Provided Courtesy of Dean Boys

THE DEATH OF THE GREAT BIRD

*Her engines coughed and came to life
As new blood rushed through her wings.
And readied for her routine flight
while the sun slowly settled out of sight.*

EC-121H "WARNING STAR" RADAR PATROL PLANE (SUPER CONSTELLATION) FLYING OVER THE CAPE COD CANAL NEAR OTIS AIR FORCE BASE. IMAGE IS IS REVERSED.

*The sea breeze blew across the field
As the great bird climbed aloft.
To no one has fate revealed
To death this plane is doomed to yield.*

*No other creature roamed the sky,
Above the sea only silence looms,
Save the singing of the engines - and why?
This great bird was doomed to die.*

*Suddenly her wings were enveloped in flame
As the silence is broken by a deafening roar.
She twisted and turned and frantically strained
But she cannot fight death: she is fatally maimed.*

*Her engines die and she slowly descended,
Against death she could fight no more,
From this she could not be defended,
To her doom she limply soared.*

Christopher Cobb

NOTE: *This poem was written by Chris Cobb, a twelve-year-old, the evening after he learned of the crash of an Air Force C(121)Radar Picket Plane in which A3C Dennis R. Cole of Westboro, Massachusetts, was killed. The plane crashed off Nantucket Island shortly after taking off on a patrol flight to defend our nation's North Atlantic frontier, April 25th, 1967.*

The poem was sent by the parents of Dennis R. Cole, Mr. & Mrs. Richard Cole to Mrs. Joan Walsh, the wife of AlC William M. Walsh, who also was killed aboard the radar plane. The poem now has been passed on by James P. Walsh, the son of Joan and William Walsh, who was 8 years old when his father died.

NOTE: THE AIRCRAFT PICTURED IS NOT 53-0549 ABOUT WHICH THE POEM WAS WRITTEN

REMEMBERING DENNIS "SKIP" COLE
BY
WALTER G. TROY II

Dennis, or "Skip," as I and his friends called him, was from Westboro, Massachusetts. Dennis and I were close friends at Otis Air Force Base and were in the process of getting ready to move in together as roommates in the 962nd AEW& C Squadron. Skip had a great sense of humor and a catchy smile. He also had a great laugh so that when he started laughing, you started too. We spent a lot of our off-duty times together in the Boston area, visiting little "coffee houses" there. Once we were asked by the Shore Patrol to leave Boston. We were in uniform and just having a great time. Being new to the Air Force we were proud to be wearing our uniforms. However, I guess the Shore Patrol thought we were drunk or something, although we didn't even drink then.

I arrived at Otis before Skip, and we sort of struck up a friendship once he arrived there. We both were student radar operators and were just learning about the aircraft, our mission, and our duties. I had a car, and Skip used it periodically. The day of the crash [April 25, 1967] Skip used my car most of the day to take care of his personal business on the base. In fact, I thought he was going to be late for a mission which he had been assigned to, which was to brief around 1700 hours.

Skip came back to the barracks and while getting ready for the flight said something to me to the effect, "Walt, you know we are not coming back tonight. We are going to crash and burn, and I'm going to get out, swim all the way to Australia, and start a new life." Of course I told him not to talk like that, but I said, "If you do get to Australia, let me know, so I could come too."

Needless to say, soon afterwards that same evening the news reported that the plane [an EC-121H Super Constellation 53-0549] went down just off Nantucket. There was only one survivor--not Skip. I remembered what Skip told me just before the flight, and I tried to think that he was out there swimming like crazy trying to make it to Australia. He had his work cut out for him--that's a long swim. Of course, Skip was killed along with 15 others.

From that point on I knew that we were not infallible and that things could happen to us. I was, frankly, scared to death to fly. We had had other things happen to us like losing hydraulic fluid, hand cranking down landing gears, having an engine blow up on us, aborting take offs many times, etc. But when the plane went down, so did my heart. We were told by those at the 551st Wing, as I recall, that flying was purely voluntary, and I was honestly thinking about getting off flying status. For several days, maybe even weeks, I tried hard not to fly if I didn't have to.

There was a Major there who, for some reason, took an interest in me and my feelings. He told me one day that he had to get in some flying time on one of the "G" model Connies and asked me to fly with him. I was real hesitant. He said he wanted to get me back into the air. Once we were airborne, he flew over the site of the crash and told me to come up to the flight deck. He said, "What do you see down there?" I told him nothing but water. The Major said, "That's right, so long as you can see that water below you, you are still flying. As long as you get back in the airplane and realize that it could happen to any one of us, but do it -- you'll be alright." I guess it worked. I started flying and did pretty well, if I do say so myself.

An interesting note. I later transferred to the "BatCat" outfit, the 553rd Recon Wing, which went to Thailand and flew the EC-121R from 68-69. I had a small cubicle at the barracks which was shared with three other roommates (Ron Deforrest, Mark Steeley, Gerry Orth). Ron and I were the best of friends, doing everything together. He was the "plain clothes hippy" of the area. I really disliked him at first, but for some reason things changed and we became the closest of friends, planning to go back to college together in his hometown of Salem, MA. In not so many words, Ron had a feeling that something was going to happen to him while we were flying our Combat Support Missions. I told him not to talk like that.

On 25 April 1969, two years to the day and approximately the same briefing time as Skip had, as I recall, Ron Deforrest and Mark Steeley were killed in a Connie [EC-121R Super Constellation 67-21493] that went down on take-off in bad weather. I kept flying, but my spirit died for quite a while along with Ron and Mark.

Walter G. Troy II, 975 Banks Lane, Newport News, VA 23608, (757)874-4751, cwf@atel.net

PHOTOGRAPH FROM BOSTON TRAVELER April 26, 1967

AIRMAN DENNIS R. COLE - AGE 19

PHOTOGRAPH DATED 9-4-54 OF COLONEL JAMES P. LYLE. PHOTOGRAPH FURNISHED COURTESY OF JANA TREVINO, DAUGHTER OF COLONEL LYLE.

COLONEL JAMES PERKINS LYLE - COMMANDER, 551ST AIRBORNE EARLY WARNING AND CONTROL WING, OTIS AIR FORCE BASE, MASSACHUSETTS. COLONEL LYLE LOST HIS LIFE WHILE COMMANDING 53-0549 WHICH DITCHED AT NANTUCKET ON APRIL 25, 1967. FOURTEEN OTHER CREW MEMBERS ALSO LOST THEIR LIVES - ONE SURVIVED.

JAMES LYLE JR., REMEMBERS HIS FATHER COLONEL JAMES P. LYLE

Where were you when...? All men and women of my age and older when asked, "Where were you when Kennedy was assassinated?" will remember exactly where they were, what they were doing, and what happened. The details of that event are indelibly etched in our memories. I share such a memory with a handful of other people of an event that changed our lives.

It was in April of 1967. I was playing bridge with my college roommate at Texas A&M and two other friends. A small television was on in the corner of the room. A picture of a AWACS Constellation was being televised. Interrupting the game, I turned up the volume to hear what was being said. A plane had crashed in the Atlantic; one of my Dad's planes! I immediately telephoned home to Cape Cod to inquire about the story. An unrecognized man's voice answered the phone. I apologized, "wrong number." I dialed again and the same voice answered. I asked to speak to my mother and was told that she could not come to the phone. Then and only then did it strike me that my father might be the pilot! I identified myself and the phone was handed to another officer who told me as much as was then known; my father's plane had gone down shortly after takeoff into the Atlantic and they were conducting a search for survivors. I called my uncle Glynn in Houston, told him what little I knew, asked him to arrange for an airplane ticket home, and quickly packed a bag. The next day I was on a plane to Boston and home to my mother and sister. Our lives would no longer be the same.

Before the accident, we were a career Air Force family. We moved every couple of years to new assignments in the United States and overseas. We changed schools, made new friends, and adjusted to new surroundings. It was hard for some of us and easier for others, but it was part of the job that my father was doing; an important job. He was Colonel Lyle, Wing Commander of the 551st Airborne Early Warning and Control Wing stationed at Otis Air Force Base, Massachusetts. My sister, Jana, was in school, my mother at home. I was a senior AFROTC cadet at Texas A&M looking forward to graduation. Soon after the accident, my mother and sister moved to Denton, Texas where my mom had grown up and had family. I went back to school to take my finals and graduate. We are grown up now, with careers, families and children of our own. Jana is a respiratory therapist and I am a college professor. My mother still lives in Denton.

We were not alone. Other families lost their fathers, sons, and brothers that night. Their lives changed by the events of that night that we will always remember.

Someone asked me about my dad. A small town boy from Texas. He was the youngest of four children and the only child to go to college. He graduated from North Texas State University before enlisting in the U. S. Army Air Corps and going off to flying school. During the Second World War, he flew heavy bombers in the European Theater. He also flew combat missions in Korea. He was a hero who didn't talk about the dangers he was exposed to. He loved to fly and loved his country very much He was a great father to me and my sister, as well as a loving husband to our mother. We all miss him greatly. Last year marked the thirtieth anniversary of that night.

James Lyle, Jr.
December 1998

I ALWAYS WILL REMEMBER MY FATHER - I WAS MY DADDY'S LITTLE GIRL

I remember the night of the accident, April 25, 1967. I was 14 years old. That's the night my father, Colonel James P. Lyle, died.

That night I was talking on the phone in my parents' room to my boyfriend, Harvey Delaware. My dad told me good night as he was getting ready to go on a routine flight. A little later, Harvey called me back and asked where my dad was flying that night and told me that his dad, Sergeant Delaware, had been called to report to duty, that there had been a plane crash.

I went into the living room to ask mom where daddy was flying and found Mrs. Kaltenbacher, the base commander's wife, there. When I asked mom, she broke down. She immediately knew something was wrong because Mrs. Kaltenbacher never came to visit at night. Mrs. Kaltenbacher wanted to know who told me. She said nothing had happened and for me to get off of the phone. A little later, she came to my parents' room and again told me to get off the phone.

By then, there were more people at our house. I do not remember any more of that night. The next day I got up and dressed for school, but the people at the house would not let me go.

I believe we stayed on Cape Cod for three or four weeks and then came to Denton, Texas. I was told that my boyfriend's father, Sergeant Delaware, got into trouble for telling his family why he was called to duty that night and because Harvey told me.

Because I never saw any physical evidence of my father's dying, I don't know if I have ever really come to terms with his being gone. We were told that my father's remains were found when the plane was recovered from the ocean.

I was told that my dad was not required to fly the Connies, but he loved flying so much and he would not ask anyone to do anything he would not do himself. I wonder if the planes were really safe --why did they ground them after the third crash?

The grave side funeral service in San Antonio was June 6, 1967, just two days prior to my 15th birthday. I have been back to visit the grave site at the cemetery on two occasions.

My mother never remarried. She was so much in love with my father no one could ever have filled his shoes.

Until recently I did not fully understand what people thought of my father and how they remembered him as a hero. I remembered hearing people at the time of the accident saying what he did was heroic and reading it in the newspapers. I thought they were just saying nice things until a couple of years ago when one of Mom's friends from Cape Cod sent us a clipping from a Memorial Day paper which highlighted three heroes. My father was one of them. That was when it hit me that it must have been true. Two of the men featured were from the Cape, and they also had included my dad from Springtown, Texas. My dad was very modest and humble and never talked of his medals or honors. It was not until his death that I learned of these things.

My father's retirement from the Air Force and my graduation from high school would have been the same year. He always told me that we were going to go to North Texas State University in Denton together. He was going to get his Masters and teach.

My brother James and I, and my being 14 and being the only girl, I was very much Daddy's girl. My mother and I were jealous of each other and the attention my father gave to the other.

My mother is very stoic, but to this day I have difficulty discussing the loss of my father. I get teary eyed and choked up. I read things about my father to my mother, whose eyesight has failed, and I get choked up and have difficulty finishing. I think my mother knows when I cry, but she doesn't say anything.

Jana [Lyle] Trevino
December 1998

NOTE: On December 26, 1998, soon after this article was written, Mrs. Juanita Lyle, the wife of Colonel James P. Lyle, of Denton, Texas, died after a lingering illness. Mrs. Lyle's daughter, Jana Trevino, wrote that Mrs. Lyle was buried in San Antonio where Colonel Lyle is buried. Jana wrote: Like my father, Mom was a very special person who cared deeply for her friends and family. She never complained about her health or loss of eye sight. She was always positive and determined to be well. She was always more concerned about others and wanting to help in any way possible.

A MAN YOU COULD LOOK UP TO... A GENTLE HERO
OUR FATHER - CAPTAIN FRANK R. FERGUSON
BY
TODD FERGUSON

How do you define a successful life? Is it number of years? Amount of wealth and fame? Or, is it not measured more accurately by the impact it has made on others? Someone once said, "That man is a success who has lived well, laughed often, and loved much." This describes our father, Capt. Frank R. Ferguson II. He made every moment count, living a lifetime in 27 years.

My brother and I have always looked up to our father as Mom kept his memory alive for us, since Daryn was not yet three years old and I was only three months old when he died. As Mom raised us, she often remarked, "You are becoming just like your dad," or "Your dad would be so proud of you." Words like those have meant so much to us, and continue to grow in meaning as we learn more about the man who was our father.

He was a natural leader, even in his service to others. In college, he became president of his fraternity, and led them to move and renovate a house. He was a leader at home, and a strong presence Mom could lean on. In the Air Force, he rose quickly in rank as a young officer, attaining Captain by age 27. He helped train other navigators after they arrived on base. In his spare time, he led a troop of Boy Scouts, trained them in wilderness skills, and embodied the principles of honor and integrity for them. Soon there was a waiting list for his troop, boys wanting to join the 50 Scouts who shared their dreams with him, and who looked to him for emotional support and encouragement sometimes not received from their fathers. We know of one of his Scouts who followed his example and is now a Scoutmaster. Daryn and I also participated in Scouting, achieving the rank of Eagle Scout, an accomplishment Dad would have been very proud of. One of his dreams was to become a Scout Executive when he finished his Air Force career.

The love that Dad and Mom shared was strong and wonderful, and it showed in every honeymoon moment of their marriage. It is no coincidence that he wrote a long letter to Mom expressing his love for her just a week before the accident. Mom remembers when funds were low they "window shopped" while holding hands, or stopped what they were doing to drive somewhere for no other reason than to just be together. They dreamed and planned their future together, looking forward to watching Daryn and me grow up, and making plans to find two little girls to adopt along the way.

Mom found that in "her Frank," she had a strong presence to lean on, a partner who would help her through two difficult, premature births, then giving Daryn and me the extra care we required. In return, he had a loving and caring wife who would rub his aching muscles after long hours at the navigator's station during the flights. He did not complain, though many times after a 14-hour mission, the phone would ring asking if he could come immediately to take the place of another navigator for another 14 hours in the air. He always replied, "No problem."

Dad found much joy working on projects in his basement workshop, as evidenced by the whistling and humming Mom heard up in the kitchen. His creativity found expression in toys, furniture, curio shelves, and other items he crafted from wood for the enjoyment of his family. Daryn has found that he loves to do projects with his hands, as well as sing in choir, just like his Dad.

Dad's final opportunities to put others first came during the ill-fated mission on April 25, 1967. We do not know if the pilot had time to consult with the crew, but we know the decision Dad would have made. Rather than risk the lives of hundreds below on Nantucket Island, he would also have chosen to try a water landing. He encouraged the frightened young airmen as he helped them into their survival suits during his final moments before, as the Air Force Hymn says, "Reaching out and touching the face of God." There is a verse in the Bible that says, "Greater love hath no man than this, that a man lay down his life for his friends" (John 15:13). He could be at peace with the possibility of death because of his strong Christian faith, knowing God would continue to be with his family.

The hardest parts of a tragedy such as this are all the unknowns, and the loss of many tomorrows together. What could Mom say to Daryn when he asked, "Mommy, when is Daddy coming home?" How would she explain that Dad wouldn't be there to celebrate his son's third birthday the very next day? That he would not get to see Daryn ride the little red tricycle he had just assembled in the hours before his final mission? It's not easy, and many questions remain unanswered. Our dad was never recovered, so it was difficult to find closure. Information on the accident has been scarce, and only *recently did we find there is a memorial dedicated at Otis to the men lost in the three accidents. Many precious memories of our life together were later lost in a house fire. Still, through it all Mom kept us close as a family with her faith and gentle strength. Our family grew when Mom remarried in 1977, and joy increased when our sister Heather was born in 1981, and again in 1995 when I married Kary.*

Here was a man you could look up to. His life was characterized by giving of himself for others, and throughout his life he left a good impression on all he met. A man who watched Dad grow up told us, "If there was anything good going on, your father was mixed up in it." Mom calls him her "gentle hero," and Daryn and I are proud to be his sons. We love him, and yes, we still miss him. Much good remained for us to be mixed up in together . . .

THE FERGUSON FAMILY - *February 1999*

Todd Ferguson
4855 Blue Heron Boulevard
West Richland, WA 99353

NOTE: Captain Frank R. Ferguson was one of the two navigators aboard 53-0549 when it ditched at Nantucket Island, MA on April 25, 1967. Captain Ferguson and fourteen other crew members lost their lives in the ditching. Captain Ferguson's remains were not recovered. The other navigator, First Lieutenant Joseph L. H. Guenet, was the sole survivor.

THE FOLLOWING PHOTOGRAPHS WERE FURNISHED COURTESY OF THE FERGUSON FAMILY

FRANK R. FERGUSON DURING HIS COLLEGE YEARS

MRS. DIANE FERGUSON, WITH CHILDREN DARYN [ON LEFT] AND TODD IN 1969

FRANK R. FERGUSON WITH HIS WIFE DIANE AND SON DARYN IN 1965

AIR FORCE PHOTOGRAPH - OTIS AIR FORCE BASE - FEBRUARY 25, 1965 - FRANK R. FERGUSON [LEFT] SHOWING SCOUTS THE PROPER USE OF A HATCHET.

[LEFT TO RIGHT] TODD - HEATHER - DARYN IN 1986

1965 - 1/LT FRANK R. FERGUSON & WIFE DIANE IN FRONT OF THEIR RESIDENCE AT 5317D ARNOLD AVENUE AT OTIS AFB, MA

REMEMBERING MY FATHER

By James Walsh of Houston, TX, who was 8 years old when his father, A1C WILLIAM MICHAEL WALSH, died shortly after 7:03 PM on Tuesday, April 25, 1967, in the crash of 53-0549 at Nantucket Island, MA. The Walsh family lived in East Falmouth, a Cape Cod town, near Otis Air Force Base, MA.

The last time I saw my father was the afternoon he left for the base. It was right after I got home from school, and I was playing in a patch of woods near our house. I remember I could hear our VW bus fire up and I knew my dad was on the way to the base. I had missed saying goodbye to him, but I was determined to not let him get away. I ran through the woods to a point on the road I knew he would be coming by. He saw me running out of the woods towards the road and stopped. I opened the door, climbed in, and gave him a hug. He told me to be good, take care of my mom and he would see me the next night. The next time I saw that VW bus it was being driven back up the road toward our house, there was an airman behind the wheel, but he was not my dad.

I do not know what happened that night. You see, a couple of people came over to the house and we were all put to bed early. No one let any of the kids know what was going on. The next morning my mom sent me and my brother Dennis off to school. I do not know if she decided this on her own, or if someone talked her into doing it. I guess everyone was holding out hope my dad would be found, and they did not want to worry the kids. I walked to school and was in a great mood I recall, it was a cool clear spring morning and I felt good. Then I walked into my class room and everyone was talking about the plane crash from the night before. I do not know why, but I knew right away it was my dad's. I felt like someone had just dropped a building on me. To make a long story short I was a wreck after that. Some of the kids in my class also had dads in the Air Force. They kept talking about how there were many planes flying at one time, and how my dad's plane was probably not the one that crashed. I actually was starting to believe that he might be okay, when the teacher told me I was wanted in the office, my aunt was there to pick me up.

We stayed on Cape Cod for only a week or so then my mom moved us all to Thompson, CT to be near her family. I think one of the main reasons we moved so fast was because of what happened when my brother and I went back to school. Seems a number of kids, (I can't imagine they were Air Force brats) started taunting us. Telling us how our dad was not going to be found and, if he was found it would be in pieces. The worst one was them telling us we would not have a Christmas that year, because our Santa had been blown up. You know kids sure can be mean.

When we moved the Air Force provided an airman to drive us to Thompson. Three days after the crash my dad's wallet was found washed up on the beach. On or about May 26th my mom was informed that my dad was recovered when they raised the last section of the aircraft. Two friends of my dads identified the body. They told my mom that it was probably best that she did not see him. She thought it was a good idea at the time, but has regretted not seeing him ever since. My dad's funeral was at St. Joseph's Church in North Grovenerdale, CT. To get to the graveyard we had to drive by my new school. It was quite a sight, and one I did not expect. My new classmates, the entire third grade, was lined up along the street leading into the cemetery. You know kids sure can be great....

Now, thirty one years after my father's death, I just came from seeing the movie "Saving Private Ryan". Watching it brought back a memory from my childhood. It was the site of the military sedan with the officer in the back, coming to tell Mrs. Ryan of the death of her three sons.

You see, even though we lived off the Air Force base, 50 percent of the families in my neighborhood were Air Force families. When you saw that sedan drive up the street, you knew it was bad news for someone. There would be a ripple of fear that would go down the street. I am sure more than a few people prayed that car would not pull into their driveway.

In August 1966, eight months before my father died, I was over at my best friend's house when that car pulled into his driveway. His dad was missing in action over North Vietnam. When the car left, the neighbors came to lend support to the family. The Air Force man who was missing was Sergeant James R. Hall who also was my dad's best friend. Sergeant Hall died in captivity in Vietnam and his body was returned in 1988. You know that no one wanted to see that car show up - just imagine how tough it was on the man who had to ride in it.

NOTE: James "Red" Hall and I [A. J. Northrup] were airborne radio operators assigned to the 961st Airborne Early Warning & Control Squadron at Otis Air Force Base, Massachusetts. We frequently were assigned together as crew members on the radar surveillance missions in the Super Constellations. James went to Vietnam a couple of years before I did. I was very sorry to learn of his having been shot down and later of his death.

MY MEMORIES OF MY DAD, A1C TED LaPOINTE, JR., BY TECHNICAL SERGEANT THEODORE LaPOINTE

I was 4 years old when the U.S. Air Force EC-121H aircraft 53-0549 went down off the coast of Massachusetts. My mother was 27 years old, and, in addition to myself, I had a younger brother of 2.

My memories of my dad are limited to 2 events. One was when he returned from the Otis AFB commissary dressed in his orange flight suit, and another was when I tied my shoes for the first time. When I finally did it, I ran into the bedroom (where he was) to show him the big event.

The Accident:

At the time of the accident, I remember lots of strangers at the house. There were many friends and family inside the house. My mom was in her bedroom with the door closed. There were people going in and out of it. I was at the dining room table and my Aunt kept me busy playing tick-tack-toe. Mr. (Technical Sergeant) Phil Wilson was there (passed away in 1998). He had flown with my dad. He and his wife, Barbara, were there the whole time. I remembered him staying outside the entire day. I found out later that he was there because the local press wanted to talk to my mom. He became the family spokesman so my mom could rest. There was a funeral that I did not attend (at the choosing of my mom).

My Family's outcomes:

My mom (Marie) never remarried. She is now 58 and very independent. My mother decided not to get remarried after my father's death. She had two reasons: 1) If she remarried, she would have lost all her benefits (recently changed) and 2) she devoted all her attention to my brother and I, and did not think that anyone could love my brother and I the way my dad loved us. I am very grateful for all she has done for us. She still lives in the same house my dad and her shared.

My brother (Michael) joined the Coast Guard and moved to Florida in 1983. He left the Coast Guard after four years and became a Policeman. He seems to be very happy there and is still single. My brother is very quiet when it comes to talking about my dad, primarily because he vaguely remembers him.

My Outcomes:

I can describe my feelings growing up as "A chase with a ghost." By this I mean, I built up such an aura of this man I never knew, like a super-hero you cannot see or touch. I hated it as a young boy. In sports I was always getting stuck with the coach during father and son tournaments. I always dreamed of my dad walking through the door one day. He was always in my thoughts. The image I had of him grew and grew.

A story I share with friends when talking about my dad is as follows. In 1982, I joined the Air Force. When I went to the Military Entrance Processing (MEP) station, there were no jobs open at the time. I wanted to leave. Instead, I enlisted in an "open" category, which meant I could have been put in any job from cook to mechanic. I knew that if I told my mother this I would never hear the end of it. Upon my return from enlisting, I told her I was going to be trained in telecommunications and sent to Germany. I went through basic and received orders to attend technical training in telecommunication with follow-on orders to Germany!

My chase with the ghost ended when I started flying EC-130H, Compass Call, aircraft. In my mind I had achieved the level my dad had. I excelled to levels I never thought of achieving while flying. During this time, I was at the same age my dad was when he died. Throughout my 27th year I was very scared, although I never shared it with my wife. At that time I too had two sons. The entire year I was consumed with the thoughts of death. It did not interfere with my daily living, but it was ever present. After the year passed I felt invincible. During IFE's (in-flight Emergencies) I never feared the worst because I knew my dad was there with me. At that same time I came to realize that my chase with a ghost was over.

I am not the most religious person, but I truly believe in my heart that my family has an angel looking out for my family and myself. His name is dad.

February 1999

THEODORE E. LaPOINTE III
Technical Sergeant - USAF

REMEMBERING MY HUSBAND

[A1C Theodore E. LaPointe Jr., USAF, Deceased]

BY

MRS. MARIE LaPOINTE

Theodore E. LaPointe, Jr. (Ted) was born on August 27, 1941 to Helen (Sheppey) LaPointe and Theodore E. LaPointe, Sr. in Pittsfield, MA. He had a half sister, Evelyn, 20 years older than he.

He attended Notre Dame Elementary School in Pittsfield. His friends knew him as Ted--his parents called him Teddy.

He joined the USAF in June 1959. After basic training and schooling for radio operator, his assignment was Otis Air Force Base, Falmouth, MA.

Ted and I met when he visited the Cape Cod Hospital School of Nursing students' home in Hyannis, MA. I was attending nursing school. We met in June but our first date wasn't until July 3, 1961. That September, he was sent to Greenland for a short tour of duty, but it felt forever for me and for him. This was the time we both realized how much love we had for one another. We had so much of our life that was similar. We were brought up by older parents, our Moms shared the same birthday, May 30th, as well as our Dads, October 15th. We both had half siblings who were 14 and more years older than us. Subsequently, we were brought up as only children. Being brought up like an only child can be very lonely, and it had been for both of us. Our Dads had passed away within 6 months of each other. So we were both raised by our older mothers, who loved us very much but struggled to make ends meet. They did a fine job.

In December 1961 I graduated from the Cape Cod School of Nursing. On March 24, 1961 Ted and I were married at St. Killian's Roman Catholic Church in New Bedford, MA. Ted continued being stationed at Otis AFB while we lived in New Bedford and I worked at Union Hospital in New Bedford as a new nurse. Life was beautiful.

On November 17, 1962, we were in heaven--our first son, Theodore Edward LaPointe, III (Teddy), was born. I can still see Ted's elated grin on his reddened face when I first saw him after he had seen our son. There was so much love and excitement in us.

Thirteen months later Ted received orders for Kimpo, Korea-- we could not go with him. This was a heartache. So, our things were put into storage. The baby and I went to stay with my mother for awhile. We had planned that I would also spend some time with Ted's sister and her family while he was gone, as well as with his Mom.

Meanwhile, Ted's Mom was diagnosed with cancer and we left for Pittsfield earlier than planned so I could help care for her. Ted's sister, Evelyn, and I took turns caring for her. As her condition worsened, Ted was summoned home to Pittsfield through the help of the Red Cross.

Ted hopped a ride with Dag Hammarskjold, who was returning to the states, which got Ted home in time. Gram-ma Pointe died just a few days after Ted arrived. I deeply believe she was waiting for him----he was her baby. This all happened in February 1964.

After Ted's return to Kimpo, we were blessed with the news we were going to have another baby. We were _thrilled_ as we were not going to have an only child!! They would be only 23 months apart and company for each other. This gave us so much more to look forward to.

Four months after, our Teddy began to develop severe respiratory problems. They became so bad that we almost lost him. September was the worst time. Teddy's condition worsened. I was due for our baby soon and Ted was in Korea. Meanwhile, Ted was bringing a plane to Florida. The doctors, with the help of the Red Cross, were able to keep him home. Teddy slowly improved. Ted got new orders to be stationed at Otis AFB again.

October 19, 1964, our second beautiful, healthy son Michael Manuel LaPointe was born. Ted's elated grin broadened. He just swelled with pride. He remarked, "Now I'll be able to see through Michael what I missed of Teddy while I was in Korea." God did let him see that. We were all together again.

Teddy continued to suffer from his unknown respiratory condition. December 1966 was the last severe bout that Teddy had.

In September 1966 Ted started school part time at Southeastern Massachusetts University, now UMass Dartmouth, while winding down his eight years with the USAF. He was going to be discharged in June 1967 and begin full time classes for his Bachelor's in Business Administration. I worked at nursing on his off days so he could watch the children while I worked. Ted also found a part-time job when I was home from work and while he was off work from flying. We were preparing for my being home for the children and for Ted while he was going full time to school. Ted's dream was to make a better life for his children.

In April 1967 Ted developed strep throat. He was off flying status. He still wasn't really well but was cleared for flying, and he wanted to fly. He wanted to go on a flight that was in the works to go to the Panama Canal. He wanted to go so he could bring back some things for his sons as he would be clearing base after that, preparing for discharge. He said "it will be <u>my last flight</u>".

Meanwhile, I developed a strange uneasiness which we thought might be due to what was ahead of us (four years of Ted in school, which could be lean years). I couldn't sleep, I would feel like something wasn't right.

Monday, April 24, 1967 was like our usual Mondays--it was our day. Ted was always home as it was at night he would have classes. We four would go out together (it was always the four of us together) to run an errand or two, visit the ducks at the nearby park, ride by the fishing boats, and always to the city airport to visit the planes. The three guys had a wonderful bond. This was our day!!

That night Ted went off to school, I got the boys into bed, and I waited up for him, as I always did even when he flew. When he flew, and it became 2:00-3:00 AM, I would go to bed so I could get up for the children and let Ted get some much needed sleep after his usually long flights.

But this night was different. When Ted came in from school, he wanted to stay up a little later. He commented that in just a few months we would be able to do this if we wanted to. So we stayed up later to celebrate the beginning of our newer life together. When we went to bed, we said good night, and when I closed my eyes, I had a vision of my Ted in a coffin. I opened my eyes, turned to him, but he looked so comfortable that I didn't disturb him or say anything to him.

April 25, 1967.

We got up as usual---never did I remember my vision of the night before. It was a busy day. Ted was preparing for the flight, I was getting ready to go to work for the 3:00-11:00 shift at a nursing home and getting things ready for the babysitter. This was the very first time we would have a babysitter for our now two-year old Michael and four-year old Teddy.

We were both not comfortable with this, but I had to work because I needed to have time off for when Ted was going TDY to the Panama Canal. Today's flight would be his last flight for what he did at Otis AFB.

Ted still wasn't feeling all that well, and I ASKED HIM TO PLEASE STAY AT HOME. He said he couldn't do that because he wanted to do the Panama Canal trip, and he had to do this trip in order to go on to Panama Canal.

I kissed our sons good-bye and Ted as he made his way down our basement stairs to retrieve some things from the dryer. That was the last time we held each other, the last I saw my sweetheart alive. Ted called me at work to say he was leaving, that he was running late, that the sitter was there, and that he loved me.

The phone at work rang around 7:00 PM. It was Teddy's godparents asking if Ted was flying. They had just seen a special announcement that another Connie had crashed off Nantucket Island, MA. I knew immediately it was Ted's plane. I was 100% sure. Why?

There was a first Connie that went down when Ted received a call from the base to report for a search party. Then, Michael's godparents called because they had just learned of a Connie crash which flashed on the television.

The second plane--Michael's godparents phoned again, but this time Ted was home after finishing a flight. However, this time Ted remembered that this flight team was the group he passed as he was coming off from his flight. I was stunned when he said that, and I remarked--My God, Ted, you passed death by.

Now it was our turn.

I immediately tried getting a nurse to cover for me at work as I was the only nurse on duty. I just needed to get home for the boys. Before leaving work, I called Staff Sgt. Phil Wilson to see if he knew anything. He had just come in from shopping, and said he would see what he could find out. On the way home, our car kept stalling --- something it had never done. One of the nurses' aides getting off duty followed me home with her husband who had come to get her.

When I got home, I found the children fast asleep in their beds. I discharged the sitter, and I immediately contacted the base.

When I called, a young sounding airman answered the phone. I asked him if the plane that went down was the one that was due for take off around 6:30-7:00 PM. He answered yes. Just as this gentle airman answered, a very firm, sturdy voice of authority took over the call. He identified himself as a Commander (his name I still can't remember). I asked him the same question I had asked the previous individual. His answer was he had no information to give me. I, in turn, said "Sir, what you really are saying to me is you CAN NOT TELL me even if you do know." His voice softened--he was already sharing our pain and answered, "No, I cannot". I thanked him and told him he had answered my question.

Now, the only thing we had left was to wait with hope in our hearts while in constant prayer.

Just at this time, S/Sgt Phil Wilson arrived and never left us until it was safe to let us be. Phil was the one to break the news to my mom. I immediately phoned Evelyn, Ted's sister, and I, for the first time, mentioned my vision of less than 24 hours. That night and throughout the morning, we kept the radio and television on continuously. Neighbors noticing our house all lit up and learning of a crash came in and shared the wait. My mom made coffee continuously and washed cups. She even took cups that were not finished to wash---just to keep busy during the wait.

During the late hour, Teddy, in his sleep, yelled out "Daddy!" I went to him, held him tight, but he was sound asleep. I guess their Daddy had stopped by. I went to Michael's crib and cradled him, too.

Around 4:00 AM, Phil put two chairs together for himself near the phone so he could be there if we got a call. I lay across the top of my bed just to rest, as I could not sleep, but prayed. I kept praying that if Ted was going to have injuries and could be the same individual he was before the accident, I prayed for that, but if Ted's injuries were so that he would never be the person he would want to be---then, Thy will be done.

My mom rested on a couch.

By 7:00 AM, the children were up, and I told them of the accident. Teddy was four and Michael was two-years old. Neighbors began to fill our home, as well as dear friends, all of whom were aching for Ted, his crew members, and their families, as well as for us.

Strange, as I sat through this, I knew exactly what to expect because one day Ted sat me down and went through the steps of what to expect if anything should ever happen to him while he was in the Air Force. His last statement was, "I am the property of the U.S. Government. When they are through with me, then they will turn me over to you".

Mid-afternoon, my boss, a nurse, came in with a shot for me ordered by Dr. Franklin Berry, so I could rest, as I had not slept nor changed my clothing since getting up at 6:00 AM April 25th. I was still in my nurse's uniform, and it was now mid-afternoon of April 26th.

After being medicated, I fell asleep and woke up a few hours later when my door opened. I asked--did they find him? The answer was,"Yes!" "He's gone, isn't he?" The answer was what I already knew. Ted was dead--he only had 60 days left for discharge after eight years of duty.

While I was sleeping, the commander of the base came to deliver the news. What a hard situation for this man to have to carry out. We learned that there was a survivor, two bodies found--Ted's and Master Sergeant Frank W. Garner, Jr., and 13 were missing.

So now it was official. Ted had died, and the Air Force had begun their Air Force procedure. A few hours later, two uniformed men of my husband's rank appeared at our door. It was after 8:00 or 9:00 P.M. I knew why they were there.

My husband had told me that the Air Force would send two airmen of his rank to be available to me for all that was to come concerning the transition from military life to civilian life. My heart went out to these men, as this had to be one of the hardest jobs they ever had to do. They apologized for not being there sooner. They could not find their way to New Bedford but finally did so by being escorted by police from one town to the next until they met the New Bedford Police at the Fairhaven/New Bedford bridge and were escorted directly to our home. Their wives had accompanied them. S/Sgt Phil Wilson and Captain Austin Ganley had been given permission to take the job over from these two men because both Phil and Austin were Ted's friends and now ours.

I thanked these men and wished them much happiness and love for them and their wives. They left. The press arrived from Boston, MA, Providence, RI, Pittsfield, MA and the television stations as well as the radio stations. The phone did not stop. The house became filled with more family and friends.

I tried to keep the children's days as near normal as possible. It was hard. Every time Teddy heard an airplane, he would run to the window and yell at us "here comes my Daddy now!"

I had to phone my pediatrician, Dr. William Downey. "What do I say to Teddy and Michael?", I asked. His advice was that each time Teddy or Michael say that their father is arriving, you have to say, "no, your Daddy isn't coming back". These were the hardest words I had to say, but I said them.

My children were not used to being cared for by others. They were being shifted from one person to another but always in our home while I attended a memorial service.

The memorial service was not just for Ted but for everyone in his plane who had lost the most valuable of property--the gift of life. Everyone under the roof of this chapel suffered their loss to the very core of their being. No words were needed. I felt so hollow, so empty, lost, and just followed what instructions Ted had prepared me for. S/Sgt. Phil D. Wilson and his wonderful wife, Barbara, Capt. Austin Ganley and his caring wife, Barbara, Teddy and Michael's Godparents and close friends accompanied me through this memorial service.

Capt. Ganley helped me through the paperwork at Otis AFB. S/Sgt Phil Wilson helped me through the funeral arrangements. It took four days before my husband's body was released from the government. Death was due to a ruptured aorta.

After viewing my husband's body in the coffin, I asked that the coffin be closed. His hair had been singed just where his only wave was on the top of his head, and the head had been cut on that same right side from the autopsy that had been performed by the government. His hands and fingers were bruised. Ted was a very proud man, and I felt he would want to be remembered as each person knew him.

I was given a beautiful gift while in the funeral home from this tall man in a white full military naval uniform [he was the gift]. *He approached me and identified himself as Coast Guard Officer Richard Ravizza stationed on a vessel based in New Bedford. He was a classmate of my husband's from St. Joseph's High School in Pittsfield, and it was his ship which carried my husband's body home. It was he who recognized my husband after receiving his body. I then learned that it was a fishing trawler [Steven R] from New Bedford that picked my husband's and Sergeant Frank W. Garner's bodies out of the sea.*

I was very thankful that Ted was accompanied by a friend out in that cold, dark world he and his crew had been in and some were still lost out there. Ted's friend offered to be a pall bearer. Ted was being honored!!

The funeral took place on May 1, 1967, from the Brooklawn Funeral Home in New Bedford, with a High Mass at St. Killian's Roman Catholic Church (where we had been married) and buried with full military honors at Sacred Heart's Cemetery because it is next to the little New Bedford Airport that Ted would take the children to see so many times. The Church of St. Mary, Our Lady of the Isle, on Nantucket had a Requiem Mass at 4:00 PM that same day for our men.

The children stayed at home with friends and family through the wake and funeral. I chose to keep them at home as I so wanted them to remember their Daddy as he was. I thought that would be what Ted would want as well.

Life never was the same. I just learned to survive life's ups and downs. The military had informed me that I would receive a veteran pension for as long as I did not remarry. Medically, I would be totally covered. I would continue to have the benefits as I had been having with the use of my military ID card. The children, until age 18 or until they finished school through college would have the same.

I was also entitled to go on to school under the GI bill, but the time of eligibility was limited. I had one year to choose if I wanted to move, and the government would pay for my move.

Promises that were made pertaining to our medical coverage are no longer effective. The medical coverage has changed. Now, in 1999, I am finally out of debt due to medical bills. I am disabled and use either crutches or canes to get about after a battle of 10 surgeries.

Since the shock of Teddy's father's death, he never experienced another respiratory problem.

Teddy graduated from GNBRVHS (vocational high school) in 1980, attended Bristol Community College for one year, and decided on his own to join the USAF. He has been all over the world. He met a wonderful wife, Cindy, in Prum, Germany and they have two handsome sons, T. J. (Theodore E., IV), born February 7, 1986, and Kevin, born May 30, 1989. On May 20, 1998, Teddy graduated from Hawaii Pacific University receiving his Bachelor of Science in Nursing. Now in his 17th year in the Air Force, he is stationed at Buckley Air National Guard Base, Denver, CO, where he hopes to retire and work as a nurse.

Michael graduated from Bishop Stang High School and did 4 years with the Coast Guard. He became a policeman in St. Petersburg, Florida, where he chose to settle down. He is divorced and has a beautiful daughter, Courtney Elizabeth LaPointe, born July 27, 1992, and a handsome son, Cameron Alden Welch, born November 15, 1995.

I returned to work after both the children started school full time. I volunteered my time at St. Mary's School (where they attended), Boy Scouts, Boys' Club, high school PTA, Big Sister program, hospice, bereavement support groups, and wherever I was needed. Because of my life experiences, people who knew me would refer individuals to me whom they felt I could help who may have had a loss of some kind.

This created my interest to enroll at Mt. Ida College in Newton Centre, MA, where on May 27, 1995, I received my Bachelor of Science in Bereavement Counseling with highest honors.

It took me 28 years to finish Ted's dream to finish college and give his family a better life.

I took 28 years to finish what Ted started, and that was to receive his degree---I did it for him, for me, and for our family.

There are still a few things I'll probably never know. I have <u>never</u> received any information of what was officially found to have caused this accident from the government or from anyone. I have always wanted to talk with the only survivor. I am so thankful for him, his family, and for us that he did survive.

Also, I understand that Ted had taken another man's place that day. I'd like so much to meet this man and tell him it's okay. I feel I need to meet with this individual. Life is a great gift, and we must all use this gift to the fullest in everything we do no matter how it was dealt to us. Living is doing what is expected of us whenever we can, and whenever we can't, we must do the next best thing. We all know that nothing ever stays the same. It becomes changed. I am so thankful for my family!

February 1999

Mrs. Marie LaPointe
163 Clifford Street
New Bedford, MA 55331
(508)998-5393
iota@gis.net

NOTE: Marie is the wife of A/1C Theodore E. LaPointe Jr., of the 962ND Airborne Early Warning and Control Squadron at Otis Air Force Base, MA. A/1C LaPointe was the radio operator on 53-0549 who lost his life along with fourteen others of the crew on April 25, 1967. The Navigator, 1/Lt Joseph L. H. Guenet, was the sole survivor of the ditching at Nantucket Island, MA.

PHOTOGRAPHS FURNISHED COURTESY OF THE LaPOINTE FAMILY

MARIE LaPOINTE AND HER HUSBAND A/1C THEODORE E. LaPOINTE JR., WHO LOST HIS LIFE IN THE DITCHING OF 53-0549 ON APRIL 25, 1967. [PHOTOGRAPH TAKEN 1963 THE DAY HER HUSBAND RECEIVED ORDERS TO GO TO KOREA FOR A YEAR]

THE LaPOINTE FAMILY - 1995

[FRONT CENTER] MARIE LaPOINTE, WIFE OF A/1C THEODORE E. LaPOINTE JR. [DECEASED]

[REAR CENTER] CINDY LaPOINTE, WIFE OF TSGT THEODORE E. LaPOINTE III

[LEFT ON END] THEODORE LaPOINTE IV - SON OF TED AND CINDY LaPOINTE

[RIGHT ON END] KEVIN LaPOINTE - SON OF TED AND CINDY LaPOINTE

[SECOND FROM LEFT] MICHAEL LaPOINTE - TED'S BROTHER

[SECOND FROM RIGHT] THEODORE E. LaPOINTE III

IN MEMORY OF MSGT FRANK W. GARNER, FLIGHT ENGINEER ON 53-0549 WHO LOST HIS LIFE ON APRIL 25, 1967

The cover of the AIR FORCE SERGEANTS Association Magazine Volume VIII, NO. 9 of September-October 1969 was in memory of MSgt. Frank W. Garner, life member Number 9.

ABOUT THE COVER

Our cover this month is in memory of a stalwart AFSA member, a man who began with AFSA from its birth and who supported AFSA in its every goal until his death: MSgt. Frank W. Garner, Life Member Number 9.

Sergeant Garner's years with AFSA should serve as a guideline for all members to follow for he amassed a record of notability. He began by helping to organize the Otis AFB Chapter in December 1961, served as chapter PIO until July 1962, appointed to the Board of Trustees in Chapter 202, August 1962, elected chapter 1st VP in January 1963, appointed chapter president in October 1964 when Joseph Brosnan was elected to National 2nd VP, elected chapter president in January 1965, elected to the office of National 1st VP in October 1965 and served on numerous committees until his death in 1967 in an aircraft accident.

At the 1967 convention, the Frank W. Garner Scholarship Fund was instituted in his memory and has awarded two $1,000 scholarships to dependents of AFSA members. The first award went to Michael N. Smith, son of CMSgt. and Mrs. Raymond E. Smith, Jr. in 1968. The second award went to Karen D. Mrotek in 1969.

The poetry depicted on the cover was written the night after Sergeant Garner's death by a very close friend, both in the AFSA and daily life, MSgt. Joe Brosnan.

A SENTINEL SLEEPS

Freedom's Eagle in your lofty place
The lowly seagull envised your grace
And Lofty Sentinel's post which was your charge
The faith and trust that people held in you

Lonely silver eagle of the sky
Sunlight sparkled on your graceful wing
A wheeling coasting ethereal thing
In dark your presence known by winking eye

A hot and stinging pain consumed your fathers
You came down to the sea to cool the flame
Now poor lonely one with black scorched wing
No more you course the endless oceans sky

So peaceful now, you sleep on oceans floor
Faithful warrior felled, you watch no more.

J. Brosnan

The following article appeared in the Air Force Sergeants Association Magazine

"We Won't Forget You"

On Tuesday night, 25 April 1967, AFSA lost one of its top leaders. National First Vice President, MSgt Frank W. Garner, Jr., was a Flight Engineer on the Radar Picket plane out of Otis AFB which crashed into the sea off Nantucket Island. Several other crew members on the aircraft were members of Chapter 202 at Otis.

AFSA has suffered a great loss in Frank's death. A big man physically, he was also a big man in his efforts to build AFSA and bring reality out of the mere idea that AFSA was in the beginning. Frank moved up to the National V.P. slot because of the hard work and leadership he had shown as a member and the President of Chapter 202. He took his position as a National Executive Council member very seriously and no amount of effort or expenditure of time was too great for Frank when he was working for AFSA. He used his cross country flying trips to great effect, and was constantly working with local Chapters at various locations to give them a boost and help them grow.

Frank was no "rubber stamp" Council member and would fight to the last second for a point if he felt he was right. On several occasions, the only thing that saved him from a beating at my hands was his size--and my fear! Once a consensus was reached, however, Frank would dig in and back the majority to his utmost. Frank was buried in Springfield, Illinois on 3 May with full Military honors. Executive Director Joe Brosnan and I were present, as were many members of the Otis Chapter, who flew out on a Connie to pay their last respects to Frank.

* * * *

I think it appropriate to say, "So long, Frank, well done, AFSA is better because of your efforts, and we won't forget you!"

NOTES ON AIRBORNE EARLY WARNING & CONTROL

Lt. Col. Joseph L. H. Guenet USAF, Ret

I begin this narrative with a discussion on the times. It is difficult for today's Americans to understand or to remember the atmosphere of the mid-60s. We were in the midst of the Cold War. The United States believed it was conceivable the Soviet Union would spring a surprise nuclear attack by air. They were certainly capable of such an attack, considering their operations with long range aircraft including a number of Bears [Note 1]. Politically, the United States and the Soviet Union were at odds on almost all issues. The Air Force had lost a number of reconnaissance aircraft to Soviet interceptors in operations near their borders, the Korean War was still a close memory, and Vietnam was beginning to intrude on our consciousness.

The Soviets operated a long range passenger mission, flying non stop from Moscow to Havana utilizing a modified Bear. This mission operated a number of times each week, and it was not unusual for us to pick up and monitor one of these missions as it traversed the Atlantic off our East Coast. We were briefed to keep a close eye on these aircraft, as it was impossible to assure that it was a passenger aircraft and not the first of a bomber group.

In the mid-50s the entire North American continent was ringed with a series of early warning RADAR stations from the Dew Line in Northern Canada and Alaska through the Pine Tree Line in mid Canada and continuing down to radar stations in our northern States. These RADAR stations transmitted their signals to the Semi Automatic Ground Environment (SAGE) sites, consisting of a number of ground stations, typically in hardened buildings, where ground control of interceptor aircraft were carried out.

The Airborne Warning and Control mission was designed to extend the warning radar coverage out over the ocean and thereby increase the warning time in the event of an air attack on the United States. Ground radar sites were only capable of "seeing" aircraft that were above the horizon, and low flying aircraft therefore could come extremely close to the shore before being painted by these sites. The AEW & C mission could add up to two hours to the warning time of a bomber attack and thereby give interceptors time to get airborne and stop the attack before it could enter our airspace.

The Air Force operated two wings of EC-121 aircraft, a specially modified version of the Lockheed Super Constellation. Each of these aircraft was equipped with a long range search radar using a large antenna mounted to the bottom of the fuselage and a height finder radar with antenna on the top of the aircraft fuselage. The aircraft airframes had been modified with the addition of fuel tanks to each wing tip, and heavy duty electrical generation capability was added to the engines. All of this modification resulted in aircraft that were heavy and radically limited in altitude and airspeed compared to their civilian counterparts.

The 552nd Wing stationed at McClellan AFB, CA, flew the EC-121D model aircraft and covered stations off the West Coast, while the 551st Wing at Otis AFB, MA, flying the EC-121H model aircraft, supported the East Coast. Another squadron of Connies operated out of McCoy AFB, FL, to cover the airspace between Florida and Cuba. Aircraft were often sent to Iceland for special duty when radar sites were out of operation. Late in 1966 the 553rd Reconnaissance Wing was activated at Otis. The aircrews of this wing were trained by the 551st, and, after training and being equipped with EC-121R aircraft, the wing was assigned to Korat RTAFB in Thailand, where it flew reconnaissance and intercept control missions. All the EC-121 aircraft were called Connies by the aircrews--short for their civilian name of Constellation.

Each AEW & C Wing had about 36 aircraft assigned and was responsible for manning specific stations off their respective coasts on a 24 hour basis. The East Coast stations were given even numbers: station 2 off Northern New England, 4 off Long Island, 6 off the Coast from Washington DC, and 8 off Charleston, SC. During normal days we kept at least two of the stations manned, and when defense conditions increased, we would man all the stations continuously.

Active Air Defense Mission duration ranged from 10-16 hours, with longer missions in the winter when we could carry maximum fuel. After takeoff from Otis we would usually fly over Hyannis, Nantucket and then to one of the "fish" points, Cod or Haddock (check points off the Coast), and from there to our station assignment. Once on station we would take up a race track pattern, typically taking an hour to traverse one circuit. The missions were flown at 12-15 thousand feet in blocked airspace, which meant no other aircraft were allowed into our area.

Winter missions over the North Atlantic tended to be somewhat violent. It was not unusual on stations that were aligned with the wind to beat upwind for 45 minutes, turn 180 degrees, fly five minutes with the wind, turn, and do it again. I recall watching the Doppler radar ground speed readout on my Nav panel crank down to negative numbers when we turned into the jet stream on one mission. The speed of the wind was higher than our aircraft air speed, resulting in our actually moving backwards over the ocean when we were in the center of the jet. Thunderstorms, extreme icing, and violent turbulence were not at all unusual. Anyone who had problems with motion sickness didn't last long.

Accumulating flying time in the Connies was not a problem; this was my initial operational flying assignment after Nav training, and in my first year at Otis I logged over 1400 hours of crew time. About a year after being assigned to Otis I met with a number of my Nav school classmates while on a cross country trip to McClellan. These classmates had gone on to Navigator Bombardier or Electronic Warfare training at Mather AFB and had accumulated 100-150 hours at that same amount of time. They were aghast at the amount of time I had logged. The longest mission in my log book while in Connies was 17 hours and 35 minutes.

Aircrew members were assigned to AEW & C Squadrons. Otis AFB had three of these aircrew squadrons: the 960th, 961st and 962nd. These squadrons were responsible for the training, administration, and support of the pilots, navigators, engineers, and radio operators required to man the missions. At Otis the squadrons rotated duty so that each day one squadron manned the missions, one had crew members on crew rest who had flown missions the prior day and the third was in training mode.

Technical crew members, including radar, comm/nav and electronic specialists, were assigned to the 551st Electronic Maintenance Squadron. These members, who made up the "rear end" crew, operated and maintained the airborne electronic equipment. A normal aircrew complement consisted of two pilots, two navigators, two engineers, and one radio operator. The rear end crew, usually six to eight airmen, consisted of comm/nav, radar, and electronic technicians.

Each aircraft had a number of bunks for off-duty personnel, a table for eating or card playing, airline-type seats, and a complete galley. One or two meals, box lunches, and/or frozen meals, coffee, juice, etc. were provided for the missions. Once on station and with all equipment functioning, the main problem for the crew was boredom. It was not uncommon to find only the navigator and, hopefully, one pilot awake on long night shifts.

The D-model aircraft assigned to the 552nd were manned by Air Defense controllers who were trained to control Air Defense intercepts between fighter aircraft and enemy bombers. In this way they were able to operate independently of ground intercept controllers.

The H-model aircraft assigned to Otis defending the East Coast were modified with a digital link, the Airborne Long Range Intercept (ALRI) capability, to send processed radar signal data to ground radio sites and then via land line to the SAGE sector. We therefore did not carry intercept controllers on the East Coast missions, as all intercepts were run from the ground SAGE site.

Background

I was born in Montreal, Quebec, Canada on 25 March 1938. My Father, Leo, was an American Citizen working in Canada. My mother Genevieve had been born in Ireland and immigrated to Canada with her family, where she met my Father. My family, consisting of two sisters, Father, Mother and myself, moved to Lyndonville, Vermont, in 1942.

I lived in that small Vermont town, completing elementary school and graduating from high school in 1956. That summer Is enlisted in the USAF, completed basic training at Lackland, and was assigned to Wright Patterson AFB (WPAFB), OH, as an altitude chamber technician. The research chamber at WPAFB was used for space research, and during that tour I was honored to work with our original Mercury Astronauts as we fitted and trained them in their space suits.

When my four-year tour was completed, I returned to Vermont and attended college. After graduation in 1963 I married Hannah Wing, whom I had met at college. I was offered and accepted a slot at Officers Training School and Undergraduate Navigator Training (UNT).

My eldest daughter, Genevieve, was born in Waco, Texas while I was attending Nav training. After graduation from UNT I attended survival school at Stead AFB, NV and reported in to my first flying assignment at Otis. Upon arrival I was assigned to the 962nd AEW & C Squadron. My youngest daughter, Melissa, was born while I was assigned to the 962nd.

Navigators Responsibilities

As navigators on the Connie, we were of course primarily responsible for the accurate positioning of the aircraft. Without an accurate position, any radar data transmitted to the Semi Automatic Ground Environment would be useless. If you don't know where the radar is, you can't plot the bogies'[unknown aircraft] position. Additionally, the ALRI antenna had to be pointed very accurately toward the ground site or the digital link would go down.

We used Loran as our primary navigation fixing tool. We were also provided with a Doppler inertial system to keep constant position information required for both the radar signal processors and the ALRI antenna. Updated weather reports were received by the radio operator hourly via HF Morse Code. The navigator reviewed these reports to assure our destination and alternates were above, and forecast to stay above, minimum landing conditions.

During winter months it was not unusual to have the weather on the East Coast fall below minimums for all our possible alternates. In these instances we would fly to Kindley AB, in Bermuda, for recovery. One winter the long range forecast indicated an extended period of bad weather. The decision was to take the majority of the wing to Bermuda and support the mission from there. As aircrew, we thought this to be a particularly delightful decision; however, upon our return to Otis a week or so later, we found our wives did not agree with our take on the matter.

My initial assignment to Otis was as a navigator with the 962nd AEW & C Squadron. This outfit was affectionately known as the Skunk squadron as a result of our baseball caps--black sides with white tops. I am not sure who picked them, but we lived with it. Because of the duty cycle, we had little chance to meet members of the other flying squadrons. In April of 1967, I was assigned to the 551st Wing as the Life Support Officer and was attached to the 962nd Squadron for flying duties. In that position I met a large number of members from the other squadrons.

The Ditching of EC-121H 53-0549

25 April 1967

This is my recollection of the ditching of USAF aircraft 53-0549, an EC-121H Super Constellation assigned to the 551st Airborne

Early Warning & Control (AEW&C) Wing, Otis AFB, MA. The aircraft was manned by aircrew members from the 962nd AEW&C Squadron, augmented by members from the 551st AEW&C Wing and the 553rd Reconnaissance Wing. The electronic technical crew was assigned to the 551st Electronic Maintenance Squadron.

Briefing, Preflight and Take Off

The aircrew, consisting of pilots, navigators, engineers, and radio operator, gathered at the 962nd briefing room about two hours prior to departure as was usual. The aircraft commander, Col. Lyle, the Wing Commander, gave the mission briefing. We were scheduled for an Active Air Defense mission on station # 4 off Long Island. I gave the standard navigational briefing, furnishing total flight duration, on station time, emergency alternates with their respective time and distance, then finishing up with a time hack for the crew. We received the weather briefing over closed circuit television from the base weather station. Weather was clear and not particularly cold for that time of year: in the high 40s, as I remember.

Once the briefing was complete, the aircrew went to the aircraft and began their preflight inspections. The electronic technicians were at the aircraft when we arrived, as their systems preflight inspections were more time-consuming than those of the aircrew. I remember little of the preflight time. The only item that was unusual was the topping off of the hydraulic system with a quart of fluid prior to engine start. I did the navigation equipment preflight inasmuch as I planned to take the initial leg and set up on station. My normal duty was the Life Support Officer assigned to the Wing rather than the 962nd Squadron. As such, I flew less frequently than aircrew members assigned to the squadrons. When I flew I tried to take the first leg, as that portion of the flight gave me more time and practice on configuring and initializing the navigation equipment.

We started engines, taxied out, and did the normal engine run. I noticed no unusual actions or items by the pilot or engineers. Just at dusk we took the active runway and began our takeoff roll. Col. Lyle was in the left seat as Aircraft Commander and Major Franklyn, the 962nd chief of standardization, was in the right seat. I was seated in the normal navigator's airline seat on the port side of the aircraft with Capt. Ferguson, the other navigator, across the aisle on my left and Airman Cook, a newly assigned radar tech, on my right. After a normal take off roll, we turned on course and began our climb.

Climb Out

As we climbed through about 2000 feet, we were cleared to move about the aircraft and to begin our flight duties. I left my assigned seat to set up the navigation station. On takeoff and landing the navigator was not seated at the Nav station but rather in an airline type seat located just aft of the cockpit facing to the rear.

The navigator's work station was on the starboard side of the aircraft at the wing root. The navigator's seat was a tall stool which was set up in the aircraft aisle, and the navigator faced to the starboard with his table and equipment arrayed in front of him. Just to the aft of the navigator's table was a narrow aisle leading to the over wing hatch with a porthole window in it. On the port side of the aircraft opposite the navigator's station was the radio operator's position.

Setting up the navigator station consisted of getting my equipment and charts set up on the table, turning on navigational equipment, checking all instruments, and assuring navigational aids such as the Doppler-inertial system were working normally. When I took my position, the Doppler-inertial system was not working correctly, and I called the Nav tech forward to look over the equipment. He indicated the system was not checking out and went to the rear to check circuit breakers and equipment. After this, I walked forward to discuss work schedules with Frank Ferguson, the other navigator. I then went back to my station and began to prepare for coast out to the over water portion of the mission.

Explosion and Emergency Actions

As I returned to the Nav position, I noted the radar tech turn on the search radar system. The circuit breaker for the search radar was positioned on a bulkhead just aft of the navigator's station. Within a few seconds there was what I believed at the time to be an explosion, and the right wing of the aircraft rose into the air a number of feet.

Immediately light smoke began to issue from the ventilation vents, and I could see indications of flames outside the over wing hatch window. I notified the Pilot over the intercom, but I received no reply over intercom for this or any other calls I made during the remainder of the flight. I then got off my seat and went to the window near the starboard wing root to look out. I could not see any flames directly but could see reflections of flames on the # 3 engine nacelle. This indicated we had a fire inboard of the engine very close to the fuselage. At this time the # 3 engine (inboard engine on the starboard side of the aircraft) was not operating and the propeller was feathered.

I estimate the aircraft was at about 6,000 feet when the explosion took place. Our position was near Hyannis, MA heading outbound toward Nantucket and station # 4. I immediately cleared my table of equipment and placed the Nav stool and my equipment bag into the latrine to clear the equipment out of the way to prepare the aircraft for return to base, as I expected an emergency landing at Otis. About the time I finished clearing the Nav station, the aircraft engines went to what sounded like METO (Maximum Except Take Off) power and we went into a steep dive. I ordered the rear end crew to don their exposure suits and prepare for emergency landing.

Frank Ferguson and I helped one of our newer crew members (Airman Cook) get into his exposure suit when he indicated he was not sure how to don it. After helping him, we donned our own suits. By this time the aircraft had leveled off at about 2000 feet and the three remaining engines continued at the high power setting.

I made a quick check of the rear end of the aircraft to ensure the radar crew had prepared themselves and the aircraft for an emergency landing. I noted all of the members in the rear had donned their exposure suits and that about half had put on their parachute harnesses.

Returning to the front area of the aircraft, I saw Master Sergeant Garner (Flight Engineer) taking a number of cans of hydraulic fluid to the flight deck. I helped him with two of the fluid cans, carrying them from the storage locker to the cockpit. Shortly after level off there was another explosion and smoke became extremely heavy, pouring out of the ventilation system. It became very difficult to breathe, and I felt if we didn't get on the ground soon few of us would survive the smoke.

From my seated position looking to the rear of the aircraft I could see what appeared to be burning hydraulic fluid flowing across the deck of the aircraft from the starboard wing position toward the radio operator's position. It may also have been fire burning through the floor from the lower compartment. In the heavy smoke, it was not possible to be certain.

About this time I noted that an over wing hatch was thrown to the floor near the Nav position. Apparently it had been taken out by the radio operator and thrown to the starboard side of the aircraft. This action helped to clear smoke from the aircraft, and it became much easier to breathe.

At this time I noticed that the galley table had a number of technical manuals on it. The table was located just to the rear of my seat location, and I decided that I should clear the books from the table as they would fly around when we landed, and I believed, would be a danger.

Ditching

I went to the table and was in the act of taking the books and throwing them into the lower baggage compartment when the aircraft hit the water. My most vivid remembrance was that of instant silence. The engines had been at high power setting, the aircraft was vibrating heavily, and then suddenly there was total silence and total darkness.

I recollect being thrown with considerable force into something fairly soft, probably my seat, hitting it with my right side, then flipping over that item and hitting something extremely hard with my left side, most likely the radio rack which was positioned just forward of my seat position

I must have been unconscious for a short while as my next recollection was that I was lying face down with something on my back pinning me down and I could hear water running. Next, I could feel the water covering me, and I struggled to get free. At first I couldn't move, but then suddenly whatever was holding me down broke loose and I found myself under the water. I swam toward the surface and remember thinking that something was wrong, as it had been dark when we ditched and now I could see a bright light at the surface.

When I broke the surface of the water, I realized the light I had seen was from a major fire totally surrounding me. I was forced to get back under the surface instantly to keep from burning.

Swimming and Surviving

My survival schools had taught me that the way to stay alive in a burning sea was to push the water up and away from your face as you did as a kid playing in the water splashing others. That may work for sailors when they are in fuel oil used in ships, but this was 115/145-octane aviation fuel. When I tried to push the water and splash it away, all I accomplished was to create an explosion in my face as I sprayed the fuel from the water surface into the air.

I quickly fixed on the following procedure: First I would go under water and stay down as long as possible. Secondly I would swim up, breaking the surface of the water as violently as I could. This would create a large splash of water and effectively throw the fire away from me. When on the surface I would wait a second to let the fuel burn off, then get a breath of air and go back under the water. In this manner I could keep from being burned. The cold water on my head, face and arms protected me from the burning fuel explosion during the moment I was on the surface.

I believe this bob and duck was necessary for about 2 to 3 minutes. After that time much of the fuel had burned off and the fire was limited - only found near any floating debris. During the time I was bobbing I was forced to take off my exposure suit as it had been torn and was filling with water and was hindering my movements. Luckily I had not taken time to put on my life preserver while in the aircraft, as it would have kept me up in the flames. Cold seawater is not difficult to keep afloat in. The density of the water is so high it seems to be more difficult to stay down than to float.

At no time after the ditching did I see or hear any other crew member or have any indication any of the others got out of the aircraft. I still don't know how I survived the impact with the water, how I got out of the aircraft, or if any one else survived the ditching and was able to get out of the aircraft.

Once the fire burned down and I was able to stay on the surface, I could hear hot metal parts that were still burning, sizzling around me. The weather was very clear and I could see the beach on Nantucket Island very clearly. A number of lighted tall antennas were visible, and I could see people standing and walking on the beach. They had come to the beach, parked their cars with the headlights on, and were on the beach in front of the headlights looking out at sea. I assume they were able to see the fires on the ocean.

I estimate I was ¼ to ½ mile off shore, and the current was moving me along parallel to the beach at a fairly rapid pace. I called for help but received no indication I was heard. I'm sure my voice was not strong enough for anyone on the beach to hear over the noise of the surf.

I was having trouble treading water. My feet kept popping to the surface, which was a very uncomfortable position to be in. After a while I realized that my boots were a winter-insulated type with air pockets, they were acting like small life preservers. Once I realized the problem I took the boots off to help me keep an even keel, and things got considerably easier.

I felt a piece of debris hit my hand. It turned out to be a piece of floating bulkhead. I was able to crawl up onto it and float on it face down like riding a surfboard, partially out of the water. While floating I was able to identify the bulkhead as the one located just forward of the nav station, distinguished by the antenna coupler mounted on it. The Air Force gave me that piece of aircraft after the investigation, and I still have it as a memento.

The seawater was about 45° F. I was beginning to lose feeling in my extremities, and I lost concentration and probably consciousness a number of times. A number of things were going through my mind. I was really angry at my predicament, that I was not going to see my children grow up, that the people on the beach were not helping me, that I was stupid enough to have taken this mission. I believe this anger was my mind's way of focusing my energies and helped in great measure to keep me alive.

Rescue

I noticed a helicopter flying nearby doing a standard search pattern about ¼ mile off. I could tell from their pattern that it would be a while before they would work their way to my position, and I wasn't sure I could hang on for that length of time. I must have been very close to losing it as the next thing I remember is that the helicopter was directly over me and was hitting me with a "horse collar" pick up device trying to rouse me from my stupor.

In my survival training I had been taught to put on the collar as though putting on a coat. The collar was put under the arms and around the back with the pick up cable in front. I remembered the instructors being very adamant that putting it on any other way would result in the helicopter crew refusing to lift you up as it was likely that the person would fall out if he were incorrectly wearing the collar. And usually falling back into the water resulted in the loss of the survivor.

I attempted to put it on the way I had been taught but was unable to lift my right arm to get into the device. I then put my left arm through the collar clasped my hands together and remember saying to myself, "Don't let go." The next thing I remember I was in the helicopter with someone asking me what my name was. I told him my name and asked him to cover me as I was so cold.

My next solid recollection was a bed in the Nantucket Cottage Hospital. Someone was asking me a number of questions about the possibility of others being in the water and whether I heard or knew of any other survivors. I was unable to make them understand me. Apparently my speaking was unintelligible or my answers didn't track with their questions. I do remember being very upset that they were not listening to my answers but just asking their interminable questions.

Aftermath

The pilot of the helicopter that picked me up told me later that he saw me floating on the bulkhead and he thought at first that it was a beach towel. The bulkhead was light gray and I was wearing an orange flight suit. I guess it looked like a beach towel with a lobster motif on it. The helicopter crew was unable to send down a swimmer to help me as they had a problem with the winch cable and didn't think it would pick up two people. When I grabbed the collar, put my arm through it, and refused to let go, they had no choice but to attempt to bring me up. Luckily my grip was stronger than my mind.

When I was checked over in the hospital back at Otis, it was determined that I had broken my clavicle, right arm and left ankle. I also had assorted bruises and contusions, areas of burned skin, and a partially detached retina. Approximately six weeks after the accident, after I had returned to work, it was discovered that I had also broken my neck between vertebra 4 and 5.

The only indication I had of these injuries while I was in the water was that my right arm wouldn't work. There was no pain that I remember, just that it wouldn't work correctly. The doctors said the cold seawater protected me another way as well as from the fire. They believe the water was so cold that my neck muscles tensed up and kept everything in place.

Obviously I was extremely lucky to have survived the ditching. Possibly hitting a number of items in succession allowed me to decelerate more slowly and therefore to survive. How I got out of the aircraft by swimming up is a mystery to me. I can only assume it broke near where I was pinned.

However, once I was on the water surface I believe that there were a number of factors that worked together to contribute to my survival. I believe the major reason I survived in the water was the fact I had a loving wife with two little girls at home whom

I needed and who needed me. This was a powerful inducement to keep trying.

Also, I had an unreasonable internal anger at everything that was in my way, which kept me focused and resulted in my refusal to give up. And finally I believe the excellent training received in a number of Air Force survival schools helped immeasurably.

Continued Career

After the accident I was medically grounded, due to the broken neck, and retrained into the Data Automation field. I left Otis in the summer of 1969 to spend a year in Thailand at Nakhon Phanom (NKP), assigned as the base Data Automation Officer. While on leave awaiting my travel to NKP, I received orders placing me back on flying status. When I arrived in Thailand I was assigned to the 56th Air Commando Wing for flying duties, where I flew missions in EC-47s, C-47s, A-26s, C-123s, OV-10s, and HH-53s.

NKP was an interesting assignment. Every aircraft assigned to the base had propellers; some were turboprops, but no pure jet aircraft were assigned. All we needed was John Wayne and it would have been just like WWII. We used to say that a tour at Nakhon Phanom was just like Boy Scout Camp, except of course the Boy Scouts have adult leadership.

During my tour at NKP I received word from my wife Hannah that we were blessed with the birth of my son Jeremy. He is now a C-130 navigator with the 914th Air Wing at Niagara Falls AFS in New York. When I returned to the States, my assignment was to Scott AFB, IL at Headquarters' Military Airlift Command as an operations officer in the D.O.'s (Director of Operations) office where I also flew for time in C-131s.

Next came a tour at Dover AFB, DE flying C-5A's. The C-5 was my first assignment as a crew member flying pure jet aircraft. After all those years and all that flying time, I finally was crewing an aircraft that didn't have propellers. As an aside, during my entire time flying C-5s we shut down one engine, and that was purely a precautionary shutdown due to oil quantity indicators. On my first ride in a Connie we shut down one in the air and a second on the runway after landing. Engine shutdowns were not unusual at all on the EC-121s.

I then returned to Scott and HQ MAC (Military Airlift Command). My final tour was as the Military Airlift Command Liaison Officer to Electronic Systems Division at Hanscom Field,

MA. I retired in 1985 as a Lieutenant Colonel after 27 years total service.

© **January 1999 - Joseph L. H. Guenet**

Joseph L. H. Guenet
Lt. Colonel USAF, Ret.
307 Smallwood Drive
Amherst, NY 14226

NOTE: Colonel Guenet wrote that after he was released from the Otis Air Force Base Hospital he attended the internment of Major Howard N. Franklyn, the Pilot of 53-0549, in Londonderry, NH.

ITEM OF INTEREST: The longest mission reported by a crew member on the EC-121 "Warning Star" is 17:35 hours by 1/Lt Joseph L. H. Guenet as a navigator in the 551st AEW&C Wing at Otis AFB, MA, on December 24, 1965, in EC-121H number 55-5262. Some seven months later on November 11, 1966, that same aircraft was lost in the North Atlantic with all its 19 member crew. Five months after the loss of 55-5262 and its crew Lt. Guenet was the sole survivor when 53-0549 ditched in the North Atlantic with the loss of 15 crew members on April 25, 1967.

[Note 1] **Bear** is the name assigned by the North Atlantic Treaty Organization (NATO) to the Russian Tupolev TU-95 Long Range Strategic Bomber. Visit the following web site to learn of the mission of Connie crews from Otis AFB in Iceland "Hunting Russian Bears":

http://www.dean-boys.com/iceland/iceland.htm

To view the following photographs on the internet go to:

http://members.tripod.com/dboys/crash/crash.htm

PHOTOGRAPH FURNISHED COURTESY OF JOSEPH L. H. GUENET - THE ONLY SURVIVOR OF 53-0549

THE PHOTOGRAPH SHOWS PARTS OF 53-0549 THAT WERE SALVAGED FROM THE ATLANTIC AFTER THE PLANE DITCHED AND EXPLODED ON APRIL 25, 1967 AT NANTUCKET ISLAND, MASSACHUSETTS. THE PARTS ARE DISPLAYED IN A LARGE MAINTENANCE HANGAR AT OTIS AIR FORCE BASE, MASSACHUSETTS WHERE THE PLANE AND CREW WERE ASSIGNED. FIRST LIEUTENANT GUENET WAS THE SOLE SURVIVOR. THE REMAINING FIFTEEN MEMBERS OF THE CREW LOST THEIR LIVES. COLONEL JAMES P. LYLE, THE 551ST WING COMMANDER, WAS PILOTING THE AIRCRAFT.

PHOTOGRAPH FURNISHED COURTESY OF JOSEPH L. H. GUENET, THE NAVIGATOR WHO WAS THE SOLE SURVIVOR OF THE DITCHING OF 53-0549 ON APRIL 25, 1967.

THE PHOTOGRAPH SHOWS WHAT REMAINED OF THE RIGHT WING ROOT AREA AND THE NAVIGATOR'S POSITION AFTER THE PIECES OF THE AIRCRAFT WERE RECOVERED AND RECONSTRUCTED IN A MAINTENANCE HANGAR AT OTIS AIR FORCE BASE, MASSACHUSETTS.

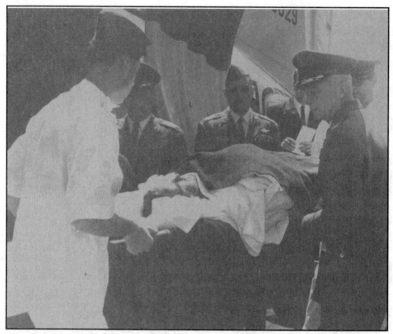

USAF PHOTOGRAPH TAKEN BY FRANK HILL WAS FURNISHED COURTESY OF JOSEPH L. H. GUENET.

HOME AGAIN

OTIS AIR FORCE BASE...4/26/67...LONE SURVIVOR [LIEUTENANT JOSEPH L. H. GUENET - NAVIGATOR] OF AIR DISASTER OVER NANTUCKET IS SHOWN BEING REMOVED FROM AIR FORCE PLANE ON WAY TO OTIS BASE HOSPITAL. OFFICERS (L TO R) COLONEL JOHN M. KONOSKY, 551ST WING COMMANDER; COLONEL ROBERT F. KALTENBACHER, BASE COMMANDER; COLONEL VIRGIL N. NESTER, DEPUTY COMMANDER FOR OPERATIONS. COLONEL KONOSKY BECAME THE NEW WING COMMANDER UPON COLONEL LYLE'S DEATH ON APRIL 25, 1967

PHOTOGRAPH FURNISHED COURTESY OF JOSEPH L. H. GUENET - SOLE SURVIVOR OF THE DITCHING OF 53-0549 ON APRIL 25, 1967

PHOTOGRAPH OF CAPTAIN JOSEPH L. H. GUENET TAKEN AT NAKON PHANTOM RTAFB, THAILAND IN 1969 - TWO YEARS AFTER THE AIR DISASTER AT NANTUCKET.

NOTES

SUMMARY OF EVENTS REGARDING THE CRASH OF EC-121H SUPER CONSTELLATION NUMBER 53-0549 PILOTED BY COLONEL JAMES PERKINS LYLE, COMMANDER 551ST AIRBORNE EARLY WARNING AND CONTROL WING, OTIS AIR FORCE BASE, FALMOUTH, MASSACHUSETTS, APRIL 25, 1967.

During the early evening of April 25, 1967, at approximately 6:58 p.m., Colonel James Perkins Lyle, Commander of the 551st Airborne Early Warning And Control Wing, Otis Air Force Base, Falmouth, Massachusetts and his crew of 15 officers and airmen took off from Otis on a Lockheed Super Constellation EC-121H on a scheduled active air defense mission.

The four-engine propeller driven aircraft was one of approximately 30 such aircraft which had been flying out of Otis Air Force Base, 24-hours a day, 7-days a week, 365 days a year, since 1955 providing an airborne radar platform as part of the nation's Distance Early Warning (DEW) air defense system.

Colonel Lyle and his crew were assigned aircraft number 53-0549. Colonel Lyle, the Aircraft Commander, and his crew performed all the required pre-flight checks, visual inspections, walk-around inspections, operational tests on all the communications and radar equipment, as well as checking the operation of the mechanical and electrical systems and completed engine run-ups. The aircraft, whose call sign was "Homey 82" then was cleared for take-off to begin a "routine" flight.

Soon after take-off, according to the only survivor, First Lieutenant Joseph L. H. Guenet, one of the two navigators, the crew felt what appeared to be "a small explosion" as the aircraft was approaching Nantucket Island climbing to its assigned altitude. The aircraft, he said, then went into a dive soon after the explosion but was pulled out of it by Colonel Lyle. "There was smoke in the aircraft that ranged from light to heavy. It considerably slowed down our preparations for the ditching," he continued. "Colonel Lyle had no time to issue any orders as such or converse with the crew. He was too busy flying the aircraft...."

Colonel Lyle, the Aircraft Commander, reported by radio about three minutes out that one of the engines was on fire and requested and received permission from Nantucket Airport to make an emergency landing there.

Eye witness reports in local newspapers reflect that "The plane came straight in towards the island, then made a loop that carried it near the jetties and then over land near Dionis as through he was making an approach for a landing."

Newspapers reported that a pilot in a small private plane watching from the air "reported seeing an engine fall from the stricken aircraft." It was further reported that "apparently, the pilot either lost control of the airplane at that point, or made a decision to head for the open ocean to spare Nantucket a fiery crash."

Newspapers reported that several witnesses saw the huge aircraft pass directly over their homes, head out to sea, and hit the water about a mile off the island only seven minutes after takeoff. Witnesses also reported seeing a hole in the wing. One engine reportedly was disintegrating and the pilot was gunning the engines in an attempt to avoid hitting the houses.

One witness, in a private aircraft, reported that he saw what was obviously an aircraft fire at about 5000 to 6000 feet altitude when the aircraft was about eight miles from the Nantucket airport. He said "It looked to me as though at least one, possibly two, of the engines dropped off the aircraft right after the burst. And it looked like parts of the structure dropped away. Suddenly, the flame was snuffed out. The pilot turned about 90 degrees left and headed a little west. He went along the north shore, turning slowly and descending slowly over Madaket, the north point. He kept turning along the shore and reached the south shore of the island and appeared to be in control. About a half mile off shore he began what seemed to be a ditching attempt. The instant he contacted water there was a tremendous burst of flame, one of the biggest things I've seen. It was just a fireball skidding about 4000 feet along the water parallel to shore. At the end of the skid she disappeared. You couldn't see a thing. You knew she was gone." He said at first the fire was small, then the smoke and fire increased. "Then there was a fireball explosion. It was a tremendous thing."

Other witnesses said "the plane was belching flames in a steep descent position heading for runway six at Nantucket Airport, when it suddenly veered 180 degrees and headed for open water." Air Force officials, it was reported, "speculated Colonel Lyle realized that any attempt to land at the airport could endanger scores of homes in the area and that he decided to ditch the plane at sea." Another witness, a pilot, who had witnessed the crash from his home, said "I am convinced that this boy fought desperately to get the plane into the water to avoid this summer colony."

Based on eyewitness reports which were documented in various newspapers at that time, it is apparent that Colonel Lyle's action as Aircraft Commander on EC-121H Number 53-0549 merits the greatest credit upon the Air Force, himself, and the crew he commanded in that he took evasive action so as not to not cause harm to the residents of Nantucket Island. His professional ability was pushed to the maximum while dealing with the life threatening problems he and his crew were encountering.

His exemplary leadership, personal endeavor, and devotion to duty is unsurpassed.

From all documented sources it appears that Colonel Lyle averted a disaster. He therefore should have received recognition for his valor.

Information used as background came from the following sources:
News Articles [Boston Traveler] [Cape Cod Standard-Times] [Cape Cod Times]
Bourne Public Schools - Lyle Middle School - Otis ANG, MA
Department of The Air Force - Headquarters Air Force Safety Center

CAN YOU RELY ON OFFICIAL RECORDS?

When I began the research into the loss of the crew members on the three aircraft I found news articles which were published immediately after the three separate aircraft mishaps occurred. Those articles also detailed events leading to the rescues of the survivors, the recovery of many of the bodies of the crew, as well as accounts of those whose bodies were never found.

In the news articles pertaining to 55-0136 which crashed on July 11, 1965, it was reported that 16 men's lives were lost and three men survived. Of the 16 who lost their lives, nine bodies were located and recovered and seven bodies were never found.

In the news articles pertaining to 55-5262, which crashed on November 11, 1966, it was reported that none of the bodies of the 19 men ever were found.

In the news articles pertaining to 53-0549 which crashed on April 25, 1967, it was reported that one man survived and 15 men died. It was further reported that of the 15 who died only two bodies (Master Sergeant Frank W. Garner Jr., and Airman First Class Theodore E. LaPointe Jr.) were found.

There were no further news articles located reflecting that the bodies of the 13 missing crew of 53-0549 ever had been found and recovered.

Documents obtained from Headquarters Air Force Safety Center at Kirtland Air Force Base, NM are not in disagreement with the news articles as to the number of men who survived, the number who died and whose bodies were recovered, and the number who died and whose bodies were not recovered.

The "Summary of Circumstances" pertaining to 53-0549 was received from the Air Force Safety Center at Kirtland AFB. It reflects that the bodies of two crew members (MSgt Garner and A1C LaPointe) were recovered. The Summary continues by stating "*The other crew members were not recovered.*"[E.S.]

The ending of the Summary reflects that "*Search and salvage operations were finally discontinued on May 31, 1967 after the majority of the aircraft wreckage had been recovered and no*

<u>additional aircrew member bodies had been located</u>." [E.S.]

Seeking to find out additional information about Colonel James P. Lyle, the 551st Wing Commander who flew as the Aircraft Commander on 53-0549 when it crashed, I was fortunate to have located his widow.

Mrs. Juanita Lyle spoke with me by telephone, and I later sent her copies of some of the information I had collected. During our conversation she mentioned that Colonel Lyle is buried in the Fort Sam Houston National Cemetery at San Antonio, TX. She said she was so distraught over his death that she permitted her brother to make arrangements for his burial and that she did not attend the internment ceremony.

Mrs. Lyle told me that no personal items worn by Colonel Lyle were returned to her (his wedding ring and "dog tags"). She questioned whether his body had been found and if the burial might not have been symbolic in nature.

I did not attribute much importance to what she said since there could have been many reasons for personal items to have been missing after a violent aircraft crash which, according to eye witnesses, had exploded upon impact in the water.

I telephoned Fort Sam Houston National Cemetery to inquire about Colonel Lyle's burial location. I was told that Colonel James P. Lyle was buried there on June 6, 1967 in Section 2C - Number 434. I asked if the burial was a memorial ceremony and was told no -- that it was a burial. I also was told that if a memorial had been placed in the cemetery, typical when no body is recovered, it would have been in a different section in the cemetery.

I also noted that information received from the Veterans Administration regarding burials reflects in part:

> Memorial monuments are provided for eligible, individual veterans whose remains are not recovered or identified, buried at sea, or are otherwise unavailable for interment. The monuments bear a "**In Memory Of**" inscription as the first line.

I also met, via the internet, James P. Walsh, whose father William M.

Walsh, A1C, AF11298681, died in the crash of Colonel Lyle's aircraft. James resides in Houston, TX, and he subsequently visited the National Cemetery at Fort Sam Houston in San Antonio where he viewed and photographed Colonel Lyle's grave marker. [See the accompanying photograph at pg. 390.]

James reported that the personnel in the administrative office at the National Cemetery maintained that there would have been a body in the grave, and they told him, as I had been told earlier, that if it had been an empty grave a memorial stone would be located in a completely different part of the cemetery.

NOTE: Colonel Lyle's aircraft crashed on April 25, 1967, and he was buried on June 6, 1967. The recovery and salvage operation was concluded on May 31, 1967.

At one point in time before James visited Colonel Lyle's grave site, he said that he had been told by his mother that the body of his father, William Walsh, had been recovered and had been identified by his dental work and by two close friends. His mother, James said, never viewed the remains and it was a closed casket funeral. James said his father is buried behind St. Joseph's Catholic Church, North Grovnerdale, CT.

Thinking perhaps I had misunderstood what was in the Summary I again contacted the Air Force Safety Center and was again told that they had no documents at the Center to show any bodies other than those of MSgt Garner and A/1C LaPointe were recovered.

I wrote Air Force Chief of Staff General Michael E. Ryan a letter in which I outlined the apparent discrepancy of whether additional bodies had been recovered of the crew of 53-0549. I urged General Ryan to cause an inquiry so that the matter might be resolved.

I subsequently telephoned the Staff Judge Advocate at Headquarters Air Force Safety Center, Kirtland Air Force Base, who told me that my letter to General Ryan had been forwarded to him and that all avenues were being pursued in an attempt to find out the answer(s) to the situation outlined in my letter.

I also contacted the Chief of Naval Operations since the Navy was in charge of the salvage and recovery operation regarding the crash of 53-0549. I requested copies of the salvage records in an attempt to determine if bodies were recovered in the fuselage of the aircraft. The response from the Navy was that the salvage records could not be located.

I wrote to the Chief of Naval Operations requesting to know if the Navy had conducted autopsies on the thirteen crew members' remains who died in the crash of 53-0549. It had been reported in the press that after the bodies of MSGT Garner and A1C LaPointe were recovered, they were taken to Chelsea Naval Hospital in Boston for autopsies. Subsequently I received a response from the Office of Medical/Dental Affairs, Mortuary Affairs Section, Great Lakes, IL that they had no information regarding my request.

I wrote to the Armed Forces Medical Examiner, Air Force Institute of Pathology in Washington, DC., requesting to know if there were records of autopsies of the crew members of 53-0549. My request went unanswered.

I contacted the Air Force Casualty Branch and Air Force Mortuary Service and told them of the apparent discrepancy about the bodies recovered. I was told by those agencies that they were pursuing the matter and would try to resolve it.

General Ryan later wrote me in part:

> Air Force Safety reports are not intended to serve as permanent records of the disposition of casualties. Therefore, the references to individuals who might have been recovered or not recovered are not authoritative for the purposes of determining their final disposition. The Air Force Mortuary Affairs Office is researching this case to see if more information is available.

I also wrote to the Nantucket Cottage Hospital at Nantucket, MA. This is the hospital where the one survivor from 53-0549 (Lieutenant L. H. Guenet) was taken for emergency treatment immediately after he was rescued from the ocean. I asked if any bodies of any members of the crew of 53-0549 were processed through that hospital before being removed from the Island. The President of the Cottage Hospital referred me to the Town Clerk of Nantucket and suggested that I ask the Town Clerk to research the death certificates for the crew members.

I furnished the Town Clerk a listing of the thirteen crew members from 53-0549 who were reported as dead and about whom there were some question of whether their bodies had been recovered.

The Town Clerk of Nantucket responded that the Town's records reflect that eight of the crew members remains had been recovered. The Town Clerk said the remains recovered for which there are death certificates in the Town's records probably were recovered on the beach at Nantucket. If other remains were recovered, they were recovered outside the Town's jurisdiction, she advised. Therefore, she said, if the remains were recovered in the ocean or in the recovered aircraft structure, they were found outside Nantucket's jurisdiction and there would be not death certificates for them filed there. The Town Clerk suggested that I contact the Massachusetts Registry of Vital Records and Statistics in Boston, MA to see if death certificates were on file there for the remaining crew members.

The Town Clerk of Nantucket furnished certified copies of the death certificates of the following crew members of 53-0549. The cause of death in each instance is shown as "Injuries sustained in airplane crash," and the date of death is shown as April 25, 1967. The place of disposition is shown below beside their names:

BEARDON, RICHARD DENNIS [Arlington Natl. Cemetery, VA]
CLAPPER, ROBERT JEFFERY [Sacred Heart No. 2, New Bedford, MA]
COLE, DENNIS RICHARD [Pine Grove, Westboro, MA]
FRANKLYN, HOWARD N. [Pleasant View, Londonderry, NH]
HAMMAN, GORDON OAKLEY [Beechwood, West Centerville, MA]
LYLE, JAMES P. [Ft. Sam Houston Cemetery, San Antonio, TX]
MULHERN, ROBERT EDWARD [Cremation, Forest Hills, Boston, MA]
WALSH, WILLIAM MICHAEL [St. Joseph, N. Grovnerdale, CT]

I informed both Colonel Lyle's wife and James Walsh of my finding the death certificates and also wrote General Ryan letting him know of my finding.

I requested copies of the death certificates for the other five crew members from the Massachusetts Registry of Vital Statistics and Records. Those are:

CAPTAIN FRANK R. FERGUSON
A1C RICHARD D. GRAVELY
A2C DENIS E. BOYLE
A2C DANNY R. BURDEN
A2C WILLIAM M. COOK

I subsequently received official notice from The Commonwealth of Massachusetts, State Department of Public Health, Registry of Vital Records and Statistics, that a search of the death records for the years 1961-1970 was done and no death certificates for the five above-named flyers were found.

I later received notice from the Chief of Air Force Casualty Branch at Randolph Air Force Base, Texas, that all avenues had been exhausted which were available to them regarding the five crew members and they were unable to provide any further information regarding them.

I was able to obtain copies of numerous news articles that were written about the three crashes. I found a large number of articles written about the crash of 53-0549 piloted by Colonel Lyle, the 551st Wing Commander. None of the newspaper articles I was able to locate mentioned that Colonel Lyle's remains were recovered nor did they mention that any of the remains of his crew, with the exception of MSGT Garner and A1C LaPointe, were recovered. Yet, according to the Town Clerk of Nantucket and reflected in records furnished by that office, at least eight recoveries were made in addition to Garner and LaPointe.

I cannot understand why the recovery of the bodies was not made public by the Air Force and reported by local newspapers that were covering the crash at that time. I am sure the fact that Colonel Lyle's remains were recovered would have been most newsworthy.

The Town Clerk of Nantucket said that autopsies of the remains of the eight crew members for which she has death certificates on file, were performed by a local medical examiner. The remains were released and transported to their final destinations for disposition.

NOTE: *I subsequently located the former wife of Captain Frank R. Ferguson (one of the two navigators on 53-0549 which crashed at Nantucket on April 25, 1967). His wife told me that Captain Ferguson's remains were never returned to her so she concluded that his body was not recovered from the crash site. I was not successful in locating the next of kin of Airmen Boyle, Burden, Cook, and Gravely to ask if their remains had been returned to them.*

CHANGES OF KEY PERSONNEL

Things appear to not have been going well at the 551st AEW&C Wing after three EC-121H "Warning Star" aircraft crashed in less than two years taking the lives of fifty officers and airmen.

Several changes of key personnel occurred immediately after the third EC-121H radar plane crashed killing the 551st Wing Commander, Colonel James Perkins Lyle. Fourteen others on his crew were killed and one survived.

Copies of the now declassified Historical Record of the 551st Airborne Early Warning and Control Wing were obtained from the Historical Research Agency at Maxwell AFB, Alabama. The report for the period ending 30 June 1967 reflects that:

Change of Key Personnel. Upon the death of Colonel James P. Lyle, 551st AEW&Con Wg Commander, Colonel John M. Konosky, Vice Commander, assumed command of the wing. On 10 June 67, Colonel Konosky was succeeded by Colonel Max W. Rogers.

Colonel Vergil N. Nestor, Deputy Commander for Operations, 551st AEW&Con Wg, was relieved of duty on 5 June 67 with a projected replacement of Colonel Max Sansing.

Lieutenant Colonel Evo Borasari, Chief of Maintenance of the 551st AEW&Con Wg, departed this station on 15 June 67. He was succeeded by Lieutenant Colonel Joseph A. Mentecki.

Colonel Robert F. Kaltenbacher, 551st Combat Support Group Commander, departed this station on 25 June 67 with a programmed replacement of Colonel Carl W. Bradford.

That same report reflects:

<u>*Flying Safety*</u>*. During this reporting period one major accident was reported to the Safety Division. The accident involved aircraft 53-0549 and 16 crew members who were aboard the aircraft when it crashed at sea on 25 April 67. Only one of the original sixteen-man crew survived; he is 1st Lt. Joseph L.H. Guenet. An extensive and thorough investigation of the accident was conducted and causative factors were determined.*

NOTE: This was the aircraft which crashed at Nantucket Island and was piloted by Colonel James P. Lyle.

The Historical Report for the period ending 30 September 1965 reflects:

Flying Safety. There was one reportable major aircraft accident on 11 July 1965 that resulted in the first loss of life in an aircraft accident during the entire tenure of this Wing. The accident report has not at this date been finalized by higher headquarters, USAF.

NOTE: This refers to aircraft 55-0136 piloted by 1st Lt. Frederick H. Ambrosia which crashed with the loss of 16 lives and had three survivors.

The Historical Report for the period ending 31 December 1966 reflects:

Flying Safety. During this reporting period only one major accident, and three minor aircraft incidents were reported to the Safety Division. The major accident involved the loss of aircraft 55-5262 and 19 aircrew members who were aboard the aircraft when it ditched at sea on November 11, 1966. An extensive and thorough investigation of the accident was held; however, conclusive causative factors are being withheld pending salvage of the aircraft.

Some of the news articles reporting the Connie accidents questioned whether the Connies were becoming obsolete.

Colonel Max W. Rogers was reportedly a former trouble shooter with the Strategic Air Command and was "affectionately" known as "Max The Axe." He took over command of the 551st AEW&C Wing soon after Colonel Lyle's untimely death.

Colonel Rogers commanded the 551st AEW&C Wing from June 5, 1967 to January 31, 1969.

Wanting to find out information about the crash of Colonel Lyle's aircraft and possibly the other two, I located Colonel Rogers, now retired and residing in Arizona. A large volume of research information pertaining to the crashes was sent to him but he did not respond.

Colonel John M. Konosky (who became the Wing Commander upon Colonel Lyle's death and who was replaced shortly afterwards by Colonel Max Rogers) is now retired and residing in Colorado. I contacted him in an attempt to get information about the accidents and particularly the one in which Colonel Lyle was killed (53-0549 on April 25, 1967).

I sent a package to Colonel Konosky and during subsequent telephone conversations with him he revealed that he has had two strokes which have impaired his memory and speech. During those conversations with him, and later by a letter from his wife, it became apparent that he could not now recall the accidents.

THEY KNEW THEY WOULD RETURN

Most of the crew members on the Super Constellations had flown the same type radar surveillance missions over and over until it had become a routine with them. I recall it was that way for me. Each time you prepared to go on a flight and said good bye to your family or your friends at the squadron, you knew you would return to fly again.

After all, you did this regularly, and you were well qualified in your job aboard the aircraft. You had all the confidence in the world in the rest of the crew and in the aircraft. You had a lot of faith in the skill of the pilots who would fly the aircraft, in the navigator who would guide the plane day or night over the ocean. Likewise, you knew that the flight engineers who watched over all aspects of the plane were professionals, as were the radar technicians, the radio operators, and the radar operators who made up the rest of the crew. You also relied on the professionalism of the maintenance and support personnel who maintained the aircraft mechanically. You also relied on the plane's electronic equipment, as well life saving devices installed in the aircraft and your own personal lifesaving equipment issued prior to each flight.

You got to know the men who flew with you and to trust them. A friendship existed that is difficult to describe to outsiders who were not on flight crews. You also got to know the families and friends of the crew members.

Most likely good byes on the three occasions were the same as they always had been. Everyone was aware that there always was some danger, but they had become accustomed of living with it. All believed they would return to fly another day.

It became a nightmare come true when military officers and clergy began knocking at the doors of the families of the missing flyers. There was hope, there was despair, there was sadness, and there was grief no one should ever have to bear.

For the families of fifty of the fifty-four, there were memorial services to attend and burials of those whose remains were recovered. Although with a heavy heart for the families of the fallen flyers, the families of the four who survived doubtless also rejoiced at their own good fortune.

Soon afterwards the wives and children of these men began their lives anew as they moved to most all parts of the country. Two years after the last accident the military unit for which they flew was deactivated, the base from which they departed on their fatal flights was renamed, the planes became obsolete and were put aside and few, with the exception of the remaining immediate family members and friends of the flyers, remember this tragedy ever happening at all.

CONDOLENCES

I hope that all the families of the flyers who died in the three EC-121H crashes received letters of condolence from the President of The United States, Air Force Chief of Staff, and dignitaries from the flyers' home states and home towns. I am sure there were many cards, letters, and offers of kindness given by those who knew the individual flyers in some capacity. The memories of kindness and respect received at such a terrible time are cherished by the families who suffered the loss of their loved ones.

CONDOLENCE LETTERS SENT REGARDING THE DEATH OF COLONEL JAMES P. LYLE ON APRIL 25, 1967 IN THE DITCHING OF 53-0549.

The first letter of condolence is from the Air Force notifying Senator John Stennis of the death of Colonel Lyle, his cousin.

The second letter of condolence is from Senator Stennis to Colonel Lyle's mother.

LETTERS FURNISHED COURTESY OF DEAN BOYS

DEPARTMENT OF THE AIR FORCE
WASHINGTON 20330

WASHINGTON OFFICE
RECEIVED MAY 11 1967
JOHN STENNIS

OFFICE OF THE SECRETARY

MAY 9 1967

Dear Senator Stennis:

Permit me to express our deepest sympathy over the recent loss of your cousin, Colonel James P. Lyle, as the result of an aircraft accident near Nantucket Island, Massachusetts.

Colonel Lyle was held in the highest esteem by his many friends and colleagues in the Air Force. He served his Country with courage, honor, and fidelity throughout his long and distinguished career which is replete with significant accomplishments. Indeed, the Nation is profoundly indebted to men of his intrepid valor and dedication.

Copies of his biographical sketch are attached for your information.

Again, our heartfelt condolences to you.

Sincerely,

LAWRENCE S. LIGHTNER
Major General, USAF
Director, Legislative Liaison

Attachment

Honorable John Stennis
United States Senate

United States Senate
COMMITTEE ON ARMED SERVICES

May 16, 1967

Mrs. C. H. Lyle
Springtown, Texas

My dear Cousin:

This letter is to you and to all members of your family and his family, to extend my condolences and my heartfelt sympathy in the earthly loss of your fine son James, who gave his life in defense of his country.

Certainly, he had a wonderful record and reflected credit on his mother and father as well as all of his family, with his devotion to duty and highly outstanding military record, in which I have such pride.

Jerome Kerby of Fort Worth wrote me about Colonel Lyle's death, and the Air Force wrote me a letter recently, a copy of which I enclose. Your family in Texas has always been appreciated by our branch of the family in Mississippi. We love you all, and I wish so much that our paths could cross for a visit.

Please extend my words of interest to the members of James' family and the other members of your fine family.

With esteem and good wishes, I am

Your cousin,

John Stennis

JS:eh
Enc.

LETTERS OF CONDOLENCE SENT FROM PRESIDENT JOHNSON, AIR FORCE CHIEF OF STAFF, AND THE GOVERNOR OF MASSACHUSETTS TO THE WIFE OF A1C WILLIAM M. WALSH UPON HIS DEATH ON APRIL 25, 1967 IN THE DITCHING OF 53-0549.

LETTERS FURNISHED COURTESY OF JAMES WALSH, SON OF A1C WILLIAM M. WALSH

THE WHITE HOUSE
WASHINGTON

May 8, 1967

Dear Mrs. Walsh:

Please accept my personal sympathy in the death of your husband, Airman First Class William M. Walsh, near Nantucket Island, Massachusetts.

The responsibility that I bear as Commander-in-Chief is made heavier by the sorrow I share with our bereaved families. I pray, however, that the memory of your husband's service in the defense of freedom will be as much a source of strength and pride to you as it is to me.

Mrs. Johnson joins me in offering heartfelt sympathy and admiration to you, your children, and the other members of the family.

Sincerely,

Lyndon B. Johnson

Mrs. William M. Walsh
53 Corte Real Avenue
East Falmouth, Massachusetts

OFFICE OF THE CHIEF OF STAFF
UNITED STATES AIR FORCE
WASHINGTON

May 2, 1967

My dear Mrs. Walsh:

    We of the Air Force share your sorrow in the death of Airman First Class William M. Walsh.

    Your husband rendered loyal and devoted services to his country. I hope this memory will bring increasing comfort to you as time passes.

    My deepest sympathy is extended to you and the other members of the family.

Sincerely,

J. P. McCONNELL, General, USAF
Chief of Staff

Mrs. William M. Walsh
53 Corte Real Avenue
East Falmouth, Massachusetts

THE COMMONWEALTH OF MASSACHUSETTS
EXECUTIVE DEPARTMENT
STATE HOUSE, BOSTON

JOHN A. VOLPE
GOVERNOR

May 3, 1967

Mrs. William M. Walsh
53 Carte Real Avenue
Falmouth, Massachusetts

Dear Mrs. Walsh:

I would like to extend my personal condolences to you and to your family on the tragic passing of your husband, William.

Airman Walsh has made the greatest sacrifice which a man can offer to his country, and I join with all Americans in expressing the profound debt of gratitude which is due your husband and his many comrades.

I know this is a time of deep sorrow for you, and Mrs. Volpe and I wish to offer our sympathy and our prayers.

Sincerely,

Governor

The following letters of condolence were sent to the Brody family upon the death of Captain Murray J. Brody in the ditching of 55-0136 on July 11, 1965. The letters were provided by Captain Brody's daughter, Deborah.

THE WHITE HOUSE
WASHINGTON

July 21, 1965

Dear Mrs. Brody:

I was deeply grieved to learn of the death of your husband, Captain Murray J. Brody, United States Air Force, as the result of an aircraft accident near Nantucket, Massachusetts.

Mere words can bring little consolation, but I want you to know that Captain Brody's many friends feel privileged to have been associated with such a fine officer. Your husband upheld the highest traditions of our country, and of its military forces. Captain Brody's skill and precision as a pilot made him a highly valued member of our Air Force. His achievements merit the highest praise.

It is my sincere hope that you will gain comfort from the knowledge that your loss is shared by a nation grateful for your husband's praiseworthy contributions.

Mrs. Johnson and I extend our heartfelt condolences to you, Karen, Deborah, Paul, and the other members of the family.

Sincerely,

[signature: Lyndon B. Johnson]

Mrs. Murray J. Brody
121 Marquand Avenue
Bronxville, New York

LETTER FROM THE PRESIDENT OF THE UNITED STATES - LYNDON B. JOHNSON

OFFICE OF THE CHIEF OF STAFF
UNITED STATES AIR FORCE
WASHINGTON

July 16, 1965

My dear Mrs. Brody:

  We of the Air Force share your sorrow in the death of Captain Murray J. Brody.

  Your husband's cooperative and sincere interest in his assignments earned him the respect of all those with whom he served. You can be proud of his creditable performance of duty in the Air Force.

  My deepest sympathy is extended to you and the other members of the family.

Sincerely,

J. P. McCONNELL
General, USAF
Chief of Staff

Mrs. Murray J. Brody
5415D Carpenter Avenue
Otis Air Force Base, Massachusetts

LETTER FROM THE UNITED STATES AIR FORCE CHIEF OF STAFF - GENERAL J. P. McCONNELL

Dear Ms. Brody - May I express my deepest regret in learning of the accident that took the life of your husband. There is little we can do to alleviate your suffering, but you should know, we are sharing your loss. Murray was a valuable crew member with the prospect of a promising career. He was a true professional and had won the respect of all for his outstanding duty. May your wonderful memories of him help to console you in the difficult days ahead. Call on us for assistance when needed. Sincerely - Herbert Thatcher.

[LIEUTENANT GENERAL - COMMANDER OF THE AIR DEFENSE COMMAND]

HEADQUARTERS
26TH AIR DIVISION (SAGE)
United States Air Force
Stewart AFB, New York 12554

Office of Commander

JUL 16 1965

Mrs. Murray Joseph Brody
5415D Carpenter Avenue
Otis AFB, Massachusetts

Dear Mrs. Brody

It is with the deepest personal feeling that I express to you my sincere sympathy in the loss of your husband, Captain Murray Joseph Brody.

Upon hearing of the tragic accident near Otis Air Force Base, I went immediately to the scene. Under the prevailing conditions, every rescue effort conceivable was effected. I realize the shock and irreplaceable loss you suffer, as tragedy befell my son at the time when he was entering into young manhood. Losing men of my Command is always a personal tragedy, and because of this I sorrow with members of their families.

The adjustment to a loss such as yours cannot be made without great difficulty, but I earnestly hope that this expression of condolence may help in some small measure to ease the grief you bear.

Sincerely

VON R. SHORES
Major General, USAF
Commander

LETTER FROM MAJOR GENERAL VON P. SHORES - COMMANDER OF THE 26TH AIR DIVISION

```
                    HEADQUARTERS
       551ST AIRBORNE EARLY WARNING AND CONTROL WING (ADC)
                  UNITED STATES AIR FORCE
              OTIS AIR FORCE BASE, MASSACHUSETTS
```

20 July 1965

Mrs. Claire Brody
5415D Carpenter Street
Otis AFB, Massachusetts

Dear Mrs. Brody:

I would like to add my personal condolences to those expressed by the Squadron Commander, Lt Colonel Robert V. Mitchell, and by the Combat Support Group Commander, Colonel R. F. Kaltenbacher, for the loss of your husband, Captain Murray J. Brody. The officers and men of my command, the 551st AEW Con Wing, of which Murray was a member, also wish you to know their sorrow and deepest compassion at this time.

You can be justifiably proud of Murray's record, as his achievements while assigned to Otis AFB were most honorable to you and the United States Air Force. He lost his life on an active air defense mission in defense of this country just as surely as if he had been a combat casualty.

Please do not hesitate to call on me if I may be of assistance to you.

Sincerely,

RAYMOND K. GALLAGHER
Colonel, USAF
Commander

LETTER FROM COLONEL RAYMOND K. GALLAGHER - COMMANDER OF THE 551ST AIRBORNE EARLY WARNING AND CONTROL WING AT OTIS AIR FORCE BASE, MASSACHUSETTS

HEADQUARTERS
551ST COMBAT SUPPORT GROUP (ADC)
UNITED STATES AIR FORCE
OTIS AIR FORCE BASE, MASSACHUSETTS, 02542

15 July 1965

Mrs. Claire Brody
5415D Carpenter Street
Otis Air Force Base, Massachusetts

Dear Mrs. Brody,

It is with profound and heartfelt sadness that I must officially inform you of the death of your husband, Captain Murray J. Brody, a member of my command. The officers and airmen of the 961st Airborne Early Warning and Control Squadron join me in offering you our deepest compassion and condolence. Although Murray had been assigned to the 961st only a little over three months, all of those with whom he worked respected and admired him for his integrity, pleasant demeanor and airmanship.

On the night of 11 July 1965, your husband died honorably and courageously in the performance of his assigned duties as Pilot of an Airborne Early Warning Constellation type aircraft. While flying at 15,000 feet altitude approximately 115 miles east of Cape Cod, the aircraft and crew were performing their mission of providing radar data to the United States air defense system when, due to a serious in-flight emergency, it became necessary to ditch the aircraft at sea. Once the emergency developed, the aircraft made contact with the water within a few minutes. Impact occurred at 1022 P.M. Some of the details of the ditching are still unknown at this time; however, your husband did not survive.

Although I know that everything will be done officially that can be done at this time, do not hesitate to call on me in the future if I may be of assistance.

Sincerely

R. F. KALTENBACHER
Colonel, USAF
Commander

LETTER FROM COLONEL ROBERT F. KALTENBACHER - COMMANDER OF THE 551ST COMBAT SUPPORT GROUP AT OTIS AIR FORCE BASE, MASSACHUSETTS

961st AIRBORNE EARLY WARNING AND CONTROL SQUADRON
551st AIRBORNE EARLY WARNING AND CONTROL WING (ADC)
UNITED STATES AIR FORCE
OTIS AIR FORCE BASE, MASSACHUSETTS
02542

Mrs Claire Brody
5415D Carpenter Street
Otis Air Force Base, Massachusetts   20 July 1965

Dear Mrs Brody,

    Although I have talked to you personally, I want to again express to you my deepest sympathy and compassion in the death of your husband. Each of us within the squadron feels deeply your loss and each shares profoundly your sadness. Since the crews fly together as a closely knit team of officers and airmen intensely dedicated to the air defense of our country, a loss of a team member is heartfelt by every member of our squadron family.

    Perhaps you can seek encouragement and comfort in the knowledge that Murray died with valor performing an Active Air Defense mission so very vital to all Americans everywhere. He sacrificed his life so that millions can rest securely and safely. For this sacrifice, he has the gratitude and thankfulness of all of us.

    Murray had been assigned to my squadron approximately ninety days, but in that period of time he had gained the respect and admiration of all those with whom he worked. His pleasant manner, integrity, and especially his initiative and desire to know the intricacies of his aircraft left an impression on me that shall long endure.

    I shall be glad to assist you in any way I can now or in the future.

Sincerely,

[signature]

ROBERT V. MITCHELL, SR
Lt Colonel, USAF
Commander

LETTER FROM LIEUTENANT COLONEL ROBERT V. MITCHELL, SR., COMMANDER OF THE 961ST AIRBORNE EARLY WARNING AND CONTROL SQUADRON TO WHICH CAPTAIN MURRAY J. BRODY WAS ASSIGNED FOR FLIGHT DUTY AS A PILOT.

The following letters of condolence were sent to the

Barbolla family upon the death of Captain Michael R. Barbolla in the ditching of 55-0136 on July 11, 1965. The letters were provided by Captain Barbolla's wife, Diane Barbolla.

WASHINGTON

July 28, 1965

Dear Mrs. Barbolla:

I was deeply saddened to learn of the death of your husband, Captain Michael R. Barbolla, United States Air Force, as the result of an aircraft accident near Nantucket, Massachusetts.

Your husband distinguished himself by his superior technical ability as a navigator, and his devotion to his career made him a respected and valued member of our Air Force. I hope the knowledge that our country is sincerely grateful for Captain Barbolla's outstanding contributions as an instructor in the Reserve Officers' Training Corps program at Manhattan College will be a source of comfort to you.

On behalf of our nation, may I express our gratitude for your husband's unselfish dedication, which is worthy of the highest praise.

Mrs. Johnson joins me in extending our heartfelt condolences to you and the other members of the family.

Sincerely,

Lyndon B. Johnson

Mrs. Michael R. Barbolla
5900 Arlington Avenue
Riverdale, New York

LETTER FROM THE PRESIDENT OF THE UNITED STATES - LYNDON B. JOHNSON

OFFICE OF THE CHIEF OF STAFF
UNITED STATES AIR FORCE
WASHINGTON

July 20, 1965

My dear Mrs. Barbolla:

    We of the Air Force share your sorrow in the death of Captain Michael R. Barbolla.

    Your husband's cooperative and sincere interest in his assignments earned him the respect of all those with whom he served. You can be proud of his creditable performance of duty in the Air Force.

    My deepest sympathy is extended to you and the other members of the family.

Sincerely,

W. H. BLANCHARD
General, U. S. Air Force
Vice Chief of Staff

Mrs. Michael R. Barbolla
5900 Arlington Avenue
Riverdale, New York

LETTER FROM THE UNITED STATES AIR FORCE VICE CHIEF OF STAFF - GENERAL W. H. BLANCHARD

AIR FORCE ROTC
AIR UNIVERSITY
UNITED STATES AIR FORCE
MAXWELL AIR FORCE BASE, ALABAMA

OFFICE OF THE COMMANDANT

19 JUL 1965

Mrs. Diane B. Barbolla
5900 Arlington Avenue
Riverdale, New York

Dear Mrs. Barbolla

I am deeply grieved by Michael's untimely death. Though no words can bring you consolation for your tragic loss, my staff and I want you to know that our hearts reach out to you and that you will be remembered in our prayers.

I would consider it a privilege to be of assistance to you and, again, express our deepest, hearthfelt condolence.

Sincerely

William C. Lindley

WILLIAM C. LINDLEY
Brigadier General, USAF
Commandant

LETTER FROM THE COMMANDANT OF THE AFROTC - AIR UNIVERSITY - GENERAL WILLIAM C. LINDLEY

```
                    HEADQUARTERS
              551ST COMBAT SUPPORT GROUP (ADC)
                 UNITED STATES AIR FORCE
            OTIS AIR FORCE BASE, MASSACHUSETTS, 02542
```

19 July 1965

Mrs. Michael R. Barbolla
2550 Independence Avenue
Bronx, New York 10463

Dear Mrs. Barbolla:

1. It is with heartfelt and profound sadness that I must officially inform you of the death of your husband, Captain Michael R. Barbolla, a member of my command. The officers and airmen of the AFROTC Field Training Unit join me in offering you our deepest compassion and condolence. In the six weeks he had been assigned to the Field Training Unit he had gained the respect of all those with whom he worked. He supported the unit in many ways including participation in all programs.

2. On the night of 11 July 1965, your husband died honorably and courageously in the performance of his duties as Navigator on an Airborne Early Warning Constellation type aircraft. While flying approximately 115 miles east of Nantucket, the aircraft and crew were performing their mission of providing radar data to the United States Air Defense System, when due to a serious in-flight emergency, it became necessary to ditch the aircraft at sea. Once the emergency developed, the aircraft made contact with the water within a few minutes. Some of the details of the ditching are still unknown, but your husband did not survive. An extensive air and sea search was conducted for five days after the crash and although all possible efforts were made to recover the body, they were to no avail.

3. A representative from a nearby Air Force Base will call on you shortly to assist in any way possible.

4. Although I know that everything that can be done officially will be done at this time, do not hesitate to call on me in the future if I may be of assistance.

Sincerely

R. F. KALTENBACHER
Colonel, USAF
Commander

LETTER FROM COLONEL ROBERT F. KALTENBACHER - COMMANDER OF THE 551ST COMBAT SUPPORT GROUP AT OTIS AIR FORCE BASE, MASSACHUSETTS

HEADQUARTERS
AFROTC Field Training Unit
UNITED STATES AIR FORCE
Otis Air Force Base, Massachusetts

Mrs. Diane Barbolla   19 July 1965
5900 Arlington Avenue
Riverdale, New York

Dear Mrs. Barbolla:

Accompanying this letter is an American Flag which was accepted on your behalf at a Memorial Service held at Otis Air Force Base on Friday, 16 July 1965.

The Flag is symbolic of the devotion to duty and country displayed by Captain Barbolla throughout his military career and was presented as a token of sincere appreciation on behalf of the People of the United States of America.

I would like to add my heartfelt condolences on behalf of the officers and men of the Air Force ROTC Field Training Unit at Otis Air Force Base, and offer any assistance which may be of value to you in the future. Please feel free to call upon me at any time.

Sincerely

EARL E. PUTMAN
Lt Colonel, USAF
Commander

LETTER FROM LIEUTENANT COLONEL EARL E. PUTMAN, COMMANDER OF THE AFROTC FIELD TRAINING UNIT AT OTIS AIR FORCE BASE, MASSACHUSETTS

THE "SILENT BATTLEFIELD"

Al Perusse of Hampden, MA, a former member of a flight crew in the 961st AEW&C Squadron at Otis AFB, MA, knew William Walsh, who lost his life on 53-0549 at Nantucket Island on April 25, 1967.

Al had attended the 551st AEW&C Wing reunion in September of 1997 and saw a picture of a flight crew in which he recognized himself and William Walsh (see photograph titled "A Typical Connie Crew" at pg. 288).

Al found out that James Walsh of Houston, TX, the son of William Walsh, had sent the photograph to the reunion hoping someone would contact him who knew his father.

Al wrote James that although it had been 30 years since his [William's] loss, "I was deeply saddened to know he was among the airmen who were lost." He further wrote James that:

> *In closing I know you should be proud to know your dad served his Country and made the supreme sacrifice in protecting our County and joins the* **'unsung heroes'** *who gave their lives.*
>
> *Someday I hope our Country will have a special honor for all the service people who died in the line of duty on the* **SILENT BATTLEFIELD**.

LISTING BY RANK, IN ALPHABETICAL ORDER, THE FIFTY CREW MEMBERS WHO LOST THEIR LIVES IN THE DITCHING OF 55-0136, 55-5262, AND 53-0549.

COLONEL	JAMES PERKINS LYLE	FR4846
MAJOR	ROBERT ABNER BAIRD	FV682603
MAJOR	HOWARD N. FRANKLYN	FV820985
CAPTAIN	EDWARD N. ANAKA	74134A
CAPTAIN	MICHAEL R. BARBOLLA	58086A
CAPTAIN	MURRAY J. BRODY	71909A
CAPTAIN	FRANK R. FERGUSON	FR75950
1/LT	FREDERICK H. AMBROSIA	70494A
1/LT	THOMAS FIEDLER	69998A
1/LT	RICHARD K. HOPPE	FV3139354
1/LT	EDWARD WILLIAM TAYLOR	FR75727
1/LT	LARRY DENNING RUCKER	FR79991
2/LT	IRA J. HUSIK	A03147737
SMSGT	ROBERT E. MULHERN	AF12191742
MSGT	ARMAND HENRY DiBONAVENTURA	AF11166476
MSGT	FRANK W. GARNER, JR.	AF11214357
MSGT	CLARENCE DAVID HENDRICKSON	AF37806596
MSGT	ROBERT ALLEN THIBODEAU	AF13105504
MSGT	JOHN JOSEPH NEROLICH	AF33260111
TSGT	GILBERT L. ARMSTRONG	AF31339667
TSGT	GORDON O. HAMMAN	AF13257903
TSGT	ARTHUR JOSEPH LAMBERT	AF1119334
TSGT	EUGENE J. SCHREIVOGEL	AF17240566
SSGT	RICHARD D. BEARDEN	AF14494389
SSGT	FRANCIS J. GRIFFIN	AF10602510
SSGT	JOHN L. HOWARD	AF14602848
SSGT	LAWRENCE ELTON McNEILL	AF11266991
SSGT	JAMES ROBERT PATER	AF16234964
SSGT	ROBERT JAMES SIMMONS	AF12358174
SSGT	ROBERT SPARKS	AF15449495
SSGT	RAYMOND M. WASHAM	AF13316653
A1C	JOSEPH FRANK ADAMICK, JR.	AF21279785
A1C	ROBERT J. CLAPPER	AF12623437
A1C	RICHARD D. GRAVELY	AF13603943
A1C	THEODORE E. LaPOINTE JR.	AF11358214
A1C	JAMES DWIGHT RODGERS	AF14743876

A1C	CHARLES K. SAWYER	AF14666776
A1C	WILLIAM M. WALSH	AF11298681
A1C	GEORGE R. WEST	AF16728130
A2C	DAVID NORMAN BAILEY	AF13844241
A2C	DENIS E. BOYLE	AF12725223
A2C	DANNY R. BURDEN	AF15707069
A2C	WILLIAM M. COOK	AF11452889
A2C	WILLIAM E. HOWE	AF14792536
A2C	ROGER PAUL KAY	AF12719058
A2C	LARRY LEE STONER	AF13826950
A2C	JAMES DAVID WILBUR	AF12709949
A2C	CHARLES H. WILLIAMS	AF11413043
A3C	DENNIS R. COLE	AF11960224
A3C	CHARLES J. PODIASKI	AF16810785

The following are the two officers and the two airmen who were the only survivors

1/LT	JOSEPH L. H. GUENET	FR80047
1/LT	BRUCE E. WITCHER	72954A
A1C	JOHN N. PUOPOLO	AF11346448
A2C	DAVID A. SURLES	AF13784150

I WOULD LIKE THE FAMILIES OF THE FIFTY DECEASED FLYERS TO KNOW THAT I HAVE FAITHFULLY REMEMBERED THESE BRAVE MEN IN MY DAILY PRAYERS SINCE THE RESPECTIVE DATES OF THEIR CRASHES. MAY THEY REST IN PEACE.

JOHN N. PUOPOLO
SURVIVOR OF 55-0136

GRAVE MARKER [LOCATED IN SECTION 2C - NUMBER 434] AT FORT SAM HOUSTON NATIONAL CEMETERY IN SAN ANTONIO, TEXAS OF COLONEL JAMES PERKINS LYLE.

[Photograph courtesy of James M. Walsh of Houston, Texas, whose father - A1C WILLIAM M. WALSH - also lost his life on Colonel Lyle's ill-fated flight]

PHOTOGRAPH FURNISHED BY MSGT DEAN BOYS - USAF RETIRED - A PERSONAL FRIEND OF TSGT HAMMAN. BOTH WERE RADAR TECHNICIANS IN THE 551ST ELECTRONICS MAINTENANCE SQUADRON AT OTIS AIR FORCE BASE.

TSGT HAMMAN WAS ONE OF THE 15 CREW MEMBERS KILLED ON APRIL 25, 1967 IN THE CRASH OF 53-0549 AT NANTUCKET ISLAND, MA. HIS REMAINS ARE INTERRED IN BEECHWOOD AT CENTERVILLE, MA.

OTIS MEMORIAL PARK - OTIS ANG BASE, MASSACHUSETTS

EACH OF THE THREE BOULDERS SET AROUND THE FOUNTAIN HAS A PLAQUE ATTACHED HONORING THE CREW MEMBERS WHO LOST THEIR LIVES IN THE DITCHING OF THREE EC-121H AIRCRAFT IN THE ATLANTIC OCEAN.

AIRCRAFT 55-0136 ON JULY 11, 1965 WITH THE LOSS OF 16 CREW MEMBERS.

AIRCRAFT 55-5262 ON NOVEMBER 11, 1966, WITH THE LOSS OF 19 CREW MEMBERS.

AIRCRAFT 53-0549 ON APRIL 25, 1967 WITH THE LOSS OF 15 CREW MEMBERS.

PHOTOGRAPH FURNISHED BY AMY RILE - PHOTOGRAPHER - 102nd FIGHTER WING - VISUAL INFORMATION OFFICE - OTIS ANG, MA

MEMORIAL MARKER TO THE CREW MEMBERS WHO PERISHED IN 55-0136

PHOTOGRAPHS OF OTIS MEMORIAL PARK TAKEN BY CARL WENBERG AND FURNISHED VIA DEAN BOYS

MEMORIAL MARKER TO THE CREW MEMBERS WHO PERISHED IN 55-5262

MEMORIAL MARKER TO THE CREW MEMBERS WHO PERISHED IN 53-0549

FOR ADDITIONAL INFORMATION ABOUT THE LOST CONNIES VISIT THE WEB AT:
http://www.dean-boys.com/lconnie/lconnie.htm

AWARDS AND DECORATIONS

It is my hope that this book will have convinced the reader, as it did me, that the fifty-four officers and airmen who experienced the three crashes described made enormous sacrifices in the defense of their country. It goes without saying that the fifty who lost their lives made the ultimate sacrifice. All four survivors suffered prolonged exposure in the frigid North Atlantic. One survivor received a broken neck, broken clavicle, broken right arm and left ankle, assorted bruises and contusions, a partially detached retina and areas of burned skin from fuel which ignited on the top of the water. Another survivor received "severe lacerations" to his foot and leg for which he was hospitalized for 10 days. Moreover, there is substantial evidence of hardships and bravery, as previously related, that all survivors endured.

The superiors in the chain of command of the flyers surely must have made recommendations for appropriate awards to honor these men. It would have been their duty to have done so.

Trying to find out what recommendations were made and if any awards and decorations were given was a frustrating task. It seemed that every avenue I approached to try to get answers to this question was blocked by red tape as well as archaic beliefs, policies, and excuses.

I experienced frustration in my contacts with the Air Force as well as with the National Personnel Records Center (NPRC). When answers were not forthcoming, I wondered if perhaps I was creating embarrassment for persons who had failed to do what was just and expected of them in recommending awards for the crew members.

I came to believe, however, that the true cause was the multi-level bureaucracy within the Air Force and the NPRC and with policies which appear to be contrary to the Freedom Of Information Act and the Privacy Act. Not wanting to ignore the men who gave their lives for our country, I appealed to higher authorities within the Air Force and the NPRC. Eventually the NPRC forwarded me the information which is shown below regarding awards.

Following are the crew members of 53-0549, 55-0136, and 55-5262 who died in the crashes

(*)   Denotes received Airman's Medal
(**) Denotes received Air Force Commendation Medal

COLONEL	JAMES PERKINS LYLE	FR 4846
MAJOR	ROBERT ABNER BAIRD	FV682603
MAJOR	HOWARD N. FRANKLYN	FV820985
(**)CAPTAIN	EDWARD N. ANEKA	74134A
(**)CAPTAIN	MICHAEL R. BARBOLLA	58086A
CAPTAIN	MURRAY J. BRODY	71909A
CAPTAIN	FRANK R. FERGUSON	FR75950
1/LT	FREDERICK H. AMBROSIA	70494A
1/LT	THOMAS FIEDLER	69998A
1/LT	RICHARD K. HOPPE	FV3139354
1/LT	EDWARD WILLIAM TAYLOR	FR75727
1/LT	LARRY DENNING RUCKER	FR79991
2/LT	IRA J. HUSIK	A03147737
MSGT	ARMAND HENRY DiBONAVENTURA	AF11166476
MSGT	FRANK W. GARNER, JR.	AF11214357
MSGT	CLARENCE DAVID HENDRICKSON	AF37806596
MSGT	ROBERT ALLEN THIBODEAU	AF13105504
MSGT	ROBERT E. MULHERN	AF12191742
MSGT	JOHN JOSEPH NEROLICH	AF33260111
TSGT	GILBERT L. ARMSTRONG	AF31339667
TSGT	GORDON O. HAMMAN	AF13257903
TSGT	ARTHUR JOSEPH LAMBERT	AF1119334
(*)TSGT	EUGENE J. SCHREIVOGEL	AF17240566
SSGT	RICHARD D. BEARDEN	AF14494389
SSGT	FRANCIS J. GRIFFIN	AF10602510
SSGT	JOHN L. HOWARD [NOTE]	AF14602848
SSGT	LAWRENCE ELTON McNEILL	AF11266991
SSGT	JAMES ROBERT PATER	AF16234964
SSGT	ROBERT JAMES SIMMONS	A12358174
SSGT	ROBERT SPARKS	AF15449495
SSGT	RAYMOND M. WASHAM	AF13316653
A1C	JOSEPH FRANK ADAMICK, JR.	AF21279785
A1C	ROBERT J. CLAPPER	AF12623437
A1C	RICHARD D. GRAVELY	AF13603943
A1C	THEODORE E. LaPOINTE JR.	AF11358214
A1C	JAMES DWIGHT RODGERS	AF14743876
A1C	CHARLES K. SAWYER	AF14666776
A1C	WILLIAM M. WALSH	AF11298681
A1C	GEORGE R. WEST	AF16728130
A2C	DAVID NORMAN BAILEY	AF13844241
A2C	DENIS E. BOYLE	AF12725223
A2C	DANNY R. BURDEN	AF15707069
A2C	WILLIAM M. COOK	AF11452889
A2C	WILLIAM E. HOWE	AF14792536
A2C	ROGER PAUL KAY	AF12719058

A2C	LARRY LEE STONER	AF13826950
A2C	JAMES DAVID WILBUR	AF12709949
A2C	CHARLES H. WILLIAMS	AF11413043
A3C	DENNIS R. COLE	AF11960224
A3C	CHARLES J. PODIASKI	AF16810785

NOTE - [National Personnel Records Center could not locate SSGT John L. Howard's records]

The following are the two officers and the two airmen who were the only survivors

1/LT	JOSEPH L. H. GUENET	FR80047
(**) 1/LT	BRUCE E. WITCHER	72954A
(*) A1C	JOHN N. PUOPOLO	AF11346448
(*) A2C	DAVID A. SURLES	AF13784150

The *Airman's Medal* was awarded *posthumously* to TSGT EUGENE J. SCHREIVOGEL, AF17240566, Flight Engineer on 55-0136. [See citation below]

The *Airman's Medal* also was awarded to A/1C JOHN W. PUOPOLO, AF11346448, Surveillance Technician and A/2C DAVID A SURLES, AF13784150, Radar Technician, both of whom survived the ditching of 55-0136.

[Citation to accompany the award of the Airman's Medal to Puopolo and Surles was not available at the National Personnel Records Center]
Source - National Personnel Records Center

AIRMAN'S MEDAL

This decoration, one of several Air Force awards established by Congress on July 6, 1960, takes the place of the Soldier's Medal for Air Force personnel. It is awarded to any member of the armed forces of the United States or of a friendly nation who, while serving in any capacity with the United States Air Force after the date of the award's authorization, shall have distinguished himself or herself by a heroic act, usually at the voluntary risk of his or her life but not involving actual combat.
Source - Air Force Personnel Center

CITATION TO ACCOMPANY THE AWARD OF
THE AIRMAN'S MEDAL
TO
JOHN N. PUOPOLO

Airman First Class John N. Puopolo distinguished himself by heroism involving voluntary risk of life 100 miles east of Nantucket Island, Massachusetts, on 12 July 1965. On that date, Airman Puopolo and two other crewmen of an EC-121H aircraft that had ditched into the ocean, were together in the water. With complete disregard for his own personal safety, Airman Puopolo assisted another crew member who was injured and whose life preserver was only partially inflated. Despite his own injuries and at a great risk to his own survival, Airman Puopolo supported his fellow crew member for six hours until he expired. By his courageous action and humanitarian regard for his fellow man, Airman Puopolo has reflected great credit upon himself and the United States Air Force.

Source - John N. Puopolo

CITATION TO ACCOMPANY THE AWARD OF
THE AIRMAN'S MEDAL
TO
DAVID A. SURLES

Airman Second Class David A. Surles distinguished himself by heroism involving voluntary risk of life 100 miles east of Nantucket Island, Massachusetts, on 12 July 1965. On that date, Airman Surles and another crew member of an EC-121H aircraft, that had ditched into the ocean, were together in the water. Shortly after dawn, his fellow crew member lapsed into unconsciousness due to the effects of prolonged exposure and injuries sustained during the ditching. With complete disregard for his own safety, Airman Surles used his remaining strength to support his fellow crew member for over two hours until they were rescued. By his courageous action and humanitarian regard for his fellow man, Airman Surles has reflected great credit upon himself and the United States Air Force.

Source: David A. Surles

CITATION TO ACCOMPANY THE AWARD OF THE AIRMAN'S MEDAL (POSTHUMOUS) TO EUGENE J. SCHREIVOGEL

Technical Sergeant Eugene J. Schreivogel distinguished himself by heroism involving voluntary risk of life near Nantucket Island, Massachusetts, on 11 July 1965. On this date, Sergeant Schreivogel was the off-duty Flight Engineer on an EC-121 aircraft which was forced to ditch in the North Atlantic. Without regard for his own safety, Sergeant Schreivogel aided other members of the crew in preparation for ditching of the aircraft. Because of his concern for other crew members, time did not permit Sergeant Schreivogel to prepare for the ditching which resulted in the loss of his life. By his courageous action and humanitarian regard for his follow man, Sergeant Schreivogel has reflected great credit upon himself and the United States Air Force.
Source: National Personnel Records Center

AIR FORCE COMMENDATION MEDAL

This medal was authorized by the Secretary of the Air Force on March 28, 1958, for award to members of the Armed Forces of the United States who, while serving in any capacity with the Air Force after March 24, 1958, shall have distinguished themselves by meritorious achievement and service. The degree of merit must be distinctive, though it need not be unique. Acts of courage which do not involve the voluntary risk of life required for the soldier's Medal (or the Airman's Medal now authorized for the Air Force) may be considered for the AFCM.
Source - Air Force Personnel Center

CITATION TO ACCOMPANY THE AWARD OF THE AIR FORCE COMMENDATION MEDAL (POSTHUMOUS) TO MICHAEL R. BARBOLLA

Captain Michael R. Barbolla distinguished himself by meritorious service while performing duty as Tactical Officer with the Air Force Reserve Officer Training Corps Field Training Unit, Otis Air Force Base, Massachusetts, from 6 June 1965 to 11 July 1965. During this period, the exemplary ability, diligence, and devotion to duty of Captain Barbolla were instrumental factors in the successful accomplishment of the cadet training mission of that unit. The distinctive accomplishments of Captain Barbolla reflect credit upon himself and the United States Air Force.

Source: Diane E. Barbolla

CITATION TO ACCOMPANY THE AWARD OF
THE AIR FORCE COMMENDATION MEDAL
TO
BRUCE E. WITCHER

First Lieutenant Bruce E. Witcher, distinguished himself by an act of courage while assigned to the 961st Airborne Early Warning and Control Squadron from 11 July 1965 to 12 July 1965. 1st Lt. Witcher was the Lead Navigator on an EC-121H aircraft which ditched into the North Atlantic as a result of a serious in-flight emergency. Although injured himself, Lt. Witcher went to the aid of several other injured crew members. He attempted to keep them together and to give them courage and hope until a rescue could be accomplished. By his example and his humanitarian regard for his fellow man, 1st Lt. Witcher has reflected credit upon himself and the United States Air Force.

Source - National Personnel Records Center

[Commentary] - All branches of the military give awards, decorations and even medals to their members. Military members are regularly permitted to wear awards and decorations that have been awarded them for their having been in a particular unit or having been in a particular place at the right time.

In fact the Otis Notice, a newspaper published for the military at Otis Air Force Base, Massachusetts, wrote:

> Change of Command Ceremony - Colonel Max W.

Rogers, who departed for Stewart AFB, NY, after the ceremony, was awarded the Legion of Merit, with first oak leaf cluster, for meritorious performance as Commander of the 551st AEW&C Wing from June 5, 1967 to January 31, 1969. He was praised for having been directly responsible for resolving many complex problems of the wing. [Also see Changes of Key Personnel]

While I do not begrudge Colonel Rogers having been recognized, I find it difficult to understand why Colonel James P. Lyle, the former wing commander, who lost his life in the crash of 53-0549 was not even considered for recognition, let alone a decoration. Colonel Lyles' actions, as heretofore described, would appear to have been more than meritorious.

How does the military and particularly the Air Force, recognize their members who give their lives in the performance of duty for our country? How were the members of the families of the flyers honored other than by the routine presentation of the American Flag?

How, with the passing of time, will the legacy of these acts of self-sacrifice be passed on to future generations? Why weren't recommendations made for each and every one of these flyers? While the Air Force apparently forgot these brave men, it is my fervent hope that they will not be forgotten.

I brought this information to the attention of the Chief of Staff of the Air Force and to the Chief Master Sergeant of the Air Force and, although they assigned it to their staff for evaluation, my attempt to get those men recognized was unsuccessful.

As a Life Member in the Air Force Sergeants Association (AFSA), I asked that they join in my effort to gain recognition for the enlisted crew members since several of their members were killed in the crashes. My request went unanswered.

In my attempts to get the Air Force to give proper recognition to the flyers I was informed that:

Although the time limit for submitting decorations has

> been waived by the Fiscal Year 1966 National Defense Authorization Act (NDAA) Section 526, the awards criteria require the written recommendations (1) be made by someone other than the member himself, in the member's chain of command at the time of the incident, and who has firsthand knowledge of the acts or achievements and (2) be submitted through a congressional member who can ask a military service to review a proposal for a decoration based on the merits of the proposal and the award criteria in existence when the event occurred.

I also was informed as follows:

> In order for a request to be reasonably considered under the provisions of this act [NDAA] by the military service involved, it is important [that] the recommendation be accompanied by signed eyewitness statements attesting to the act(s), sworn affidavits, certificates, and any other official documentation. As a general rule, corroborating evidence is best provided by former commanders, supervisors, and fellow comrades who had personal knowledge of the circumstances and events relative to the recommendation. Unfortunately, newspaper articles and historical accounts do not serve the purpose or take the place of written recommendations for decorations.

Additionally, I was informed that:

> Although the Privacy Act of 1974 does not apply to the records of deceased individuals, Department of Defense instructions indicate that we must have the written consent of the next of kin if the individual is deceased.

Although the Air Force placed a burden on me which I felt I could not carry, I tried not to forget those men. I was able to locate a former commander, but due to his health he could not reasonably be expected to write a recommendation. The fact that those accidents which took the flyers' lives happened 33, 32, and 31 years ago presents severe difficulties in trying to locate the required people, even if they still are alive today.

I wrote prominent members of the U.S. Senate trying at the very least to get recognition for the flyers in The Congressional Record and this too was unsuccessful.

I eventually made a plea to the President of the United States that he take action independent of the Air Force to honor the flyers. However, in this instance my request was once again forwarded to the Secretary of the Air Force and once again the Air Force provided me the procedures and requirements relating to the award of military decorations. Additionally, the Air Force informed me that ....*[it would be inappropriate for the President to intervene, since such a recommendation would result in preferential treatment not available to others in the same or similar circumstances....*

I eventually conceded that I could not accomplish today what the Air Force and its Commanders and Supervisors failed to accomplish all those years ago in what I believe was a dereliction of their duty not to bestow on all these men the proper awards and decorations honoring their sacrifice. Those responsible should be ashamed of themselves for doing nothing.

NOTE: A more recent example shows what happens when someone cares. An aircraft accident occurred on September 22, 1995 when the United States Air Force and Canadian Forces lost 24 of their flyers with the catastrophic accident of an Air Force E-3 Airborne Warning and Control System (AWACS) aircraft. That is the type aircraft which replaced the EC-121H.

The aircraft known by its call sign "YUKLA 27" crashed after taking off from Elmendorf Air Force Base, Alaska. This was the first crash of the U.S. E-3. The AWACS aircraft was headed out on a seven-hour surveillance mission.

The Air Force investigating officer determined that the crash resulted from the aircraft's two left-wing engines ingesting several Canada geese. According to the investigator, engine number two lost all power and engine number one experienced severe damage after encountering the geese shortly after takeoff. The resulting loss of thrust rendered the aircraft uncontrollable, and after a slow, left-climbing turn, the aircraft pitched downward and crashed.

Air Force Chief of Staff General Ronald Fogleman signed the order awarding each member of the crew of YUKLA 27 the Meritorious Service Medal.

Why wasn't each and every member of the three crews of the earlier EC-121H accidents given recognition for their bravery and self-sacrifice?

Why weren't there recommendations made and medals or recognition bestowed on all the 54 brave men?

How does one justify Airman's Medals for two survivors from one accident while the only other survivor from the same accident received a lesser award, the Air Force Commendation Medal, even though each experienced the same ordeal?

Why was the only survivor of the crash of 53-0549 not even recommended for a medal?

Why was the pilot of 53-0549 not even recommended for a medal when numerous eyewitnesses provided information attesting to his bravery in avoiding a potential catastrophe on Nantucket Island?

Why did the Air Force disapprove the recommendation for the posthumous award of medals to five officers and 15 enlisted men?

****
THE FOLLOWING RECOMMENDATIONS FOR POSTHUMOUS AWARD OF MEDALS WERE DISAPPROVED

****

THE CITATION TO ACCOMPANY THE AWARD OF THE DISTINGUISHED FLYING CROSS (POSTHUMOUS) TO FREDERICK H. AMBROSIA

First Lieutenant Frederick H. Ambrosia distinguished himself by heroism while participating in aerial flight as

Aircraft Commander 100 nautical miles east of

Nantucket Island, Massachusetts, on 11 July 1965. On that date, Lieutenant Ambrosia was piloting an EC-121H aircraft engaged in an active air defense mission, when, at 2200 hours, compounding in-flight emergencies resulting from a fire in the accessory section of number 3 engine and an additional malfunction in number 2 engine forced Lieutenant Ambrosia to ditch the aircraft at sea. Lieutenant Ambrosia, at great personal risk, maneuvered the crippled aircraft through extremely hazardous weather and zero visibility to impact. Although Lieutenant Ambrosia lost his life in the ditching, twelve crew members were able, in one manner or another, to escape the ditched aircraft. The outstanding heroism and selfless devotion to duty displayed by Lieutenant Ambrosia reflect great credit upon himself and the United States Air Force.

NOTE: A Headquarter Air Defense Command (ADC) letter dated 9 May 1966 was signed by W. B. Keese, Major General, USAF, Chief of Staff "FOR THE COMMANDER". The letter read:

"After full consideration of the recommendation, it was decided that award of the Distinguished Flying Cross (Posthumous) to Lieutenant Ambrosia is not warranted".

****

Each of the 19 members of the crew of 55-5262 which ditched on November 11, 1966 with the loss of all aboard were recommended for the Award of the Air Medal (Posthumous). The citation to accompany the award of the Air Medal for each member reflects that:

[_____NAME] distinguished himself by meritorious achievement involving the loss of his life 11 November 1966 while participating in an aerial flight over the North Atlantic on an Active Air Defense Mission essential to the air defense of the North American continent. On that date, the EC-121H aircraft on which [_____NAME] was [_____CREW POSITION] experienced an inflight emergency of unknown origin and magnitude and crashed into the sea approximately 125 nautical miles east of Nantucket

Island, Massachusetts. The professional skill and airmanship displayed by [_____NAME] reflect great credit upon himself and the United States Air Force.

Following are those crew members of 55-5262 recommended for the Air Medal posthumously:

> MAJOR ROBERT A. BAIRD
> 1ST LT RICHARD K. HOPPE
> 1ST LT LARRY D. RUCKER
> 1ST LT EDWARD W. TAYLOR
> MSGT ARMAND H. DiBONAVENTURA
> MSGT CLARENCE D. HENDRICKSON
> MSGT JOHN J. NEROLICH
> MSGT ROBERT A. THIBODEAU
> TSGT ARTHUR J. LAMBERT
> SSGT LAWRENCE E. McNEILL
> SSGT JAMES R. PATER
> SSGT ROBERT J. SIMMONS
> SSGT ROBERT SPARKS
> A1C JOSEPH F. ADAMICK, JR.
> A1C JAMES D. RODGERS
> A2C DAVID N. BAILEY
> A2C ROGER P. KAY
> A2C LARRY L. STONER
> A2C JAMES D. WILBUR

A Headquarters Air Defense Command letter dated 26 July 1967 signed by W. B. Keese, Major General, USAF, CHIEF OF STAFF, "FOR THE COMMANDER" and addressed to 1 AF (CCR) reflects that:

> After full consideration of the below listed recommendations for posthumous award of the Air Medal, it has been determined that the achievements cited, though noteworthy, do not warrant award of the Air Medal. The recommendations are being returned for consideration of a lesser award.

Headquarters Air Force Personnel Center wrote that:
The record does not contain any documents showing a lesser award was considered or approved and that the record does not contain a copy of the chain of command endorsements or identify the official that made the recommendations.

AIR MEDAL

The Air Medal is given to any person who, while serving with the armed forces of the United States in any capacity subsequent to Sept. 8, 1939, shall have distinguished him or herself by meritorious achievement while participating in aerial flight. It is given for combat or non-combat action, and conferred in recognition of single acts of heroism or merit for operational activities against an armed enemy, or for meritorious services, or for sustained distinction in performance of duties involving regular and frequent participation in aerial flights.
Source: Air Force Personnel Center

After having located the four survivors from the three accidents, I again contacted the Air Force in an attempt to have the Air Force contact them as the source for justification to make appropriate awards and decorations to the crew members.

Matthew J. Arth, Major, USAF, Chief, Recognition Programs Branch at Headquarters Air Force Personnel Center, Randolph Air Force Base, Texas, wrote:

This is in response to your 13 Aug 98 letter to Colonel Fryman concerning your continued attempts to receive recognition for crew members who perished in the EC-121H Radar Constellation aircraft accidents. Colonel Fryman's response in his 15 Apr 98 letter was clear and precise into the avenues you must seek to gain recognition. We have provided you a copy of that letter.

Although we cannot stop you from submitting statements from survivors of the crashes in your attempt for recognition, the other requirements (i.e.,. NOK [next of kin] concurrence and submittal of your case through a congressional member) are not waiverable.

Again, we know this is not the response you had hoped for; however, these procedures must be followed. Further correspondence received in this office without the correct procedures being followed, will not be acted upon. Thank you for your continued patience and understanding in this matter.

AIRMAN'S MEDAL

AIR FORCE COMMENDATION MEDAL

MEDALS CAN BE SEE IN COLOR AT:
http://www.afpc.randolph.af.mil

TOWN OF NANTUCKET, MASSACHUSETTS

Nantucket is an island located south east of Massachusetts and is approximately 15 miles long and famous for summer vacations. It was a landmark for years to the crews of the radar patrol planes flying from Otis Air Force Base, Massachusetts, who regularly flew over it, near it, or around it on their way to and from their assigned North Atlantic patrol areas.

It was during the early evening on April 25, 1967 that one of the EC-121H radar patrol planes named the "Warning Star" fell from the sky and crashed into the Atlantic Ocean approximately one mile south of the western tip of the island of Nantucket. The fiery crash took the lives of 15 of the 16 crew members. In command of the aircraft was Colonel James P. Lyle, the Commander of the 551st Airborne Early Warning and Control Wing at Otis Air Force Base.

From all documented sources it appears that Colonel Lyle averted a disaster when he took evasive action to not cause harm to the residents of Nantucket Island. Therefore, I expected that he would have received an award for his valor.

However, that was not so. **The Air Force acknowledges that Colonel Lyle never received any award or decoration for his apparent act of bravery.**

I wrote to Ms. Libby Gibson, the Town and County Administrator at Nantucket, explaining what happened there thirty-one years ago and asked if there was any memorial plaque erected, proclamation made, or other action taken by the Town or County to honor Colonel Lyle and his crew.

The Town and County Administrator subsequently told me that there was nothing found honoring either Colonel Lyle or his crew. However, I was told the material I had sent was being presented to the Town Selectmen for their consideration.

At the meeting of the Town Selectmen on April 22, 1998, three days short of the 31st anniversary of the crash, the Town Selectmen formally recognized the bravery of Colonel Lyle in taking evasive action to avoid harming the citizens of Nantucket. The minutes of that meeting reflect:

> *Chairman (Arthur Descrocher) gave recognition (posthumously) to the late Air Force Colonel James P. Lyle who died on April 25, 1967 along with fifteen fellow crew members in a plane crash off Nantucket. Chairman Descrocher noted that Colonel Lyle is credited with taking evasive action to avoid crashing the plane on Nantucket and causing harm to the residents of the island.*

The Assistant Town Administrator for the Town and County of Nantucket, Ms. Nancy S. Oliver, wrote:

> *On behalf of the Board, I thank you for bringing this event to the attention of many individuals, presently living on the island, who were unaware that this tragic event took place.*

Some months later I contacted the Town Clerk of Nantucket, Ms. Catherine Flanagan Stover, to request her to review her files to determine if any death certificates were on file there for any of the members of Colonel Lyle's crew. Ms. Stover wrote in part:

> Your fax transmission brought me to tears this morning. It has been many years since I have thought about the plane crash. It was mentioned recently in the newspaper, of course, when our selectmen recently honored Col. Lyle. I was a freshman in High School and I was in my room doing my homework. An airplane going over my house was not an unusual occurrence, so when I heard the Constellation go over I knew immediately that this was the sound of an airplane in trouble. I jumped up and looked out my window and could see the plane, which seemed enormous, heading out toward Madaket. I realize now, of course, that it seemed so large because it was so close. There was a slight flame coming out of it and the engines sounded really jerky and hesitant. I knew it was going to crash and I ran downstairs to tell my parents. They didn't pay any attention to me. Then my Dad, who was on the Fire Department, heard the horns blowing a short while later. I remember the next day,

they were requesting citizens assistance to walk the beaches to help recover victims. I will never forget it. I think, when I look back on it now, that experience is one of the reasons I went to Mortuary College and became a funeral director and embalmer. (I am still licensed. I practiced until seven years ago when I moved back to the Island.)

My sympathies to you and to all the families.

MAP OF NANTUCKET ISLAND PROVIDED COURTESY OF HILLIARD WOOD - GIS COORDINATOR TOWN OF NANTUCKET, MASSACHUSETTS

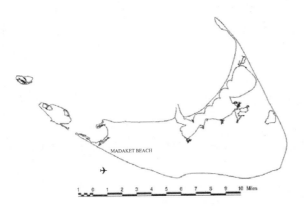

MAP OF NANTUCKET ISLAND, MASSACHUSETTS

ON THE EVENING OF APRIL 25, 1967 AN EC-121H [NUMBER 53-0549] CRASHED AND WAS DESTROYED APPROXIMATELY ONE-MILE SOUTH OF MADAKET BEACH OFF THE WEST TIP OF NANTUCKET ISLAND, MASSACHUSETTS. ONLY ONE OF THE 16 MEMBER CREW SURVIVED. OTIS AIR FORCE BASE IS LOCATED APPROXIMATELY 35 NAUTICAL MILES NORTH WEST FROM NANTUCKET ISLAND.

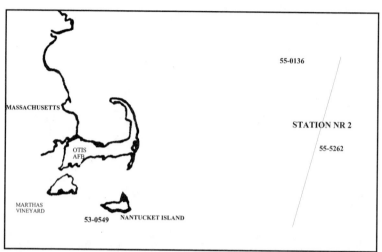

MAP DEPICTING THE DITCHING SITES OF 55-0136, 55-5262 AND 53-0549 OFF CAPE COD MASSACHUSETTS AND THE ISLAND OF NANTUCKET.

The distance from Otis Air Force Base to Nantucket Island is 35 nautical miles. The first of the three EC-121H Super Constellations (55-0136) which ditched had been assigned to man Station 2, a point in the Atlantic Ocean approximately 100 miles from Nantucket. That aircraft ditched with the loss of 16 of its 19-man crew on July 11, 1965, after experiencing engine problems and an engine fire. The second aircraft (55-5262), also assigned to man Station 2, ditched on November 11, 1966, for unknown reasons after going off radar and with no communications being received, with the loss of its entire 19-member crew. The third aircraft (53-0549) which ditched was en route to man Station 4 but experienced an engine fire and ditched at Nantucket Island on April 25, 1967, with the loss of 15 of its 16-member crew.

55-0136 ditched at the approximate coordinates of 41 degrees 45 minutes north - 67 degrees 37 minutes west and 41 degrees 43 minutes north - 67 degrees 41 minutes west. The three survivors were picked up at 41 degrees 40 minutes north, 67 degrees 37 minutes west.

55-5262 ditched ½ mile east of station track 5 ½ miles south of station center point.

53-0549 ditched one-mile south of the west end of Nantucket Island off Madaket Beach.

HOUSE ARMED SERVICES COMMITTEE REPORT AND A SPECIAL REPORT ORDERED BY THE SECRETARY OF THE AIR FORCE

In reading the news articles pertaining to the crash of 53-0549, I realized that the cumulative loss of 50 crew members and three aircraft in a period of 21 months had suddenly become a matter of concern. Perhaps it was because the 551st Wing Commander (Colonel James P. Lyle) was killed while piloting the aircraft when it crashed on April 25, 1967 and perhaps it was due to the fact, reported in those news articles, that Representative Hastings Keith of Massachusetts mourned the loss of Colonel Lyle, a personal friend.

Representative Keith, it is reported, questioned whether the giant radar planes had become obsolete and he, along with Senator Edward M. Kennedy, urged the House Armed Services Committee Chairman (Representative L. Mendel Rivers) to appoint a special subcommittee to investigate the crashes of the Super Constellations.

A special subcommittee headed by Representative Richard Ichord was appointed by Chairman Rivers. Representative Ichord was reported as saying, "When 50 airmen and three airplanes, each valued at some $7,000,000, are lost within such a short period, such conditions warrant the serious consideration of both congress and the military".

I contacted the House National Security Committee [note at end of next page] and requested a copy of the above-mentioned subcommittee's report. After an extensive search it was determined that the subcommittee had existed for a period of two months. However, no record has been located of the sub-committee ever having made a report of their investigation to anyone or that they documented their investigation in any manner as a matter of record.

I also sent a copy of the news articles to Senator Edward Kennedy and requested information about the special subcommittee report, but my request was not acknowledged.

The news reports also mentioned "*that the Air Force is preparing a special report on the crash at the request of Air Force Secretary Harold Brown who was said by [Representative Philip] Philbin [D.- Mass] to have raised some questions when he heard the news. The exact nature of Brown's inquiries could not be determined but Philbin said he had been promised a copy of the special report when it was submitted to the secretary"*.

I made a request under the Freedom of Information Act to the Secretary of the Air Force for a copy of the "special report" allegedly requested by former Secretary Brown and was informed that "no records were found".

I also made a Freedom of Information Request to the Air Force Safety Center requesting to know if a copy of the report by the above-described sub-committee was on file there. The Center responded that "We have no information here at the Air Force Safety Center dealing with this Special Sub-Committee investigation of the three EC-121 aircraft mishaps."

Note: The House Armed Services Committee now is named the House National Security Committee.

THOSE WHO WISH TO MAKE CONTACT

Following are some relatives of the deceased flyers who have expressed an interest in making contact with anyone who knew their loved ones. Also shown are the three survivors from 55-0136 which ditched on July 11, 1965, and the one survivor from 53-0549 which ditched on April 25, 1967. They are willing to communicate with relatives who lost loved ones in those two accidents.

Joseph L. H. Guenet - The only survivor of 53-0549 which ditched on April 25, 1967:

Joseph L. H. Guenet
307 Smallwood Drive
Amherst, NY 14226
E-Mail: naviguesser@adelphia.net

The daughter of Colonel James P. Lyle - Jana [Lyle] Trevino

Jana Trevino
1201 Greenbriar Street
Denton, TX 76201
E-Mail: jana.trevino@tx.columbia.net

The son of Colonel James P. Lyle - James L. Lyle Jr.

James L. Lyle Jr.
619 Eight Place
Hermosa Beach, CA 90254
(310)376-0087
E-Mail: jlyle@beachnet.com

The son of A/1C Theodore E. LaPointe, Jr., Radio Operator, who lost his life on April 25, 1967 on Aircraft 53-0549:

TSGT Theodore LaPointe
5845 South Quatar Circle
Aurora, CO 80015
(303)699-5551
E-Mail : tedncindy@earthlink.net

The son of A/1C William M. Walsh, Radar Operator, who lost his life on April 25, 1967 on aircraft 53-0549:

James P. Walsh

4909 Park Drive
Houston, TX 77023
E-Mail: jwalsh@netropolis.net

The family of Captain Frank R. Ferguson, Navigator, who lost his life on April 25, 1967 on 53-0549:

(Diane, Daryn, Todd, Heather)
% Todd Ferguson
4855 Blue Heron Blvd
West Richland, WA 99353
E-Mail: tkferguson@aol.com

The daughter of Captain Murray J. Brody, Pilot, who lost his life on July 11, 1965 on aircraft 55-0136:

Deborah A. Brody
Director, Support Center for New Health Foundations
Grantmakers in Health
1100 Connecticut Avenue, NW
12th Floor
Washington, D.C. 20036
(202)452-8331
FAX (202)452-8340
E-Mail: dbrody@gih.org

John N. Puopolo, Radar Operator, who survived the ditching of 55-0136 on July 11, 1965:

John N. Puopolo
6830 Crystalwood Drive
Liverpool, NY 13088-5902
(315)451-1731

David A. Surles, Radar Technician, who survived the ditching of 55-0136 on July 11, 1965:

David A. Surles
12417 Glenfield Avenue
Tampa, FL 33626
(813)891-0700
E-Mail: drifter22@prodigy.net

Bruce E. Witcher, Navigator, who survived the ditching of 55-0136 on July 11, 1965:

Bruce E. Witcher
74-5588-C Pawai Place

Kailua-Kona, Hawaii 96740
(808)334-0322
(808)334-0831 (FAX)
E-Mail: bewitch@ilhawaii.net

Former wife of Captain Edward N. Anaka - AFROTC Instructor, who lost his life in the ditching of 55-0136 on July 11, 1965:

Judith C. Wallingford
P.O. Box 136
Windham, ME 04062
(207)892-3335

Wife of Captain Michael R. Barbolla, AFROTC Instructor, who lost his life in the ditching of 55-0136 on July 11, 1965:

Diane Barbolla
8183 Via Mallorca
La Jolla, CA 92037
(619)453-2247
(619)627-2953
E-Mail: barbolla@ix.netcom.com

"COLD WAR RECOGNITION CERTIFICATES"

In accordance with Section 1084 of the Fiscal Year 1998 National Defense Authorization Act, the Secretary of Defense approved awarding Cold War Recognition Certificates to all members of the armed forces and qualified federal government civilian personnel who faithfully served the United States during the Cold War era, from September 2, 1945 to December 26, 1991.

Certain documents are required as proof of service for both military and civilian personnel.

For information on the availability date of the certificates, for submitting your request for the certificate and the required documentation to be submitted, please contact the nearest military or Department of Defense installation or visit the following web site:
> http://147.103.18.232/

ABBREVIATIONS

AAD	Active Air Defense
AC	Aircraft Commander
ADC	Air Defense Command
AEW&C	Airborne Early Warning and Control
AEWA	Airborne Early Warning Association
AF	Air Force
AFB	Air Force Base
AFI	Air Force Instructions
AFROTC	AF Reserve Officers Training Corps
AFSA	Air Force Sergeants Association
ALRI	Airborne Long Range Input
ANG	Air National Guard
APS	Airborne Search Radar - USAF
ASAP	As Soon As Possible
ATC	Air Training Command
ATC	Air Traffic Control
AWACS	Airborne Warning & Control Sys.
BOADS	Boston Air Defense Sector
CADS	Continental Air Defense Command
CICO	Combat Information Center Officer
CP	Command Post
CRT	Cathode Ray Tube - Engine Analyzer
CW	Continuous Wave
D	Democrat
DD	Department of Defense
DEFCON	Defense Condition
DEW	Distant Early Warning
DME	Distance Measuring Equipment
EMS	Electronics Maintenance Squadron
EST	Eastern Standard Time
FAA	Federal Aviation Agency
FAX	Facsimile
FL	Flight Level
FMS	Field Maintenance Squadron
FOIA	Freedom Of Information Act
FPM	Feet Per Minute
HF	High Frequency - Communications
IFF	Identification Friend or Foe
IFR	Instrument Flight Rule

KIA	Killed In Action
LASI	Lockheed Air Service Incorporated
LAX	Los Angeles Airport
LORAN	Long Range Navigation System
LPU	Life Vests - Inflatable
METO	Maximum Except Take Off
NATO	North Atlantic Treaty Organization
NAV	Navigator
NCO	Non Commissioned Officer
NDAA	National Defense Authorization Act
NORAD	North American Air Defense Cmd.
NPRC	National Personnel Records Center
OMS	Organizational Maintenance Sqdn
OSI	Office Of Special Investigations-AF
PA	Public Address - Amplified
PCS	Permanent Change of Station
PRT	Power Recovery Turbines
R.	Republican
RET	Retired
RICMO	Radar Input Counter Measure Officer
RO	Radio Operator
ROTC	Reserve Officer Training Corp
SAGE	Semi-Automatic Ground Environment
SIF	Selective Identification Equipment
SONAR	Sound Navigation Ranging - NAVY
SOS	An International Emergency Signal
SSB	Single Side Band - Communications
STOP	Strategic Orbit Points
TACAN	Tactical Air Navigation Aid
TECH	Technician - Radar/Nav
UHF	Ultra High Frequency
USAF	United States Air Force
USNR	United States Naval Reserve
VHF	Very High Frequency
VOR	Visual Omni Range - Nav Aid

USAF MILITARY RANK REFERENCED

BG . . . . Brigadier General
COL . . . . Colonel
LT. COL . . . . Lieutenant Colonel
MAJ . . . . Major
CAPT . . . . Captain
1/LT . . . . First Lieutenant
2/LT . . . . Second Lieutenant
SMSGT . . . . Senior Master Sergeant
MSGT . . . . Master Sergeant
TSGT . . . . Technical Sergeant
SSGT . . . . Staff Sergeant
SGT . . . . Sergeant
A/1C . . . . Airman First Class
A/2C . . . . Airman Second Class
A/3C . . . . Airman Third Class
AMN . . . . Airman

MILITARY AIRCRAFT REFERENCED

A-26 . . . . Douglas "Invader" Tactical Bomber
AC-47 . . . . . . Converted Douglas "Gooney Bird" to Gun Ship
B-17 . . . . Flying Fortress Bomber by Boeing - WWII
B-24 . . . . Liberator Bomber - WWII
B-25 . . . . North American - Mitchell Bomber -WWII
B-52 . . . . Boeing Stratofortress Jet Bomber - USAF
C-5 . . . . Lockheed "Galaxy" Four Engine Jet Transport
C-5A . . . . Lockheed "Galaxy" Four Engine Jet Transport
C-47 . . . . Douglas Two Engine Transport "Gooney Bird"
C-119 . . . . . . "Flying Boxcar" by Fairchild
C-121 . . . . . . Lockheed Constellation - USAF
C-123 . . . . . . Fairchild "Provider" Cargo Aircraft
C-124 . . . . . . "Globemaster" by Douglas Aircraft
C-130 . . . . . . Lockheed "Hercules" Cargo Aircraft - USAF
C-130H . . . . . Lockheed "Hercules" Cargo Aircraft - USAF
C-131 . . . . . . Convair Two Engine Transport
EC-47 . . . . . . Douglas "Gooney Bird" for Reconnaissance
EC-121 . . . . . Lockheed Super Constellation - USAF
EC-121H . . . Lockheed Super Constellation - USAF
EC-121R . . . Lockheed Super Constellation - USAF
F-94 . . . . "Starfire" Fighter Interceptor by Lockheed
F-100 . . . . . . "Super Sabre" Fighter by North American - USAF
F-101 . . . . . . "Voodoo" Fighter by McDonald - USAF
F-102 . . . . . . "Delta Dagger" Fighter by Convair - USAF
F-105 . . . . . . "Thunder Chief" Fighter by Republic - USAF
HU-16 . . . . . "Albatross" NAVY Amphibious by Grumman
HH-53 . . . . . Sikorski Aircraft "Super Stallion" Helicopter
KB-50 . . . . . . "Superfortress" Aerial Tanker by Boeing - USAF
KC-97 . . . . . . Boeing "Stratofreighter" - Aerial Tanker
KC-135 . . . . . "Stratotanker" USAF Aerial Refueling by Boeing
ME-109 . . . . "Messerschmitt" German Fighter Plane - WWII
OV-10 . . . . . Boeing "Bronco" Twin-Turboprop
P-3 . . . . Lockheed "Orion" - US Navy Submarine Warfare
RC-121D . . . Lockheed Super Constellation Radar Aircraft
SA-16 . . . . . . "Albatross" Amphibious Aircraft by Grumman
S2F . . . . US Navy submarine tracker by Grumman
TC-121 . . . . . Lockheed Super Constellation - USAF
TC-121C . . . Lockheed Super Constellation - USAF
TU-95 . . . . . . Tupolev Russian Long Range Bomber "Bear"

PHOTOGRAPHS AND ILLUSTRATIONS

Photograph of Missing Man Flyover - Formation flying of the
Super Constellations at the Memorial Services for the crew of 55-0136 138

Photograph of EC-121 Super Constellation 42

Photographs of A.J. Northrup [1956] and [1998] xx

ADC and 551st AEW&C Wing emblems 31

Unit patches of the 551st AEW&C Wing 32

Photograph of Colonel Oliver G. Cellini - first Wing Commander 35

Photograph of BG Gibson, Colonel Cellini, Colonel McCartan,
Colonel Hook, and Colonel Havey "Commanders" 36

Photograph of RC-121D and F-94 "Starfire" interceptors 37

Photograph of Colonel Cellini, Secretary of the Air Force, and the
Governor of the Commonwealth of Massachusetts at an Otis AFB
flight line ceremony 38

EC-121 Specifications 43

Photograph of Major Robert A. Bostick - "A" Flight Commander of
the 961st AEW&C Squadron 53

Photograph of EC-121H in flight over the Cape Cod Canal 62

Photograph of Arthur D. Kerr - Former Connie Pilot in 961st 74

961st Airborne Early Warning and Control Squadron - Unit Patch 75

551st Electronics Maintenance Squadron - Unit Patch 86

Photograph of Dean Boys - MSGT USAF Retired 86

United States Air Force Seal 117

Photo of 1/LT FREDERICK H. AMBROSIA [Deceased July 11, 1965]
Aircraft Commander of 55-0136 122

Photo of 1/LT THOMAS FIEDLER - [Deceased July 11, 1965]
Co-Pilot of 55-0136 122

Photo of A2C CHARLES H. WILLIAMS [Deceased July 11, 1965]
Radar Technician on 55-0136 122

Photo of A1C JOHN N. PUOPOLO [Survivor of ditching of 55-0136]
Surveillance Technician/Assistant Crew Chief 122

Photo of CAPTAIN MURRAY J. BRODY [Deceased July 11, 1965]
Pilot on 55-0136 123

Photo of 1/LT BRUCE E. WITCHER [Survivor of ditching of 55-0136]
Navigator 123

Photo of A2C WILLIAM E. HOWE [Deceased July 11, 1965]
Radar Technician on 55-0136 123

Photo of 2/LT IRA J. HUSIK [Deceased July 11, 1965]
Navigator on 55-0136 124

Photo of CAPTAIN EDWARD N. ANAKA, AFROTC Instructor
[Deceased July 11, 1965] while flying as an Observer on 55-0136 124

Photo of CAPTAIN MICHAEL R. BARBOLLA, AFROTC Instructor
[Deceased July 11, 1965] while flying as an Observer on 55-0136 124

Photo of COLONEL RAYMOND K. GALLAGHER, Commander of the
551ST Airborne Early Warning and Control Wing - Holds model
of Constellation that ditched July 11, 1965 125

Photo of Air Force Constellation crew after returning from sea search
for survivors of 55-0136 125

Photo of 1/LT BRUCE E. WITCHER, Navigator, Survivor of the
ditching of 55-0136 on July 11, 1965, arriving at the Otis Air Force
Base Hospital 126

Photo of body of Airman (one of 16 casualties) being lifted from Air
Force bus-ambulance at Chelsea Naval Hospital, Boston, MA 127

Photo of two of the three survivors of the ditching of 55-0136 at a news
conference [A/2C DAVID A. SURLES and 1/LT BRUCE E.
WITCHER] with their Commander, LIEUTENANT COLONEL
ROBERT V. MITCHELL SR. 128

Photo of A1C JOHN N. PUOPOLO's wife and daughter 129

Photo of A1C JOHN N. PUOPOLO's parents 130

Photo of SSGT FRANCIS J. GRIFFIN's wife and daughters. SSGT
Griffin, Radio Operator on 55-0136, lost his life on July 11,1965 131

Photo of TSGT EUGENE J. SCHREIVOGEL's family - Sergeant
Schreivogel, Flight Engineer, lost his life during the ditching
of 55-0136 on July 11, 1965 132

Photo of A1C JOHN N. PUOPOLO shown at a radar scope like
those aboard the EC-121H aircraft 133

Photo of A1C JOHN N. PUOPOLO, one of three survivors of the
ditching of 55-0136 on July 11, 1965, arriving at Otis Air Force
Base Hospital 134

Photo of 1/LT BRUCE E. WITCHER, Navigator, one of three
survivors of the ditching of 55-0136 on July 11, 1965 135

Photo of A2C DAVID A. SURLES, Radar Technician, one of
three survivors of the ditching of 55-0136 on July 11, 1965 135

Photo of Super Constellation and US Navy Destroyer *Vesole*
searching the North Atlantic for survivors of the ditching of
55-0136 on July 11, 1965 136

Photo of JOHN N. PUOPOLO and wife in 1997 137

Photo of JOHN N. PUOPOLO and family in 1997 137

MEMORIAL SERVICE PROGRAM FOR CREW OF 55-0136 139

Photo of CAPTAIN EDWARD N. ANAKA
[Deceased July 11, 1965] AFROTC Instructor lost his life on
55-0136 while flying as an Observer 144

Photo of CAPTAIN EDWARD N. ANAKA's wife and his
mother receiving the Air Force Commendation Medal
[Awarded Posthumously to Captain Anaka for his AFROTC
accomplishments] 144

Photo of CAPTAIN EDWARD N. ANAKA's children 145

Photo of CAPTAIN MICHAEL R. BARBOLLA's wife and son.
Captain Barbolla, an AFROTC Instructor, lost his life on July 11,
1965 while flying as an Observer on 55-0136 145

Photo of Diane Barbolla and family 1988 151

AFROTC Emblem 154

Photo of CAPTAIN MURRAY J. BRODY's family - Captain
Brody, Pilot, lost his life during the ditching of 55-0136 on July
11, 1965 158

Photograph of the West German destroyer Z1 which rescued the
three survivors of 55-0136 181

Photographs of 1/Lt Witcher and A/2C Surles meeting the Skipper
of the ZI and the sailor who pulled them from the Atlantic 182

Photograph of 1/Lt Witcher and A/2C Surles meeting the Skipper
of the Z1 and sailor who pulled them from the Atlantic with an
unidentified German Navy Officer 183

Photograph of Lt. Colonel Robert V. Mitchell, Sr, Commander
of the 961st AEW&C Squadron with 1/Lt Witcher and A/2C
Surles being greeted by a West German Counselor 184

Photograph of 55-5262 218

Photo of COLONEL JAMES P. LYLE, Commander of the 551st
Airborne Early Warning and Control Wing at Otis Air
Force Base, Massachusetts at the time 55-5262 ditched
on November 11, 1966. 219

Photo of MAJOR ROBERT A. BAIRD [Deceased November 11,
1966] Aircraft Commander of 55-5262 220

Photo of 1/LT RICHARD K. HOPPE
[Deceased November 11, 1966] Navigator on 55-5262 220

Photo of 1/LT LARRY D. RUCKER
[Deceased November 11, 1966] Pilot of 55-5262 220

Photo of 1/LT EDWARD W. TAYLOR
[Deceased November 11, 1966] Navigator on 55-5262 220

Photo of A2C LARRY L. STONER and wife. Airman Stoner,
Radar Operator, lost his life in the ditching of 55-5262
on November 11, 1966 221

Photo of A2C ROGER P. KAY and wife. A2C Kay, Radar
Operator, lost his life in the ditching of 55-5262 on Nov 11, 1966 221

Photo of COLONEL JOHN H. PEASE who headed the Air
Force Board of Inquiry regarding the loss of 55-5262 on
November 11,1966 222

MEMORIAL SERVICE PROGRAM FOR CREW OF 55-5262 223

Photo of COLONEL JOHN M. KONOSKY, Vice Commander of the 551st Airborne Early Warning and Control Wing at Otis AFB when the Wing Commander, COLONEL JAMES P. LYLE, lost his life in the ditching of 53-0549 on April 25, 1967 286

Photo of a typical Connie crew who flew the EC-121H Super Constellations - One Airman, A1C WILLIAM M. WALSH, Radar Operator on this crew later lost his life on April 25, 1967 while flying on a different crew in the ditching of 53-0549 287

Photo of A1C WILLIAM M. WALSH [Deceased April 25, 1967] being congratulated in August 1965 by COLONEL ROBERT F. KALTENBACHER, Commander of the 551st Combat Support Group, upon WALSH's recent promotion 288

Photo of MAJOR HOWARD N. FRANKLYN [Deceased April 25, 1967] First Pilot on 53-0549 289

Photo of TSGT GORDON O. HAMMAN's children 290

Photo of TSGT GORDON O. HAMMAN, Radar Technician, was one of 15 crew members who perished in the ditching of 53-0549 on April 25, 1967 290

Photo of witness R. ARTHUR ORLEANS of Nantucket, Massachusetts, who saw 53-0549 ditch and explode into the Atlantic Ocean on April 25, 1967 291

Photo of witness MICHAEL LAMB of Nantucket, Massachusetts, who saw 53-049 ditch and explode into the Atlantic Ocean on April 25, 1967 291

Photo of airmen at Otis Air Force Base, Massachusetts, viewing a newspaper story of the loss of 53-0549 at Nantucket Island on April 25, 1967 292

Photo of a standby plane crew awaiting orders to search for possible survivors of 53-0549 293

Photo of 1/LT JOSEPH L. H. GUENET, Navigator and the lone survivor of 53-0549 shown recovering at the Cottage Hospital at Nantucket 294

MEMORIAL SERVICE PROGRAM FOR CREW OF 53-0549 297

Photo of A3C DENNIS R. COLE, Student Radar Operator, who perished in 53-0549 on April 25, 1967 303

Photo of COLONEL JAMES P. LYLE, Commander of the 551st Airborne Early Warning and Control Wing lost his life while piloting 53-0549 as Aircraft Commander 304

Photograph of Frank R. Ferguson during his college years [he perished in the ditching of 53-0549 on April 25, 1967] 313

Photograph of Mrs.Diane Ferguson with children 313

Photograph of Frank R. Ferguson, wife Diane and son Daryn 314

Photographs of Captain Ferguson with Scouts at Otis AFB 314

Photograph of the Ferguson children [Todd, Heather, Daryn] 315

Photograph of Frank R. Ferguson and wife Diane 315

Photograph of Maire LaPointe and A/1C Theodore E. LaPointe Jr., [who lost his life in the ditching of 53-0549 on April 25, 1967] 331

Photograph of the LaPointe family 332

Photo of pieces of 53-0549 recovered and displayed in a hangar at Otis AFB, MA 350

Photograph depicting damage to the Navigator's station and the right wing root based on the reconstruction of pieces recovered from the ditching of 53-0549 351

Photograph of First Lieutenant Joseph L. H. Guenet being removed from a C-47 aircraft at Otis AFB upon being transferred from Cottage Hospital at Nantucket 352

Photograph of Joseph L. H. Guenet as a Captain in 1969 while stationed at Nakon Phantom RTAFB, Thailand 353

Condolence Letters received from Government Officials by Colonel Lyle's family upon the death of COLONEL JAMES P. LYLE in the ditching of 53-0549 on April 25, 1967 370

Condolence Letters received from Government Officials by the Walsh family upon the death of A1C WILLIAM M.. WALSH in the ditching of 53-0549 on April 25, 1967 372

Condolence Letters received from Government Officials by the Brody family upon the death of CAPTAIN MURRAY J. BRODY in the ditching of 55-0136 on July 11, 1965 375

Condolence Letters received by Diane Barbolla from Government Officials upon the death of her husband Captain MICHAEL R. BARBOLLA in the ditching of 55-0136 on July 11, 1965 382

Photo of grave marker of COLONEL JAMES P. LYLE 390

Photo of grave marker of TSGT GORDON O. HAMMAN 391

Photo of Otis Memorial Park established in honor of the fifty men, who perished in the loss of three EC-121H aircraft 392

Photo of Memorial Plaques at Otis Memorial Park honoring those crew members who lost their lives 393

Airman's Medal - Air Force Commendation Medal 407

Map of Nantucket Island depicting the ditching location of 53-0549 411

Map of the area off Cape Cod depicting the ditching locations of 55-0136, 55-5262, and 53-0549 412

NOTE: Originals of many of the photographs and documents no longer exist and best available copies were used.

GLOSSARY OF UNCOMMON WORDS & PHRASES

Air Force Brats .. Dependent children of members of the Air Force.

Bag Drags ...... Dragging one's fly away bag of personal equipment across the aircraft parking ramp from one aircraft to another when for various reasons re-assignment of aircraft occurred.

Bear .... Russian Tupolev TU-95 Long-Range Bomber

Cape Codders ... Old time residents of Cape Cod Massachusetts.

Class VI .... Military Package Store.

COD Intersection Off shore navigational check points.

Connie .... A name given to the Super Constellation aircraft.

Cross Rip .... A navigational check point/route for flyers.

Diverts .... Diversion to a secondary location [divert to].

Squawk .... Emergency Squawk - an emergency code set into a transponder of an aircraft to identify on radar scopes that an emergency condition exists aboard the aircraft.

Feathered ...... When an engine was shut down in flight the propeller blades were [feathered] rotated into a position to let air pass through them without causing them to rotate.

Goon .... Slang for [C-47 aircraft] also Gooney Bird.

Morse Code ..... A communications code devised of clicks and spaces - long and short sounds [dots and dashes] or flashes of light for the alphabet and numbers [devised by Samuel F. B. Morse].

Painted .... To reflect a radar signal back from a target.

Prop .... Propeller attached to an aircraft reciprocal engine.

Radome .... A dome-shaped device used to house a radar antenna

Warning Star .. Lockheed's name for the EC-121H.

MILITARY CONSTELLATIONS [TOTAL LOSS] DURING 1953-1978

07.07.53 Lockheed R7V-1 Super Constellation
Bu128440 (4107) United States Navy
location: Chesterton (USA)

30.10.54 Lockheed R7V-1 Super Constellation
Bu128441 (4108) United States Navy
location: Atlantic Ocean

09.12.54 Lockheed WV-2 Super Constellation
Bu131387 (4307) United States Navy

17.01.55 Lockheed C-121J Super Constellation
Bu131639 (4140) United States Navy
location: Newfoundland Naval Air St. (Canada)

17.09.56 Lockheed WV-3 Super Constellation
Bu137893 (4380) United States Navy

30.12.56 Lockheed C-121C Super Constellation
54-0165 (4184) United States Air Force - USAF

17.04.57 Lockheed WV-2 Super Constellation
Bu141314 (4438) United States Navy

23.12.57 Lockheed WV-2 Super Constellation
Bu143197 (4471) United States Navy

14.01.58 Lockheed R7V-1 Super Constellation
Bu128436 (4104) United States Navy
location: Patuxent River Naval Air Station (USA)

28.02.58 Lockheed WV-2 Super Constellation
Bu141310 (4434) United States Navy

14.05.58 Lockheed R7V-1 Super Constellation
Bu131652 (4153) United States Navy

25.05.58 Lockheed RC-121D Super Constellation
55-0123 (4396) United States Air Force - USAF
Burned up on ramp during preflight

18.10.58 Lockheed WV-2 Super Constellation
Bu141294 (4418) United States Navy

28.02.59 Lockheed C-121G Super Constellation
54-4069 (4149) United States Air Force - USAF

29.03.59 Lockheed WV-2 Super Constellation
Bu141332 (4456) United States Navy

02.04.59 Lockheed WV-2 Super Constellation
Bu141303 (4427) United States Navy

31.10.60 Lockheed WV-2 Super Constellation
Bu126513 (4302) United States Navy

22.01.61 Lockheed WV-2 Super Constellation
Bu143193 (4467) United States Navy

22.03.61 Lockheed TC-121C Super Constellation
51-3842 (4118) United States Air Force - USAF
location: Marysville (USA)

12.04.62 Lockheed C-121G Super Constellation
54-4066 (4146) United States Air Force - USAF

22.05.62 Lockheed EC-121M Super Constellation
Bu131390 (4310) United States Navy

31.08.62 Lockheed C-121G Super Constellation
54-4057 (4138) United States Air Force - USAF
location: Oakland (USA)
nature: phase: Ground

31.07.63 Lockheed EC-121K Super Constellation

Bu141329 (4453) United States Navy

01.08.64 Lockheed WC-121N Super Constellation
Bu137891 (4378) United States Navy

03.11.64 Lockheed C-121J Super Constellation
Bu131625 (4126) United States Navy
location: Patuxent River Naval Air Station (USA)
nature: phase: Landing

11.06.65 Lockheed EC-121K Super Constellation
Bu141321 (4445) United States Navy

11.07.65 Lockheed EC-121H Super Constellation
55-0136 (4409) United States Air Force - USAF

20.08.65 Lockheed EC-121M Super Constellation
Bu135747 (4314) United States Navy

27.01.66 Lockheed EC-121M Super Constellation
Bu135751 (4318) United States Navy

11.11.66 Lockheed EC-121H Super Constellation
55-5262 (4413) United States Air Force - USAF

25.04.67 Lockheed EC-121H Super Constellation
53-0549 (4364) United States Air Force - USAF

24.01.69 Lockheed EC-121R Super Constellation
67-21476 (4441) United States Air Force - USAF

15.04.69 Lockheed EC-121M Super Constellation
Bu135749 (4316) United States Navy

25.04.69 Lockheed EC-121R Super Constellation
67-21493 (4489) United States Air Force - USAF

16.03.70 Lockheed EC-121K Super Constellation
Bu145927 (5508) United States Navy

25.08.70 Lockheed EC-121K Super Constellation
Bu145928 (5509) United States Navy

08.10.70 Lockheed C-121J Super Constellation
Bu131644 (4145) United States Navy

19.07.73 Lockheed EC-121K Super Constellation
Bu145936 (5517) United States Navy

15.03.78 Lockheed EC-121T Super Constellation
55-0121 (4394) United States Air Force - USAF
Burned up after landing gear collapsed

Source: http://aviation-safety.net/
Copyright By Harro Ranter
hranter@inter.NL.net

Permission granted by Harro Raner for use of Copyrighted material

431

THOSE WHO HAVE ATTENDED OR HAVE REQUESTED INFORMATION ON THE 551ST WING REUNIONS

List furnished courtesy of Joanna DaSilva, 551st AEW&C Wing Reunion Coordinator

ABBOTT, DONALD
208 BRYANT ST APT 6
MALDEN, MA 02148-4244

ADAIR, BILL
485 BOURNE ROAD
PLYMOUTH, MA 02360

ADAMCZYK, MATTHEW
185 DAVISVILLE ROAD
EAST FALMOUTH, MA 02536

ADAMO, FRANK
37 PORTSIDE DRIVE
POCASSET, MA 02559

ADAMS, RICHARD C.
139 LAKEVIEW AVENUE
FALMOUTH, MA 02540

ALBRYCKT, CASMIR
27 DOLPHIN DRIVE
FARMINGDALE, NY 11735

ALEXANDER, JAMES
524 GREENBRIAR DRIVE
RAVENNA, OH 44266

ALEXANDRAKOS, PETER
12524 FANLEAF COURT
FAIRFAX, VA 22033

ALLEN, AARON
812 BLOSSOM COURT
LAFAYETTE, IN 47905-5600-12

ANDEREGG, JOHN
12912 IRONGATE AVE
AUSTIN, TX 78727-4313

ANDERSEN, ROBERT
22 PIEPER DRIVE
WALLINGFORD, CT 06492

ANDRADE, WILLIAM
P. O. BOX 255
ONSET, MA 02558

ANDREWS, RAYMOND
875 POINT ROAD
MARION, MA 02738

ANGLEA JR., WILLIAM
604 HAMBLEN DRIVE
MADISON, TN 37115

ARENO, ROCCO
97 MAPLE STREET
BUZZARDS BAY, MA 02532

ASCHER, DAVID
105 WICKSFORD GLEN
DUNWOOD, GA 30350

ASSELIN, DONALD R.
RT 2, BOX 1597
LITCHFIELD, ME 04350

ATWOOD, RICHARD
204 MAIN STREET
SANDWICH, MA 02563

AUGUSTYNIAK, EDWARD F.
44 SALLY LANE
E. FALMOUTH, MA 02536

BAADE, WALTER
11524 SEMINOLE S.W.
TACOMA, WA 98499

BAKER, JOHN
9051 HERRING ROAD
LITCHFIELD, MI 49252

BAKER JR., HAROLD L.
P.O. BOX 585
FALMOUTH, MA 02541

BALDRIDGE, WILLIAM
132 WINSLOW COURT
MELBOURNE, FL 32934

BANNER, JOHN
RUSSELL STREET
FALMOUTH, MA 02520

BARBER, THOMAS
27485 THREE MILE POINT RD
CHAUMONT, NY 13622

BARIL, RAYMOND
149 W. WRENTHAN ROAD
CUMBERLAND, RI 02864

BARLEY, CHARLES
20320 BAYNES ROAD
BURLINGTON, NC 27217

BARNES, DONALD
4347 ORTEGA FARM CIRCLE
JACKSONVILLE, FL 36489

BARON, MARY V.
P.O. BOX 505
POCASSET, MA 02559

BARROS, RICHARD
101 WHIPPOORWILL RUN
PINEHURST, NC 28374

BARROW, FRANKLIN
2444 DUNCAN DRIVE
NICEVILLE, FL 32578

BARS, ED
P.O. BOX 218
E. KILLINGLY, CT 06243-0218

BASHAW, JACK
11048 M 5TH STREET
PHOENIX, AZ 85020

BASQUE, PATRICIA E.
30 MAPLE AVENUE
SHALIMAR, FL 32579

BATES, KENNETH
2705 EAST PIKE
ZANESVILLE, OH 43701

BECKER, DENNIS
36 WALL ST
BUZZARDS BAY, MA 02532

BECKFORD, WILLIAM
93 CENTRAL STREET
FRAMINGHAM, MA 01701

BEEBE, ROBERT
103 DAWNSHIRE COURT
SUMMERVILLE, SC 29485

BENNETT, ART
20 ELIOT DRIVE
LAKE GROVE, NY 11755

BERNARD YOUNG
949 SANDWICH ROAD
E. FALMOUTH, MA 02536

BERNHARDT, ANGIE
T-126-661 FALMOUTH ROAD
MASHPEE, MA 02649

BERNKLOW, DAVID
102 THOMPSON ROAD
THOMPSON, CT 06277

BESSE, PHILLIP
9 ROY STREET
FAIRHAVEN, MA 02719

BIBBER, RONALD E.
62 SHAWS MILL ROAD
GORHAM, ME 04038-2136

BIRD JR., LEWIS L.
16222 MONTEREY LANE SPC #79
HUNTINGTON BEACH, CA 92649

BISHOP, RUSSELL & BARBARA
115 GEGGATT ROAD
E. FALMOUTH, MA 02536

BLAIKIE, THOMAS
12401 W. OKEECHOBEE RD #496
HIALEAH GARDENS, FL 33016

BLAIR, BOB
57 IOWA DRIVE NE
FORT WALTON, FL 32548

BLAIR, GEORGE
19 PORTSIDE CIRCLE
E. FALMOUTH, MA 02536

BLANCHARD, ROBERT
310 RAFAEL DRIVE
ELVERTA, CA 95626

BLANK, GEORGE W.
840 ENFIELD STREET
BOCA RATON, FL 33487

BLOMMER, BOB
RIVER ROAD
LINCOLN, RI 02865

BLOSS, NORMAN
32 MARILYN ROAD
MONUMENT BEACH, MA 02532

BOCK, WALDEN H.
P.O. BOX 764
POCASSET, MA 02559

BOND, LESTER C.
BOX 145A RIVERDALE ROAD
RT 4
MILLSBORO, DE 19966

BONIN, RUDY
9 MILL WHEEL LANE
POCASSET, MA 02559

BOSTICK, ROBERT
RT #7 BOX 91A
CANTON, TX 75103

BOSTWICK, JAMES
12 ABEGAIL'S WAY
SANDWICH, MA 02563

BOWDEN, WILLIAM
237 MIDDLE ROAD
SAYVILLE, NY 11782

BOYKIN RR., NEWTON C.
7711 REMMICK LANE
HUBER HEIGHTS, OH 45424

BOYNE, WILLIAM D.
150 SPRINGER LANE
W YARMOUTH, MA 02673

BOYS, DEAN
RR 3 BOX 193
SHELBYVILLE, IL 62565

BRACCO, PAUL
1712 HOLIDAY LANE
FAIRFIELD, CA 94533

BRADT, CARMEN
104 E WOODLAND RIDGE APT21
VALMEYER, IL 62295

BRANTON, WILLIAM
595 PHINNEY'S LANE
CENTERVILLE, MA 02632

BRIGGS, RAYMOND
56 CRYSTAL SPRING ROAD
MATTAPOISETT, MA 02739

BRIGGS, ROBERT
SO WEYMOUTH NAVAL AIR STATION - FIRE DEPT.
SO WEYMOUTH, MA 02190

BRION, LEONARD L.
107 HOPE TERRACE
CARLISLE, PA 17013

BRODY, DEBORAH
2250 CLARENDON BLVD
APT 825
ARLINGTON, VA 22201

BROGDEN, ELLIOTT P.
3904 DU BOSE DRIVE
COLUMBIA, SC 29204

BROOKS, DEAN
2440 SO LYNDONVILLE RD
LYNDONVILLE, NY 14098

BROSNAN, JOSEPH
P. O. BOX 495
POCASSET, MA 02559

BROW, ROBERT D.
P. O. BOX 298
6004 N MT. MARIA ROAD
HUBBARD LAKE, MI 49747

BROWN, THOMAS G.
17 BURBANK STREET
MILLBURY, MA 01527-2401

BROWN, NORMAN R.
37 CONCORD DRIVE
FAIRVEIW HEIGHTS, IL 62208

BROWN, RALPH
282 BARLOWS LANDING ROAD
P.O. BOX 538
POCASSET, MA 02559

BROWNELL, PETER
111 NORWOOD PLACE
STERLING, VA 20164

BRUNET, PAUL M.
384 REDONDO AVENUE #305
LONG BEACH, CA 90814

BRYANT, JAMES
10 LOUISE LANE
E. FALMOUTH, MA 02536

BRYD, WILLIAM I.
1048 PETERSBURG COVE
COLLIERVILLE, TN 38017

BUCKO, EDWARD P.
14829 E. EVANS AVENUE
AURORA, CO 80014-4518

BUENO, JUAN J.
525 MAIN STREET
FALMOUTH, MA 02540

BURGER, ROBERT S.
9 SNOWBERRY ROAD
BALLSTON SPA, NY 12020

BURGESS, PHIL
P.O. BOX 133
1051 SHORE ROAD
POCASSET, MA 02559

BURKETT, ARTHUR
527 SANUEL HUNTINGTON ST.
ORANGE PARK, FL 32073-8567

BURNELL, SAN
BOX 101
POCASSET, MA 02559

BURNS, DALE
1340 KNOLL ROAD
REDLANDS, CA 92373-7035

BURRIS, JOHN
HIGHRIDGE ROAD
READING, CT 06896

BURROUGHS, ROBIN
24 ORCHARD ROAD
MASHPEE, MA 02649

BURRY, FRANK J.
22 TURTLE POND ROAD
FALMOUTH, MA 02540

BURTYK, ANDY
BOX 277
129 WILLIAMS AVENUE
POCASSET, MA 02559

BUTCH, DAVID
P. O. BOX 9222
PENSACOLA, FL 32513

BUTTERS, JAMES A.
40 TRENTON STREET
KINGSTON, MA 02364

BUXTON, CAROL
P.O. BOX 162
W BOOTHBAY HARBOR, ME 04575

BYRNES, FRANK
P.O. BOX 1297
CANNAE, TX 77305

BZIBZIAK, WALTER
23 OLD FORGE ROAD
N. FALMOUTH, MA 02556

CALDWELL, RUTH
P.O. BOX 3
BUZZARDS BAY, MA 02532

CALHOUN, JOHN
286 OAK COURT
SEVERNA PARK, MD 21146

CALL, LEONARD
14 STOWERS STREET
E. FALMOUTH, MA 02536

CALLAND, DON
462 ST LUCIA COURT
SATELLITE BEACH, FL 32937

CAMAROTA, THOMAS
162 SEACOAST SHORES BLVD
E. FALMOUTH, MA 02536

CAMPBELL, ERNEST K.
1307 WICKS AVENUE
CHARLESTON, SC 29412

CANNATA, RICK
RT 1   BOX 576
LEE, MA 01238

CARETTE, NORMAN
465 CARRIAGE SHOP ROAD
E. FALMOUTH, MA 02536

CARLSON, OLWYN
1906 PARKSIDE PLACE
INDIAN HARBOUR BEACH, FL 32937

CARLTON, ERNIE
17615 NATHAN'S DRIVE
TAMPA, FL 33647-2273

CARMODY, MIKE
4107 142ND AVENUE N.E.
LAKE STEVENS, WA 98258

CARNEY JR., SHAUN
37 PROSPECT ROAD
MATTAPOISETT, MA 02739

CARON, GEORGE
16 CRANBERRY ROAD
BUZZARDS BAY, MA 02532

CARSON, K. N.
5100 JOHN D. RYAN BLVD #1602
SAN ANTONIO, TX 78245

CASH, LEE W.
211 NORTH BRIDGE STREET
WETUMPKA, AL 36092

CAVALLARO, VINCENT S.
21 METTLER STREET
WOODBRIDGE, CT 06525

CELLINI, OLIVER G
3020 E. FULLER ROAD
COLORADO SPRINGS, CO 80920

CHABOT, GEORGE
23 KAYAJAN AVENUE
BUZZARDS BAY, MA 02532

CHAMPAGNE, HENRY
5 BURNSIDE STREET
N. PROVIDENCE, RI 02911

CHANCELLOR, LUCILLE
24 MEADOW LARK DRIVE
WAREHAM, MA 02571

CHANCELLOR, ROY
607 BELL HURST DRIVE
MONTGOMERY, AL 36109

CHAPPELL, RICHARD
1001 STARKEY ROAD LT. 627
LARGO, FL 34641

CHARNESKI, PAUL C.
14309 10TH AVENUE S
TACOMA, WA 98444-2069

CHASE, JERRY
297 AUTUMN TRAIL
PORT ORANGE, FL 32119

CHASE, CHARLES
5040 CASTLEDOWN ROAD
COLORADO SPRINGS, CO 80917

CHILDRESS, FREDDIE
2615 WALTON WAY
AUGUSTA, GA 30904

CHILDRESS, HOWARD O.
6614 GARY LANE
CHATTANOOGA, TN 37421

CHROSTOWSKI, EUGENE
14 ENGLAND WOODS DRIVE
WEAVERVILLE, NC 28787-9006

CINQUEGRAMA, ANTHONY
17 DEVONSHIRE LANE
LONDONBERRY, NH 03053

CLARK, JACK R.
13 SOUTH LAVON AVENUE
KISSIMMEE, FL 32741

CLARK, ROBERT W.
1556 HAPPINESS DRIVE
COLORADO SPRINGS, CO 80919

CLEMENT, ARTHUR
269 TEATICKET PATH
TEATICKET, MA 02536

CLONINGER, ROBERT
47 RIDDLE HILL ROAD
FALMOUTH, MA 02540

COBIA, RAY
317 MESA LANE
W. COLUMBIA, SC 29170

COLE, CHARLIE
1385 S. MAPLE AVENUE
FAIRBORNE, OH 43324-3553

COLEMAN, JUSTIN
555 CURRIER ROAD
E. FALMOUTH, MA 02536

COLLINS, RAPHAEL C.
504 COTUIT ROAD
MASHPEE, MA 02649

COLLINS, JAMES
71 YORK STREET
DARTMOUTH, MA 02747

CONKLIN, DONALD
46 BETTY'S PATH
W. YARMOUTH, MA 02673

CONNOLLY, JOHN Q.
355 BELAIR STREET
NEW BEDFORD, MA 02719

COOK, GLADYS
615 SEA PINES LANE #405
NEWPORT NEWS, VA 23503

COOKE, ROY L.
484 HATCHVILLE ROAD
E. FALMOUTH, MA 02536

COOLEY, CARROL R.
8 COURT STREET
WINDSOR, VT 05089

COOPER, GEORGE J.
348 BRIAR DRIVE
MILLVILLE, NJ 08332

CORNELIUS, JOHN J.
3 WHIPPLTREE LANE
OLD LYME, CT 06371

CORREIA, JOHN
P. O. BOX 256
ONSET, MA 02558

COSTA, JAMES
3 BAHIA LANE
E. FALMOUTH, MA 02536

COSTANZO, LAWRENCE G.
4537 W. BOBBIE TERRACE
GLENDALE, AZ 85306

COSTIDIO, JIM
875 DEER RUN DRIVE
MELBOURNE, FL 32940

COVILLE, PAUL
117 ½ EAST MAIN STREET
SOUTH PARIS, ME 04281

CRABLE, ARTHUR
123 BAKER ROAD
RAYNHAM, MA 02767

CRAFTS, LEWIS G.
26 FAITH STREET
LISBON FALLS, ME 04252

CROBAR, JAMES
4520 COUNTY RT 6
OGDENSBURG, NY 13669

CROZIER, DICK
242 TOMPKINS STREET EXT
CORTLAND, NY 13045

CULLEN, MICHAEL
P.O. BOX 62E
EAST FALMOUTH, MA 02536

CURRENCE, SAM
39 SHORE ROAD
BOURNE, MA 02532

CURTIS, RICHARD E.
328 PAPERMILL ROAD
WESTFIELD, MA 01085

CUSSON, A. J.
60 MAIN STREET
ACUSHNET, MA 02743

CUSTER, JOSEPH
P.O. BOX 498
FALMOUTH, MA 02541

CYR, JOSEPH A. R.
41 BENNETTS NECK DRIVE
POCASSET, MA 02559

DaSILVA, JOANNA
P.O. BOX 226
E. WAREHAM, MA 02538

DAHER, JOSEPH T.
59 BURNS STREET
NEW BEDFORD, MA 02740

DAIGNAULT, ERNEST
1101 S. 92ND ST #664
MESA, AZ 85208

DANIEL, WAYNE L.
6028 SO. LAKEVIEW STREET
LITTLETON, CO 80120

DAVIS, ROLAND L.
202 HILLTOP DRIVE
MADISON HEIGHTS, VA 24572

DAYTON, RANDALL
302 THIRD AVENUE EXT.
RENSSELAER, NY 12144

DEAN, WALLACE D.
10004 STEWART DRIVE
BAINBRIDGE, GA 31717

DeBOER, RICHARD
P.O. BOX 3005
BOURNE, MA 02532

DeCOSTA, JOE
9814 REYNOLDS ROAD
LOUISVILLE, KY 40223

DeCOSTA, JOHN
32 PART STREET
MATTAPOISETT, MA 02739

DeCOSTA, LEONARD
3411 S. CAMINO SECO #251
TUCSON, AZ 85730

DEERY, KAY
22 BLANCHARD STREET
NASHUA, NH 03060

DeFEMBACH, GEORGE
US ARMY CORPS OF ENG
CAPE COD CANAL BOX J
BUZZARDS BAY, MA 02532

DeGOWIN, DON
BOX 56
WEST WAREHAM, MA 02576

DeGRAFF, JAN
RR2 BOX 1039
DINGMANS FERRY, PA 18328

DELOZIER, WINSTON
216 PINE GROVE ROAD
NEWPORT NEWS, VA 23601-1632

DEMIJOHN, RONALD S.
2893 QUEENS WAY
THOUSAND OAKS, CA 91362

DENEAULT, R. J.
2835 LINDEN LANE
FALLS CHURCH, VA 22042

DENIS, JAMES-BERRY
700 FRONST STREET 1304
SAN DIEGO, CA 92101

DENKEWITZ, ROBERT P.
7 NOTTING COURT
NESCONSET, NY 11767

DENNIS, DAVID F.
3400 N. E. WASHINGTON ROAD
CLAREMORE, OK 74017

DENNIS, TOM
43 VICTORIA CIRCLE
DOVER, DE 19901

DEPIAZZA, JOHN R.
5265 WOODVALE WAY
CARMICHAEL, CA 95608-1669

DERATANY, DAVID & SANDY
7 JONATHAN WAY
OSTERVILLE, MA 02655

DeROSA, PETER G.
104 PARK
HYANNIS, MA 02601

DeSANAO, COSIMO

825 IRVING AVENUE
ENDICOTT, NY 13760

DESROSIER, CLINTON L.
6671 RIVER RUND BOULEVARD
WEEKI WACHEI, FL 34607

DeVAUGHAN, BOBBY
49 OAK STREET
W. BARNSTABLE, MA 02668

DeWAN, OTIS K.
122 ALLEN AVENUE
FALMOUTH, MA 02540

DILLON, TIMOTHY
607 OAKLAND AVENUE
STATEN ISLAND, NY 10310

DIONNE, LAURA
RR 5 BOX 13B
RUTHERFORDTON, NC 28139

DIXON, TRAVIS
3 PLYMOUTH STREET
LAKEVILLE, MA 02347-2440

DOERR, BOB
RD 1 BOX 65B
ANDREAS, PA 18211

DONALD, BETTY
CHANDLER NURSING CENTER
RT 2 BOX 2334
CHANDLER, TX 75758

DONNER, PAUL G.
2714 BEACON COURT
LAVARRE, FL 32566

DONOVAN, JOHN A.
107 HARRISON DRIVE
VINCENNES, IN 47591

DOUCETTE, ROBERT
17 MIDWAY ROAD
P.O. BOX 1004
MONUMENT BEACH, MA 02553

DOUCETTE, LORETTA
P.O. BOX 572E
E. FALMOUTH, MA 02536

DOW, MAURICE M.
STAR ROUTE BOX 308
BRADFORD, NH 03221

DOWLER, JAMES B.
227 LAFAYETTE STREET
WOOD DALE, IL 60191

DOWNEY JR., PAUL L.
38 DOWNEY DRIVE
WAYNESVILLE, NC 28786

DRAPER, HENRY
83 HANDY ROAD
POCASSET, MA 02559

DRISCOLL, JAMES C.
9323 BRAMBLY LANE
ALEXANDRIA, VA 22309-3009

DROUIN, NORMAN R.
401 SANDWICH ROAD
E. FALMOUTH, MA 02536

DRYER, DAVE
694 SAGE CIRCLE
HIGHLANDS RANCH, CO 80126

DUBEY, ORAM
COTUIT ROAD
MARSTON MILLS, MA 02648

DUDEK, WALTER J.
P.O. BOX 697
HERNANDO, FL 34442

DUFFY, TOM
2863 WEST 1600
NORTH CLINTON, UT 84015

DUGAN, DIXIE
99 QUEENS ROAD
FALMOUTH, MA 02540

DUGEAU, CHARLIE
14 COUNTRYWOOD LANE
E. FALMOUTH, MA 02536

DUNCAN, DANIEL F.
62 CAMERON AVENUE
W. SOMERVILLE, MA 02144

DUPONT, LENNY
155 CAROLINE STREET
NEW BEDFORD, MA 02740

DUPUIS, PAUL
4 TUCY AVENUE
BUZZARDS BAY, MA 02532

DUPUY, WILLIAM L.
3244 CHADBOURNE ROAD
SHAKER HEIGHTS, OH 44120

DUROCHER, ANDRE
198 WINDSWEPT DRIVE
W. WAREHAM, MA 02576

DZIOBECKI, BILL
319 COTUIT ROAD
MASHPEE, MA 02649

D'ANDREA, GENE D.
P.O. BOX 8674
WARWICK, RI 02888

EDWARDS, WORTH A.
RT 5 BOX 317
GALAX, VA 24333

EDWARDS, WILLIAM
7668 THUNDERBIRD LANE
COLORADO SPRINGS, CO 80919

EDWARDS, JOHN B.
75 HANDY ROAD
POCASSET, MA 02559

ELLIS, ALBERT
7 LOWELL STREET
BUZZARDS BAY, MA 02532

ENGLIS, CHARLES
17 BROOKFIELD DRIVE
BROCKTON, MA 02402

ERHARDT, DAVID
8 DONNA AVENUE
DERBY, CT 06418-1018

ERWIN, WILLIAM H.
7617 GERONIMO CIRCLE
NO. LITTLE ROCK, AR 72116

ETHIER, OMER
964 BROOKVIEW DRIVE
VALDOSTA, GA 31602

EVERS, ROBERT L.
3512 WINDSOR LANE
WICHITA FALLS, TX 76308

FABIAN, JOHN
1170 DUTTON STREET
NEW BEDFORD, MA 02745

FELD, DAVID
541 ROCK SHADOW COURT
STONE MOUNTAIN, GA 30087

FERRI, JEAN
533 HIGHLAND HILLS DRIVE
HOWARD, OH 43028

FICKLING, ROBERT M.
12158 COUNTY ROAD 4017
KEMP, TX 75143-3774

FIGUEIREDO, JOHN A.
100 WEST HILL ROAD - APT D
NEW BEDFORD, MA 02740

FINDLING, MARVIN
P.O. BOX 32129
PALM BEACH GARDENS, FL 33420-2129

FIRDA, NICK
RFD #1
SAND HILL ROAD
PETERBORO, NH 03458

FISHER, RAYMOND R.
33 HEAD OF THE BAY ROAD
BUZZARDS BAY, MA 02532

FITZGERALD, JOHN C.
15 IRA ALLEN DRIVE
ESSEX JUNCTION, VT 05452

FLANAGAN, JOHN F.
22 CAPTAIN'S LANE
E. FALMOUTH, MA 02536

FLEISHER, MARK
3 LLOYD DRIVE
HORSEHEADS, NY 14845

FLEURENT, RENE
30 BRIGGS ROAD - P.O. BOX 55
WESTPORT, MA 02790

FLORY, BERNARD
169 UPPER PATTAGANSETT RD
EAST LYME, CT 06333

FLYNN, JUNE
54 ST MARGARET ST
BUZZARDS BAY, MA 02532

FOGG, GEORGE
2240 S.E. 110TH
PORTLAND, OR 97216

FORD, CLAYTON
9719 BROADRIPPLE DRIVE
SAN ANTONIO, TX 78230

FORSTER, LYNDEN
3000 JOHN HARDEN DRIVE
JACKSONVILLE, AR 72076

FORTUNE, RICHARD
125 SIERRA WOOD CR
FOLSOM, CA 95630

FOUGERE, DONALD J.
5 WEBSTER AVENUE
SANDWICH, MA 02563

FOWLIE, DONALD A.
119 PLEASANT STREET
FAIRHAVEN, MA 02719

FRANKLIN, FRANK C.
11 PATRICIA AVENUE
E. FALMOUTH, MA 02536

FREDEROSKI, HARRY
20 BLUEBERRY STREET
E. FALMOUTH, MA 02536

FREEDMAN, BERNARD
10907 SHORT CUT ROAD
APISON, TN 37302

FRIEDRICHSEN, MARIE
1051 BANFIELD ROAD
PORTSMOUTH, NH 03801

GABREY, FRANK
199 HATHAWAY ROAD
WAREHAM, MA 02571

GAGNON, LEO A.
120 PURITAN ROAD
BUZZARDS BAY, MA 02532

GAINES, WILLIAM A.
1122 CAMERON WAY
STOCKTON, CA 95207

GALLA, MARIO
18 SHIRLEY STREET
NEW BEDFORD, MA 02746

GAMAGE, PHILIP
P.O. BOX 81
FARMINGTON, NH 03835

GARDNER, JAMES R.
1037 MARION LANE
SUMTER, SC 29153

GATZIMOS, GEORGE
17 MT. VERNON STREET
LOWELL, MA 01854

GEGGETT, ROY
1550 HORTON STREET
N. DIGHTON, MA 02764

GEOGHAN, THOMAS
100 PARK AVENUE
GETTYSBURG, PA 17325

GEORGE, ROBERT
620 LAKEVIEW DRIVE
WILLOW GROVE, PA 19090

GERACE, JOSEPH
227 CLUB VALLEY DRIVE
E. FALMOUTH, MA 02536

GIAMMATTEI, TONY
#2 FELSEN STREET
HIGHLAND, NY 12528

GIANGERELL JR., TOM
37 CRANE COURT
SAFETY HARBOR, FL 33572

GIARRAPUTO, EDWARD P.
79 HANDY ROAD
POCASSET, MA 02559

GILBERT, BRUCE
4011 N. WATERBRIDGE CIRCLE
PORT ORANG, FL 32119

GILLIS, MAILON A.
6223 SHADY BROOK
SAN ANTONIO, TX 78239

GILMORE, CHESTER
9 IVY LANE
FALMOUTH, MA 02540

GLASS, ANDRE
RD 2 BOX 4273
JONESTOWN, PA 17038

GLICK, JOHN
228 LIVE OAK STREET
BOYNTON BEACH, FL 33436

GOBBI, VICTOR
10 CAROLINE DRIVE
MILFORD, MA 01757

GOERSHEL, DON
18 ONEIDA ROAD
ACTON, MA 01720-2316

GOLDSTEIN, BILL
21 BECKERT AVENUE
REVERE, MA 02151

GONNEVILLE, PAUL
21 NECK ROAD
ROCHESTER, MA 02770

GONSALVES, ROBERT
NEW BEDFORD FIRE DEPT.
NEW BEDFORD, MA 02740

GONYON, DARYL
76 FROST STREET
FALL RIVER, MA 02721

GOOD, CHARLES
106 ALLERTON STREET
PLYMOUTH, MA 02360

GOODLEY, GRADY
918 LAMAR STREET
SAN ANTONIO, TX 78202

GORDON JR., RICHARD W.
RD #2 CARLTON ROAD #2231
WHITEHALL, NY 12887

GORE, ROBERT
1202 DOGWOOD LANE
BLOOMINGTON, IL 61701

GOUGE, ROY
3161 CRANBERRY HIGHWAY
BUZZARDS BAY, MA 02532

GOURLEY, EDWIN
903 MINUTEMAN CAUSEWAY
COCOA BEACH, FL 32931

GRAHAM, JUSTIN
P.O. BOX 457
BURLINGTON, KS 66839

GRANDY, LLOYD G.
155 GRANDY ROAD
HERMON, NY 13652

GRANT, THEO E.
4804 HOLLY PARK DRIVE
PASADENA, TX 77505-2123

GREANEY, ROBERT
58 CIRCLE DRIVE
CAYCE, SC 29033-1729

GREEN, DAVID
17 KRAUSE STREET
BAYSHORE, NY 11706

GREENE, RICHARD
P.O. BOX 39
HARRISVILLE, NY 13648

GREGORY, DONALD
12 JOWICK STREET
MATTAPOISETT, MA 02739

GREMLIPZ, WALTER
#3 WILDWOOD DRIVE
MILFORD, MA 01757

GRIFFIN, LEO J.
11447 HATCHET PASS
SAN ANTONIO, TX 78245

GRIFFIN, LAWRENCE
567 CRESCENT AVE LOT - 10A
HIGHLAND, NY 12528

GRIMM, JAY
2454 FIVE SHILLING ROAD
FREDERICK, MD 21701

GRUNWALD, KEN
1375 ABBEY WAY
BENSALEM, PA 19020

GUSLEY, JOHN R.
7 GREENWOOD VILLAGE ROAD
NO. EASTON, MA 02536

HABEGGER, HARLEY
1462 BARNS DRIVE
WOOSTER, OH 44691

HABER, JOE
4318 THORNHILL PLACE
PITTSBURGH, CA 94565

HACK, CARLTON B.
4 PORTSIDE DRIVE   BOX 304
POCASSET, MA 02559

HACKLER SR., TED H.
208 WALTON COURT
MELBOURNE, FL 32934

HAGGETT, DAVE
6 PEPPER POND TRAIL ROAD
SHERMAN, CT 06784

HALL, JOSEPH
106 LINCOLNSHIRE DRIVE
NICEVILLE, FL 32578

HALL, LIONEL & MARGARET
80 VIDAL AVENUE
E. FALMOUTH, MA 02536

HALL, WEBSTER
525 ASHLEY BOULEVARD
NEW BEDFORD, MA 02745

HALL, DICK
1771 SEVERN STREET
GROSSE POINT, MI 48236

HALL, VIRGIL
11040 TAMERIX AVENUE
PORT RICHIE, FL 34668

ALLIDY, HUGH D.
1 BESSIES LANDING DRIVE
POQUOSON, VA 23662

HALLWASS, KARL
P.O. BOX 3144
BOURNE STATION
BUZZARDS BAY, MA 02532

HALPENNY, ROBERT P.
5650 FLINT RIDGE DRIVE
COLORADO SPRINGS, CO 80918

HALVERSON, LEONARD
427 LOCUST FIELD ROAD
E. FALMOUTH, MA 02536

HAMMOND, GEORGE JR.
P.O. BOX 111
E. WAREHAM, MA 02538

HANSON, JAMES R.
8 PONTES AVENUE
E. FALMOUTH, MA 02536

HARASIAK, EUGENE J.
15 SABBOTT ROAD - BOX 234
POCASSET, MA 02559

HARBAUGH, JANET
478 PRESTWICK COURT
MELBOURNE, FL 32940

HARDWICK, STAFFORD E.
14 WALL STREET
BUZZARDS BAY, MA 02532

HARRIS, HUGH
1225 KAREN ROAD
MONTGOMERY, AL 36107

HARRISON, NORMAN
JULY STREET - P.O. BOX 280
LIMINGTON, ME 04049

HARRISON JR., HOWARD
32945 33RD AVENUE S W
FEDERAL WAY, VA 98023-2733

HARTI, GABE
11800 RIDERS LANE
RESTON, VA 22091

HATTAWAY, THOMAS L.
3612 QUANDO DRIVE
ORLANDO, FL 32812

HAWKINS, EDDIE
P.O. BOX 15
ALTUS, AR 72821

HAWORTH, WALTER
162 MAIN STREET
FAIRHAVEN, MA 02719

HAYES JR., JOSEPH S.
17 EDGAR ROAD
BILLERICA, MA 01821

HEALY, MICHAEL J.
11 MICHAEL ROAD
POCASSET, MA 02559

HELLER, ARCHIE
501 VINCENT AVENUE
FT. WALTON BEACH, FL 32547

HEMMER, DONALD
785 BEDFORD HILL DRIVE
EARLYSVILLE, VA 22936

HENDERSON, ERNEST
62 LOCUS STREET
FALMOUTH, MA 02540

HENRY JR., GEORGE A.
9607 MUIRFIELD DRIVE
UPPER MARLBORO, MD 20772

HESLER, RICHARD T.
9517 PORTLAND AVENUE
TACOMA, WA 98445

HICKEY, CORNEILUS J.
P.O. BOX 727
FALMOUTH, MA 02541

HICKS, CHARLES R.
BOX 162
GREAT NECK ROAD N.
MASHPEE, MA 02649

HILL, LEVI
132 ARROWHEAD DRIVE
HYANNIS, MA 02601

HITCHCOCK, CALVIN
P.O. BOX 398
W. WAREHAM, MA 02576

HOFFMAN, HENRY T.
148 HOMESTEAD LANE
TEATICKET, MA 02536

HOLLAND, HOWARD
73 GUILD ROAD - BOX 328
FORESTDALE, MA 02694

HOLLOWAY, JERE
4727 KITTY DRIVE
MEMPHIS, TN 38128

HOLT, SAM
229 BARLOWS LANDING ROAD
BOX 402
POCASSET, MA 02559

HOPKINS, NORMAN
1037 QUEENS ROAD
VINELAND, NJ 08360

HORHSAW, VERNON
1627 CONLYN STREET
PHILADELPHIA, PA 19141

HORTON, HOWARD
309 WILD HARBOR ROAD
N. FALMOUTH, MA 02556

HUBBARD, LYMAN
3320 BUNNELL DRIVE
OAKLAND, CA 94602

HUGHES, DAN
1308 AMERICAN PLANT ROAD
WASKOM, TX 75692

HUGO, VANE
4319 APPLE TREE WOODS
SAN ANTONIO, TX 78249

HUOT, RAY
1315 CHAGAL AVENUE
LANCASTER, CA 93535

IBBTSON, GEORGE
208 ELM STREET
HANSON, MA 02341

INGLIS, EDWIN B.
100 HIBBERT STREET
ARLINGTON, MA 02174

ISAACSON, WAYNE G.
25 CRESTA WAY
HOT SPRINGS VILLAGE, AR 71909

IVERSON, WILLIAM J.
56 PROFFITT STREET
COOKEVILLE, TN 38501

IVES, DAVID V.
20 SALT RIVER ROAD
E. FALMOUTH, MA 02536

IZDEPSKI, NORBERT V.
8105 SUNSET AVENUE
FAIR OAKS, CA 95628

JACKSON, GLENWOOD R.
21 TWIN HILL ROAD
E. FALMOUTH, MA 02536

JAMES, BILL
P.O. BOX 638E
FALMOUTH, MA 02536

JANUARY JR., JACK
179 RAMADA LANE
APTOS, CA 95003

JASINSKI, JOHN M.
7 BERRY DRIVE
N. CHELMSFORD, MA 01863

JAWORSKI, WALTER J.
7 PORTSIDE DRIVE
POCASSET, MA 02559

JEWELL, LYLE
6660 CROWN RT VISTA
GRANITE BAY, CA 95746

JOHNSON, DUANE
72633 TRAMWAY VISTA DR NE
ALBUQUERQUE, NM 87122

JOHNSON, EARL
P.O. BOX 1052
CLAY POND ROAD
MONUMENT BEACH, MA 02553

JOHNSON, EARL
121 6TH AVENUE
SHALIMAR, FL 32579

JOHNSON, HAROLD
251 S.E. FIELDS TERRACE
PORT CHARLOTTE, FL 33952

JOHNSON, ROBERT W.
15326 FLORWOOD AVENUE
LAWNDALE, CA 90260

JOHNSON, MARY
234 SOUTH STREET
MILFORD, NH 03055

JOLIN, BOB
1319 B STREET
COEUR D'ALENE, ID 83814

JONES, GRAEME
431 CARDINAL AVENUE
FT. WALTON BEACH, FL 32548

JONES, CLARENCE H.
252 CARROL STREET
NEW BEDFORD, MA -2740

JONES, RICHARD
1017 NORTH CRYSTAL WAY
MUSTANG, OK 73064

JONES, MARIE
MONUMENT BEACH, MA 02553

JOYCE, WILLIAM A.
BOX 38
FALMOUTH, MA 02541

JOZWIAK, TOM F.
3012 LYNNWOOD DRIVE
ARLINGTON, TX 76013

JUBE, HERBERT W.
210 LAKE HARBOR CIRCLE
HOT SPRINGS, AR 71901

JUSZCZYK, WALTER
44 RUSSELL STREET
FALMOUTH, MA 02540

KAPLAN, DONALD
775 DUNLAP CIRCLE
WINTER SPRINGS, FL 32708

KARCZEWSKI, CHARLES
9242 ARLINGTON BOULEVARD
FAIRFAX, VA 22031

KARRAM, CALVAN
78 BLUEBERRY LANE
MARSTONS MILLS, MA 02648

KELLER, PAUL
91 MARINERS LANE
FALMOUTH, MA 02540

KENDRICK, BILL
232 MORGAN CIRCLE
GAFFNEY, SC 29341

KENNEDY, EVERETT
7500 BELLE PLAIN DRIVE
DAYTON, OH 45424

KENNEDY, JACK
19 MAPLE AVE
CENTERVILLE, MA 02632

KENYON, LESLIE J.
943 E. NEWTON
PLACENTIA, CA 92670

KERCHER, GERALD F.
P.O. BOX 168
QUAKER HILL, CT 06375

KERR, ARTHUR D.
22133 NE 26 PL
REDMOND, WA 98053

KERR, ROBERT C.
2519 SILVER RIDGE
SAN ANTONIO, TX 78232

KESTER, VICTOR H.
297 PALMER AVENUE
FALMOUTH, MA 02540

KEUREN, DONALD VAN
1013 ROUND HILL CIRCLE
NAPA, CA 94558

KILGORE, ROBERT
16 CONNELLY CIRCLE
BRAINTREE, MA 02184

KIMBROUGH, THOMAS
3178 RIVER FOREST ROAD
MONROE, GA 30655

KIMMEL, WILLIAM B.
RR #4 BOX 476
WEST PITTSTON, PA 18643

KIRBY, WILLIAM
22832 CYPRESS TRAIL DRIVE
LUTZ, FL 33549-4153

KLINE, DALE
402 GUNTER STREET
OZARK, AL 36360

KLOPFER, RICHARD
810 N. EGLIN PARKWAY #5
FT. WALTON BEACH, FL 32548

KLUBERTANZ, JEAN
117 NURSERY ROAD
FALMOUTH, MA 02540

KNIGHT, DAVID
11180 FRY ROAD
EDENBORO, PA 16412

KNIGHT, DOUGLASS R.
P.O. BOX 955
SALEM, NH 03079

KNISPEL, RAYMOND
11 RIBBON FALLS DRIVE
ORMOND BEACH, FL 32174

KOCH, JOHN
100 BRANCH STREET
ARLINGTON, MA 02174

KOELLN, WERNER R.
C/O CINDY KOELLN
1371 NORMANDY DR. NE #2
ATLANTA, GA 30306

KOLBERT, ROBERT J.
6 WALL STREET
BUZZARDS BAY, MA 02532

KONOSKY, JOHN M.
2620 ORO BLANCO DRIVE
COLORADO SPRINGS, CO 80917

KORONKIEWICZ, GEORGE A.
550 COUNTY ROAD
POCASSET, MA 02559

KRESAGE, JAMES
139 BRALEY ROAD
E. FREETOWN, MA 02717

KROL, SYLVESTER
P.O. BOX 060773
PALM BAY, FL 32906

KRZYSKO, JOSEF & EDYTH
19 SEVERENS DRIVE
NEWPORT, VT 05855

LABARGE, RAYMOND
674 LORD DUNMORE DRIVE
VIRGINIA BEACH, VA 23464

LaBELLE, WALTER
3151 OTTAWA COURT
MELBOURNE, FL 32935

LaBRANCHE, WILLIAM
1521 AVENIDA FIESTA
N. LAS VEGAS, NV 89031

LACROIX, JOSEPH
62 RABIDEAU STREET
MORRISONVILLE, NY 12962

LAFFEY, "PAT" THOMAS
3903 SHADY TERRACE
KINGWOOD, TX 77345

LANEY, CLIFFORD W.
305 N. MANTUA STREET
KENT, OH 44240

LaPOINTE, TED
5845 S. QUATAR CIRCLE
AURORA, CO 80015

LaPORE, WILLIAM
BOX 96
SAGAMORE BEACH, MA 02562

LARSEN, ROLAND
1402 S.W. 54TH TERRACE
CAPE CORAL, FL 33914

LASS, LEO
49 MOON COMPASS LANE
SANDWICH, MA 02563

LAWYER, JAMES L.
BOX 3286
POCASSET, MA 02559

LE BLANC, ART
1 ALERVINE FARMS ROAD
KENNEBUCK, ME 04043

LEE, RICHARD C.
2613 S. ROSE STREET
TACOMA, WA 98405

LEGAN, JOSEPH
1807 BOX ELDER COURT
INDIANAPOLIS, IN 46260

LEHNER, NORMAN
519 SUN LAKE DRIVE
PORT ORANGE, FL 32127

LEIN, ERNEST
6342 FLAT RIVER ROAD
GREENE, RI 02827

LEMANSKI, CHESTER
18 NICK VEDDER ROAD
BUZZARDS BAY, MA 02532

LEONARD, DEAN A.
5 FOREST STREET
SO. BURLINGTON, VT 05403

LONG JR., LYNN J.
2802 MILLBROOK ROAD
FAYETTEVILLE, NC 28303

LORSON JR., (NICK) RALPH
P.O. BOX 985
NO. FALMOUTH, MA 02556

LOYKO, ED
14 ELDONA AVENUE
FALMOUTH, MA 02540

LUMLEY, JIM
P.O. BOX 766
ONSET, MA 02558

MacCORMACK, DONALD
85 PURITAN ROAD
BUZZARDS BAY, MA 02532

MacDOUGAL, GREGORY
144 MINNESOTA STREET
ROCHESTER, NY 14609

MADDOX, HARRY
439 PITCHERS WAY
HYANNIS, MA 02601

MAGNUSKI, BILL
P.O. BOX 269
STATEN ISLAND, NY 10310

MAGNUSON, JOSEPH E.
24 WHORTLEBERRY LANE
DENNISPORT, MA 02369

MAHER, EDWARD D.
14219 MINORCA COVE
DEL MAR, CA 92014

MAHONEY, JOHN M.
26 COTTAGE STREET
FAIRHAVEN, MA 02719

MANNERING, WILLIAM
12915 EAST 36TH TERRACE
INDEPENDENCE, MO 64055

MARCOTTE, ROGER E.
28 DUNCAN STREET
NEW BEDFORD, MA 02745

MARGARET ENDRES
3411 COUNTY ROAD #70
PALM HARBOR, FL 34683

MARINOFF, HYMAN
4 SKYLINE DRIVE
N. DARTMOUTH, MA 02747

MARQUES, STEVE
12 SMITH AVE
METHUEN, MA 018440

MARR, GERALD
BOX 100093
NASHVILLE, TN 37284

MARSCHOLL, GERALD
P.O. BOX 704E
E. FALMOUTH, MA 02536

MARSHALL, FRED
P.O. BOX 140
WILLSEYVILLE, NY 13864

MARTIN, LAVERNE & JEROLD
117 WAYCROSS DRIVE
ROUTE 4
GEORGETOWN, TX 78628

MARTINKA, HENRY
RT 7A BOX 102
SHASTSBURY, VT 05262

MASAPOLLO, GUY
16 MERRILL AVE
TAUNTON, MA 02780

MATICE, RICHARD
P.O. BOX 1
GARDINER, NY 12525

MAY, RICHARD D.
22 ALDEN AVENUE
BUZZARDS BAY, MA 02532

MAYER, VICTOR I.
5403 HUNTERS GLEN
AUSTIN, TX 78745

McCALL, JAMES L.
2083 S. BROADWAY
GRAND JUNCTION, CO 81503

McCAULEY, GERARD
42 WYMAN AVENUE
MONUMENT BEACH, MA 02553

McCLAID, SHERMAN & LOUISE
52 VIDAL AVENUE
E. FALMOUTH, MA 02536

McCLANNAHAN, REESE
1295 ISLAND DRIVE
MERRITT ISLAND, FL 32952

McCLUNG, SPENCER
3617 RED OAK DRIVE
RD #4
DENTON, TX 76205

McCONNELL, JOHN
5 SYLVAN DRIVE
HYANNIS, MA 02601

McDONALD, LEROY
10 RUE DE LE ROI STREET
FORT WALTON, FL 32547

McDONOUGH, PETER J.
4537 BARRETT ROAD
CARMICHAEL, CA 95608

McGUIRE, M. R.
6041 GEORGIA DRIVE
N. HIGHLANDS, CA 95660

McINTOSH, BRUCE
1104 NO. HIGHLAND AVENUE
ARLINGTON HEIGHTS, IL 60004

McKAY, GEORGE W.
360 SUMMER HAVEN LANE
HENRY, VA 24102

McLAMB, WALLACE F.
P.O. BOX 65882
HAMPTON, VA 23665

McLAUGHLIN, HERBERT
26 SCOTT DRIVE
\MANOMET, MA 02345

MEDEIROS, ROBERT
5601 PHLOX COURT
SACRAMENTO, CA 95842

MEIKLE, WILLIAM K.
11524 WOODLAND AVENUE E
PUYALLUP, WA 98373-4662

MELONE, JOHN
4 HILLCREST DRIVE
CECIL, PA 15321

MELTON, KENNETH
11526 SPICEWOOD PARKWAY
AUSTIN, TX 78750-2602

MENKER, GENE
440 LAKE OF THE WOODS DR
VENICE, FL 34293

ENTZ, THOMAS
2934 SHAWN WAY
RANCHO CORDOVA, CA 95670

MERKEY, HARRY
347 NEW 22 EAST
JONESTOWN, PA 17038

MIKLOS, JOHN
4435 E. GLENROSA AVE
PHOENIX, AZ 85018

MIKSCH, JOSEPH
913 CENTRAL AVENUE
E. BRIDGEWATER, MA 02333

MILLER, BOB
1332 KESSER DRIVE
PLANO, TX 75023

MILLER, MELVIN
25 SAO PAULO DRIVE.
FALMOUTH, MA 02536

MILLER, WILLIAM G.
130 HADLEY STREET
NEW BEDFORD, MA 02745

MILSKY, PETER W.
CEDAR LANE
EASTHAM, MA 02642

MIRANDA, ALVIRINO
374 RAYMOND STREET
NEW BEDFORD, MA 02745

MITCHELL, MRS. GEORGE
16 CAMBRIDGE AVE NE
FT. WALTON BEACH, FL 32548

MITCHELL, CHARLES
33 HARBOR ROAD
HYANNIS, MA 02601

MITCHELL, EDWARD
39 SALLY LANE
E. FALMOUTH, MA 02536

MITCHELL SR., ROBERT V.
ROUTE 1   BOX 233
MOUNTAIN ROAD
JAFFREY, NH 03452

MITCHELL, JOHN E.
23 FALMOUTH HEIGHTS ROAD
FALMOUTH, MA 02540

MONCEVICZ, DONALD
40 POND STREET
W. DENNIS, MA 02670

MOON, JACK
6416 HEATHER MARIE LANE
CALLAWAY, FL 32404-8307

MOORE, EDWARD SHERRY LANE
P.O. BOX 458
MONUMENT BEACH, MA 02553

MARYLAND, BENJAMIN
38 VIDAL AVENUE
E. FALMOUTH, MA 02536

MORGAN, BILLYOH
208 HOLLY DRIVE
CAMP HILL, PA 17011

MORIN, RAY
P.O. BOX 213
MONUMENT BEACH, MA 02553

MORRIS, A.E.
2279 PORT MALABAR BLVD NE
PALM BAY, FL 32905

MOSER, DONALD D.
250 PINEHURST CIRCLE
NAPLES, FL 34113

MOVINSKI, JAMES F.
28594 WESTWOOD LANE
CARMICHAEL, CA 95608

MULLINAX, GEORGE
191 PERSHING STREET
SPARTANBURG, SC 29302

MURPHY, JEAN
64 OLD MEETING HOUSE ROAD
E. FALMOUTH, MA 02536

MURPHY, MAURICE
P.O. BOX 126
WEST OSSIPEE, NH 03890

MURPHY, HENRY
35 LINWOOD AVENUE
P.O. BOX 97
MONUMENT BEACH, MA 02553

MURRAY, WILLIAM D.
7 WEST WOLFE STREET
AVON PARK, FL 33825

MUSSER, MARTIN R.
1450 CAMBRIDGE
NOVATO, CA 94947

MUSTAFA, AHMED
530 CARRIAGE SHOP ROAD
E. FALMOUTH, MA 02536

NADEAU, JAMES E.
263 HUCKINS ROAD
CENTERVILLE, MA 02532

NAGY, GARY N.
87 WASHBURN AVENUE
WASHINGTON, NJ 07882

NEAL, J. W.
4122 MARLIN STREET
PANAMA CITY BEACH, FL 32408

NELIPOWITZ, THOMAS R.
40 BERWICK ROAD S
SYRACUSE, NY 13208

NELSON JR., ALLEN H.
2913 ALTA VISTA LANE
SAN ANGELO, TX 76904

NEYMAN, DAVID
5701 BLACKJACK ROAD
OKLAHOMA CITY, OK 73150

NOLAN, BILL
11 N CLAREMONT
COLORADO SPRINGS, CO 80909

NORTON, BARRY
24 MOORE STREET
FALL RIVER, MA 02721

NOYES, RON
16000 PHILMONT LANE
BOWIE, MD 20716

NUCKOLES, WILLIAM O.
ROUTE 1   BOX 600
STUARTS DRAFT, VA 24477

OBER, MARTIN
BOX 3015
2718 CRANBERRY HIGHWAY
WAREHAM, MA 02571

OLEY, LEO F.
7753 FARMGATE WAY
CITRUS HEIGHT, CA 95610

OLIOSI, EDITH
6 BLUEBERRY ROAD
BUZZARDS BAY, MA 02532

OLIVE, DAVID
5905 N.W. PINEWOOD PL
CORVALLIS, OR 97330

OLIVEIRA, JOSEPH
50 PAGE STREET
NEW BEDFORD, MA 02740

OLIVER, DAVID
830 LIGHTSTONE DRIVE
SAN ANTONIO, TX 78258

ORLIK, PETER
401 BARRYMORE DRIVE
OXON HILL, MD 20745

OSBORNE, ARTHUR D.
6 MEEHAM DRIVE
CHELMSFORD, MA 01824

OSTENDORF, TED
19795 E. TOP O' THE MOOR DR.
MONUMENT, CO 80132

OTTAVIANO, ROBERT
33 PERCH POND CIRCLE
E. FALMOUTH, MA 02536

OTTEY JR., EARL R.
BOX 537
N. FALMOUTH, MA 02556

OYER, KEN
1374 CYPRESS TRACE DRIVE
MELBOURNE, FL 32940

O'BRIEN, ROBERT H.
40 JILMA DRIVE
EST DENNIS, MA 02641

O'BRIEN, ROBERT J.
162 HOLLINGSWORTH ROAD
OSTERVILLE, MA 02655

O'DONNELL, JOHN
P.O. BOX 336
OSTERVILLE, MA 02655

O'REILLY, FRANK J.
1519 E. LAKE LANE
SEBASTIAN, FL 32958

PABILONIA, R.
3822 ENCINO DRIVE
COLORADO SPRINGS, CO 80918

PACHICO, GEORGE
9 ALGNAN WAY
E. FREETOWN, MA 02717

PALMER, EDWIN
138 SPRING STREET
HOPE VALLEY, RI 02832

PARK, ALEXANDER C.
2865 REGAL CIRCLE, APT H
BIRMINGHAM, AL 35216-4688

PARKER, BRIAN T.
3700 OLD HEARNE ROAD
BRYAN, TX 77803

PARSONS, LOUIS
27 LINCOLN AVENUE
BUZZARDS BAY, MA 02532

PASQUINI, FRANK H.
8821 OLD WALNUT ROAD
OCEAN SPRINGS, MS 39564

PASSOA, BENJAMIN
4712 GREENLEIGH ROAD
RICHMOND, VA 23223

PATTERSON, HARRY C.
1964 POINT WINDWARD PL. SW
SHALLOTTE, NC 28470

PEINE, LESLIE A.
109 ANDREWS DRIVE
LUBBOCK, TX 79416

PELEHACH, STEVE
1705 FAIRWAY LANE
ROCKLEDGE, FL 32955

PELIZZARI, PAUL
18 RICHARD STREET
ANSONIA, CT 06401

PENNEY, DORA
7 LEE LANE
OLD TOWN, ME 04468

PERCY, NEWELL
3455 PELICAN CIRCLE
TITUSVILLE, FL 32796

PERUSSE, AL
35 FERNWOOD DRIVE
HAMPDEN, MA 01036

PHILBRICK, SCOTT
P.O. BOX 100
ORRINGTON, ME 04474

PHILLIPS, CARL
51 PARKER ROAD
E. FALMOUTH, MA 02536

PICCOLO, SAMUEL T.
86 PERCH POND CIRCLE
E. FALMOUTH, MA 02536

PICHT, CLYDE W.
3708 KELVIN AVENUE
FORT WORTH, TX 76133

PIEPER, BRUCE
374 IDAHO ROAD
LEOMA, TN 38468

PINKSTON, NELL
4341 THOMAS DRIVE
PANAMA CITY BEACH, FL 32408

PIPKINS, LEMAR
30 CENTER AVENUE
BUZZARDS BY, MA 02532

PITTS, JAMES R.
1815 4TH AVENUE S
IRONDALE, AL 35210

PITTSLEY, HOLLUS
1516 SASSAQUIN AVENUE
NEW BEDFORD, MA 02745

POLEK, WALTER S.
38 EMERY STREET
NEW BEDFORD, MA 02744

POLKEY, ERNEST
182 TWIN BRIDGE ROAD
SANDY NOOK, MS 39478

POORE, EDWARD & CLARE
P.O. BOX 352
SAGAMORE, MA 02561

POSAKA, GERALD R.
41 WOODHULL ROAD
E. SETAUKET, NY 11733

POSTOSKY, ANDREW
6406 KILLARNEY STREET
CLINTON, MD 20735

POTACK, WALTER J.
3525 COUNTRY HILL DRIVE
FAIRFAX, VA 22030

POWERS, ELLIOTT
2309 WOLD AVENUE
COLORADO SPRINGS, CO 80909

PREGONY, DOUG
23 SUNRISE AVENUE
GREENFIELD, MA 01301

PRIEST JR., CHARLES
15 HOOVER ROAD
TWEKSBURY, MA 01876

PRUDEN, JESSE E.
1514 BRITTLE DRIVE
SUFFOLK, VA 23434

PUBICOVER, JOE
21 EDITH AVENUE
BUZZARDS BAY, MA 02532

PUOPOLO, JOHN N.
6830 CRYSTALWOOD DR
LIVERPOOL, NY 13088

QUINN, RANDALL
P.O. BOX 11540
LAS VEGAS, NV 89111

QUINN, PATRICK D.
2433 CYPRESS DRIVE
BETTENDORF, IOWA 52722

QUINTAL, EDWARD A.
16 SCONTICUT NECK RD #195
FAIRHAVEN, MA 02719

RAIMOR, DAVID
P.O. BOX 19396
CLEVELAND, OH 44119

RANDALL, JOHN M.
1417 JACKSON STREET
STOUGHTON, WI 53589

RATTI, REGINA E.
2602 WATERFORD WAY #A
PALMETTO, FL 34221

RAY, ROBERT E.
RR3   BOX 807K
DRUMS, PA 18222

RAYMOND, ADELARD, JR.
44 SADY'S LANE
E. FALMOUTH, MA 02536

RAYMOND, ROBERT
132 EASTON STREET
NEW BEDFORD, MA 02746

REDDEN, MILDRED
HC 60   BOX 39
QUINWOOD, W.VA 25981

REDDING, BEN
117 LAKESHORE DRIVE
FREDERICKSBURG, VA 22405

REED, RICHARD
17 BLUEBERRY LANE
E. FALMOUTH, MA 02536

REESE, BEN
565 WESTMOND ROAD
SAGLE, ID 83860

REESE, JAMES
4 WOODSPRING FARM LANE
SANDWICH, MA 02563

REEZE, JIM
1498 BUTTER BRANCH DRIVE
FAYETTEVILLE, NC 28311

REGAN, BERNIE
6 LINWOOD ROAD
FORT WALTON BACH, FL 32547

REILLY, PATRICIA
90 HILLMAN STREET - APT 3
NEW BEDFORD, MA 02740

REILY, BOB
BOX 462
MONUMENT BEACH, MA 02553

RESCIGNA, FRANK
376 GAREBOLDI AVENUE
LODI, NJ 07644

REUTER, NORMAN
PO BOX 5253
INCLINE VILLAGE, NV 89450

RICE, ART
5641 DENNER AVENUE
KLAMATH FALLS, OR 97603

RICHARD, SID
479 KARLO COURT
DELTONA, FL 32725

RICHARD, JIM
120 JAMES STREET
ACUSHNET, MA 02743

RICKEY, JIMMY
9316 N.E. 16TH
MIDWEST CITY, OK 73130

RIDLEY, JAMES
33 PORTSIDE CIRCLE
E. FALMOUTH, MA 02536

RITTER, KEITH
7143 TANGERINE ROAD
ALTA LOMA, CA 91701

RIZZUTO, JOHN
9651 E. CROSBY STREET
GARDEN GROVE, CA 92644

ROACHE, THOMAS
40 OAK STREET
E. FALMOUTH, MA 02536

ROBARGE, JOHN
P.O. BOX 451
WAREHAM, MA 02571

ROBERTS, ANDUS E.
43 HANDY ROAD
POCASSET, MA 02559

ROBIDOUX, ROBERT
P.O. BOX 3156
WAREHAM, MA 02571

ROBIDOUX, THEODORE
P.O. BOX 325
FISKDALE, MA 01518

ROCHA, RICHARD
558 MOUNT PLEASANT STREET
NEW BEDFORD, MA 02745

ROCHA, MANNY
30 CHASE STREET
HYANNIS, MA 02601

RODRIQUEZ, PAUL
6837 TREEBARK WAY
CITRUS HEIGHTS, CA 95621

ROGERS, GENE
RR2 BOX 608
BRIDGTON, ME 04009

ROGERS, LUTHER
343 CLUB HOUSE DRIVE
HATCHVILLE, MA 02536

ROGERS, PHIL
234 SOUTH STREET
MEDFIELD, MA 02052

ROGERS, ROBERT B.
198 CLINTON STREET
SAYRE, PA 18840

ROGERS, WILLIAM
18 TOBY ROAD
WAREHAM, MA 02571

ROGGE, DERWOOD L.
24 RACE LANE
SANDWICH, MA 02563

ROISMAN, BARRY P.
3201 FOOTHILL STREET
WOODBRIDGE, VA 22192

RONCARATI, ALBERT
240 BLACK CAT ROAD
PLYMOUTH, MA 02360

ROOD, RICHARD F.
P.O. BOX 1713
BUZZARDS BAY, MA 02532

ROSE, LAWRENCE G.
11 VILLAGE DRIVE
NO. DARTMOUTH, MA 02747-2038

ROYER, JOHN H.
54 NOTTINGHAM DRIVE
CENTERVILLE, MA 02632

RUFO, BOB
46 REGAL STREET
HOLLISTON, MA 01746

RUUD, EINAR
131 HEATHER LANE
N. FALMOUTH, MA 02556

SACHS, ROBERT L.
RFD 3 BOX 207E
PLYMOUTH, NH 03264

SADLER, ROBERT J.
105 SURREY AVENUE
COUNCIL BLUFF, IA 51503

SAMPSON, WILLIAM
65 GREAT HILL ROAD
SO. SANDWICH, MA 02563

SARGENT, H.J.
P.O. BOX 693
MILTON, W.VA 25541

SARGENT, EILEEN
5 SHAW STREET
MATTAPOISETT, MA 02739

SAWYER, BRUD
BILLINGTON SEA ROAD
PLYMOUTH, MA 02360

SAWYER, BUZ
1495 ALMADEN VALLEY DRIVE
SAN JOSE, CA 95120

SCHADWILL, ED
RR 5 BOX 64
QUEENSBURG, NY 12804

SCHALTENBRAND, EUGENE
11501 NW 30TH STREET
CORAL SPRINGS, FL 33065

SCHEDLER, HAL
3712 HAVEN GLENN PLACE
SACRAMENTO, CA 95821

SCHNEPP, C.M.
933 GARDINIA
DEL RAY, FL 33444

SCHULTZ, WILLIAM
510 GREENE STREET
FAIRBORN, OH 45324

SCHULTZ, DONALD
27 LEXINGTON DRIVE
LIVINGSTON, NJ 07039

SCHWARTZ, ROBERT L.
3418 W. DALKE AVENUE
SPOKANE, WA 99205

SEARS, JOSEPH & PAULINE
12 WOODKNOLL DRIVE
NO. HAMPTON, N.H. 03862

SENNA JR., MANUEL
4403 MARBLE WAY
CARMICHAEL, CA 95608

SEYREK, JOSEPH J.
9 CLIFF ROAD
MONUMENT BEACH, MA 02553

SHAFFER, THEODORE C.
68701 CLARK ROAD
ST. CLAIRVILLE, OH 43950

SHANK, FLOYD I.
66 KING POND PLAIN ROAD
PLYMOUTH, MA 02360

SHERARD, WRIGHT J.
1532 INDEPENDENCE AVENUE
MELBORURNE, FL 32940

SHERBLUM, CARL
5 VERA ROAD
COVENTRY, RI 02816-4302

SHERIDAN, JOHN J.
84 MARNISTA EXT
TEATICKET, MA 02536

SHIELDS, RICHARD
7942 MOONMIST CIRCLE
HUNTINGDON BEACH, CA 92648

SHORT, WILLIAM
P.O. BOX 346
KIMBERLING CITY, MO 65686

SHURMANEK, TONY
279 WYOMING STREET
WILKES-BARRE, PA 18705

SIERSDALE, DAVID
51 MORSTON STREET
NEEDHAM, MA 02194

SIMMONS, RICHARD J.
597 CHURCH STREET
NEW BEDFORD, MA 02745

SLABENSKI, EUGENE J.
335 PHILLIPS ST LYNWOOD
WILKES-BARRE, PA 18702S

LAUSON, THEODORE W.
5805 SOUTHGROVE DRIVE
CITRUS HEIGHTS, CA 95610

SMITH, KENNETH K.
3821 BUCKSKIN TRAIL E
JACKSONVILLE, FL 32277

SMITH, KENNETH
4 DOGWOOD COURT
DOVER, DE 19904

SMITH, RALPH F.
508 TODD AVENUE
ELLWOOD CITY, PA 16117

SMITH, NORMAN E.
2137 HAFER ROAD
FAYETHVILLE, PA 17222

SMITH, NORMAN
42 NORTH READING STREET
MANCHESTER, NH 03104

SMITH, GILBERT E.
37025 QUEBEC STREET
DENVER, CO 80237

SMITH, WILLIAM
670 CASMAN STREET
SATELLITE BEACH, FL 32937

SMITH, JAMES R.
116 JEFFERSON ROAD
BOURNE, MA 02532

SOLIMINE, ANTHONY R.
194 ACAPESKET ROAD
E. FALMOUTH, MA 02536

SOMERVILLE, WILLIAM
460 SAND BARKELY DRIVE
CADIZ, KY 42211

SOMMERFELT, RICHARD
68 HOLLY RIDGE DRIVE
SANDWICH, MA 02563

SOTRINES, FRANK
7160 FOUNTAINDALE ROAD
TOPEKA, KS 66614

SPANNER, DAVID
14913 WANNAS DRIVE
ACCOKEEK, MD 20607

SPENCER, STANLEY JR.
RR 1 BOX 2010
SKOWHEGAN, ME 04976-9721

SPENCER, CLAUDETTE
63 UNION STREET
NEW BEDFORD, MA 02740

SPENO, NICK
144 GARROW STREET
AUBURN, NY 13021

SPRADLIN, JOSEPH
3242 YORK ROAD
ST JAMES CITY, FL 33956

SPRING JR., ROLLAND
489 CROWN POINT
SANDFORD, NC 27330

SREMANIAK, STEVE
P.O. BOX 127
OZARK, AL 36361

ST. GEORGE, RALPH
28 GREENVILLE DRIVE
FORESTDALE, MA 02644

STABLER, TARLTON B.
317 MATLOCK CREEK ROAD
FRANKLIN, NC 28734

STANIS, JOHN J.
50 WYCHUNAS AVENUE
BUZZARDS BAY, MA 02532

STANY, PAUL
11299 MURCHIE ROAD
NEVADA CITY, CA 95959

STEFANOS, JOHN
470 HARKNESS ROAD
PERU, NY 12972

STEPHENS, WILLIAM
P.O. BOX 658
INTERCESSION CITY, PA 33848

STETCH, JOSEPH
136 E. EMMAUS AVENUE
ALLENTOWN, PA 18103S

STOELZLE, WILLY
46 GROUSE STREET
FALMOUTH, MA 02540

STOMA, A. J.
92 LEWIS POINT ROAD
BUZZARDS BAY, MA 02532

STONE, ROBERT
39 VICTORIA STREET
CENTERVILLE, MA 02632

STOPKA, HENRY
225 CUSHMAN ROAD
ROCHESTER, MA 02770

STUDLEY, ROBERT C.
35 PORTSIDE DRIVE   BOX 996
POCASSET, MA 02559

SULLIVAN, JOSEPH
2 PERRY VENUE
MALLAPOISETT, MA 02739

SULLIVAN, WILLIAM
P.O. BOX 373
ALFRED, ME 04002

SWAN, KAYE
12630 HUNTERS CHASE
SAN ANTONIO, TX 78230

SWEENEY, THOMAS
50 DONE COTTAGE ROAD
FALMOUTH, MA 02540

SYLIA, DOMINGO
419 CHASE ROAD
NO. DARTMOUTH, MA 02747

SYLVESTER, PATRICK
452 GALENA STREET
AURORA, CO 80010

SYLVIA, JOSEPH
NORTH STREET
MALLAPOISETT, MA 02739

TADRZAK, CHESTER
5659 LINCOLN
DEARBORN HEIGHTS, MI 48125

TAGG, JAMES M.
1205 NORTH 6 EAST
MOUNTAIN HOME, ID 83647

TARDY, ALDEN
RR 3 BOX 4209
NEWSPORT, ME 04953

TASTULA, ALLAN
20 SPRUCE STREET
HUDSON, NH 03051

TAYLOR, DONALD
832 MAIN STREET
YARMOUTHPORT, MA 02675

TAYLOR, FRAN
4421 FOXWOOD LANE
SANTA MARIA, CA 93455

TAYLOR, VIRGINIA S.
903 SANDWICH ROAD
E. FALMOUTH, MA 02536

TENCZA, C.S.
23 QUAIL RUN ROUTE 7
SHERMAN, TX 75090

THERRIAULT, NORMAN B.
22 BENNETTS NECK ROAD
POCASSET, MA 02559

THIBEAULT, RAYMOND
913 RUSSO DRIVE
MT. HOLLY, NJ 08060

THOMAS, JOHN W.
2051 WILLIAM PENN WAY
LANCASTER, PA 17601

THOMPSON, MAYNARD R.
2 WHIMBREL DRIVE
CATAUMET, MA 02534

THOMPSON, ROBERT H.
91 BRICK KILN ROAD
E. FALMOUTH, MA 02536

THOMPSON, JAMES
918 WOODLANE ROAD
MT. HOLLY, NJ 08060

THOMPSON, DOROTHY
53 COTUIT ROAD
BOURNE, MA 02532

THRASHER, DICK
BOX 49   338 SHORE ROAD
MONUMENT BEACH, MA 02553

TIBBETS, CHARLES
BOX 1022
ONSET, MA 02558

TIBBLE, WILLIE
2708 LANGSTON DRIVE
GOLDSBORO, NC 27530

TILL, JERALD J.
13302 WILDWOOD DRIVE
TOMBALL, TX 77375

TIMMS, CHARLES R.
615 CHICKASAW DRIVE
WESTMINISTER, SC 29693

TIPPING, LESTER
59 BOURNE VENUE
E. FALMOUTH, MA 02536

TORREY, ROGER A.
4713 SE 47TH STREET
OKLAHOMA CITY, OK 73135

TOWERS, KEN
58 WEST AVENUE
ST. THMS ONTARIO, CANADA
N5R3P7

TRACHTA, JAMES
2975 EL CAPITAN DRIVE
COLORADO SPRINGS, CO 80918

TREVINO, GILDARDO H.
314 SILVER FOX LANE
GOOSE CREEK SC 29445

TREXEL, RICHARD
BOX 123
MONUMENT BEACH, MA 02553

TROY, WALT
975 BANKS LANE
NEWPORT NEWS, VA 23608

TRUSAL, SHIRLEY
18703 MARYANN WAY
QUEEN CREEK, AZ 85242

TURKE, TONY
BOX 3386   4 COACH ROAD
POCASSET, MA 02536

TURNER, JAMES O.
443 BRYANT DRIVE
PITTSBURGH, PA 15235

TURNER, JACK
785 RIVERBEND PARKWAY
ATHENS, GA 30605

TURNER, JOHN S.
RR 3   BOX 91
WELLSBORO, PA 16901-9438

TYLER, NANCY (WHEELER)
100 AARON PLACE #3
LYNCHBURG, VA 24502

VALENTE, MARIO
1701 COMMERCE AVE W
LOT 229
HAINES CITY, FL 33844

VALENTINO, RUDOLPH A.
130 RIDER AVENUE
LANCASTER, PA 17603

VALKENBURG, WILLIAM VAN
7121 100TH AVENUE
CLEAR LAKE, MN 55319-9607

VALLESIO, VINCENT R.
8 CLIFF ROAD
BUZZARDS BAY, MA 02532-4204

VANDINI, LAWRENCE
ATLANTIC AVENUE
PLYMOUTH, MA 02360

VAUGHN, ROY
96 MAIN STREET
KINGSTON, MA 02364

VAYDA, ROBERT S.
510 BEACH DRIVE
DESTIN, FL 32541

VELDHOVEN, JOHN
226 DALY DRIVE EXTENSION
STOUGHTON, MA 02072

VERNOOY, RUSSELL
BOX 1115
POCASSET, MA 02559

VICKERS, CLIFTON T.
1276 CIBOLO TERRACE
UNIVERSAL CITY, TX 78148

VILANDRY, LEO
6 HILL STREET
FAIRHAVEN, MA 02719

VIVEIROS, JOHN
9 CATTAIL LANE
NO KINGSTOWN, RI 02852

VOGEL, RICHARD A.
2208 ADMIRAL CIRCLE
VIRGINIA BEACH, VA 23451

WAIT, TOM
274 SCHOOL STREET
MARSTON MILLS, MA 02648

WAITE, CLYDE
36 WOODBURY STREET
BUZZARDS BAY, MA 02532

WALKER, GARY
33 KENSINGTON DRIVE
SANDWICH, MA 02563

WALKER, JANE
2 SANDPIPER CIRCLE
E. FALMOUTH, MA 02536

WALKO, WALTER A.
25736 E. JAMISON CIRCLE
AURORA, CO 80016

WALKUP, L. G.
5008 ST. MARIE AVENUE
ORLANDO, FL 32812-1069

WALKUP JR., CLYDE W.
43 HARTFORD AVENUE
MARSTONS MILLS, MA 02648

WALSH, GEORGE
P.O. BOX 2375
GLEN FALLS, NY 12801

WALSH, JAMES
111 E. 25TH STREET
HOUSTON, TX 77008

WALTER, ALICE
903 SANDWICH ROAD
EAST FALMOUTH, MA 02536

WALZ, RODNEY
7 MORSE POND ROAD
FALMOUTH, MA 02540

WARD, NEIL
466 MOLINO AVENUE
MILL VALLEY, CA 94941

WARNER, DAVID
533 LAKE JOY ROD
KATHLEEN, GA 31047

WARREN, JIM & POLLY
8 NECTARINE LANE
LIVERPOOL, NY 13090-3045

WARREN, JIM
8150TH 61ST AVE #1033
GLENDALE, AZ 85302

WATERFIELD, EUGENE
34 FORTALIZA AVENUE
E. FALMOUTH, MA 02536

WATSON, FLOYD
7112 UDINE AVENUE
ORLANDO, FL 32819

WEISBARTH, IRWIN
1555 FINCH AVE E   APT 2503
WILLOWDALE, ONTARIO
CANADA M2J4X9

WEIST, FORREST DALE
5754 ORTEGA STREET
SACRAMENTO, CA 95824

WENDELL, SGT & MRS VIVIAN
1918 CHIMNEY WOOD COURT
ABILENE, TX 79602

WENZ, DAN
200 CHELL ROAD
JOPPA, MD 21085

WERTANEN, MARTIN
1866 MAIN STREET
W. BARNSTABLE, MA 02668

WHITE, ROBERT G.
GREAT HERRING POND ROAD
CEDARVILLE, MA 02532

WHITEHEAD, CHARLES W.
16124 OAK MANOR DRIVE
TAMPA, FL 33624

WHITELEY, WILLIAM
68 LINDEN LANE
OSTERVILLE, MA 02655

WHITTEN, ROOSEVELT D.
1972 BIRCH COURT
MARYSVILLE, CA 95901

WILLIAMS, CLARENCE
6070 CAPRI
CINCINNATI, OH 45224

WILLIAMS, GARY
C/O RICHARD GREENE
HARRISVILLE, NY 13648

WILLIG, JEAN E.
1354 PILGRIM VENUE
MELBOURNE, FL 32940

WILLNER, WILLIAM
19 KETTLE HALE ROAD
FALMOUTH, MA 02540

WILSON, WALTER F.
P.O. BOX 426
SO SALEM, NY 10590-0426

WINFIELD, TOM
103 SHAWMUT VENUE
NEW BEDFORD, MA 02740

WINLING, JACK
8 FISHERMAN'S COVE ROAD
E. FALMOUTH, MA 02536

WINOSKI, LILLIAN
342 CASTLEWOOD DRIVE
HYANNIS, MA 02601

WITCHER, BRUCE E.
75-5588-C PAWAI PLACE
KAILUA-KONA, HI 96740

WOOD, DONALD
50 PART STREET
MATTAPOISETT, MA 02739

WOOD, KEN
5050 KLARE DRIVE
KEYSTONE HEIGHTS, FL 32656

WOODCOCK, HERBERT
23 CASWELL DRIVE
GREENLAND, NH 03840

WOOLARD, SAM
P.O. BOX 107
E. WAREHAM, MA 02538

WOOLF, MICHAEL B.
1594 SILVER DELL ROAD
LAFAYETE, CA 94549

WOOMER, VAN O.
306 ALDERSGATE DRIVE
SUMTER, SC 29150

WUNSCH, EDWARD
45 INDIAN ACRES
HINSDALE, NH 03451

WYNN ,JAMES S.
575 TRAVIS DRIVE
DAYTON, OH 45431

XIARHOS, GEORGE
21 VILLAGE AVENUE
ACHUSNET, MA 02743

YATES, BILL
690 FOREST LAIR
TALLAHASSEE, FL 32312

YOUNG, WALTER
38 WALLACE AVENUE
BUZZARDS BAY, MA 02532

YOUNG, RUSSELL A.
231 W. LORRAINE   DR
MARY ESTER, FL 32569-1827

ZANOTTI, ANTONE
20 BRAUNACKER ROAD
PLYMOUTH, MA 02360

ZIEGLER, DONALD
15174 EAST WESLEY AVENUE
AURORA, CO 80014-2544

ZIEGLHOFER, FRED
207 WESTLAND AVENUE S. W.
MASSILLON, OH 44646

ZILINSKY JR, ANTHONY J.
P. O. BOX 263
DURHAM, CT 06422

ZIMBA, RICHARD
373 COUNTY ROAD
WEST WAREHAM, MA 02576

ZLOGAR, JOSEPH
8 ALDERBERRY ROAD
BUZZARDS BAY, MA 02532

ZOIA, LAWRENCE
4 WINDY HILL DRIVE
W. WAREHAM, MA 02576

NOTES

ORDER FORM

Additional copies of *FIFTY FALLING STARS* are available. Please use order form below.

SEND BOOK TO:

NAME: _____
ADDRESS: _____
CITY/STATE: _____
ZIP CODE: _____

NUMBER OF COPIES _____

PRICE PER BOOK $19.95

TOTAL $_____

TOTAL FOR ORDER $_____

FLORIDA RESIDENTS ADD
7% SALES TAX [$1.40] $_____

FINAL TOTAL $_____

MAKE CHECK
OR MONEY ORDER
PAYABLE TO: A. J. NORTHRUP

MAIL TO: A. J. NORTHRUP
                       1976 HICKORY TREE LANE
                       TALLAHASSEE, FL 32303

AJN02[1]

NOTE: A COPY OF THIS ORDER FORM ALSO MAY BE PRINTED FROM THE FOLLOWING INTERNET LOCATION:

http://web.one-eleven.net/~deanboys/northrup/fifty.htm